This biography is for readers who wish to know the true story behind Isak Dinesen's tale, *Out of Africa*.

The Danish writer, twice nominated for the Nobel Prize, artfully related her efforts to run a coffee farm in East Africa between 1914 and 1931. She described her love for Africans and for farming and her tragic loss of the farm in the Great Depression. Her story is notable for its lyrical description of Africa and the larger-than-life friends she made there.

Isak Dinesen's book was a memoir: that is, she related the story in part and gave it certain flourishes that were only approximately true. The Hollywood film "Out of Africa" was loosely based upon her rendition and four other books by or about Isak Dinesen, whose real name was Karen Blixen.

This book is the first to show by detailed analysis the development of Karen Blixen/Isak Dinesen's relationship with the legendary hunter, Denys Finch Hatton. The friendship, which lasted thirteen years, was strongly influenced by the presence or absence of another Kenya settler, Berkeley Cole. Karen Blixen twice believed she was pregnant with Finch Hatton's child.

She was married, for a time, to a lovable rogue, her cousin, Baron Bror Blixen, who gave her syphilis in their first year of marriage. He was, physically, the love of her life, while Finch Hatton remained her romantic ideal.

Karen Blixen's medical history has been widely misunderstood. She suffered only briefly from syphilis, and many of her later medical problems are attributable to the arsenic she took for years as a tonic. She also suffered from panic attacks, vividly described in *Out of Africa*, and a life-long fear of living alone.

Karen Blixen's many fictional works were not previously well understood because her life and character remained an enigma.

This book, told from Karen Blixen's point of view, focuses upon the events that inspired her early writing.

Out of Isak Dinesen in Africa

in Africa

the untold story

Out of Isak Dinesen in Africa

the untold story

by Linda Donelson

Coulsong List

Iowa City, Iowa

Published in the United States by:
Coulsong List, P. O. Box 1938, Iowa City, IA 52244

First Edition, April 1995

Donelson, Linda
    Out of Isak Dinesen in Africa:the untold story /
    by Linda Donelson. — 1st ed.
        p. cm.
    Includes bibliographical references and index.
        ISBN # 0-9643893-0-4 Cloth
        ISBN # 0-9643893-1-2 Paper

Publisher's Cataloging in Publication Data
        1. Dinesen, Isak, 1885–1962—Biography. 2. Dinesen, Isak, 1885–1962—Homes and haunts—Africa. 3. Authors, Danish—20th century—Biography. I. Title.
PT8175. B545Z.*LD1* 1994
839.8 1372—dc20   Library of Congress Catalog Card Number: 94-69465
[B]

Grateful acknowledgment is made for permission to reprint from *Letters from Africa: 1914–1931* by Isak Dinesen, ed. by Frans Lasson, trans. by Anne Born, copyright © 1981 by the University of Chicago Press; for permission to reprint from "Kaerlighed og okonomi," by Else Brundbjerg, *Kritik* no. 66, copyright © 1984 by Gyldendal; and to Gyldendal for permission to reprint from *The Power of Aries: Myth and Reality in Karen Blixen's Life*, by Anders Westenholz, trans. by Lise Kure-Jensen, copyright © 1987 by Louisiana State University Press.

Cover photograph from *Out of Africa* by Isak Dinesen, compilation copyright © 1985 by Century Publishing Co. Ltd., courtesy the publisher.

Out of Isak Dinesen

in Africa

the untold story

Contents

Frank • I Have Never Felt Anything Like It Before • A Dirty Trick • Taking Stock • Teaching Denys a Lesson • Uncertainty • Black Buffaloes • An Essay on Sexual Morality • The Gold Ring

Je Responderay • Three Generations of Wives • The Stork • A Vending Machine Tycoon • Something the Matter with His Heart

Italian Colonial Atrocities • Kasparson • Lions in the Coffee Field • The Indian High Priest • Marienbad Pills • The Prince of Wales • The Ngoma • Kamante's Meal • The Prince's Safari

A Rage • Market Crash

A Scene of the First Water • Dickensian Dilemmas • A New Bookcase • Beau Geste • A Letter from a King • Leaving Things to Themselves • The Most Transporting Pleasure in Africa • She Can Fly

A Loan • Locusts • A Talk with Mohr and Denys • The Quarrel • Love, Denys • I See • Grey Geese • Blackened Oranges • An Appreciation • Pellegrina Leoni

Center

Photographs
Map of Karen Blixen's World
List of Karen Blixen's Journeys to Africa
Family Chart
Chart of "The Years in Africa"

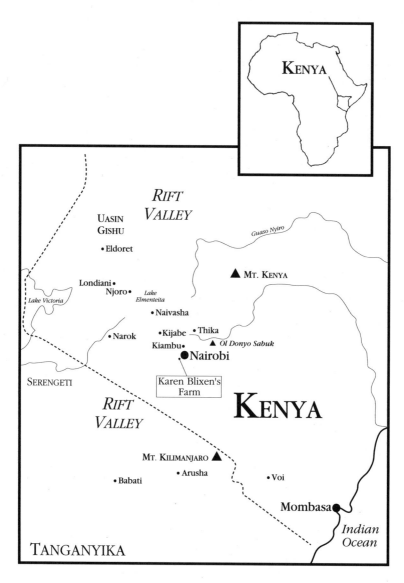

Circa 1925

Key to References

The following abbreviations are used, with the page numbers of the citations, for references in the text.

DFH to KB	Letters of Denys Finch Hatton to Karen Blixen
DFH to KR	Letters of Denys Finch Hatton to Kermit Roosevelt
AH	*African Hunter*, Blixen-Finecke
AL	*The Africa Letters*, Blixen-Finecke
B	*Boganis*, T. Dinesen
CEPT	*Carnival: Entertainments and Posthumous Tales*, I. Dinesen
DOE	*Daguerreotypes and Other Essays*, I. Dinesen
ID	*Isak Dinesen*, Thurman
IDKB	*"Isak Dinesen" & Karen Blixen*, Hannah
KBS	"Karen Blixen's Sygdomshistorie," Fog
KO	"Kaerlighed og okonomi," Brundbjerg
LB	*The Living Bible Paraphrased*
LDID	*The Life and Destiny of Isak Dinesen*, Lasson
LFA	*Letters from Africa*, I. Dinesen
LFD	*Longing for Darkness*, Gatura
LFTH	*Letters from the Hunt*, W. Dinesen
LT	*Last Tales*, I. Dinesen
MSID	*My Sister, Isak Dinesen*, T. Dinesen
MWWL	*The Man Whom Women Loved*, Aschan
OA	*Out of Africa*, I. Dinesen
OMM	*On Modern Marriage*, I. Dinesen
OMS	*Out in the Midday Sun*, E. Huxley
PA	*The Power of Aries*, Westenholz
SE	*The Settler Economies*, Mosley
SGT	*Seven Gothic Tales*, I. Dinesen
SH	*Sex in History*, Tannahill
SOTG	*Shadows on the Grass*, I. Dinesen
SOTM	*Straight On Till Morning*, Lovell
SWS	*Silence Will Speak*, Trzebinski
T	*Titania*, Migel
TP	*The Pact*, Bjornvig
VLT	*Victorian Lady Travellers*, Middleton
WBM	"Who is Beryl Markham?," Fox
WM	*White Mischief*, Fox
WMC	*White Man's Country*, 2 volumes, E. Huxley
WT	*Winter's Tales*, I. Dinesen
WWTN	*West with the Night*, Markham

Note: In quotes from *Letters from Africa* in this volume italics are used both where Isak Dinesen underscored her words and where she inserted English words into the Danish.

"In a hundred years your works will be read much less than today . . . But one book . . . will be rewritten and re-read, and will each year in a new edition be set upon the shelf."

"What book is that?" Lord Byron asked.
"Life of Lord Byron," said Pippistrello.

—Karen Blixen
"Second Meeting"

Introduction

1

In 1938 booksellers in America featured an exciting new work entitled *Out of Africa*. Written by a Danish author with the enigmatic name Isak Dinesen, the book described the author's life on a coffee farm in Kenya. The reading public was captivated by the story, for it conjured up a sense of romance seldom found in non-fiction. The author's tone was nostalgic, leisurely, with vivid metaphors, luxurious recollection of scenes, and the entire recitation given as though the author were recounting a dream. In an epoch burdened by the effects of world war and the most disastrous economic slump in history, the dream of pastoral living in a land of noble tribes and exotic animals appealed to the most jaded readers. The story seemed a metaphor for the age: the struggle to accept fate in the face of war and drought, economic chaos, loss of loved ones, and the failure of idealism. The author touchingly described her ambitious plans to raise coffee, and the affection that developed between herself and her African workers. Even after the farm was lost to creditors, readers were left with optimism that the Ngong Hills, the Masai, the giraffe and lions, and the spirit of Africa would persist despite man's misfortunes, and that a new ideal would arise, representing true happiness. Yet the story could not be read without sadness, for in the end the author lost not only her farm, but her greatest friends.

Featured by the Book-of-the-Month Club, *Out of Africa* became a bestseller in a time when few could afford to buy books. Libraries with meager budgets allowing them to buy only one copy could not keep up with the demand to read it. Its author was not altogether unknown, for, two years before, the Book-of-the-Month Club had introduced a collection of stories by Isak Dinesen entitled *Seven Gothic Tales*. Readers—who assumed Isak Dinesen was a man— received the tales with enthusiasm. It was mysterious to them that a Danish writer should write so well in English. Some thought the author was Jewish, since the name Isak in Hebrew means "the one who laughs." *Out of Africa* was different from the tales, in fact, so different it was hard to recognize the author, save that the writing in both cases was carefully turned.

The memoir whetted readers' appetites to know more about Isak Dinesen. Indeed, some aspects of *Out of Africa* are so mysterious as to leave the reader frustrated at what lies behind them. Once or twice the author mentions "my husband" but says nothing more about him. Several times she refers to being away from Africa "on home leave" but does not explain how much time she was away, and when. How much time did she spend in Africa? Was she really an aristocrat? How much help did she have in initiating this great plan of living in Africa? What role did her friend, the hunter Denys Finch Hatton, play in her life? Were they lovers? What happened to her after she left Africa? How did she come to be writing books?

While readers in America, and soon those in England, were fascinated with speculations about the author of *Out of Africa*, the Baroness Karen von Blixen-Finecke, nee Dinesen, was living in Denmark with her mother on the estate where she was born. She laughed at the curiosity of readers, and soon revealed she wrote under a pen-name, but she elaborated no further on the burning questions readers were asking about her life in Africa. For twenty-five years she continued to write stories, including the collections *Winter's Tales* and *Last Tales*, and the novels *Ehrengard* and *The Angelic Avengers*, as well as several stories for the *Ladies Home Journal*. By the time she began reading stories on the radio in the late 1940s she had established a public persona.

People were led to understand that she was a member of the aristocracy, and of the higher society of European writers. She was nominated for the Nobel Prize for Literature in 1954 and 1957, and visitors who made the pilgrimage to Denmark to meet her were greeted by a gracious, thoroughly aristocratic writer—a charming hostess, and most intriguing conversationalist. A spare, oddly beguiling woman nearly seventy years old, with grippingly luminous dark eyes, she was also one of the most intelligently sensitive listeners they had met. She liked to greet visitors outside her large stucco and timber estate house, where they would stroll among the flower gardens, cross a white wooden bridge over a pond, and follow the footpaths in the woods outlining her mother's land. She seemed content living there, and except for the occasional far-away gaze did not appear to miss Africa. Inside the house, there were few memorabilia from the African years. In the summer lace curtains cascaded from the height of the windows and pooled over the polished wooden floors. The furniture was elegant yet comfortable. In each room a coal stove of elaborate design existed as an object of art as well as practicality. Only in the sunroom where the baroness did her writing was there evidence of her life in Africa: on the writing desk, a picture of Denys Finch Hatton, looking ingenuous at the age of eighteen or twenty; on the wall, some Masai swords and shields; and in the corner, the very screen covered with oriental images—sultans and servants, palm trees and Africans— that inspired the tales she had invented for her friends when they returned from safari.

The baroness had for some years ridden her bicycle almost daily to the village of Rungsted. She enjoyed brisk walks around the grounds of her estate. She was famous among the local children for her playfulness and interest in their affairs. Her nieces and nephews, who lived nearby, adored her ability to join in their fantasies. This playfulness extended to her adult friends, whose hair she sometimes decorated with flowers. Even in old age she loved a masquerade, and occasionally went so far as to dress herself as a figure, Pierrot, in the Commedia Dell'arte. She was famous for her table, and her conversation, as she had been in Africa, and authors from all over the world came to visit her.

However, she was often unwell. She suffered from strange crises of the stomach which took her to the hospital from time to time for surgeries that never eliminated her symptoms. To intimate friends she expressed her conviction that the symptoms related to an unmentionable disease contracted in Africa from her husband. She spent periods as long as several months in bed, during which she dictated stories to a loyal secretary named Clara Svendsen.

In 1961 Karen Blixen published a second, shorter memoir of her years in Africa, *Shadows on the Grass*, in which she elaborated on some of the themes of *Out of Africa*. But she made no further revelations about the personal questions readers wished to know. Within a few years *Out of Africa* would be understood to be partly fictional, for it was recognized that Karen Blixen had romanticized the account of her life in Africa. So readers were even more intrigued to learn the truth behind the story.

Eventually some biographies of her were written. However, little new information came to light about the mysterious relationship between Karen Blixen and Denys Finch Hatton. Readers still yearned for answers to their questions about Karen Blixen's affection for her husband and about her love affair with Finch Hatton. The movie "Out of Africa" added greatly to the curiosity and also to the confusion about which aspects of the story were genuine. The film recreated the ambiance of colonial Kenya, and vivified the characters of Karen Blixen's friend Berkeley Cole, and her husband, Bror Blixen. However, where the story concerned Denys Finch Hatton, the Hollywood version proved suspect.

The Kenyan writer Beryl Markham, a friend of Finch Hatton, describes how his character was shaped by education in the British public schools. He was, above all, a product of Eton and Oxford, and what stood out to anyone who met him was his broad range of knowledge and his English comportment. He was a gentleman—but one of great sensitivity, good humor, and surprising vulnerability. His skills of repartee were famous, yet he was also exceptionally thoughtful. He was a hunter for lack of another trade, but he loved the out-of-doors and was as observant as a naturalist. He has been described as a

Peter Pan, as an avoider of commitment, as someone too restless for an ordinary life, but if this were so, then anyone who chooses not to marry may be similarly accused. There were, and are still today, men and women so intrigued by life upon the African plains that they devote themselves to it. Denys Finch Hatton was less of a wanderer than many, since he returned to England for six months nearly every year, and limited his travels to the route to and from East Africa. He was committed to this routine, and although he was not one to marry, it appears that he was true to his friends—men and women.

Beryl Markham's connection to this story remains controversial. Although various recent accounts talk about an affair between her and Denys Finch Hatton, several biographers who interviewed her in the 1970s, before age had taken its toll on her mind (she died in 1986), were unable to elicit from Beryl an acknowledgment that such an affair took place. The sources who suggest there was indeed an affair are questionable: an elderly woman whose account cannot be documented, two friends who met Beryl many years after Denys's death, and one acquaintance of Denys who also insisted that Bror Blixen never had syphilis.

Rumors about Beryl Markham's relationship with Denys Finch Hatton have expanded in direct proportion to public admiration for her book, *West with the Night*, but Denys's inclusion in the story seems likely to have involved poetic license. Beryl wrote the book immediately following the early popularity of *Out of Africa*, and a mention of Denys was certain to pique readers' interest. She says Denys invited her to fly with him often, and this is surely true; he invited everyone to ride. But she also says he asked her to go with him on his final flight, and this is surely not true, unless, as with another woman, it was done in jest. Denys seldom traveled in Kenya without a servant, he was taking the Somali Hamisi (not the Kikuyu Kimau as stated in other accounts) with him to the coast, and there was no room in the airplane for anyone else.

Denys and Karen generally agreed about people. At the time she knew them, Beryl was a "child," as Karen put it. She was neither their age (fifteen years younger) nor as well educated. It is easy to imagine Denys bemused at the strange convolutions of Beryl's love affairs and lifestyle.

* 2 *

You may wonder at not finding in this volume certain anecdotes from other biographies of Karen Blixen. There is, for example, a story that Denys Finch Hatton once flew his airplane from Nairobi to London merely to attend the ballet (or the opera, as is variously reported). Denys Finch Hatton was a legend in his own time, but this story is apocryphal. The flight, one-way, in Denys's time took a minimum of six days—for a seasoned pilot who had obtained permission to land for refueling at numerous exotic stations across the breadth of Africa. Denys, who had owned his airplane little more than six months, could not have undertaken such a journey upon a whim.

In a letter to her sister from Africa, Karen Blixen once wrote, "There are some artists, and in fact human beings in general, and no doubt usually those who possess marked personal charm, or *charming* personality, who have the gift of 'making myths'; their personalities remain alive in people's consciousness as well as their works, and the particular kind of poetry that they have represented or expressed goes on gathering or maturing around them; people continue to add to it" (*LFA*, 394). So it was for Karen Blixen, who became a mythical figure in her own time, even to her friends and family. With age her nose grew more prominent and her eyes more luminous, so that she herself thought she looked like a witch, and others, who had come under the spell of her stories, believed there was something of the supernatural about her. Those who met her often described her as "histrionic." She spoke and dressed in a dramatic way; her appearance and behavior were also dramatic—her deep voice an effect of the cigarettes she smoked constantly, her mannerisms exaggerated and given with a flourish. Her striking thinness enhanced her piercing gaze and rendered her spiritual energy almost diabolic. She encouraged this impression, and in fact believed the only route to greatness was by means of illusion. In order to be remembered, she thought, one must make oneself memorable, and this can be accomplished by hiding one's bourgeois upbringing and becoming an aristocrat, that is, a person above mere mortals, someone who fascinates. "Truth is for tailors and shoemakers" (*SGT*, 24), she said. "Make poetry, use your imagination, disguise the truth (*SGT*, 25) . . . there never was a great artist who was not a bit of a charlatan . . . " (*SGT*, 58).

Her memoir *Out of Africa* enhanced the impression that she lived more romantically than the average person. She commented to her sister about the nature of remembrances: "God knows if it is always true, but it is truth in a higher sense, it is myth" (*LFA*, 395). For many years it was believed, as she related in *Out of Africa*, that Karen Blixen had shot the magnificent lion whose skin she bestowed on the king of Denmark in 1930. However, letters to her mother reveal that Denys Finch Hatton shot the lion, and that Karen Blixen wished the king to believe the trophy had been won by a Danish subject.

"It is difficult to estimate a human life; it is quite impossible to do so according to definite rules, and as time goes by one grows very cautious about it," Karen Blixen told her sister. "The things that happen do not have the same value for everyone" (*LFA*, 351). Biographies, and memoirs, differ widely in the stories they tell. Anecdotes are enlarged upon by acquaintances, emotionally distorted by family, and, like the story of the lion skin, enhanced by the subject for the sake of romanticism. The better one knows the subject, the easier it is to separate truth from myth, but one must remain wary of anecdotes. So, for the most part, this book contains information collected, in letters and other writings, from the persons described.

We are fortunate to have Karen Blixen's extensive letters from Africa. She was cautious in writing to her family about Finch Hatton, but it is possible to trace the evolution of her relationship with him, which lasted thirteen years. Although it is necessary to make educated guesses about the context of some of the events, it will be seen that, as in any relationship, their affection for each other evolved through various stages of intimacy; it appears they did not become lovers, nor even close friends, until they had known each other for some time.

Karen Blixen's relationship with her husband, Bror Blixen, has long been an enigma. She was found to have syphilis in 1915, only a year after their marriage, and neither her family nor her doctors doubted that her husband was the source of contagion. Several of her closest friends knew her husband had given her syphilis; indeed, she wrote to her brother concerning the matter in 1926, making it clear that her family knew the circumstances surrounding her illness. In recent years a fashionable rumor has arisen that Bror Blixen never had syphilis, but this rumor appears to have originated with another of his wives, who said he never told her he had the disease. Why he would avoid mentioning it to her seems clear, since he knew from consultations with doctors that his syphilis was no longer contagious. By all accounts, Bror was physically irresistible, and a warm, generous, engaging, humorous, and considerate adventurer, to whom Karen Blixen was bound by love and kinship and romantic memories until the end of her days.

* 3 *

I first became interested in this story in 1978 when my husband, a scientist, and I were living on a research farm west of Nairobi, overlooking the Ngong Hills. I often took friends to visit Karen Blixen's house. When you sit on the terrace at her millstone table, you feel Africa still echoes a song of Karen Blixen, because the view of the quiet grounds and the blue hills has changed little: great birds soar in the clouds, and one listens amid their calls for the voice of Denys Finch Hatton or for the sound of his car coming up the drive.

The atmosphere in Nairobi in 1978 in many ways resembled that of Karen Blixen's time. It still seemed like a colonial town. Even today the architecture of some streets is unchanged from the rows of stuccoed buildings with pillared overhangs that Karen Blixen knew. Many of the shops are still owned by Indians, selling cloth and spices, hardware and pots and pans, jewelry and native carvings, safari hats, souvenirs, and custom-tailored tropical suits. The mosque, the market, and the McMillan Library still dominate the center of town, where natives of many lands intermingle in a wide variety of attire: whites in safari gear, African politicians in business suits, Masai in red blanket cloaks and dangling earrings, Indians in sari and sandals, Kikuyu women in colorful cloth wraps, and working girls in elaborately plaited hairdos. Lepers with stumps of feet bound in rags ask for alms on the pavement in front of neoclassical, pillared banks. Some of the best tomatoes and onions, garlic and ginger, eggs and oranges are sold in the outdoor markets. Souvenirs and trinkets are laid out on the sidewalks and displayed for tourists. The Somali ghetto of Karen Blixen's time has been replaced by streets lined with Indian shops and crowded with "Asians," as Indians are referred to in this town begun as an outpost of the British empire.

Nairobi was in the beginning nothing more than a frontier base camp for construction of the Uganda railroad. The site itself may have been chosen by a few errant railroad engineers in the throes of delirium, for the altitude, 5,200 feet, gives a feeling of ecstasy, and the weather contributes a fresh clearness that is seductive. Despite the latitude, only 4 degrees south of the Equator, the heat is seldom noticeable, and evenings can be cold. Ten or fifteen miles to the north are juniper forests, but on the hills adjacent to Nairobi—for the town itself was built on low-lying, swampy ground—are rich *shambas* (farms) where the Kikuyu raise corn and spinach, tomatoes and sweet potatoes. As a source of food supply for railroad workers, the site could not have been better chosen.

Extending south from Nairobi towards Tanzania is a vast plain which becomes the Serengeti. The variety and numbers of wildlife inhabiting this plain are still astonishing, although at the time Karen Blixen came to Africa the zebra and rhino, lion and gazelle were so numerous that advertisements urging tourists to use the Uganda Railroad depicted animals peering curiously into the windows of the trains while they stopped for refueling.

A few miles to the northwest of Nairobi, on the other side of the Ngong Hills—a row of four blue peaks rising to over 8,000 feet near the town—the elevation falls steeply toward the Rift Valley, a vast depression in the earth, in places sixty miles wide. Here on the plains live the Masai who do not plant crops—an idea perhaps too bourgeois for a wandering, aristocratic people who live off their cattle and sheep, but at the same time a wise decision, for the land in this area is too dry for agriculture, the rains too uncertain. In particularly dry years, the Masai used to move their herds up into the hills and, by invading the greener territories of the Kikuyu to the east and the Kipsigis to the west, instigated wars, for the tribes understood that this high, East African land could support only a limited number of people.

When Karen Blixen came here in 1914, the colony was barely fifteen years old. Little was known about crop-raising in the tropics, even less about the history of the region, its pattern of rainfall and drought, the record of crop and animal diseases, the vagaries of climate and altitude. It has been said Karen Blixen was foolish to undertake farming in such an untried region of the world, but then there must be many like her, for nearly all pioneers face similar uncertainties.

* 4 *

Karen Blixen was born in 1885, at a time when new frontiers were opening in many parts of the world. The industrial revolution was changing the structure of society. Transportation had been revolutionized by steam trains and ships, and these, along with the wireless, made communication and commerce overseas effortless by previous standards. Raw materials were needed for burgeoning industry, and an increasingly wealthy middle class demanded consumer goods, like tea and spices from India, china and silks from the Orient, and rubber and coffee from the tropics. Karen Blixen's maternal grandfather, Regnar Westenholz, had begun life as a humble clerk in a dockside warehouse, but soon he made enough money to purchase his own shipping business, and his rise to wealth typified that of many members of the middle class who benefited from economic prosperity.

No longer did the aristocracy hold its centuries-old grip on political power. Money allowed men like Regnar Westenholz to increase their social position and to exert influence as never before. Ownership of land, the symbol of status, began to pass from titled aristocrats to the wealthier bourgeois, as the middle class emulated the aristocracy by escaping the city for country estates. Regnar Westenholz was among those who bought several farms.

Karen Blixen's paternal grandfather, Adolph Dinesen, also owned land, but he had come to his legacy by different means. He was descended from a line of Danish professional soldiers who had striven for greatness according to the Napoleonic ideal. This ideal, in which success derives from heroism, was also the means by which a man without a title might become an aristocrat. While none of the Dinesens had ever been knighted, Karen Blixen's great-aunt Thyra, sister to Adolph Dinesen's wife, had married into the aristocracy, becoming Countess Frijs. This close association with nobility inspired the remainder of the family to yearn even more ardently for a title— although in Karen Blixen's time dreams of becoming an aristocrat were part of the fantasies of every member of the middle class, including, one may be sure, the less socially advantaged Westenholzes. (Even Americans were consumed by the passion for a title, and over five hundred wealthy entrepreneurs found the means to marry their daughters to European noblemen. One of these, a Philadelphia banking tycoon named Anthony J. Drexel, married his daughter to Guy Finch Hatton, Viscount Maidstone, later Earl of Winchilsea—Denys Finch Hatton's brother, Toby. As in so many of these marriages, including Karen Dinesen's marriage to Bror von Blixen-Finecke, bourgeois money was greatly appreciated by aristocratic families suffering from the threat of financial extinction.)

Karen Blixen's father, Wilhelm Dinesen, originally a soldier like his father, was the second son, so he did not inherit the family estate. However, a devastating agrarian slump in the 1870s made farms available to investors, and he was able to buy land. His holdings lay halfway between Copenhagen and Elsinore, along the Oresund, the channel dividing Denmark and Sweden; and this is where Karen Blixen grew up.

Her life at home was typical for wealthy families of the day. A large number of children was the rule, since there were plenty of servants to help care for them, and, anyway, Victorian morality dictated that sexual intercourse between married people exist strictly for the procreation of children. One did not give oneself over to sensuality or to the practice of contraception, in theory at least.

The existence of large families meant that people like the Dinesens had many relatives: Karen Blixen's father had six sisters and one brother; her mother, two sisters and two brothers. This created a large number of cousins, added to numbers of second cousins. Like so many upper-class Europeans, Wilhelm Dinesen chose his closest friends from among his relatives, the two most prominent being his cousin, Count Mogens Frijs of Copenhagen, and his cousin Clara's (Frijs) husband, Baron Frederik von Blixen-Finecke of Sweden.

The distance in miles between their estates could be covered in a few hours. While men assembled throughout the seasons for hunting, women accompanied them to see the other relatives in summer, the families exchanging visits, often lasting weeks at a time, at their cousins' country estates.

To understand Karen Blixen's upbringing one must imagine a time when the richer a woman was, the less likely she was to be sent to school. It was considered more genteel, in an age when striving for status was the goal at all levels of society, for girls to be taught at home by a governess. Schools for girls existed, but they were seldom attended by girls of rank, but rather were filled with daughters of the middle class, whose fathers could not afford to accommodate, in a modest house, a "Mademoiselle" to attend to their education. So a well-bred family like the Dinesens educated its girls at home.

University education for girls was considered avant-garde but had been available since the 1870s. However, few women sat for the entrance examinations. Most were obliged to educate themselves by reading the books in their fathers' often capacious libraries. A few women achieved acclaim for entering professions previously accorded to men—Ethyl Mary Charles became the first qualified female architect in Britain in 1898—but such a goal existed only in the fantasies of most Edwardian women.

The heroines of the age fell into two categories: those who belonged to the much aggrandized aristocracy, and those who ventured into courageous travels. Karen Blixen lived in admiration of both ideals. She yearned to follow in the stylish and entertaining footsteps of the goddesses of the age, Queen Alexandra of England and Princess Marie of Rumania. Yet she was mesmerized by accounts of the exploits of world travelers like Isabella Bird Bishop, Marianne North, and Fanny Bullock Workman. May French Sheldon had studied the native customs of the Masai in East Africa, and Annie Taylor had traveled alone in China as an Inland Missionary. Kate Marsden had toured Siberia and Eastern Europe in the cause of treating leprosy. Mary Kingsley had explored the West African jungles, establishing that women could perform exploits similar to those of men.

The women's movement had been under way since the 1830s, so that by the early 1900s women had accustomed themselves to counting their strides and outlining their future. But the right to vote had yet to be won. Goals were belabored in lectures and public meetings, and accentuated in the writings of female journalists—since, besides nursing, journalism had become a favorite entry for upper- and middle-class women into the marketplace. However, the majority of women were obliged to content themselves with marrying respectable gentlemen, providing a good example to their children, and laying the comfortable foundation for the advancement of men in their professions and their entertainments.

Karen Blixen had written a few stories before she went to Africa, and she had learned to paint, but writing and painting, like flower-arranging and entertaining, were common pastimes in an age when all except the lowest classes had servants. She did not need to make a living from writing, since her family lived on the annuities from their modest estate; nor was she serious about writing until after she had spent some years in Africa.

As she prepared to leave Denmark in 1913, the political climate in Europe was far from her thoughts. By many accounts, people had never been happier, and, anyway, politics had never interested her. At home there was prosperity, and flourishing of the arts. The success of the Diaghilev Ballet in London was the talk of the aesthetic upper class. Indeed, art, music, dance, astronomy, archaeology, and natural history of all kinds were the passions that consumed the educated classes, who were wealthy and well traveled in these times, and patrons of libraries and museums. These were the things Karen Blixen hesitated to leave, as she set out for Africa.

She gave little thought to the possibility of war in Europe. Although the German kaiser had taunted the British for two decades—forcing a strengthening of the navies of both countries—and although there had been disagreements between England and Germany over colonial rights, and struggles for influence over Russia and the Balkan countries, these issues were regarded by most Europeans as little more than wrangling among relatives. The kaiser and most of the crowned heads of Europe were cousins, Queen Victoria having married many of her children to their royal families. Karen Blixen was fascinated by the personal lives of the royalty, but not by their politics.

At twenty-eight, she thought of herself as an old maid who had finally consented to marry. There is no evidence she had experienced any adolescent infatuations, but it was not that she did not believe in romance; it was that she was perhaps too romantic. She had read a great many books, enough to recognize the ideal love when he appeared. At the age of twenty-four, she fell in love with Hans von Blixen-Finecke, twin brother of Bror. She perhaps aimed too high, since he was a champion horseman and outstanding young officer, and she, with a bourgeois upbringing, had no great confidence in her looks or her talents. Moreover, she did not understand that she was too bright for him. But she was attracted to Hans because he fulfilled an ideal of the kind of person she wished to be. Later she said in a story that "the part of ideals" in one's life was "that of an unseen directive force" guiding people toward paradise, "an elysium of dignity, grace, and brilliancy" and immortality (SGT, 361). She believed in surrounding herself with the finest sort of people, for friends act as mirrors to one's virtues, and as a spur toward great achievements. By marrying Hans Blixen's brother Bror she would acquire a title and associate herself intimately with the family of the man whom she most admired; but by going to Africa, thus rejecting bourgeois married life, she challenged herself with the dual ideal of making her name as an aristocrat and as a legendary heroine of travel.

1913

Karen Dinesen had always imagined herself in the role of the great romantic heroine. It was this vision that gave her the strength, in December 1913, to board a steamship in Naples bound for East Africa.

As she walked up the gangway she struggled with the leash of a large Scottish deerhound, and perhaps considered how admirable the bourgeois dames in Denmark would find it for a lone woman to be traveling out to Africa. This act alone—striking out on her own—ought to win her immortality, at least in the minds of the village wives of Rungsted, few of whom could imagine having the courage to go off and marry in the wilds of Africa.

Her courage seemed to her even greater because she had not been well for some weeks. In light of earnest discussions among her family about the risks of disease in Africa, she had resolved to appear gay in leaving.

Looking appropriately chic in her traveling clothes, she concentrated on maintaining the debutante slouch—shoulders rounded, hips thrust forward—in vogue that season. Her suit was a fashionable length, allowing her ankles to show demurely in cream-colored stockings. She wore cloth-covered pumps to match her suit. Her wide-brimmed hat made her hair look as though it could not all fit underneath, and she had pinned her chignon so as to let the hair puff around her face. The few curls in front set off her large eyes, the same deep brown as her hair. Her face was too round, her chin too small, to be beautiful. But she was not unattractive. In fact, the other women in the family insisted she was the most attractive among them. She was presently thinner than usual; this satisfied her, for she was concerned with maintaining her figure.

As she steered the deerhound into the throng on deck, several well-dressed young men—friends of her fiancé—tipped their hats and made genial comments to her. They were a party of Swedish aristocrats accompanying Prince Wilhelm of Sweden on a big-game hunting expedition to East Africa. The idea of traveling with royalty had piqued Karen's imagination. By marrying Bror she herself was to become a member of the aristocracy, for she would take the title of Baroness von Blixen-Finecke. It was a sublime idea. If she had had any doubts about making the trip alone, they were dispelled by thoughts of grandeur; and she had overcome her family's reservations through confident assertions that she herself had no qualms. She could see that the dog amused the men. They arranged a place for her at the railing, and—not without difficulty—she made the dog sit. It made a few excited yaps as the steam whistle blew.

Karen's mother and sister Elle had traveled with her by train to Naples. She might have boarded the ship in Germany, but she did not like to travel alone, and, because of her recent illness, her mother and Elle had insisted upon accompanying her overland as far as Italy.

The family had always doted upon Karen; she was the most adventurous, the most interesting, the most stylish of them all. Of the five children, she was the most like her father. And like her father, she was the most restless. The family supported her dream of living in Africa, but they did wonder whether the experiment would succeed. What troubled them was Karen's decision to marry Bror. They had discussed with her quietly but persistently their misgivings. They had always known Bror. Their grandmothers—Karen's father's mother and Bror's mother's mother—had been sisters. At gatherings through the years her family had watched Bror grow up, and they did not feel that she and Bror were alike. Bror was never serious. He loved athletic games, hunting, and giving parties. He had not lasted in school. Karen had spent much of her time at home; she liked poetry and conversation. She had displayed talents for painting and writing that might bear fruit and that Bror little appreciated. Yet there existed a streak of adventurousness in Karen that fit well with Bror's inclinations. Karen had always tried to be different, to create challenges for herself. She had perhaps read too many epic poems: she wanted to see the world, and have others admire her for it.

* *

Karen and Bror had announced their engagement in December 1912. In coming to this decision, she had made Bror realize they could not devote themselves to bourgeois life at home. Uncle Aage Westenholz had encouraged them to try their luck in the colonies, and he had suggested they might like to manage his rubber plantation in Malaya. They had agreed enthusiastically. But when Uncle Mogens Frijs heard this scheme, he shook his head and said, "Go to Africa, you two. A well-run farm in East Africa just now ought to make its owner a millionaire" (*AH*, 7).

Uncle Mogens had just returned from a safari in Africa and had seen its potential. There existed vast areas of unoccupied land which looked ideal for farming. To protect their colonies and guard the source of the Nile, the British had built a railroad nearly 600 miles long from the Indian Ocean to Lake Victoria. Constructing and maintaining it had been so expensive that detractors had dubbed it the Lunatic Express. Thousands of lives of Indian laborers had been lost to lions and tropical diseases, while drought, desert, and precipitous escarpments in the African highlands seemed to turn the empire's scheme of introducing the railroad to East Africa into a fool's undertaking. Now the colonial government was offering incentives to settlement, ninety-nine- and nine-hundred-ninety-nine-year leases on land, at cheap prices, in order to make the railroad pay. From what Uncle Mogens had heard, only a few hundred settlers had arrived since the railroad opened in 1901. The land was virtually free to the takers—much more land than the Africans knew what to do with. But Bror would find particularly attractive the opportunities for hunting. Uncle Mogens emphasized this; the country was teeming with game—so full of antelope, buffalo, lion, and elephant as to defy the imagination. Bror could make money on the sale of ivory and trophies, without considering the wealth to be gained from farming. Uncle Mogens had heard that the climate was excellent for growing coffee. But from what he had seen of mile upon mile of grassland, cattle might be a shrewd investment.

This idea of cattle-raising appealed to Bror. He knew nothing about coffee-growing, but he understood livestock. He was at the time running his father's dairy farm in Skaane, and he exhibited a flair for working with livestock. A large cattle farm in Africa would suit him.

As to the development of the country, Uncle Mogens said that Nairobi was just starting to grow. More and more luxuries were arriving by ship and train, and a number of merchants—mostly East Indians who had immigrated when the railroad was built—sold dry goods, cloth, and spices. Some settlers lived in thatched houses with earthen floors, but in Nairobi Uncle Mogens had seen rather comfortable stone houses with wooden floors, built by Indian craftsmen. Bror could go out to Africa ahead and arrange for the building of a good house.

The climate was of great concern. Would not the heat be oppressive? Uncle Mogens pointed out that the altitude in the farming areas was high, several thousand feet above sea level. There was not the heat one would expect at the Equator, and there were snow-capped mountains—Mt. Kenya to the north and Mt. Kilimanjaro to the south.

Yet Bror anticipated that farming in Africa would depend on getting enough workers. What were the natives like? Could they be trained to work? Uncle Mogens knew that the tribes had been at war until the recent British intervention. The Masai, a proud tribe of the plains, had had to be brought to heel. They were proficient at spearing lions, and they drank the blood of cattle to maintain superior strength as warriors. From time to time they raided their neighbors, and sometimes they killed entire villages. But in recent years, subdued by drought and disease, they had not seemed hostile to whites. In Uncle Mogens's view, the Africans needed to be taught to work; this would eliminate their need to fight each other. Certain tribes of the highlands, particularly the Kikuyu, maintained a tradition of agriculture. As one traveled through the hill country, one saw countless small plots of land under cultivation in sweet potatoes and maize, legumes and bananas. Doubtless, sufficient workers could be recruited who understood the principles of crop-raising.

Uncle Mogens knew of a Swede named Sjögren, an engineer who had gone out to East Africa in 1910 as head of the Swedish Zoological Expedition. He had brought back trophies for the museum in Stockholm—leopard skins, elephant tusks, and various species of antelope, stuffed and mounted—and then he had returned to Nairobi as Swedish consul. More recently he had started a coffee plantation near Nairobi. Perhaps he could be of help to Bror.

After some correspondence, Bror received word from Africa about excellent land available for stock-breeding. A suitable parcel of 700 acres was suggested, and Bror cabled his agreement to buy. He invested some of his own money, but his primary backing was from Karen's uncle, Aage Westenholz, and Karen's mother. They were skeptical of buying land sight-unseen, but Bror insisted they could not risk losing this parcel to someone else. The investment appeared especially fine—not far from the railroad, and close to that of other settlers. That Sjögren's word could be trusted, Uncle Mogens would guarantee.

Once the question of the land was settled, Bror was determined to go out to Africa and look at the farm. He saw to the packing of his hunting gear—and a small amount of farming equipment—and he told Karen that he would send her instructions when he had sized up the situation. She was to choose her trousseau and begin selecting furniture. The festive wedding she hoped for could take place when he came back for her.

But no sooner had Bror arrived in Nairobi than he sent word that the land he had bought was unsuitable. He had had an earful of the experiences of the country's most prominent settler, Lord Delamere, who had used up nearly all his inheritance trying to breed livestock in the Kenya highlands. His merino sheep, his English-bred cattle, and his expensive dairy herds had succumbed to African diseases—East Coast fever, sleeping sickness, and pleural pneumonia. Bror had thought better of his scheme of owning a dairy farm.

In addition, he had discovered that his parcel of land was not much more than a kitchen garden compared to Delamere's 100,000 acres. Several farmers owned greater than 10,000 acres. He was not wealthy enough to aspire to an enormous holding, but he took Sjögren's advice, sold his grazing land, and bought instead 1500 acres of wooded ground near Nairobi. The farm was said to be perfect for coffee: high-altitude forest loam. Coffee had become like gold in Africa; Catholic missionaries living on the northern outskirts of Nairobi had been raising coffee for over ten years—at rumored enormous profits. Bror was especially pleased with the setting of the new land: wooded like Denmark, mountains on the horizon, the great plains in the distance, and the game reserve across the river from the farm.

He was relieved to have sold the other piece of land because of his difficulty in persuading the African chiefs there to promise workers, despite his having spent weeks camping in the hills, negotiating and offering them gifts. The new farm lay in populous Kikuyu land. These agricultural people were used to the white man's needs, and if one treated them right, workers showed up in good numbers. Bror was proud to have already signed a few hundred to work. He had also hired two white men as foremen and was beginning to clear land for coffee.

Finally he wrote to say he could not leave the farm just as he was getting it started, and Karen should come to Africa to join him. He knew she did not like to travel by herself, but he had it on good authority that Prince Wilhelm would be coming out to Africa at the end of the year. Bror would see to arrangements for her to travel on the same ship.

* *

All Karen's furniture had finally been stowed on board—months had been required to prepare and crate it. She was taking along her father's old Bornholm clock, a small chest of drawers given to her by her grandmother, Mama Westenholz, and a number of paintings—in addition to the settee, and a desk, and the dining room set, two suites of bedroom furniture, and her silver and linen. Bror had written there was a good house, and plenty of Africans to work on the farm. She hoped some were also trained to work as servants.

She was at last embarking, after an exhausting journey to Naples, and two weeks of preparations and last-minute purchases. From the ship's deck she looked out at the faded façades of Naples, and perhaps found the city nostalgically splendid and the warm breezes of the Mediterranean an inspiration, compared to the icy winds of Denmark in this season. As the ship pulled away from the quay, she watched the faces of her mother and Elle slowly fade amid the waving handkerchiefs, until they were no more distinct than if she had been looking into a snowstorm.

* 2 *

In those times one could go out to Africa on a steamer from several European ports—Antwerp or Marseilles, Genoa or Naples—although many preferred to travel across Europe by train to shorten the time aboard ship, since putting into port at various points in the Mediterranean was tedious, and travel by ship uncomfortable. Even the journey from Naples took nearly four weeks, and the food and company aboard ship left something to be desired. Traveling out to the colonies were functionaries of His Majesty's government, soldiers on their way to commission, an occasional wandering naturalist intrigued by the challenges of Africa, and rich adventurers intent on shooting safaris. There were few women, although Aunt Fritze Frijs had made the journey with her husband a year or two earlier. Some colonial functionaries brought their wives out, even though the climate was known to be dangerous. It was said one's health could be ruined simply from exposure to the sun—not to mention the multitude of tropical ailments, such as malaria, sleeping sickness, and dysentery.

Karen found the wives of civil servants without style. They belonged, in general, to a certain element of the middle class. Their fathers had been clergymen, professors, or farmers, or had spent their lives, like the wives' unfortunate husbands, in government service. Their education was limited; they were little interested in lofty or creative conversation. They seemed to prefer rumor and speculation, and began to complain about conditions in Africa—on the basis of surmises—while still aboard ship. How were they to cope with heat and insects, with dirt and smells, with naked natives, poor supplies, and inferior servants? Their talk consisted almost entirely of complaints. She could learn nothing from them. Was there anticipation for the wonders of Africa? Were there fantasies about the splendor of the great wild country ahead? Was there curiosity about the tribes and the flora, the mountains and the game-covered plains? Not from them. They hoped to train their servants properly and keep a good house.

Entertainment aboard ship consisted of shuffleboard and bridge, charades in the evening, and occasionally a costume ball. Readings were given; sometimes someone sang or performed at the piano; skits were devised. Karen found the input dreary and would have preferred conversation about Africa, its exotic rewards, or even coffee farming. The food aboard ship—limited to fish and foods that would keep without ice during the four-week journey—was bland; nothing could rescue the meals save an interesting dinner partner.

Each evening Karen selected one of the dinner gowns hanging in her large steamer trunk. She had not reached the age of twenty-eight without acquiring charm. In fact, charm was her proudest asset, although her mother and aunts would have preferred that she stress her other qualities. It was her goal as she dined to make an impression, and she thought of her white shoulders as part of the effect. But she believed it was her conversation that really counted and, in the end, made her dinner partner remember her.

In addition to Bror's friends—whom she knew all too well—the passenger list included a charming German commandant, Paul von Lettow-Vorbeck, who devoted much attention to her en route. He was in his early forties and rather attractive, although he had lost his sight in one eye, in a battle to crush an uprising in South West Africa, and he wore an eye patch. Karen found his conversation delightful, and wrote to her mother that he came from a fine old German family. He was on his way to assume command in Tanganyika, the territory Germany claimed in East Africa. They talked of horses—Karen esteemed herself a good judge of them—and she offered to find some good Abyssinian ponies for his regiment once she reached British East Africa. Bror had written about the excellent horses available from the north.

When her health permitted, Karen spent her days on deck, watching the shores of Suez slip by and joining in an occasional game of shuffleboard. She had been ill enough before leaving home that weakness overshadowed her voyage, and her exhaustion intensified with the heat as they passed through the Red Sea. One evening at dinner the captain remarked that she looked pale. She explained she was really unfit to travel, and he commented sympathetically that she could do with a personal maid. This thought had occurred to Karen before—though not to her mother. A Victorian guidebook entitled *Hints to lady travelers* had advertised that lady's maids were "a great nuisance" to women wishing to see the world (*VLT*, 7). Although "even quite a modest home," like that owned by Karen's family in Denmark, had at least "a cook, two maids, and a groom, as well as a washerwoman and a gardener" (*MSID*, 27–8), Ingeborg Dinesen had not thought it seemly for Karen to travel with a servant. However, with the captain's urging, Karen agreed to hire one of the ship's German stewardesses as her personal maid. As a future baroness, she thought it only proper to have one. They devised a plan for the stewardess to stay with Karen for some weeks in Africa to help train her house staff. Karen was in despair over how to train African servants; she had never trained a servant at home.

When the ship called at Aden, Britain's large military port, Karen went ashore in the thick heat. Suddenly out of the Arab crowd stepped a statuesque black man in a white robe and red turban. His nose was so straight and his features so soft that Karen thought he was Indian. He touched his hand to his forehead, made a brief salaam, and, in English so halting she could barely understand, said he was called Farah (*LFA*, 1). Bror had received word of Karen's recent illness and, knowing she was reluctant to travel alone, had sent his most valued servant to accompany her.

* 3 *

Farah fascinated Karen in three ways: first, he was her own personal servant, an exalted luxury; then, he was a member of those exotic races hitherto known to her only in epic literature; and finally, he was Bror's gift to her—a wedding present to rival the gifts of legend, for it was creative. In Bror's thoughtfulness she discerned brilliant understanding of herself, and she was glad for choosing this husband.

Farah, she judged, was nearly her own age. He was only slightly taller than she, but seemed imposing because of his carriage—"like a Spanish grandee" (*LFA*, 4). She spoke gently to him, as one might to a child—the child of a king. He understood little of her language, but obeyed, as though sensing her needs out of superior instinct. Truthfully, she did not herself know what she wanted him to do; having one's own servant would require experience.

He brought her tea in the morning, knocking softly before entering the small stateroom; in a grave way, as though damned—because Allah would not approve—he cared for her dog; he stood by her deck chair, willing to fetch what she had forgotten and to carry her wrap if the sun grew too warm. When she did not need him, he disappeared into the mysterious culture of servants, below decks.

That Bror should have chosen this servant for her intrigued Karen. Why had she been so long in realizing how much she and Bror thought as one? He had asked her to marry him more than once before she assented. Why had she not understood earlier his creative imagination? It was she, not Bror, who had instigated this emigration to the colonies. Yet Bror had seized upon her fantasy with an adventurer's instinct. He had enlarged upon the idea as though it were his own, so that now it was difficult to say who displayed the greater enthusiasm for it. In fact, he had taken over the wings of her fantasy and was gliding, unafraid, in a direction unknown to them both.

This was taking a gamble, agreeing to be Bror's wife. Karen was unsure of her skills. She would make his life comfortable and be a good companion for him, provided she could survive the hot climate—a factor which up until now she had failed to consider. But it was not possible to worry about that now, because she had already made up her mind. She was going to Africa to seek her destiny.

She was convinced one could never become a heroine by staying at home. She had always imagined herself playing a great role in history. She wished to take her place among the figures of legend, to be a name upon the lips of children, to live experiences romantic to generations to come. One could not achieve greatness by undertaking domestic life—a quiet home, a brood of children, a husband earning a dignified living—in Denmark. There, it seemed to her, the greatest challenges encompassed little more than serving tea to esteemed members of the community and maintaining one's position in society.

Yet, exotic aspirations aside, she could not forget that her main purpose in going to Africa was to become a wife—a role she accepted reluctantly because she was trained for no other livelihood. Thanks to her mother and aunts, who had pampered her and her sisters, she had not even learned household skills.

Having witnessed her mother's devotion, Karen envisioned her role of wife as one of serving her husband. This ageless idea was a particular feature of Edwardian times, when England's adored Queen Alexandra—the King's Danish wife—set the style for wifely behavior. As Alexandra had summoned the King's mistress to his death bed, so did women live to serve their husbands. Beyond this understanding, however, Karen had little idea what it meant to be a wife, for there were no men in her family. Her father had died by suicide when she was ten years old. Perhaps she longed to live adventurously, *like* a man, to fulfill her father's dreams for himself.

* *

Wilhelm Dinesen, like his daughter, had held a heroic vision of his destiny. His life had been characterized by a restless striving for greatness. The family's daguerreotypes show his proud posture and face—bearded in later years, vaguely reminiscent of King Edward VII. Wilhelm Dinesen had been trained as a soldier, like his father. He fought in the Dano-Prussian war of 1864, in which Denmark lost, and later he joined the French side in the Franco-Prussian war of 1870–71, in which France was defeated. Afterwards he wrote a book about his war experiences, entitled *Paris under the Commune*. In 1872, at the age of twenty-eight, he left Denmark for America. There he traveled and took odd jobs, and finally he camped for some time in a log cabin in Wisconsin, where his closest neighbors were the Chippewa Indians. He lived intimately with them; they gave him the name Boganis— "hazelnut" in the Chippewa language—later used as his pen-name.

It was said by members of the family that Wilhelm Dinesen had been in love with his cousin Agnes Frijs, who died of typhoid shortly before he left for America; but he might have gone to America anyway, for he was, like his contemporaries, romantically drawn to the life of the "noble savage" described by the French writer Chateaubriand. It was common for sons of the wealthy to travel as part of their education. Those interested in commerce went to India, Africa, or the Orient, but those pursuing a romantic ideal sought to live with the American Indians, in contact with nature.

Wilhelm Dinesen had not expected to make his fortune in America, but to experiment with a different philosophy of life. However, in 1874, because his parents were ill, he returned to Denmark. He re-entered the army, and eventually volunteered to fight in the war of 1877–78 with Turkey against Russia, but he was never assigned to active duty. Finally, after both his parents had died, he left the military for good. He did not inherit his father's country estate—Katholm in Jutland—but he did receive a small inheritance. His older sister, Alvilde, recently a widow, had also come into money and agreed in 1879 to invest in an attractive property with him: the Rungstedlund, Rungstedgaard, and Folehave farms, on the Oresund, fifteen miles north of Copenhagen. This land, with a view of Sweden across the channel, was bordered by coastline for three kilometers. The property seemed a shrewd investment and a romantic setting for a home, where Wilhelm Dinesen hoped to live out his ideal of a pastoral life. He had begun to court Ingeborg Westenholz, the sweetly beautiful daughter of the widow of a wealthy shipping merchant. Despite, or perhaps because of, Wilhelm's having poured out to her the story of his amorous adventures with other women, she was very much attracted to him. They exchanged poems with each other, and became engaged.

* *

Ingeborg Westenholz came from a family of five children. (A sixth Westenholz child died in infancy.) Her mother, Mary Westenholz, who had been widowed at the age of thirty-three, was grateful for the arrival of a suitor for her daughter, for she had never been comfortable with managing her own affairs and longed for a man to take them over again. Wilhelm Dinesen offered his new mother-in-law a house on his own estate, only a few miles from his own. His sister, Alvilde, lived in the Rungstedgaard house, his mother-in-law and her daughters in the house at Folehave, and he and his new wife at Rungstedlund, by the sea. The modest manor house of timber and stucco, surrounded by barns, had once been an inn. The renowned Danish lyric poet, Johannes Ewald, had lived there in the 1700s, and it was for this that Wilhelm Dinesen was romantically attracted to it. The house was drafty, taking in wind from the sea, but it suited him and his serenely adoring wife.

Although he was never perfectly content there, he oversaw the farms, supervised the grooming and training of his horses and dogs, and devoted himself to hunting and to keeping a journal of the life of outdoor sport. His journals were published as *Letters from the Hunt* and received literary acclaim. He captured the spirit of the hunting life in a way with which men could identify. Women did not play a part in the essays, in the same way they were not welcome to join in hunting. Wilhelm Dinesen wrote that there were certain times of the year "when the black cock keeps to himself or is with one of his comrades. He can't stand childish nonsense, and he can't stand female chatter, and he will have nothing to do with family life. And as for the dried-up old hens, they have to amuse themselves as best they can—alone or with each other—but without him" (*LFTH*, 1).

The five Dinesen children were born over a span of eleven years. There were first three girls: Inger ("Ea"), born in 1883; Karen ("Tanne"), in 1885; and Ellen ("Elle"), in 1886; and then two boys: Thomas, born in 1892; and Anders, in 1894. Of the girls, only the second, Karen, shared Wilhelm Dinesen's love of the out-of-doors. She was an attractive child, vivacious, with dark eyes and curls. He would sometimes take her with him, setting out along the path to the woods, he in his tweed hunting clothes with his rifle under his arm, and she in brown, high-buttoned boots and long woolen coat, skipping behind him through fallen leaves. His dogs went, too; they were like people to him—his passion second only to hunting.

Although the family pleased Wilhelm Dinesen, and he never found discontent with his wife, he was a moody man. He had always been restless, and after some years of living in the country, had taken up politics and won a seat in parliament—a not uncommon course of action in these times for a member of the wealthy middle class. He stayed in Copenhagen when parliament was in session, and became an influential politician. However, he suffered intermittently from depression. His sisters remarked that even in his youth he had often been withdrawn. He would stay apart from others in the drawing room and, while meditating on some unresolved course of action, would sometimes drop down in a faint, the effect of standing rigidly for many minutes. In 1895, at the age of 50, he talked of going away for awhile, perhaps taking a trip around the world. But one evening while staying in his apartment in Copenhagen, he hanged himself. That he should have chosen to die by hanging, like a traitor, appeared to be an admission of guilt for abandoning his family. Although never confirmed, the romantic tradition in the family maintained he suffered from syphilis and could not face a life of gradual debilitation. (The family came to this conclusion naturally, for one out of three men living in Copenhagen contracted venereal disease, in one form or another [*SH*, 366]. Because the Victorian ethic emphasized sexual restraint at home, the era was characterized by high levels of prostitution.)

That her husband had been unfaithful did not appear to disturb Ingeborg Dinesen as much as one might have expected. Perhaps she was resigned to the customs of the times, when, like hunting, paramours were the accepted recreation of men. Wives were to be treasured and sheltered from base, sexual desires. One's spouse's role lay in the procreation of children and upholding the family name. Fru Dinesen never lost her esteem for her husband, nor did his suicide change her serene approach to life. Left alone with five children under the age of twelve, she was well provided for. Her own inheritance and Wilhelm Dinesen's estate, more valuable since the completion of the railroad between Rungsted and Copenhagen, allowed her and her children to continue living as wealthy, country gentry. Nearby she had the support of her mother, Mama Westenholz, and her unmarried sister, Bess.

The Westenholz women, who had lost their own father at a young age, were accustomed to the absence of a man in their household. Ingeborg's sister, Lidda, eventually married, but Bess, like Queen Alexandra's daughter, Princess Victoria—and many spinster daughters of the age—was destined to remain at home and devote herself to the care of Mama. Aunt Bess had won the family's gratitude in this, for Mama Westenholz, as everyone recognized, was simply "not very self-sufficient"—she was almost child-like in her inability to manage on her own (*MSID*, 25–6).

At times Karen reflected that Aunt Bess had assumed her role with rather exaggerated seriousness—she being a person who viewed life as a mission to reform others. Aunt Bess had been overseer of her fatherless younger brother and sister, Aage and Lidda, a fact that perhaps ever afterwards shaped her interactions with people. When her own siblings had gone, she turned her governance to Ingeborg's family, offering them moral supervision. Fru Dinesen and a governess saw to the education of the girls, in the subjects with which they were familiar: history, literature, social studies, and geography. Mathematics and science were thought to be of interest only to boys, and were taught to Karen's brothers later when they attended Rungsted Boarding School. The girls were encouraged to express themselves, both in writing and conversation. They were coached to speak logically and to write clearly. They were aided in this by endless parlor games designed to polish their verbal skills: skits and rhyming competitions, poetry and essay contests, recitations and story-telling.

In 1898, three years after Wilhelm Dinesen's death, a great fire broke out in the old Rungstedlund manor and destroyed the entire south wing and all the barns. Much of the house had to be rebuilt. With the encouragement of Mama Westenholz and Aunt Bess, who offered to care for her small sons, Ingeborg Dinesen took her three girls to Switzerland for a change of air. Accompanying them was Else Bardenfleth, the daughter of long-time friends Rear Admiral Frederik and Ida Bardenfleth. Karen was then thirteen years old. There for the first time she attended school, where she learned French, and took drawing and painting lessons. Later in Denmark, at the age of seventeen, she was sent, along with her sisters, to Miss Sode's Drawing School. Of the three girls, Karen showed the most aptitude for art. Her mother and Aunt Bess encouraged her to take up painting, suggesting that perhaps she had found her *métier*. Thus in 1903, when she was eighteen, Karen enrolled in classes at the Academy of Art in Copenhagen. Her interest in studying art was, as could be expected for one of her age, only slightly greater than her enthusiasm for the opportunities for social contact at school. She soon became vice-chair of the Student Union, a position whose responsibilities included planning dances and other festive events. Painting never became for her more than a serious pastime.

In her more reflective moments she also demonstrated talent for writing. When she was only six or seven years old, she began inventing stories for her younger sister, Elle, who later remembered listening to them in bed and begging Karen to stop when she grew too sleepy to listen. Karen later wrote down her stories, as dramatizations to be performed for the family. Over the years, she had favorite ones that she changed and polished, until the year 1907—she was twenty-two years old—when two of them were published: "The Ploughman," in *Gad's Danish Magazine*, and "The Hermits" in *The Spectator*. "The de Cats Family" appeared in *The Spectator* in 1909.

During three years of art classes in Copenhagen, she had established a friendship with her cousin, Countess Daisy Frijs, one of Copenhagen's most prominent young socialites. Daisy was one of four daughters of Count Mogens Frijs. Frequently Karen was welcomed to stay at the Frijs mansion rather than take the evening train to Rungsted. The Frijs home represented a different world compared to the staid maternal atmosphere at the Dinesen house. Uncle Mogens with his cigars set a masculine tone; Aunt Fritze was the quintessential feminine antidote—gay, chic, a little flighty—the fashionable Queen Alexandra type.

The Frijses were wealthier than Karen's family, and being part of the aristocracy, lived on a higher social plane. Although they were relatives, Karen never ceased to feel her visits to the Frijses were privileges. Daisy, three years younger than Karen, had not yet made her society debut when Karen first began spending time in Copenhagen. Therefore, in the years Karen went to art school she participated in Daisy's coming out. Privy to the aristocratic milieu, she observed with fascination a titled girl's search for an appropriate suitor. Daisy's sister, Inger, married Count Julius Wedell in 1908, and honored Karen by asking her to be a bridesmaid. Karen joked loftily of the wedding, "I sacrificed myself to high society" (*MSID*, 23). She continued to spend more and more time with Daisy's fashionable set, was invited to balls, hunting parties, and evenings of bridge, and went skating and sailing with them in season.

Among the young aristocrats joining in these activities were Daisy's cousins—Karen's second cousins—the twins, Hans and Bror von Blixen-Finecke. Karen's father had spoken well of Baron Blixen in his *Letters from the Hunt*. Karen was intrigued by the atmosphere at Näsbyholm, the Blixen country estate, where she was invited from time to time with other young people. The atmosphere resembled life at home when her father was alive. Aunt Clara subjugated all her desires to those of Uncle Frederik. Her husband and sons received the utmost deference. The days of the hunt, to which women were invited only as spectators, were a good example. Karen's impression at Näsbyholm was that the lives of women consisted of waiting backstage for a summons to a part in the vigorously ongoing drama in which men engaged. She later described the women as "civilized slaves of good-natured barbarians" (*OA*, 190). Yet the devotion of the women fascinated her. They were supporting an ideal. She yearned to play such a role herself. It was this yearning to take her place as a devoted partner in a titled marriage that had brought her to her present situation. Her ideal included travel, riches, adventure, and children, but, most of all, the title, *Baroness*. Gaining a title represented life's most sublime accomplishment, and she had not been willing to marry without it.

As for going to Africa, she was eager to escape boredom at home—Sunday tea with Mama Westenholz and conversations limited to her family's views had begun to suffocate her. But she had had other chances to escape, and had not availed herself of them. She had traveled with her brothers and sisters to Germany, England, and Norway, and had gone to Paris once for six weeks with her sister Ea— but she always returned homesick. She had never been willing to travel alone, nor been desperate enough to get away to become a nurse in China. In fact, she had had suitors, yet her mother's home had sufficed until she reached the age of twenty-eight. She would have easily renounced her yearning to see exotic places to marry Hans Blixen—who showed every sign of living just the kind of bourgeois life she planned to escape with Bror.

She would not have gone to Africa, indeed could not have considered going, without Bror. Bror was necessary to consummate the adventure. Bror was to be the farmer; she was to be his wife and companion. She was marrying to satisfy a physical longing, and to make her life meaningful, but she had chosen Bror, not just because of his title, but because he was willing to do what she wanted. From now on her talents for writing and painting would be subjugated to those needed to support their joint ideal. Her talents for conversation, for entertaining, for dressing and looking well must be used to make Bror proud. She thought she had mastered these well. Nevertheless, she had reason to wonder if her talents were adequate to being a devoted wife in Africa.

Something may have reminded her of a fight she and Bror had, as child cousins at Näsbyholm. While visiting there with her family, she was perhaps teased into an argument by the boy, Bror Blixen. She wrote about such a conflict in the fictional tale, "Peter and Rosa." Unable to settle their differences verbally, the two children in the story end by wrestling. "She had pulled his hair with all her might while, with his tough boy's arms round her, he had tried to fling her to the floor. She laughed at the memory, with her eyes closed" (*WT*, 269).

1914

1914

1

After leaving Denmark, where in December there are only seven hours of daylight, arriving in Africa has the effect of a bright light turned on when you have been asleep in the dark. You cannot get used to the glare. You would like to appreciate the fruity, flower-laden aroma of the coastal forest, and to rejoice in the chanting of the porters as they unload the ship—large bundles on top of turbaned heads, brown legs in loin cloths wading from the log canoes to the beach. You would like to stare up at the baobabs, the elephants of the tree world, and wonder why they have been planted, as it appears, upside down. You would like to touch the brown shining-eyed children and ask their names, and to peer inside the stuccoed buildings lining the tunnel-like streets. You would like to know how this Muslim colony came to be here, and why a great coral fort rises over the entrance to the town. You would like to think about the slave and the ivory trade that has passed through Mombasa port, and the coffee, sisal, and tea being shipped to England and points abroad from this small tropical island, joined by a bridge to the African mainland. But it is so bright that you only wish to get away, anywhere, out of the sun.

There is a strange, thick, musty smell at the African coast that may have seemed ominous to Karen—who was perhaps yearning to have her mother beside her as she readied to leave the ship. The sight of palm trees and bougainvillea, of minarets and African fishing canoes did not arouse her excitement as she had expected; she was fainting from the heat. There being no quay, Bror, in a rumpled white suit, was rowed out to greet her. He was robust and tanned, and roughly affectionate—but she wished he would not embrace her so openly in front of the others. His greeting matched the enthusiasm of the crowd onshore to welcome Prince Wilhelm to Mombasa.

As a friend and titled compatriot, Bror was part of the official delegation. Karen was impressed by the honors to her associated with arriving with the Prince. Stepping ashore from the canoe, she was introduced to the American millionaire Northrup McMillan, entrepreneur in East Africa and leader of the delegation to welcome the royal figures. McMillan—dignified and imposing despite weighing at least 300 pounds—assured her that Bror was setting an outstanding example for new settlers and she would be amazed at all he had done to prepare for her arrival (*LFA*, 3–4). McMillan guided them, along with the royal party, on a brief tour of Mombasa. They climbed the cobblestone street that gave entrance to the massive coral walls of Fort Jesus—a relic of Portuguese military domination, abandoned when the Portuguese were driven out by the forces of the Sultan of Oman in the 1700s. The sultan retained nominal jurisdiction over the Kenya coast—as long as he cooperated with the British. His representative in Mombasa, Ali bin Salim, greeted the dignitaries and invited them to honor him with a visit on any occasion on which they came to Mombasa. The sultan himself, whose ancestors controlled the northern Arab emirate of Oman, now lived on the island of Zanzibar, where he was said to have grown rich from the spice trade. Rumor maintained he had not altogether given up, at British bidding, his most lucrative business as the greatest slave trader of them all.

As they made their tour, Karen was less concerned about learning coastal history than about what was happening to the expensive shoes she had bought in Paris. The streets were filled with pineapple remnants, coconut shells, banana peelings, and peanut waste. Everywhere was the smell of rotting garbage, urine, and mule and camel manure. Dusty, naked children played in the streets; women in black veils hid their faces furtively as they passed; the rows of white stuccoed buildings with heavily studded doors faced each other so closely that only a man and a donkey had room to walk. Karen was weak from the effort to be gracious.

At the arranged hour, the party made their way to the office of Charles Hobley, the British District Commissioner, who had agreed to marry Karen and Bror. The building, a corrugated iron bungalow, was sweltering at eleven A.M. when the ceremony took place. Karen perspired in the shántung suit and silk blouse she had chosen for her wedding. With some sense of at last arriving in exotic climes, she had donned a safari helmet; she had been warned the sun could be fatal to whites, for whom God had never intended such brightness. Prince Wilhelm and his aides, Boström and Lewenhaupt, served as witnesses to the ceremony, and Sjögren, the Swedish consul, as best man. The wedding was over in less than ten minutes; then the party adjourned by rickshaw to Hobley's seaside villa for drinks.

As the lone woman in the company, Karen may have been aware that she was creating a sensual effect. Although her shoes added height, she seemed small beside Bror, and her figure was generous: one might say, *ripe*, as one might expect of a bride. She had taken off her hat, revealing her thick, brown hair. Her face and dark eyes were sweet and alluring. The men may have judged that Blixen had chosen well. They perhaps wondered if he had tasted the fruits.

As a matter of fact, it is likely he had. Bror Blixen was not one to be reticent when it came to women. In his twenty-seven years he had already known quite a few, and he clearly had a way with them.

* *

He had always known Karen, but he had begun to find her particularly interesting some four years previously when she fell in love with his twin brother Hans. Hans was a few minutes older and a little better looking, and Bror had made his life a game of drawing attention from Hans to himself. Hans had become a soldier and expert horseman. Bror had gone to agricultural school, which he never took seriously, and, for lack of another trade, afterwards took up management of the family's dairy farm. He had not done too badly at it, because he had a knack for working with animals. But his greatest talent was for the pleasurable pursuits—parties, hunting, and women.

Karen had had a teasing relationship with both twins since they were children, for they saw each other at family gatherings. If she eyed her cousins with the possibility of marrying one of them, she would have chosen Hans naturally, for, in his uniform, with his medals for horsemanship, he was decidedly the hero of the twins. And it was a hero she was seeking; she would have nothing else—unless it were to be the hero herself.

The family knew about Karen's infatuation with Hans. For several years she believed she might win him. Her best friend and cousin, Daisy, encouraged her in this fantasy. The fact that Daisy's and Hans's mutual grandmother and Karen's grandmother were sisters, and the fact that the cousins by virtue of wealth were part of the same social set, had prepared the stage for girlish intrigue. Karen and Daisy had used some deviousness to bring Hans and Karen together.

"I fell very, very deeply in love when I was quite young,—it was in 1909," she later wrote (*LFA*, 225). She was then twenty-four years old. In the tale "The Deluge at Norderney," she provides a description, elegantly concealed, of a loss of virginity—portrayed as a loss of "voice":

> . . . the court physician, who was attending
> me, told me that I had lost my voice and that I had no
> hope of getting it back. While I was still in bed I was
> much worried by this, not only by the loss of my voice
> itself, but by the thought of how I should now
> disappoint and lose my friends . . . I was even
> shedding tears about it . . . He had to get up from his
> chair and pretend to look out of the window to hide
> his laughter. I thought it heartless of him, and did not
> say any more to him . . . . he said, "I have reason to
> laugh, for I have won my bet. I held that you were
> indeed the simpleton you look, which nobody else
> would believe . . . . It will not make the slightest

24

difference in the world to you that you have lost that voice of yours." (*SGT*, 32)

In "The Old Chevalier" the narrator falls in love while spending an autumn hunting weekend with young friends in the country (*SGT*, 82). It would have been a good joke to Hans Blixen to flatter and deceive the brightest—and the most upright—of the girls.

Bror could never stand for his brother to have anything he did not. He had spent his life refusing to be outshone, and he made up his mind to pursue Karen himself. Fortune was in his favor. By 1912, Hans had found a wealthy debutante—eight years younger than Karen—who interested him. This created an emotional crisis for Karen; despite not having had Hans's attentions for some time, she continued to fantasize about marrying him. She was obsessed with the idea that she would never be happy in life without Hans. Later she said, "More than anything else, a deep, unrequited love left its mark on my early youth" (*LDID*, 65).

Her depression at the news of his coming marriage was worsened because Daisy had already married, in 1910. Even though she had impetuously—and from some spite toward a former suitor—married an older man entirely unsuited to her, she had achieved by marrying what Karen had not. Daisy's new husband, Henrik Castenskiold, was appointed Danish ambassador to Rome, and their departure left Karen's social milieu disturbingly silent. She had lost her source of contact with titled suitors, of which there were anyway precious few. After Hans's engagement Karen went to Daisy in Rome, staying several weeks, and came back willing to be courted by Bror Blixen.

Bror was of average height, and muscular—some would have said, stocky. He had a round, congenial face with ruddy skin and mischievous blue eyes. His blond hair waved away from a broad forehead. He was not quite as attractive as his twin brother, but he seemed in one respect his equal, and this was in his ability to charm. Content to be Karen's second choice, he was persistently gallant, offering himself to her in a tenderly humorous way, one may imagine, as not a bad alternative to Hans. But it was his sensuousness that finally wore her down, for her sexual instincts had been primed by her experience with Hans, and Bror showed himself capable of satisfying her longings.

For Bror there was apparently more to the competition than sexual conquest. Karen had something to offer him which was particularly advantageous to him at his stage of life, and this was, quite simply, money. Not to say that Karen was not also a fascinating and pretty woman, but Blixen had been moved to propose primarily by what she offered in financial security. His family, though titled, was not wealthy, but Karen's merchant forefathers had left her well-off.

To say the couple did not love each other would have been putting it too strongly. Indeed, Karen suggests in the tale "The Pearls," modeled after her life with Bror, that the wags were mistaken: "The gossips of Copenhagen would have it that the bridegroom had married for money, and the bride for a name, but they were all wrong. The match was a love affair . . . " (*WT*, 108–9). But the Swedish friends who witnessed their marriage in Mombasa may have suspected there were some conveniences in the marriage arrangement between Karen and Bror.

* 2 *

The British governor had sent his private train to Mombasa to escort Prince Wilhelm to Nairobi, and the wedding party trailed the Swedish delegation as it boarded the train. Karen could not but consider how grand it was, being treated like royalty within hours of her marriage. However, despite the grandeur, she felt exhausted. The train, for all its official pomp, had no sleeping car, so she was forced to stretch out on one of the cushioned, horsehair-covered benches, in sheets Bror had kindly brought along.

The first leg of the journey led away from the coast, past coconut palms and tiny farms cut into thick vegetation. Here and there a small African boy could be seen tending goats. Adults had taken shelter from the mid-day heat. Soon the terrain gave way to a desert of scrub and dust—the Taru. Here the sparse and diminutive trees were gnarled and twisted, as though growing in fits and jerks. There was no grass, only hard-baked ground. Dust hung in the railroad car. The sun

set at six o'clock, disappearing without twilight—a year-round phenomenon of sunset near the Equator. Heat still blanketed the train,
but now a slight breeze came up.

Toward eight o'clock the heat diminished enough to allow
Karen to move about without feeling she was swimming against a
current. She changed into a gown for dinner. One could reach the other
cars only while the train was stopped, and the meal was served while
the train remained stationary on the tracks. Northrup McMillan's
personal chef and kitchen staff had laid what Karen later described to
her mother as an "absolutely splendid" meal (*LFA*, 2). After dinner
they returned to their own car and slept until dawn. By this time the
train had reached the plains of the Athi River, southeast of Nairobi, and
they could see lush grass, low trees, and blue mountains in the
distance, while thousands of wild animals grazed within easy range.
There were large flocks of zebra and gnu, tall, slow-moving giraffe,
many types of antelope, small troops of gray baboon, and ostriches,
warthogs, and guinea fowl. Once or twice they caught sight of a lion or
cheetah stalking its morning prey. As the sun came up, the animals
seemed to teem and fade in the shimmering light. Bror said he had
hunted most of these animals and had collected good trophies. Karen
asked if she could learn to hunt them, and he said, of course, he would
teach her. This perhaps seemed fitting to her, since she had grown to
love him on hunting weekends at home. Bror knew how to study the
best of the herd and capture it for himself. He gave Karen the
impression she would be equally valuable as his wife and as his friend.

* 3 *

As she stepped off the train at Nairobi, Karen's first impression was how clear and soft the air was. It gave her a sense of elation
which she interpreted as sheer joy in being there. She had never before
seen such a variety of dress as existed in the throng on the station
platform—white men in khaki shorts and knee stockings, Africans in
bright cloths, English women in fancy hats and Edwardian skirts,
Kikuyu women in leather aprons, with babies on their backs, Swahilis
in long cotton robes and skull caps, Masai in red cloaks, earrings

drooping to their shoulders—and the governor and his delegation, lined up in strict pomp and white uniform, ready to escort the Swedish royal entourage to Government House.

At luncheon, feeling shy at the honor, Karen sat beside the governor, on one hand, and the vice-governor on the other. Everyone called her "Baroness," and she was embarrassed, because, as she wrote to her mother, "to start with I didn't realize they were addressing me" (*LFA*, 3). After luncheon the royal party was to be escorted to Parklands, a suburb of Nairobi, where they would stay as guests in the home of the Honourable Denys Finch Hatton. The arrangements had been made by Northrup McMillan, who had owned this palatial residence for some time. (An entry in the newspaper saying that Finch Hatton had bought the house is questionable; buying such a property was out of character for him. He had never owned a house before, and, as Karen Blixen points out in *Out of Africa*, never owned a home while she knew him.) However, Bror Blixen and his wife were not to be among the visitors at Parklands, since Bror was eager to show Karen their farm.

Bror had borrowed a car for the occasion—one of only a few in Nairobi in 1914. The car moved joltingly along the red laterite road grooved with wagon ruts accumulated during the rains. This track led out of town, past shanties roofed with corrugated tin, which served as shops and stores of Nairobi, and into lush countryside, where round thatched huts clustered near patches of maize, and Africans lingered amidst their goats and cows. Children, naked, ran to the road to watch them pass. They sang greetings and waved, and Karen waved back. The car passed old women bent with loads of wood on their backs; they stood aside, staring as the car passed, too fatigued to smile. Their bundles of wood were attached by leather straps around their fore-heads and their long, flaccid breasts hung free. Here and there near the huts were two or three men wearing loin coverings and earrings, seated on the packed red earth in the shade. Occasionally, in a field, Karen saw a woman bent double, hoeing—bobbing up and down as she worked with a baby on her back. In front of one of the huts, two women stood pounding corn with long, thick poles in a wooden mortar. Smoke rose from cooking fires, and fat babies wearing strings of beads around their waists crawled nearby. Karen was in rapture. Through the trees along the road, she could see a cluster of low blue mountains; the rounded summits ran in a line along the horizon, like the knuckles of a hand. These were the Ngong Hills, at the foot of which, Bror said, lay the farm.

The trees became thicker as they approached. Karen was impressed by the beauty of the woods; it reminded her of the deer parks at home (*LFA*, 3). When they rounded a bend in the road she caught sight of a large moving display and heard an ear-splitting welcome as 1200 Africans, lined up on either side of the lane to the house, chanted and saluted. As Karen came nearer, she saw that their faces were painted with white stripes and they were gesturing with spears.

They crowded around the car as it stopped. Karen stepped out into a sea of Africans wearing only beads and loin covers and leather aprons. Afterwards what stayed in her mind was the sight of hundreds of woolly heads dancing around her. She wrote to her mother that they "surrounded us when we got out of the car and insisted on touching us . . . " (*LFA*, 3). Among the throng were six white men, foremen of the farm and the neighboring plantation, the Swedo-African Coffee Company, owned by Sjögren. They had seen to the preparation of a lavish welcome—cakes and sandwiches and tea—and wedding gifts. The house was a gray fieldstone bungalow with many-paned windows— not an enormous house, but comfortable. There was a lavatory off Karen's bedroom; she told her mother it was the only one in East Africa—most settlers having to content themselves with a "long drop" behind the house. She sized up the grounds and made plans for a garden that first day. They would stay in Nairobi at the Norfolk Hotel until their furniture had been unpacked and arranged.

That night she and Bror shared a quiet dinner in their room. Karen later wrote home: "It was wonderful to be with someone one feels one belongs with again . . . " (*LFA*, 2).

* 4 *

Bror had planned for them a honeymoon on safari. A friend named Hopcraft offered to let them use his hunting lodge in the grasslands, near Lake Naivasha, where Bror hoped to teach her how to shoot. Karen described it as ". . . a little log cabin, two rooms with wooden floors, with a fireplace in one of them and all around on every side the most magnificent and wonderful scenery you can imagine, huge distant blue mountains and the vast grassy plains before them covered with zebra and gazelle, and at night I can hear lions roaring like the thunder of guns in the darkness" (*LFA*, 2). In the East African highlands, even the air seemed seductive, as though setting the stage for a great love affair.

Sexually speaking, Karen was not very experienced, but she had become aware of the power of her charms. In the tale "The Deluge at Norderney," she describes a situation in which a naïve young woman so yearns to be a boy that she wishes to cut off her breasts. This yearning ceases at the moment she achieves an understanding of her sexual attractiveness (*SGT*, 46). Bror introduced her to the world of men's interests by teaching her to hunt, and expanded her understanding of sexual love, and she took up both her husband and hunting with passion. The rifles were erotic symbols, and the ardent conquest of each other was far more significant than the trophies—skins and tusks of animals—earned through hunting. Years later Karen said that if she could relive any portion of her life, it would be safariing with her husband, Bror.

But, in some ways, it was painful to love at once so passionately and so constantly. Karen said later that the ecstasy experienced on a honeymoon is so excruciating, one would simply expire if it were to continue indefinitely. In "The Roads Round Pisa," the hero is troubled by reflecting upon this dilemma on his wedding night. In "The Caryatids," newlyweds make love in the woods: "At times then he had alarmed her by the violence of his love for her, as if there were no moment to lose, as if death were threatening to separate the two" (*LT*, 148). Although she perhaps felt "melting tenderness" for Bror and "groaned under his caresses"—descriptions of lovemaking she later wrote to her brother—her health was not up to the strength of his ardor, nor to the incessance of his desire. She describes distress in the tale "The Dreamers": "This is too much; the sweetness is killing me, and I cannot stand it" (*SGT*, 332). Her mother had likely never spoken to her of the sexual aspect of marriage, and Karen, who believed that marriage stood for two people joined for spiritual perfection, had not realized the importance of sexual intercourse in what she had before viewed as a partnership for a far less physical ideal.

1914

In "The Poet" she says, ". . . fatigued by exquisite pleasure . . . where pleasure goes on forever, we run the risk of becoming blasé . . ." (*SGT*, 387), and in *Out of Africa* she describes a young bride's signal of disinterest: she turns her cheek to his kiss "in a pretty forbearing way, like a young wife who pertly permits her husband a caress" (*OA*, 74). After a day or two, this may have led to Bror's announcement that it was time they got back to the farm. There were projects at home that could not be managed without him.

* 5 *

Although Bror had established himself in the house, known as Mbagathi, before Karen's arrival in Africa, his arrangements were little better than those of a safari camp. Until his wife came from Denmark with the furniture, one may imagine he had been sleeping on a camp cot. In the room that served as office and sitting room, he had a couple of native-made cane chairs and a wooden table for estimating farm expenses. He made do with meals designed by his African cook: sweet potatoes, beans, bread, and game Bror shot himself, but he spent as many evenings as he could in Nairobi, where the cuisine at the hotels was more varied—if no better than the usual colonial fare. Karen's first task was to get the house in order, and to oversee the preparation of meals.

Her experience of housekeeping was rudimentary, for servants had done their work invisibly at home, and her knowledge of cooking had been acquired by sitting in the kitchen at Rungstedlund, watching the cooks. She understood only a little about gardening, having followed her mother in the flower beds, talking to her while she thinned the perennials. Her lack of experience exasperated her; she wondered how she had reached the age of twenty-eight with so little practical knowledge. She entered into housekeeping, taking as much off-hand advice as Bror could offer, and getting a few arch suggestions from neighbors—who perhaps thought her questions naïve.

Their furniture was brought from the railway station by oxcart and unloaded at the farm amid heated exchanges between Karen and the men; some of it was of course damaged, but Bror assured her they could get Indian craftsmen in Nairobi to make repairs.

The house had come with a servant, a Somali named Juma whose mother was Masai. Bror had managed to find an old African named Ismail ("Esa" in *Out of Africa*), who had once worked for a European, as cook. And there was Farah, also Somali, one of many from the aristocratic Mohammedan tribe who came south to seek work in the colony. The German stewardess from the ship had not, after all, accompanied Karen, so she had to train the servants on her own. Fortunately, Farah had an instinct for the job. In other ways, too, he was her mentor, since he knew the universal language of East Africa, Swahili—a vestige of slave-trading and the only means of communicating with the staff. The Africans spoke little or no English, so Karen began taking lessons in Swahili from Farah, and went around the farm greeting people in broken phrases and gestures. Her efforts were a pleasant joke to the Africans, and their laughter bonded her to them.

She spoke to Bror about the need for a kitchen garden; the lack of variety in vegetables was becoming intolerable to her. He had a small area plowed near the house, and a fence put around it to keep out the native sheep. Although Bror sometimes brought in game— birds and antelope from the nearby reserve—the rest of their food had to be bought in Nairobi. They made the trip twice a week when the roads were dry, in a wagon drawn by mules, with an African riding in the back surrounded by the market baskets. They could get spices, paraffin (kerosene), matches, and cloth from Indian merchants; flour, sugar, rice, and tinned goods at McKinnon's store; and tomatoes, bananas, spinach, and ground corn in the teeming native market. There was a bakery of only fair quality; one was much better off making one's own bread and pastries. Fish and cashews, pineapples and coconut came to Nairobi by train from the coast. Meat was sold from a single carcass hanging in the open—beef on Mondays, Wednesdays, and Thursdays; and lamb on Tuesdays, Thursdays, and Saturdays—or some similar variation. A few people sold chickens and eggs, but butter was very hard to come by, available only in tins, since Delamere's dairying scheme had failed.

Karen put together rudimentary menus—she had to grope in her taste memory for recipes, then teach the cook to prepare them. He worked in a hut separate from the house, over a charcoal stove, with a limited number of utensils. Hunger drove Karen to be creative; the variety of food was poor, and she was always craving the sweet and hearty dishes of home. When the rainy season began, toward the end of March, the trip to Nairobi became unpleasant. The mud was too thick for the wagons, so Bror would go on horseback, bringing back what he could carry. But he was glad for the rain, for it meant he could now plant coffee.

* 6 *

When Bror bought land in Africa, he was only twenty-seven years old—a year younger than Karen—but he had enough experience with agriculture, from running his family's dairy farm, to understand the pitfalls of farming. He had heard about Lord Delamere's financial losses and was persuaded he ought to stick to a crop like coffee that had already proved itself in the tropics. Grassland was no good for coffee. What was needed was good forest loam, and he believed he had bought excellent land. It was sheltered by the surrounding forest and the nearby Ngong Hills, and it sloped gently and would not become boggy, even in the rainy season. He had been told coffee did not like excessive moisture and would not do well with wide swings in temperature. The rainfall near Nairobi had been variable over the previous years. However, Bror was hoping for an average of fifty inches a year, and had no reason to think there might be less. The temperature of the region was fairly constant, seldom dipping below fifty-five degrees Farenheit at night. He would have preferred one additional thing—a better source of running water on the farm. But there was a small stream; with good rains, the farm should do well. Jesuit priests at St. Austin's Mission on the high outskirts of Nairobi had been successfully growing coffee since 1900, and Bror had reason to believe his land was every bit as well suited to the crop. In other parts of the tropics, coffee grew well at altitudes between 5,000 and 6,500 feet. Bror's farm, at 6,100 feet, presented just the type of soil and climate coffee entrepreneurs were said to dream of. His neighbors—Sjögren, with his 4,500-acre Swedo-African Coffee Corporation, and Johnnie van de Weyer—certainly thought so.

The French priests had been experimenting with different types of coffee; and while the ideal planting strain had yet to be developed, one or two seemed to be more resistant than others to the coffee blights of East Africa: bugs, borers, thrips, and fungus. Bror was advised to clear and plant at least fifty acres the first year, and to continue to put in about twenty-five acres each of the next few years. The coffee bushes would not bear for three to five years, and they must be planted with their taproots straight, in moist soil, if they were to do well.

The greatest problem Bror faced was finding workers to help him. His first task in Africa, once he had had a look at his land, was to hike into the Kikuyu hills and find the chief, Kinanjui. It took weeks of negotiations and many exchanges of gifts before Kinanjui guaranteed him a few hundred warriors willing to set down their spears for wages. The length of the planting season extended from February to June, coinciding with the long rains. Bror told Karen the incentives he had offered: He had given the Africans a place for their huts and grazing for their cattle, as well as food and blankets, and wages—amounting to a few rupees per month. According to regulations established by the Resident Native Labourers Ordinance, each worker willing to stay beyond the planting season would receive two acres of *shamba* (native farm) to cultivate as his own, provided he worked at least 180 days out of the year and agreed to bring his family to help with the harvest. Bror had seen to it that each African placed his mark on a contract promising to work at least six months. He preferred that "squatters" live on the farm rather than leave at the end of the planting season, so he would know how many workers he could count on.

Many white farmers had difficulty keeping workers, but it seemed to Bror that if the Africans were treated well they would stay. One of the chief concerns of any farm in the colony was making sure its workers remained in good health. The settlers' wives made it their custom to keep a daily check on the sick and injured. It would be up to Karen, as far as she was able, to attend to the medical needs of the Africans. If she felt at sea about ointments and bandaging, she was to do for the Africans what she would do for herself. This was why Bror had asked her to bring out from Denmark a chest of medicines. At any rate, Bror knew a little first aid, and if there was anything that together they could not manage, the Protestant mission hospital was only twelve miles away.

In preparing to plant coffee, Bror first directed that the land be cleared. He had the trees cut down and made a contract to sell them to neighboring Swedo (the Swedo-African Coffee Company), where there was a sawmill. Bror's foremen supervised the removal of the stumps and the turning of the soil—it was a labor that required all of the twelve hundred Africans hired to work on the farm. Even with these workers, Bror's goal was only to plow enough ground this year to plant a fifth or so of the acres he envisioned devoted to coffee. Gradually, the farm would be developed to its full potential.

By March 1914, when the rainy season began, Bror and his foremen had seen to the clearing of a portion of the forest, the tilling of the land, and the preparation of seedlings. No coffee could be planted without the rains, since there must be at least three inches of moisture in the soil for the coffee to do well. Bror and the foremen went around measuring the rows for the coffee bushes and showing Africans how to plant the seedlings. They must scoop out the soil deeply so as to plant the taproot perfectly straight. Placing a stake against the side of each hole, they set the seedling beside it, pushed the red humus around the root, and then, with the stake, gentled the plant upright.

By April several hundred seedlings had been planted. Karen wrote to her mother, "When I recall how it looked when I arrived I can hardly recognize it; great areas of land that were then virgin forest are now like a stretch of garden with all the new little coffee plants in dead straight rows and the soil between them without a single weed" (LFA, 6). She and Bror had developed a vision of the money the coffee would bring. As Bror put it later, "The only anxiety was how I should be able to put all the money into the bank" (AH, 7). Yet coffee is a crop one must wait for; they could expect no ripe berries for three years, and the bushes might not reach their potential for five. While they waited, they must live on money belonging to Karen's family, but they were confident the wait would yield far beyond their investment.

* 7 *

Things might have gone differently between Karen and Bror if she had not been stricken with malaria in the middle of April 1914, while still in the honeymoon period of her marriage. But her malaria was perhaps inevitable, because malaria preys most easily on those whose health cannot stand up to it. Karen had never recovered her strength from illness in Denmark, and, unused to African food, she was thin and anemic. The fever brought her down hard.

Malaria was less common at the higher elevations, but Bror had noticed from the beginning that the swamps around Nairobi were unhealthy. The rainy season, while good for the crops, brought on mosquitoes. Shaking chills sent Karen to bed. She lay shivering violently for what seemed like hours. One may imagine that Bror directed Farah to bring every blanket in the house, then he lay down beside Karen himself to warm her. After some time, she would have grown hot and—unable to tolerate touch—pushed him away.

The fever came and went. Bror brought Burkitt, the doctor from Nairobi. He wondered why Karen had taken no quinine, and warned Bror about fatal anemia and brain fever. He prescribed what he could, and she did get better; at least the fever subsided. But she could not seem to get over her weakness; for weeks she had hardly the energy to get out of bed. She languished, and longed to go outside with Bror. At night it rained and she listened to it drumming on the roof. In the morning when the sun came out, Bror would be off on errands.

She grew restless. It made her cross to be cooped up so long. She had little to read and she yearned to read something Danish. Bror brought what books he could find, but they were mostly English novels, and Karen could not bear the plots. Bror was in and out of Nairobi and sometimes stayed all night. When he came home, he often had friends with him. They would sit in the parlor, discussing the future of the colony and filling the house with cigar smoke. Karen was too weak to dress, and too uninterested in their conversation to care to join them. But she was irritable with the noise and the feeling of being

confined to her room. Sometimes Bror's friends brought women with
them. They came in to greet her wearing khaki skirts and suede
pumps; she disliked the look of them and the sound of their laughter
(*LFA*, 10).

She had little good to say about the whites of the colony. They
treated their servants and workers poorly; they took little interest in
speaking Swahili; they behaved badly toward the Kikuyu chief,
Kinanjui; and they were, in general, boorish and overbearing in their
attitudes toward Africa. She did not exempt the Swedes; even Sjögren
had adopted the same "English stupidity"—on one occasion "guffaw-
ing and blustering, playing up to all of us and emphasizing that he was
condescending to talk to a native . . . " (*LFA*, 5). As for the women of
the colony, she had no friends among them. On the farm, she was too
far from Nairobi to see them often, and it was just as well, for she said,
"I think you could count the decent women in this country on one hand
. . . "(*LFA*, 7). One day the governor's wife paid her a visit. It was not
necessarily the beginning of an intimate friendship, but at least Lady
Belfield could maintain a sensible conversation.

A major factor in Karen's isolation was her difficulty in
speaking English, a failing which embarrassed and humiliated her. She
was exasperated by her inability to communicate gracefully. Expressing herself was more trying when she was ill or tired, and she found it
impossible to follow a conversation if there was more than one other
person involved. She could not seem to find the correct progression of
words, and she had the impression that people were amused by the
awkwardness of her phrasing. She was particularly at a loss to express
herself when she wanted to make important points, especially concerning her respect for the Africans and their customs. Her discouragement was compounded by the fact that in Denmark conversation had
been her forte. Not understanding the language was like being deaf,
a feeling disturbing enough to engender paranoia. When people
smiled patronizingly at her, she felt they were deprecating not only her
speech but her ideas.

Still out of sorts from illness, Karen directed her exasperation
toward the house, which she found unbearably hot. She could not
understand why there was no veranda on the south, and complained
she would suffocate without some air in the afternoons. She sat up in

bed and made sketches of changes, then wrote to her mother to announce plans for renovations. She had hired Indian workmen to build a new veranda, to extend around the house on the west and south, enclosing the old veranda into a new, cooler sitting room—separate from Bror's. She regretted using her mother's money for the project, but—considering how poorly she was standing up to the heat—the project must not be delayed.

For lack of anyone to talk to, and in an effort at optimism, she wrote letters home, describing the things that delighted her about Africa. She talked about the nearby tribes—the Kikuyu, an agricultural people of the highlands, and the Masai, wandering and pastoral, living on the plains; she spoke of lions that came onto the farm at night; she explained her fascination with the Islamic customs of the Somalis, how they prayed on little mats outside the kitchen. She expressed her greatest admiration for the "native"—her "greatest interest" in Africa (*LFA*, 4). She said, ". . . one loses a good deal of racial superiority out here; it seems obvious to me that the natives surpass us in many ways" (*LFA*, 8).

Near the end of May 1914—nearly two months after she had fallen ill—no longer willing to be an invalid, she insisted that Bror take her to Dr. Burkitt to demand a cure. Burkitt examined her and discovered she was anemic, as he had suspected, since malaria thins the blood. But he shrewdly diagnosed that her main problem was depression. Under the circumstances, he gave her his standard prescription: "a change of air" (*LFA*, 12).

* 8 *

Bror had conceived of a new approach to going on safari: instead of using African porters carrying burdens on their heads, he would take loaded wagons pulled by mules. The two of them, Karen and Bror, started off with three wagons and nine servants toward the grasslands of the southern Guaso Nyiro River. With them they took Farah, a cook and his helper, and six servants to help with hunting and skinning the trophies. The road led northward, past the forests and trout streams of the Aberdare Mountains, then across drier territory to grasslands, where before them appeared, like mirages in the shimmering air, the dark moving forms of thousands of grazing zebra and wildebeest.

Karen wrote to her brother Thomas, "Just before I left Bror gave me a rifle, a 256, with a telescopic sight, a splendid gun that I was scared stiff to fire at first but that I gradually learned to handle. Bror is an excellent instructor . . . It is very tempting out here to shoot from too great a distance, but Bror was strict and stopped me doing that and was very good at getting one close up to the game" (*LFA*, 18). At night they listened together for the approach of lions, while sitting inside a *boma*—a protective enclosure of thorn branches. They had shot a gazelle as bait and laid it out in front of the boma (*LFA*, 18). In the moonlight—and it was no good going on safari without the moon—they could see the lions clearly, and managed to shoot some fine specimens.

It was cool at night; Karen wrote her brother, "I must say that in fact I suffered more from cold than heat on this safari . . . Then by midday the sun is blazing, it is hard to shoot because the air is shimmering in the heat" (*LFA*, 19). Mid-morning they would leave the boma, and after making sure the men had properly skinned the night's trophies, they would have tea and breakfast, then retire to their tent. The boys would bring hot water for them to bathe. Toward dusk, when it was cooler and they might expect game to be coming to the river to drink, they hunted again, stalking on foot behind an African scout, sometimes scaring up warthogs and guinea fowl, often alerting and shooting gazelle, occasionally coming upon a cheetah eating its prey. Karen told her brother that this was a delightful time of day, "between 4:30 and 7, when all the colors are wonderful and the air delicious . . . There are many flowers on the plains, especially purple ones and almost everywhere masses of forget-me-nots" (*LFA*, 19).

They dined at a camp table under the stars, eating antelope meat, bread baked on stones, and tinned fruit, with wine. The only trial was the flies, which sat on their lips and eyelids and seemed to stick there, even while they tried to sleep, and the chiggers—four of which burrowed into Bror's great toe and had to be removed by the servants with a needle, to prevent his foot from oozing with infection.

Describing to her brother the success of the safari, Karen had no complaints, only rapturous praise. She said she had been "strengthened by the air of the high mountain region, tanned by its sun, filled with its wild, free, magnificent beauty in heat-dazzling days, in great clear moonlit nights" (*LFA*, 18). They ventured 130 miles from Nairobi and were out traveling and camping for nearly six weeks. Their trophies included twenty different types of game, including four lions, two leopards, and a cheetah.

One of the trophies was a marabou stork. This last Karen may have regretted shooting, for a stork had always been to her a great sign of happiness. She had taken the idea, from an old volume of Danish fairy tales in the nursery at home, that the trials of life meant nothing in themselves, but from the whole of them would come something as wonderful as a stork. In *Letters from the Hunt*, her father had written that the stork was a "symbol of luck," and that to kill one was to challenge and defy fortune (*LFTH*, 46). Thus, shooting the stork may have caused her to wonder if she should have been more careful with her happiness.

* 9 *

Sixty-five kilometers north of Nairobi, on a grassy land bridge in the Rift Valley, there was a town called Naivasha, a station along the Uganda railway. In this rolling country farmers owned Abyssinian horses so legendarily fine that a law was later passed to forbid taking them out of the colony. At a sale on one of these farms shortly after their safari, Karen selected ten of the finest mares to send on to Von Lettow in Tanganyika—in fulfillment of the promise she had made to him on the voyage out. In return, she hoped to receive one or two splendid Persian carpets brought into Dar es Salaam by the ancient wooden sailing vessels of the Indian Ocean, the dhows.

But the horses she bought were never shipped as far as Tanganyika. Before they could be sent, they were confiscated by His Majesty's army; on August 5, 1914, within a few days of Karen and Bror's return to their farm, England declared war on Germany.

1914

It was not a war the colonists could ignore. To the south, Kenya bordered Tanganyika for 300 miles; the German army, under Von Lettow, was mustering there for attack. Alarmed, the colonists had to contrive their own defenses. They abandoned their farms and came to Nairobi to offer their services as irregulars in the colonial army. The Swedes met at Blixen's coffee farm to discuss their private strategy, since, not being British citizens, their position was delicate. They preferred to remain neutral, as long as Sweden stayed out of the war, but they must show their loyalty to the colony, or be arrested as German sympathizers. There was much serious discussion, with Bror as leader, and many cigars smoked, as the argument seesawed over what was to be done. At last it was decided: with no telegraph between the border and the northern railway, some means would be needed of getting messages from the frontier to the capital. Delamere was taking a troop of irregulars down to the border to gather intelligence. Bror and the others could put together a human telegraph, using motorcycles and bicycles, to operate between troop headquarters and the telegraph terminus at Kijabe—and thus keep Nairobi informed and insure that needed supplies reach the army. This plan Bror jokingly referred to as "unfighting"—a commitment without really taking sides (*LFA*, 13).

Work on the farm had been halted, the agricultural wagons had been requisitioned by the army, and Africans were being recruited as regimental porters. The Indians renovating the house had abandoned their work, leaving an unpleasant rubble where the new veranda should be. The steps were missing, the door had yet to be repaired, and debris nearly prevented one from climbing inside the house. Karen wrote to her mother that the house had been designated as a shelter for whites in the district in the event of a native uprising, and added, "... that I can well understand since it is almost impossible to get into" (*LFA*, 17).

In *Out of Africa* Karen says that it was rumored that the white women would all be sent to a concentration camp where they could be protected in wartime against native uprisings. She felt that, were she confined with women, she would die (*OA*, 276). The fear of restless natives reflected her lack of confidence in the colonial system, but the idea that the English would isolate their women seems peculiarly inconsistent with their history. Karen was certainly frightened, as she said, but not because all white women were to be confined. There was a far greater danger that she would be jailed for being a German sympathizer—a threat that became clear within a day of Bror's leaving for the front. When Karen went to Nairobi on errands, she feared for her life. Hatred materialized in the streets, where unruly crowds of recruits shouted at her, and contemptuous white women made rude remarks. Shopkeepers refused to serve her. One or two said she ought to be arrested. Word had spread that only a few days before war broke out she had been buying horses for the German army.

Karen retreated to the farm, shaken and afraid to be without Bror. She evidently kept her horse saddled and rode over to Swedo to consult Nils Fjaestad, who announced he was soon to leave to join Bror. She insisted upon accompanying him. Taking along Farah, as well as her Scottish deerhound Dusk, her old cook, Ismail, and a few other servants, on August 13, 1914, she rode away on her horse Aimable, with Fjaestad to Kijabe. Fortunately, her destination was familiar to her, since she and Bror had just spent a few days at Kijabe's Mountain Resort on their way home from safari.

* 10 *

Kijabe lay northwest of Nairobi about forty miles over a rough, hilly track. The town was the last station of the railroad before its descent westward into the Rift Valley. Running roughly north and west on its course from the coast to Lake Victoria, the rail line paralleled the border with Tanganyika. There were fears the Germans would blow up the rails at strategic locations or attempt to destroy the bridges. Delamere's intelligence unit was designed to forestall such maneuvers.

From a lip of the escarpment, the village of Kijabe overlooked a series of terraces patched with green and gold African *shambas*, and beyond, the hazy gray floor of the Rift with Longonot volcano resting in the distance. Karen directed the servants to pitch her tent in an unromantic but protected setting beside the railway station, between the stacks of wood for fueling trains. From there she kept track of

Bror's whereabouts by visiting the telegraph office, where messages were brought from the front by runners and wired on to Nairobi. The telegraph was operated by a chatty Indian, whose conversation she found amusing. But she had not been in Kijabe long when a crisis occurred in which she was only too willing to take charge. Bror had written to request that two wagonloads of supplies, which he listed—mostly food and petrol—be sent to Delamere's regiment. They were not to be sent without a white escort, since the Masai in the region could not be trusted.

A South African named Klapprott had been put in charge of the supplies, and he was readying a convoy to leave for the border when police arrived. They accused him of being a German spy and arrested him. Eighteen Africans waited near the wagons, ready to accompany the supplies south. Karen evaluated the situation: she herself might well be arrested like the unhappy Klapprott. Even in Kijabe she was not safe (*OA*, 277). Nearby stood two heavily loaded wagons, each with a team of sixteen oxen, plus nine extra oxen for the army. She saw an obvious escape from the threat of imprisonment, as well as an excuse to look for Bror, and she announced that she herself would escort the supplies. And so it happened, as she describes in *Out of Africa*, that she went into the bush to transport supplies for the army.

Her safari with Bror the month before had been a rehearsal. Now they were descending into the Rift Valley and using oxen instead of mules, but with the help of the servants, she could manage the animals. She said that taking a wagon into the Rift was like negotiating a track down the side of a pyramid (*LFA*, 14). The wheels teetered and jolted over boulders. In places the path was so narrow that the wagons could barely squeeze through the passes. Here there was greatest danger from lions, since they could leap from above onto the backs of the oxen and claw them to death before being driven off. Just such an incident occurred at dusk one evening when one of the wagons became lodged on a boulder. They were working to free it when a commotion occurred, and a terrifying growl signaled the arrival of a lion. Karen frightened it off with a rifle (*LFA*, 14) hastily handed to her by Farah [not with a whip, as she says in *Out of Africa*] (*OA*, 280). Later, when Bror heard the story, and chided her about the danger, she said,

"What else could I do?" (*AH*, 92). Unable to free the wagon in the dark, she and the Africans built a *boma* of thorn branches and sat up all night anticipating the return of the lion.

Karen had become accomplished with her rifle and used it to kill antelope to feed the servants. They thought she was an extraordinary shot, she said; she overheard them bragging about her shooting talent to a white man they passed on the trail. They took four days to cover the seventy-three miles from Kijabe to their destination, Narok Boma. Karen walked most of the way—her mule had been requisitioned by the army, and she said this was no country for horses. In a letter she bragged a little about the journey, comparing it to Uncle Mogens Frijs's more comfortable trip; he and Aunt Fritze had covered the same route on their hunting safari a few years before (*LFA*, 14). It was a dusty trip across country with no streams or water holes; when she arrived in Narok she felt she had never been dirtier in her life. The D.C. (District Commissioner) was there to receive her, but Bror and his men had moved their camp.

She left the supplies but did not want to go back to Kijabe. Later, she said she had gone out as a "transport man" for the army (*LFA*, 15) and liked the job too much to give it up. She wrote to her mother, "I would have gone home to the farm but it is so tiresome because any news from here has to go through Nairobi . . ." (*LFA*, 16). Whatever her fears before this safari, they were dissipated by elation at being useful to the army. The longer she was out, the more her confidence grew, since the Africans looked to her for decisions and to provide them with game. She enjoyed their company. They came from a pleasing mixture of tribes—Somalis, Kikuyu, Masai, and Kipsigis, who mingled without jealousy—and she said their behavior was superior to that of "civilized" men: "I am absolutely convinced the *natives* are the '*best class*' out here; I find it quite impossible to take any interest at all in the English *middle class*, but the boys are absolute *gentlemen* . . . " (*LFA*, 15).

She was told of a cache of goods abandoned by an American hunting safari when the war broke out, so she borrowed another wagon from the camp of the army and went into the bush to collect the supplies. During this excursion Bror and his men came upon her and camped with her, helping her to load the provisions. Afterwards, unwilling to go home, she stayed in the region of Narok, hunting. She had good luck keeping the Africans supplied with meat, and shooting birds that tasted, she said, like turkey (*LFA*, 14).

Bror's attitude toward her independent safariing was a source of amazement to her; her adventurousness inspired his admiration more than anything she had done in their marriage. That she had risked her life appeared to entertain and intrigue him. He called it "wonderful feminine courage" (*AH*, 91). In the tale "The Pearls," Karen describes a marriage similar to her own in which the husband "was surprised and enchanted at the change of the demure maiden into a Valkyrie. He put it down to the influence of married life, and felt not a little proud. She herself, in the end, wondered whether she was not driven on in her exploits by his pride and praise . . . " (*WT*, 112).

After she moved her camp, Bror told Delamere he needed sick leave for dysentery, then struck out walking to find her. On this leave—and perhaps on several others—he spent a night in a Masai village. He had walked for a day, following Karen's trail, and had not found her. Having few provisions with him, and no tent, he was relieved at the prospect of shelter from lions and something to eat—although this food might be only goat's milk mixed with blood from a live cow. The Masai village consisted of a few dusty *manyattas*—houses fashioned from mud and cattle manure—surrounded by a thorn *boma*. The dwellings were rectangular with rounded mud roofs, a narrow foyer where the goats slept at night, and a low door leading to the smoke-filled interior. A fire burned in the middle of the floor for warmth, and the smoke kept the flies away. Bror's bed, like the others, was possibly a mud pallet along one wall. As was customary among the Africans, he would have been offered a Masai woman to spend the night with him.

In the first years of the century, it had been noted by the white man—and by Karen, who wrote home to her mother concerning the matter—that the Masai seemed to be dying out as a tribe. The reason given was that the women bore few healthy children. Later it became known that syphilis was endemic in the tribe since the coming of the white man. If Bror had heard the tribe harbored the disease, he perhaps did not take the idea seriously that night in the *manyatta*. At any rate, when he came upon Karen's camp the next day, he was amorous, having traveled eighty miles on foot to find her.

She was at the time camped at Narok, near the house of the D.C. She wrote to her mother that Bror had arrived "quite brown and very tired" (*LFA*, 14). She seemed pleased at his ardor. He had walked to find her camp, and she laughed at him—"his legs were completely stiff and he could not sit down unless we bent him together..." (*LFA*, 16). The next morning, Bror awakened thirsty, and finding no drinking water at hand, began rummaging in the supplies for a bottle of soda. Finding what he believed to be a soft drink, he mistakenly drank from a bottle of Lysol. His mouth and throat were badly burned. He was too ill to eat for the rest of the day, and lay awake all night with pain and fever. Yet the following day he took Karen hunting, and a day later walked twenty miles back to rejoin Delamere's army.

For nearly two months Karen stayed out on the plains as "transport man" for the army. She found other caches of supplies, including one near the Masai Reserve, a little Indian *duka* (store), strangely abandoned but still full of provisions. She delivered these supplies to Delamere and felt proud to be part of the great effort of war. But when reinforcements of regular troops arrived from India, officers declared Karen's presence near the front lines inappropriate, and she was ordered to go home. The ultimatum increased her disdain for the English. It seemed to her that they were short-sighted about the value of individual contributions like hers. She concluded they were a colorless, bourgeois people: self-righteous, heartless, and unimaginative.

11

Karen rode her horse, Aimable, home from Kijabe in discouragement. Her mood was such that every stumble of the horse seemed a near disaster, the occasional voices of the servants disturbed her brooding thoughts, and she was out of patience with her dog Dusk, who would not follow closely.

She had been happy with her sorties into the bush for the army and dreaded the moment of arriving home. She harbored the conviction that home would never again suffice, and that whatever she found there must, after what had passed, be a disappointment. What crises was she to find at the farm? She feared the sheer number of them. The last time she and Bror had returned, they discovered that all the oxen had died of disease, plague had broken out among the workers, and native sheep had got into the maize field and ruined the crop.

The sight of the grounds was the first of her discouragements: there was no grass around the house. There had been no rain, and African sheep had stripped the park clean. She had hoped to find flowers and a flourishing kitchen garden, but neither had been started. To enter the house, she had to climb over the half-finished wall of the new veranda, traverse the rubble there, and hoist herself through the door, whose lintel was still missing. She surveyed the half-painted interior, and the remnants of workmanship littering the sitting room. The rest of the house ought still to be livable, but as she went into the other rooms, she was appalled by the disorder. She spoke shrilly to Farah. They must question the houseboys. The servants had followed as she inspected the house; now she turned on them and demanded to understand how they had disobeyed her instructions.

One may imagine the tableau: Karen in her riding boots and divided skirt, carrying her double felt hat, her round face red and angry; Farah beside her in his long white *kanzu* (robe) and turban, glaring at the servants; the barefoot boys, in rough shorts, listening as Farah questioned them in Swahili. He dealt with them with the haughtiness of a king, turning to Karen to explain what was said. It seemed that certain of the servants had broken into the liquor stores, got drunk, and had a fight in the house. Karen was discouraged at the explanation, knowing she must decide upon punishment, a responsibility she detested. She ordered the offenders to be whipped with twenty strokes of the *kiboko* (hippopotamus whip), and later wrote to her mother, "I have never punished my boys with the kiboko before" (*LFA*, 17); it was the type of punishment she despised the other colonists for using.

Bror had remained at the frontier, so she had no one to whom to express her frustration. She attempted to resolve the disarray, gave orders for food to be prepared for her dinner, and directed the servants to get her bath ready. This flurry of activity was soon interrupted by a commotion outside that Farah called her to assess. Surrounded by a group of excited boys was a young herder with a gash in his buttock. He had been kicked by an ostrich while tending his father's cattle.

Such a crisis could not have occurred at a time when Karen felt less able to cope with it. She was tired and angry; this was again a problem she must manage with no experience. Why had she come out to Africa knowing no skills of nursing? Why had she not learned more in her youth? She told her mother, "He had a long wound several inches deep and I put a really good tight bandage on it, but afterward I realized that it had probably made it impossible for him to go to the bathroom" (*LFA*, 17). She had ordered Farah to tell him to return to have the dressing changed, but afterwards she brooded to her mother, "I strictly forbade him to touch the bandage and hope he doesn't die of it . . . " (*LFA*, 17).

* 12 *

Whatever she had counted on when she went out to Africa, Karen did not imagine how few friends she would have. Her innocent venture to buy horses for the German army cruelly isolated her. She could not for her life persuade the English that her friendship with Von Lettow was a naïve mistake.

When she went to Nairobi for shopping, she was bitterly snubbed. Among many insults, the wife of one government official approached and sharply accused her of stealing her African cook. The woman warned that her husband would see to it the man was drafted into the carrier corps, unless he returned to her service immediately. Karen's angry retort fell flat because her English was still awkward; the majority of her conversations in the language were with Africans, and so she could not argue effectively with the woman. When she told her old cook, Ismail, about the incident, he removed his apron and said he was going to work for the lady. At Karen's mention of the carrier corps, he was beyond listening to reason (*OA*, 264), because Africans feared the dangerous job of carrying burdens for the army. Karen would not get him back to her employ until the end of the war.

During this time mail was censored, and the government directed that people write their letters in English. All foreigners were

under suspicion, but especially the Swedes, since Sweden was suspected of leaning toward Germany. Karen admitted that most of the
Swedes in Africa sympathized with the Germans. She accused the
English of "incredible boastfulness" and "colossal self-satisfaction"
(*LFA*, 23). Frankly, she said, the Germans were not stupid like the
English in conducting warfare. Germany had troops in Tanganyika
well before the war, but the British were only just bringing some in
from India. Karen gave grudging support to England, because, she
said, the atrocities of the Huns were more to be feared than the
bungling of the English. Nevertheless, she lived in a nightmare of
bitterness toward the English, and felt isolated as she had never been
at home (*OA*, 362).

She had grown to despise even the wives of her Swedish
neighbors in the colony. From Sjögren's estate—the Swedo-African
Coffee Company—Mrs. Gethin and Fru Holmberg occasionally came
to tea. Karen listened to their complaining and overwrought conversations about the Africans—why were they afraid that the natives might
kill them? If they would stop beating the Africans over trivial complaints, and learn to speak their language, the women would not be so
fearful. They tried her patience, and she stopped making them
welcome.

During this time, while the men were gone, Fru Holmberg
reported to the police that her houseboy had tried to strike her, and she
demanded that the police arrest and flog him. "She and her bosom
friend, Mrs. Gorringe, worked themselves up into a terrible state over
this . . . ," Karen wrote to her mother. Fru Holmberg accused Karen of
harboring the boy on her farm, and it was true. She was convinced that
Fru Holmberg as usual was exaggerating the incident. "I have turned
into a law breaker now," she said. "The boy came and sought refuge
here, shaking all over with terror, and I hid him in my boys' huts . . . "
(*LFA*, 25).

In this difficult time even Farah seemed to turn against her.
Less than two weeks after their return to the farm, he asked for three
months' leave, saying he desired to earn some money through trading.
Karen wrote her mother that he was restless and worried about his wife
and child in Somaliland, but, more likely, she had been upset with him

and railing, and he was sulking because he could not satisfy her. He was willing to come back when Bror returned.

Not much mail was getting through and what did arrive carried bad news. Karen's grandmother, Mama Westenholz, had had a stroke and was dying. She was too ill to understand that a war was on in Europe. This news made Karen feel more intensely cut off from her family. Bror's absence meant that for the first time in her life she was having to live by herself. She was not used to surviving without supportive conversation and felt her mind a little unbalanced by solitude. The harshness of African life menaced her.

To drive off loneliness, she gathered her pets around her— her dog Dusk and a mother cat and kittens. But Dusk was so persistently curious with the kittens that the mother cat carried them into the woods to hide them. There they were devoured by safari ants.

* 13 *

As soon as British regular troops assumed guard over the southern border of the territory, the irregular army, including Delamere's intelligence-gathering force, was dismissed. The Swedes were especially unwelcome because of their suspected sympathies with Germany. Bror came home toward the end of October 1914 to a neglected farm whose wagons had been commandeered by the army—those same wagons Karen had used to transport troop supplies. Wagons were necessary to the farm's operation at the moment, because Bror wanted to cut down more forest to enlarge the fields, and needed to get the logs out of the way. He had made a contract to sell the timber to the Swedo-African Coffee Company for their sawmill; but now that he had no transport, he told Karen he was going to get Swedo's permission to make charcoal from the wood (*LFA*, 27).

In *Out of Africa* Karen attributes the charcoal-making scheme to a character called "Old Knudsen," but her letters clearly reveal that the idea was Bror's. He had observed charcoal being made in the north of Sweden and thought the idea a rather lucky solution to the problem. He saw to the building of eleven kilns in a forest clearing, and set about experimenting with charcoal production. Karen describes the setting in *Out of Africa* as though it were a lovely scene in a romantic drama. She was enchanted by the ring of smoking fires surrounded by the cozy woods, and she began to imagine that fairies were there at work. But things did not go so easily as Bror planned, nor so romantically as Karen described. The kilns persisted in catching fire, until Bror grew disgusted enough to declare that you can only make charcoal in a country where there is lots of snow to extinguish the flames. Moreover, he had discovered that good charcoal could not be made from logs, but only from brush. Karen was not cynical about the effort and admired Bror for attempting the experiment, however impractical it seemed. Later she viewed the results as representative of her life with Bror. The failed charcoal remnants, like her memories of their life together, remained "beautiful," "smooth," "freed of weight," and "imperishable" symbols of their romantic experiences (*OA*, 197).

The failure of the charcoal scheme reversed their finances further. They were desperate for money to carry on. They invested in some *dukas* (shanty stores improvised in villages), where people bought matches, paraffin, ointment, and tinned goods. And they managed to put together a small herd of their own African cattle and sheep, but drought made it difficult to keep livestock. The short rainy season, from September to November, failed in 1914.

Without rain there could be no further planting on the farm, but since it was the expected season, Africans showed up looking for work. Karen was proud to see them, because other farmers complained of not being able to get help. She thought their problems were due to the poor way they treated Africans, and she was sorry to turn away hundreds of workers for lack of money to pay them. Fewer farmers were hiring, since many had gone to war, but she said, "I myself would certainly not go and work anywhere where there was a risk of being thrashed" (*LFA*, 26).

Now that Ismail had left her service, she was obliged to train a new cook. Still coping with the primitive state of her African kitchen, she wrote to her mother, "If you could find a cookery book from 1830 to send me I should be overjoyed. The one that I have is too modern" (*LFA*, 25). Although ingredients were in short supply—anything that had come in by boat before the war was now an expensive luxury—she managed to get flour, sugar, and tinned butter to concentrate on what was then her favorite aspect of cooking: desserts. She taught her new cook, a Somali named Hassan, to make "custard flans, meringues, pancakes, layer cakes, various kinds of soufflé, cream horns, apple cake, chocolate pudding, [and] cream puffs" (*LFA*, 27). When he had mastered a delicacy called brown cabbage soup, she forgot her peevishness against the Swedes and began inviting people for dinner. Then she wrote home, "You may find it hard to believe that my house is renowned for good food; the Swedes out here say that it is the most well run house according to Scandinavian taste in B.E.A. [British East Africa], but then there aren't so many out here" (*LFA*, 27).

One dinner with the Swedes, however, led to some unpleasantness. Unknown to Karen, Bror had recently gone to his Swedish neighbors to beg a loan of money. When Karen learned of it, through a slipped remark of one of the guests, she was furious. She did not understand how he was going to pay back the money. She quarreled with Bror over this; the result was a silent anger between them that lasted for some time.

1915

1

The days grew hotter and drier. Christmas passed, along with the first anniversary of their wedding. Afraid the remainder of the livestock would die, Karen and Bror did not dare to leave the farm for a safari holiday. As usual, Karen was suffering from the heat, but she was not alone. On the plains, the Masai and their cattle were dying from the drought, and in the hills the Kikuyu *shambas* turned black from lack of rain. The African children who brought their sheep to graze on the sparse lawn in front of Karen's house were thin and wan from hunger. Drought and war had taken the humor out of people. Africans came to Karen and spoke of their fear of the Germans; whites speculated about the chance of a native uprising.

From the beginning, Karen had found it difficult to keep her sense of humor with Bror. Her tone with him was one of continuing exasperation. Bror was quite boyishly appealing, as long as one did not have, so to speak, jurisdiction over him. But she could not control his impulse to spend money, and there were other troublesome developments. In the early weeks of 1915, someone—possibly Olga Holmberg, for it was like her—revealed to Karen that Bror was not being faithful to her.

The news was certainly a shock to her, but Karen did not wish to be thought naïve, nor to admit to the humiliation of having been deceived. Previously she had harbored suspicions but she had refused to believe her instincts. Bror had been consistently affectionate to her. They saw life very differently, but she had been convinced that, like the fictional husband in "The Pearls," "he was in love with her, and he admired and respected her. She was innocent and pure; she sprang from a stock of people capable of making a fortune by their wits; she could speak French and German, and knew history and geography. For all these qualities he had a religious reverence" (*WT*, 111). She had not thought it possible that he would betray her, his greatest friend.

However, when she learned the names of the women, among them the wife of the man from whom Bror had borrowed money, she was forced to accept the disclosure as true. She could not have been more shaken if Bror had put poison in her coffee and offered it to her with a smile. It was, as she described in the tale "The Old Chevalier," like being left with the entire building of her pride and happiness lying in ruins. She was sick with horror and humiliation (*SGT*, 90).

When she confronted Bror, evidently he was silent, then he shrugged and said, "You are free to do likewise." Much later, in a letter to her brother Thomas, she suggested such a scenario:

> I recently heard of a conflict like this from a young wife. Her husband had in no small degree neglected to observe what in the old days was held to be the duty of fidelity in marriage, and when she remonstrated he suggested that she was perfectly free to do likewise; he would have no objection. This was completely unsatisfactory to her as she had no such desires. All right, then, they could get divorced, and what more could she want? (*LFA*, 325)

He ought to have realized how far out of the question divorce was—how humiliating the mention of it was to her, and how impossible it would be to admit to anyone that she was to be divorced, after only one year of marriage and such grand aspirations. Where would she go? What was she to do? How was she to answer for her family's money, or find someone to take her in?

Faced with such horror, she lost the ability to sleep. There were no good alternatives to staying with Bror. She could not face the whites of Nairobi, who must be laughing at how she had been deceived. And there was no question of going back to Denmark to endure the pity of her family. Night after night she went sleepless, and then one day she nearly lost her life from an overdose of sleeping tablets.

She described the incident to her mother: "I had not been able to sleep for some nights and, as you know that is not usual to me, I grew very impatient with it . . . " (*LFA*, 29). She said she had taken only four, because three tablets the night before had failed to work. But she also said, "Bror wrote a long letter to you—and in English too: but I tore it out because he was at that time very anxious about me and it was all too sad" (*LFA*, 29). Bror had come into her room in the afternoon and found her unconscious, and revived her only by frantic efforts. Karen said she vomited afterwards for two days, and Bror insisted that she see a doctor.

All of this letter, Karen knew, would be read by the censor in Nairobi, and she was careful how she phrased the story. The sleeping tablets, which went by the name Veronal, were a barbiturate used fashionably to commit suicide. (The writer Virginia Woolf had tried to end her life with Veronal in 1913, but did not succeed.) What made Karen vomit for days was likely the antidote Bror gave her to bring up the tablets. He then took her to Dr. Burkitt, who was concerned enough to prescribe several "tonics," and to insist to Bror that she have "a change of air." Karen told her mother she was going out on safari with a neighbor named Fägerskiöld and hoped to be gone two months. She said Bror had been especially kind to make all the arrangements (*LFA*, 29–30). The likely truth was that she could no longer bear the sight of him.

* 2 *

Since Karen's wartime safari, farm life seemed dreary to her. Going out to shoot with Fägerskiöld was like being released from prison. Out on the plains, the sight of zebra and wildebeest, hyena and elephant seemed to diminish her problems. Perhaps she began to think of Bror as another creature who needed freedom to act according to his instincts.

The hunting was not as enjoyable as when she was with him; moreover, while on safari she came down with fever, and then she felt the lack of his affectionate nursing. The illness began with headache, a rash, and swollen glands. She went hunting anyway; she hated complaining about being ill. Then her joints began to ache, and the rash spread to the palms of her hands and the soles of her feet. Fägerskiöld was alarmed into insisting they go back to Nairobi; he had probably never before seen an illness like this.

Dr. Burkitt examined her in his characteristic way—his bombastic reputation had earned him the nickname "Kill-or-Cure Burkitt." One who was sick cringed at the thought of consulting him; he was bound to propose a theatrical remedy. When a patient had fever causing convulsions, Burkitt stripped off the sick man's clothes, put him in his open car and, once on the road, drove him as fast as he could until the fever came down. By the time this remedy worked, Burkitt was far from Nairobi. When the patient began to shake from the chill, Burkitt took off his own clothes and put them on the sick man; he was never accused of not caring about his patients. His diagnosis of Karen's symptoms must have disturbed him. He recognized her disease all too well; it was one for which he sadly did not have a showy remedy. It was syphilis.

Syphilis was a common disease in Africa, especially among the Masai. Burkitt knew Bror well and had no illusions about the source of contagion. It did not surprise the doctor that Blixen himself had not been seriously ill; Bror was stronger and better nourished than his wife. Some weeks before, Bror had probably had symptoms—achiness, rash and fever—and accepted them as just another illness in Africa.

1915

Burkitt told Karen that her syphilis had begun several weeks before when she had noticed a firm, painless sore. The sore had disappeared without making her ill, and an interval passed before her present symptoms. What he perhaps did not mention was his suspicion that she might recover from this present stage of illness—as Bror had done—only to have symptoms return in twenty-five or thirty years, when her brain or spine began to deteriorate, or when the aorta, the great vessel leading away from her heart, might rupture. While her syphilis was contagious now, in some months it would no longer be so. The disease could progress silently for years, until she went mad, or began to lose control of her legs and her bladder, or suddenly fell dead. This same scenario would be true for Bror. Burkitt certainly advised Karen to send Bror to see him.

The doctor did not have an effective remedy and could offer only his old stand-by, mercury tablets. Some people seemed to improve with them. In Europe they were using a new treatment, developed by a German named Ehrlich, which amounted to several injections with an arsenic compound called Salvarsan. Burkitt was not experienced with it, but he had some on hand if she were willing to try it. She really had no choice but to agree.

Unfortunately, all she gained after a few days' treatment was blood poisoning in her arm—and the determination, in spite of the war, to go home. She did not at first tell Bror she had syphilis—maybe she hoped he would go mad from the disease. Indeed, she was not speaking to him, but she had to tell him she was going to Europe. She could not travel alone, with fever and the infection in her arm, and she had made up her mind to take Farah with her. When she informed Bror about this, he protested angrily. He thought she was making a histrionic gesture. She then pointed out "in a cold white rage" that he had given her *syphilis*. When Bror heard this unlikely outburst, he "stared at her incredulously for a moment" without saying a word, then "turned and left the room" (*T*, 55).

IN AFRICA

* 3 *

Since the onset of war, Bror and Karen had been living financially day by day, for they were out of money, and none was getting through from Europe. Finding passage on a ship to Europe was difficult, because ships had been commandeered for carrying military supplies, but paying for passage represented an even greater challenge. With Farah's help, Karen sold off her *dukas* to raise money. Then, in early April 1915, she and Farah boarded a train for Mombasa.

Even to those not encumbered by illness the journey was oppressive. The train was hot and dusty and stripped of comforts, the air at the coast seemed heavy and ominous, and the steamer to Marseilles, carrying coal and timber for the war effort, was militarily bleak.

According to a compromise insisted upon by Bror, who maintained he could not take care of the household staff without him, Farah left Karen at Marseilles and went back to the farm. Alone, she made her way by train to Paris to consult a specialist. She had not told her family she was coming to Europe; because she did not want her relatives to learn she had syphilis. But luck was against her, since in Paris she ran into one of her cousins, Baron Bech Frijs. She managed to appear gay and unconcerned, and formulated an elaborate explanation for why she was in Europe. But once he had seen her, she could no longer keep the news of her whereabouts from her family, so she wrote a hasty letter to reassure her mother. Bech Frijs was all too helpful in suggesting that Karen's letter be sent with a friend of his, on his way home to Sweden. This friend may have planned to deliver the letter to Bror's mother to pass along to Karen's family, for Karen was careful to send fond greetings to Aunt Clara, to assure her Bror was well, and to stress how upset she had been at leaving Bror behind (*LFA*, 31).

The specialist she consulted in Paris did not have much time for her; he had soldiers to care for. He examined her, and told her he had to be honest in saying that he doubted very much whether she would recover (*LFA*, 127). Although he was too busy to be objective, too rushed to care about helping her, and too ready with his knowledge of medicine, Karen accepted his opinion unquestioningly. He advised her to look for treatment somewhere else—England or Switzerland. She felt more ill when she left his examining room than before she had seen him.

Soon she did go on to Zurich but found no one there to help her, and she rejected the thought of traveling to England; she had no friends there. Finally she realized she would have to go home.

The Germans had mined the Mediterranean, there were zeppelins over France, and submarines patrolled the English Channel. In Zurich, Karen lay ill in her hotel bed, watching the hours go by on the town hall clock, and believed they were the last hours of her life (*LFA*, 127). Eventually she made her way by ship to Bergen, Norway, and from there returned to her mother's house.

* 4 *

There was a specialist in venereal diseases in Copenhagen, a physician named Carl Rasch. Karen asked that he keep her diagnosis in utmost confidence; she did not want her relatives to know why she was seeing him. Rasch had a fearless approach to syphilis; he knew Ehrlich's methods with the new arsenic injections and was confident that he could make her well. What he did not know, and could not tell her, were the long-term effects of the medication. He thought the disease could be cured, but because twenty-five or thirty years intervene before late symptoms of syphilis appear, he could not say the disease would never return. In the few years arsenic had been used to treat it—only since 1910—no one had been able to prove it was a permanent cure. Still, he assured her she was lucky such a treatment was available.

Relieved to have finally found someone to take charge of her case, Karen fairly collapsed in the Royal Hospital in Copenhagen. She allowed the nurses to fuss over her and the quiet atmosphere to calm her after the months of terror. Rasch exuded competence and kindness; he seemed genuinely interested in making her well. She was glad for the sound of his Danish voice. The nurses saw to it that she ate well, when she could, for the injections of Salvarsan, given weekly along with bismuth, upset her stomach. While killing the syphilis in her body, the arsenic temporarily poisoned her system. She endured headache, pain in her ears, abdominal cramps, and burning sensations in her hands and feet. But the stay in the hospital renewed her. At her request, she was not placed with the other patients with venereal disease, so that her relatives might not guess she had syphilis. Of course, she told her mother, but the others were led to believe that she had a severe case of malaria. But she did reveal her fears to her immediate family that such a severe illness might prevent her from having children (*LFA*, 31).

In reality, there was never any question of her not being able to become pregnant. The early stages of syphilis are dangerous to pregnant women, for a mother may pass syphilis to the baby in her womb; but once a woman has recovered from the early symptoms—the sores, the fever, and the rash—she would not be contagious to a baby or to a sexual partner. The disease might lurk in her brain, her great vessels, or her spine, but it would not likely keep Karen from having children. Rasch made all this clear to her during her three-month stay in hospital, after which he discharged her with instructions to return to him for reexamination.

Life in Denmark then seemed cold, remote, and gray compared to life in East Africa. Denmark had not entered the war, but all of Europe lay under a pall. Word of the shocking numbers of fatalities stunned the world. In keeping with the charged emotional atmosphere, Karen's two sisters, Ea and Elle, agreed to marry men they had previously refused. In the year 1915, Ea was thirty-two, and Elle, twenty-nine years old. Karen had complained about the dearth of eligible bachelors in Denmark, and about the impossibility of meeting them in a family with so few social contacts. But these willowy sisters with dark hair and serene faces like their mother's had little reason for remaining spinsters, except that they had preferred not to marry. Ea had studied singing for many years, and Elle had trained as a secretary, then gone to Russia briefly and involved herself in the developing Bolshevik movement there. In the altruistic spirit characteristic of the Dinesen women, she had applied to work as a nurse in England during the war, but was turned down. Both Elle's fiancé, Knud Dahl, a prominent Copenhagen barrister and book publisher, and Ea's future husband, Viggo de Neergaard, were wealthy landowners.

1915

Thoughts of the coming marriages of her sisters stirred Karen's nostalgia for her own wedding, and she began to miss Bror. He had been writing affectionate letters to her, as though to make amends, and talked of Africa in such a way that she yearned to be there with him. His letters inspired her to write a poem, "Ex Africa" ("Out of Africa"), in which she wrote evocatively of the moon shining over the African farm, the mountains, the grasslands, and the Guaso Nyiro River where she had honeymooned with Bror.

1916

In the spring of 1916, a year after Karen left Africa, Bror found passage home and reunited with her at Rungstedlund. Together that summer in Sweden and Denmark, she and Bror visited the family—the Frijses, the Blixens, the Westenholzes, and the Dinesens—and everywhere Karen listened as Bror enthusiastically expanded upon the opportunities for investment in East Africa. The war had engendered enormous profits for producers of all commodities—coffee, tea, beef, poultry, grains, and wool. Europe could not get enough of these goods. Farmers producing them were becoming rich, and richer. Farms in the Kenya Colony were luckily far from the battlefields. Farmers like the Swedes, whose nationality protected them from the draft, stood in a position to make enormous sums, while helping the war effort by supplying goods. What was needed was working capital. One ought to get into all phases of farming on a large scale to take advantage of war-time demands. What Bror would do if only he had the money!

Uncle Mogens Frijs, who knew Africa, had already invested in a farm there. Bror's sister's husband, Gustaf Hamilton, listened to his talk, and became determined to go out to Africa with Bror and buy land immediately. Uncle Aage Westenholz was also intrigued by what Bror said. He had inherited some family farms in Denmark, and owned his rubber plantation in Malaya, and he had some investment collateral. He discussed Bror's ideas with his sister, Ingeborg Dinesen. Of course, she had already helped finance the coffee farm, but she did have more money she could invest. This certainly seemed the right time to do so.

Their appetites for buying land were whetted by some specific properties that Bror described. Some were for sale because the farmers had gone to war; others had failed for lack of capital. One of these farms was the large plantation next to Bror's—the Swedo-African Coffee Company, Ltd.—now derelict, abandoned by its owner, Sjögren. Here were 4500 acres of prime land that, in Bror's view, would not only be profitable for coffee, but could also support a wide variety of other farming projects, all of which should reap huge profits for the investor.

Uncle Aage was persuaded, and Ingeborg Dinesen went along upon his advice. Against collateral offered by Uncle Mogens and Aunt Fritze Frijs, Aunt Bess and other family members, Uncle Aage borrowed a million Kroners and set up a family corporation for buying the land. Since Karen's relatives were providing the money, he insisted on naming the new venture the Karen Coffee Corporation.

Bror, who was now sole manager of this enormous sum of capital, eagerly bought passage back to Africa for himself and his wife, with joyful visions of the sheep and cattle, corn and flax, honey and sugar, pigs and poultry that would soon make him rich.

* 2 *

In her eighteen months at home, Karen's physician, Dr. Rasch, had administered several Wasserman tests. The final tests of her blood and spinal fluid showed no syphilis. Was the disease lying in wait to damage her brain or spine? Rasch could not be sure. He would examine her again in three years. But she need not worry about giving it to others; that was not possible. It would have been strange if Rasch did not also test Bror. Rasch had no way of knowing whether years later Bror might go mad or die suddenly from the rupture of the great vessel to his heart, but he would certainly have assured Bror that he was no longer contagious. Rasch saw no reason why he and Karen might not have children, but he advised them to wait at least a year for Karen to regain her strength (*LFA*, 47).

Karen and Bror left Denmark in November 1916 and traveled to London, where they were to embark for Africa on the R.M.S. *Balmoral Castle*, a ship destined for the Cape of Good Hope. They had been warned to avoid the Mediterranean because of the danger of German torpedoes. In London they gathered a number of supplies and went to see bankers and solicitors about the new land they were buying. Baron and Baroness Blixen were also presented to the Queen Mother, Alexandra. Karen wrote to her mother that the Danish-born queen had been "quite exceptionally gracious and kind" in receiving them (*LFA*, 33).

Brushing shoulders with soldiers in the streets exhilarated Karen; she saw them as part of a vast epic in which she too was involved. She loved being in London and was sorry to leave it. Their ship was carrying few passengers, and these were the boorish type of English she had met in Nairobi. They were more interested in shuffleboard than in the events taking place in Europe. Karen disliked their self-satisfied attitude toward the war. She wrote to her mother, "the English are so strange, they are always absolutely the same whatever may have happened to them, yes, in fact from the time they are ten until they are ninety" (*LFA*, 34).

Bror was delighted with the opportunity to pass by way of South Africa. He had been given the names of successful entrepreneurs, and he took the occasion to travel upcountry and visit them. He and Karen were lucky to buy a car in Durban, for there were none available in Nairobi. They drove to the ranch of the Hon. Joseph Baynes, who advised them about starting a dairy with Friesland cattle. Bror had made it known that he had a great deal of money to invest, and people began to approach him with wonderful ideas. A Belgian named Rolin was all for forming a company for making blankets, using wool produced in South Africa. Bror was urged to put up a brickworks at Ngong, and he was shown a good one already running in Maritzburg.

Bror's brother-in-law, Hamilton, had it in his mind to start a sugar plantation on the Kenya coast, and Bror's capital could finance a sugar refinery next to it. Why not also start up a coconut nursery there? Karen protested to her mother that she had little faith in the business sense of Hamilton.

They made the second leg of the trip—from Durban to Mombasa—in a small Indian vessel that called in at Zanzibar. Karen and Bror went ashore there to explore; it was a relief to get free of the ship for a few hours, for it was infested with ants. They finally arrived at their own farm on January 26, 1917. The entire trip from Denmark to Kenya had taken eleven weeks. Karen said she hoped she would never have to travel out to Africa on this route again (*LFA*, 39).

* 3 *

It was a fine arrival compared to Karen's previous return to the farm. Everywhere around the house there were grass and flowers. The veranda was completely shaded by flowering vines. Farah had seen to it that the house was in order. The Africans living on the farm turned out to greet them, crowding the lawn with chants and spontaneous dancing. To Karen the farm looked better than those in South Africa; in fact, it looked better than she had dreamed. It had been raining nearly every day for eight weeks.

Rain in December and January was unusual, and Bror was worried, for he was not ready to plant now, and he wondered if there would be rain in April when he needed it. Something else unexpected had occurred: there had been a killing frost, and this meant that the coffee had been set back. The bushes were now three years old, and Bror had counted on a crop, but this had become sadly unlikely.

Karen was glad that Bror, not she, was dealing with these problems. There were always so many unpleasant matters to attend to when one arrived home after being away. On the evening of their return, Bror's overseer, a Swede named Aake Bursell, came to discuss the affairs of the farm and candidly told Bror that he could get better pay working elsewhere. Other farmers, prospering since the war, were offering to take him on. Could Bror match their offers of £60 a month and ten percent of profits?

The suggestion was preposterous. The corporation allotted Bror himself a salary of only £50 a month, plus ten percent of profits. He told Bursell that the farm's corporate advisors would never agree to his demands. The result was that Bursell gave him notice. This was unfortunate, because Bror was dependent upon Bursell's expertise. The money Bror had raised was meant for capital improvements; he had not counted on using it to increase the wages of his crew. Now he would have to get someone else to help him—preferably a Swede whom he could trust.

Bror was now determined to embark upon cattle-raising. A month following their return, he took Karen and Hamilton to the highlands that lay within the Rift Valley to the northwest and there they traveled around looking at cattle farms and getting advice from old settlers. Karen found these colonists surprisingly engaging. These members of the peerage were the first interesting Englishmen she had met. One of them was the son of the Earl of Enniskillen, Galbraith Cole, who farmed near Gilgil and knew a great deal about the Masai. He allowed no hunting on his farm, so to Karen his land was like an enormous deer park. She and Bror dined with him, and Karen wrote to her mother afterwards, "it is a pleasanter life than on the coffee farms around Nairobi, but I do not think so profitable" (*LFA*, 41).

With the blessing of the shareholders, and advice obtained in South Africa, Bror bought a second farm of 4500 acres, on the other side of the Rift Valley, on the Uasin Gishu plateau 250 miles from Nairobi. Here lived an enclave of South Africans who grew quantities of wheat, maize, and cotton. They were eager to work land for Bror if he would put up the capital. A large area of forest would have to be cleared, but this was the best soil in the colony; Bror could not go wrong on the investment. The land had already been surveyed to accept a new leg of the railroad, which would pass near Bror's land and allow him to ship directly to Mombasa. For the moment, farmers were hauling their grain by ox-wagon to the railroad seventy-five miles away. But confidential talk maintained that as soon as the war was over, and the railway line completed, the value of land at Uasin Gishu would mount beyond anyone's dreams. People assured Bror he was indeed making a shrewd investment.

1917

By March 1917, Bror had bought some cattle and was putting in a cattle dip. A trench was dug and a cement trough constructed with a ramp down which the cattle could be prodded, single file, into a disinfecting solution. Now that he owned cattle, Bror had to dip them every three to seven days to rid them of ticks, or risk having them die of East Coast fever. The arsenite of soda used in the dip was expensive, but Bror had been advised to be rigorous. He also had the cattle vaccinated against rinderpest (a disease similar to measles in humans)—one never knew when the native stock would spread it—but the cure could be as lethal as the illness itself; some cattle died from the vaccinations. Bror had invested strictly in native cattle. These humped *zebu* cattle tolerated dry weather and resisted sleeping sickness better than European breeds. However, brown and white in color, and exactly the same species owned by the Africans, the cows might easily be added to the Masai herds, and so they were subject to theft. Bror warned the people of the farm that he would take strict measures if his stock disappeared. Then he was off to Mombasa with Hamilton to see about buying a sugar plantation.

For two months Karen had been traveling with Bror almost continuously, because he had wanted her to see "all the different branches of Karen Coffee Co" (*LFA*, 42). But she drew the line at going to the coast. She had never been able to tolerate the hot climate; and even though they could take their car on the train as far as Mombasa, the trip would mean more driving over rough roads. Besides, just then there was excitement in being at home, for she and Bror had moved to the much larger house that Sjögren had built for himself at Swedo. This house had such large rooms compared to the other, she said, that they were like receiving rooms in a palace. The floors were of cedar parquet, and the dining room was paneled with mahogany. There was a veranda on the south and east, and French doors opened onto a terrace at the back. This house was made of the same gray fieldstone as the other, but the rooms, high ceilings, and multitude of large, many-paned windows made it seem huge and airy. Best of all, it was cool, since the forest surrounding it protected it from the sun.

Sjögren's house had been empty for a time, and rain had got in, so there were repairs to be made. Part of one ceiling had come down, and the house needed to be repainted inside. Even before all this work was done, however, Karen and Bror moved in. They were there by the end of March 1917, and Karen spent the next several weeks putting things to right. Sjögren had left some of his things behind, including that which delighted her most: a large library of books, brand new and unread, including the complete works of Kipling, Stevenson, Wilde, Bret Harte, and several of the Scandinavian authors, such as Lagerlöf, Bjørnson, and Heidenstam.

Before moving in, she had asked a foreman named Anderson to look at the grounds with her and decide which trees needed to be felled. With proper clearing, they could open up a lovely view of the Ngong Hills from the terrace. Thanks to all the rain, they had just the right conditions for putting the grounds in order and starting a garden. Karen had brought with her from South Africa a number of plant cuttings from the botanical gardens at Durban. She supervised the planting of them in a pleasant arrangement beyond the terrace. From there one could look down to the tops of the acacia trees bordering the river, which formed the farm's boundary with the Masai reserve. After endless discussions with Bror, Karen had decided to name the house Mbogani, "the house in the woods"—an African name that resembled her father's Chippewa pen-name, "Boganis."

Bror had replaced his foreman, Bursell, with a new man named Von Huth. Karen wrote to her mother: "I don't think that it is easy to keep the books for Bror, as he is never very accurate about all the details; so it is a good thing that Von Huth can manage it . . . " (*LFA*, 44). In fact, Bror had not been keeping books at all, and had never prepared any financial statements in the four years since he bought the farm.

Even though the rains were good, farmers were having difficulties. Ships needed to carry their produce to Europe were filled with soldiers and war supplies, and they could get few workers because the British were conscripting more African porters for the carrier corps, as their army swept into German East Africa in pursuit of Von Lettow. The shareholders of Karen Coffee Corporation sent uneasy letters, and Karen answered sympathetically, "The fact that communications are so bad because of the war makes it very difficult for both Bror and the management at home" (*LFA*, 45).

In early June 1917 Bror claimed he needed a holiday and entrained again for Mombasa, and Karen went to bed with what she called "sunstroke." News had perhaps reached them from Sweden of the death of Bror's twin brother, Hans Blixen, in the crash of a light plane. The tragedy came only a few months following word in March of the suicide of their cousin and Karen's friend, Daisy Castenskiold.

Hans's death wrenched the thoughts of Karen and Bror toward home, and upon his return, Bror began spending long evenings brooding about the future, wondering if he should go back permanently to Sweden. Still confident of making a quick fortune in Africa, he contemplated returning to Europe afterward to buy one of the family's ancestral estates. Yet Hans's death brought out a rare streak of bitterness in Bror. Karen wrote to her mother, "Bror is right in saying that they have never given him much consideration in Sweden because he is not an officer" (*LFA*, 55). He seemed convinced that his family would not have mourned his own death so deeply as they did that of Hans.

* 2 *

In the last week of June 1917, Bror invited Karen to accompany him to Naivasha for a weekend. At the request of Uncle Mogens Frijs, he was having a hunting lodge built on his uncle's farm. Karen had been to Naivasha before and had found it a "paradise on earth" (*LFA*, 51). The lake and the mountains reminded her of Scotland. She was charmed by the view of hundreds of antelope and zebra grazing in the hills, and at night she watched the distant glowing fires of Masai herders. She had bought some paints in Durban and had taken up painting again, and she stayed on after Bror left, enjoying the quiet, and glad to paint without interruptions.

But there was an important reason for her to keep away from Nairobi, and this concerned a scandal which had arisen around the Swedish settlers. In a series of articles in the Nairobi newspaper *The Leader*, the Swedes were again being accused by the British settlers of holding German sympathies. The presence of Swedes in the colony was claimed to be dangerous because of the threat of treachery. Of course, this was a long-standing issue, but now the argument was exacerbated by three years of war. Tempers flared toward violence.

Karen had read the articles and found them contemptible. They singled out Bror, implying that he had been using "tainted" money to further his interests in Kenya (*LFA*, 51). Even the Somalis had heard about the articles and approached Karen to ask whether the stories were true. Upon her return to the farm, she insisted to Bror that something must be done. She could not understand how he remained calm in the face of this kind of attack. Could he not find someone to speak on his behalf? Bror pointed out that the writer of the articles, a man named Bromhead, had no proof for his accusations, and he, Bror, could see to it that Bromhead was embarrassed for his efforts. He intended to take the man to lunch and see about a retraction. Lord Belfield, the previous governor, had been reposted to England, but Bror planned to speak to the acting governor.

There had been no Swedish consul in Nairobi since Sjögren left. (One wonders if he left the colony because of some similar unpleasantness.) So Bror had to deal with the situation himself. This he did in his usual affable way. Karen was amazed that he did not become angry. She wrote to her mother in the last week of July 1917 that Bror had managed to quiet the whole unpleasant affair (*LFA*, 51).

* 3 *

While Bror inspected and supervised his farms, Karen contented herself with setting up her new house and keeping company with Farah and her dogs. She had arranged a new household budget with Farah, who was to keep her supplied with meat, eggs, vegetables, poultry, and butter, in exchange for retaining for himself any money left over—she sensibly realized she could not control expenses tightly if she were to entrust him with money, since, according to African custom, he would use some of the money for his own purposes. Bror encouraged Karen's inclination to buy additional furniture, some of which was more expensive than she wished to mention in her letters home. Her staff now included Farah, Juma, Esa—a houseboy—a cook named Ali, and two *totos*—children to help with the kitchen chores. Recently Bror had hired a mechanic, who was teaching Karen to drive. Behind the wheel she thought of herself as the most emancipated of women.

She had turned her dog Dusk over to Bror, who could manage him better and liked to travel with him. She now had two new deerhound puppies, born since her return from Europe. Sadly, their mother was stolen from the veranda one night by a leopard; Karen grieved as though a family member had died, and took over the care of the puppies herself. She did so with the aid of a nine-year-old Somali boy named Abdullai. "I think I love him as much as if he were my own son," she wrote to her mother (*LFA*, 54). It made her laugh to see him and the puppies following each other around the farm.

On an evening in September 1917, Bror announced to Karen that when he was rich, he intended to go back, not to Sweden, but to Denmark, to settle at Dallund, an inland estate on the island of Funen, where he had spent happy boyhood years. His family had been forced to sell Dallund only two years before. Bror thought that soon he would be wealthy enough to buy it back. This surprising belief Karen supported whole-heartedly "if it would make Bror feel really happy" (*LFA*, 55). She much preferred this plan to the idea of living in Sweden.

The two of them began to fantasize about the child they hoped to conceive. "I do still nourish the hope that I may one day have my little Wilhelm to bring up,—not so much to run Dallund as to take over our concern out here and develop it further . . . ," she wrote to her mother (*LFA*, 55). How long before they would have enough money to go back to Europe? Would their land go to one of Bror's nephews if they had no child? Would it not be grand to have a son to carry on their work in the colony?

At first Karen was not sure Bror's answers to these questions were the same as her own, for, she said, "Bror and I have very different ideas about so many things" (*LFA*, 45). She confided to her mother that she hoped he would come around to her views. But, in any case, nothing must be said to Bror's family about these speculations, since they might be taken as foolishly premature (*LFA*, 55).

Karen's sister Ea was now expecting a child. There was concern at home that Karen would find the news upsetting, but she said she was delighted to know of it. "Strangely enough it has been hearing about children that are nothing at all to do with me that has been painful," she said (*LFA*, 47).

After living with them for seven months, Bror's brother-in-law, Gustaf Hamilton, had gone back to Sweden—nothing having come of his dreams of sugar plantations and African wealth. Karen had grown weary of sharing every single meal and every hour of traveling with him. At last she was having some hours alone with Bror. To her mother, who worried about how Bror treated her, Karen wrote that for married people "the intimacy and sincerity they show each other when they are alone together is something others never see, but is infinitely more significant . . . " (*LFA*, 47). One day she and Bror were walking around the farm, talking about children and dreaming about the day when they would be rich, when they spied a twelve-foot python, barely visible except for the way it moved the tall grass. Karen was terrified, but Bror took aim and shot it in the head, and gallantly presented it to her, suggesting that she have a pair of shoes made in Paris.

Karen's sister Ea gave birth to a girl in October 1917 and named her baby Karen. There had been early rain in September, Bror was pulling flax, the land was green, and, Karen said, among the birds in the meadows around the farm, there strolled many storks.

1918

In the year since her return to Africa, Karen had begun to make enjoyable friends among the white colonists. In late November 1917, she had visited the farm of Frank Greswolde-Williams in the Kedong Valley, thirty miles west of Nairobi. Williams, a fifty-year-old English-man, had lost his son in the war and had recently been wounded in the eye in a shooting accident. Karen believed that Uncle Mogens Frijs would count him "among the dregs of society" (*LFA*, 56), but he was rich, and interesting in an eccentric way. Williams took her on a buffalo hunt and had his scouts beat the bushes so she could get a good shot. Unfortunately, she missed, because Williams's gun was too heavy for her.

Along with Bror, Karen had also been invited by Northrup McMillan and his wife for a shooting holiday on their farm at Juja. McMillan was about to be knighted by the English king for his contributions to the development of the colony. Karen enjoyed him although she could not speak so highly of his wife. Mrs. McMillan was a little too chatty, but, Karen said, "as she loves Bror that is quite all right" (*LFA*, 56). An intriguing older gentleman formed a sort of *ménage à trois* with the McMillans; he was Mr. Charles Bulpett, who had to his credits a long courtship with a famous French courtesan known as "La belle Otéro." He related to Karen a number of adventures, including his mountain climbing escapades, and claimed that in his youth he had been among the first to climb the Matterhorn.

Just after Christmas 1917 a Swedish officer, Baron Erik von Otter, visited the Blixen's farm. He had known Karen and Bror at home and had come out to Africa the same year as Karen. An officer of the King's African Rifles, he was in Nairobi on Christmas leave, and Karen found him charming. He had studied the Koran and converted to Mohammedanism, he was well read and enjoyed many of the same books as she, and he could talk endlessly about Islamic philosophy and Muslim ideals. Karen, who had been fascinated with Mohammedanism long before this, found Von Otter an exhilarating conversationalist. She went so far as to write about him to her brother Thomas: "I would think that his character resembles Father's, he is so interested in all nature, hunting and war, and particularly in the natives, their customs and ideas . . . " (*LFA*, 58).

In the first part of February 1918, Karen and Von Otter went on safari together to the Tana Plains. Von Otter said they were sure of getting rhino, and Karen was thrilled, since she had not hunted them before. Wearing a wide-brimmed double *terai*, she looked radiant, with brown curls sweetly framing her round cheeks. As for Von Otter, he was handsome and dark, but his expression was too intense to be sensual. Karen and he went away with Bror's knowledge and permission. Bror was above all a person who valued personal independence, for Karen as well as for himself. In some ways, this flexibility was among Bror's finest traits: he encouraged the people around him to do what made them happy. It made Karen very happy to go, and she said afterwards, "There is something about safari life that makes you forget all your sorrows and feel the whole time as if you had drunk half a bottle of champagne" (*LFA*, 59). She had not sat beside a campfire for three years, since she went out as "transport man" for the army. Now she and Von Otter read aloud from *The Three Musketeers* and *The Deerslayer*, gazed at the constellations, and listened to lions roaring by moonlight.

But, although she enjoyed Von Otter's company, she was not in love with him. He was too humorless for her—and too serious about pursuing her. When she came home, she thought Bror looked thin.

"Poor Bror has refused to hear anything about Mohammed between twelve and four [o'clock]," she wrote to her mother (*LFA*, 62). He was certainly tired of the subject.

* 2 *

By the middle of March 1918, a pall hung over the coffee farm at Ngong, as, indeed, over all the farms of the Athi River Valley, because the long rains had failed. Having seen almost no rain in the space of a year, the young coffee bushes, which might have been expected to give a reasonable crop in this their fourth year of life, wanly shriveled, giving out no flower buds. No longer able to stand the sight, nor to bear pacing under clouds that never brought rain, Bror left Ngong for the Uasin Gishu farm—where the weather was not so intransigent. He was not expected back until at least the end of April.

The drought had a peculiar effect upon Karen: as the Kikuyu children, the native cattle, the giraffes of the plains, and the people of the farm grew thinner, Karen, too, could not retain her weight. She was suffering from a queer kind of rheumatism that seemed to have come on with the heat and dryness, and she thought she might have lost at least thirty-five pounds since her return from Denmark; none of her dresses from Paris fit her anymore.

She was also having difficulty sleeping. Her peculiar insomnia—in the past due to jealousy—had been growing worse for months. Karen had been making a show of independence, visiting friends like Greswolde-Williams without Bror, going on safari with Erik von Otter, gaily entertaining various officers of the King's African Rifles, but there was something too frenetic about her new series of friendships— as though she were trying to run in parallel with Bror. It was as she described in the tale "The Old Chevalier": She was surrounding herself with admirers but keeping her eye on Bror, "as a competitor in a chariot race would have his eyes only on the driver just beside him" (*SGT*, 87).

Once Bror had gone to Uasin Gishu, she was lonely for him, and wrote her mother to say how much she missed him (*LFA*, 64). He had evidently been affectionate, if not necessarily faithful, since her safari with Erik von Otter. His attentions had renewed more strongly her hopes for conceiving a child (*LFA*, 61); thus his departure for Uasin-Gishu deprived her in more than one way. Only recently she had written home: "I want to earnestly beg all of you who are fond of and believe in Bror to have so much faith in him that you do not judge him quite as you would other people; he is not like others, and he must have freedom to be as he is if he is to achieve the best he is capable of . . . I beseech you, as my first and last wish, to turn a blind eye on Bror for two or three years more . . . " (*LFA*, 63).

She solaced herself by seeing something of Algy Cartwright, a farmer from Naivasha, one of a multitude of officers drifting through Nairobi on their way to wide-flung army posts. The war in East Africa was effectively over. For three years Von Lettow, an expert at strike-and-hide warfare, had made the English army chase him. Karen, like the English themselves, spoke of him with admiration: "They say that his tactics are based on the sole aim of keeping the war going out here until peace is made in Europe so that Germany can press demands for G.E.A. [German East Africa]" (*LFA*, 43). She was impressed that such a hero, a legend in his own time, had been her casual friend. But now the English army had succeeded in pushing Von Lettow's army south, out of Tanganyika, which they declared an English colony, and into Portuguese Africa. Thus, the British proceeded to deploy their troops, including Africans and officers of the King's African Rifles, like Cartwright, toward Europe and the Mediterranean.

Algy Cartwright, one of the old settlers—though, in fact, not very old, having come to East Africa only a few years before Bror and Karen—was soon to leave for the war theater in Mesopotamia (Middle East, Iraq). One afternoon he and Karen went for drinks to the Blue Post Hotel—an outpost on the road to Thika near the Chania Falls. However, it was another date with Cartwright she would remember more intensely, one that occurred the night of April 5, 1918. On that evening he took her to dinner at the Muthaiga Club—where membership was limited to the old settlers—and there she met a tall, rangy Englishman named Denys Finch Hatton.

* 3 *

The Muthaiga Club was located in an exclusive suburb of Nairobi. It was well secluded by trees and sported tennis lawns for its selective clientele. Most of its members were sons of European aristocrats who, bored with life at home, had come out to Africa to make or spend their fortunes. Established in January 1914, the Muthaiga Club provided an alternative to the Nairobi Club, whose membership consisted of functionaries in the colonial government—the people Karen had come to know and despise as boring and miserably bourgeois. There was less snobbism in her attitude than disgust that people could live in Africa and not appreciate its uniqueness. They did little but complain about how stupid were the Africans and how beastly was the climate. They took no interest in African culture or language, and spent their time trying to recreate England as closely as possible in Africa. When Karen attempted to discuss with them the interesting aspects of African life, the women tittered, and the men muttered at her foolishness.

Thus she found it charmingly different to spend time at Muthaiga, where the old settlers came to converse about the Masai and their cattle, how noble and beautiful they seemed, and how sad it was that they were dying out for lack of grazing land and from difficulties in childbirth; about the Kikuyu and their shrewdness at avoiding working for the white man, and how despicable the government was in taxing them to force them to work; and about the Luo, who did not circumcise and would not intermarry with the other tribes; and about the circumcision of women, intended to keep the wives of the Kikuyu from looking at other men. Karen could not get enough of talking of these things, and she had at last found people of like mind among the settlers who frequented the Muthaiga Club.

The club was an English idea—a place to gather in private and shut out those who did not meet one's standards. The bar at the Muthaiga Club did not admit women, but they could take luncheon in the dining room, or lounge in the overstuffed chairs, and smoke, converse, or read the newspaper—and one never knew whom one would run into. The club had several cottages for housing members from upcountry.

Karen had heard of Denys Finch Hatton; he seemed to be popular among the settler aristocracy. He was not a farmer; in fact, it was difficult to get clear what he did for a living. He owned some trading stores and held shares in one or two farms in the highlands, but before the war he had devoted himself to safariing. He was the son of Henry Stormont Finch Hatton, Earl of Winchilsea, but like many of his contemporaries in Kenya, he was not the first son, and so would not inherit his father's title or estate. He had graduated from Oxford with a poor Fourth, and left England almost immediately to see what Africa might offer. He could finance his travels from an inheritance that included some timbered lands in Norway left him by a distant relative. These gave him a small income, enabling him to live off the interest. He pursued a comfortable life, without any real occupation, while his investments were managed by caretakers. As Karen later put it, Denys belonged to "a class of people who have nothing other to do than follow their own bent . . . " (*LFA*, 67). He was no businessman; the substantial work of caring for his finances was done by a firm of solicitors.

When Karen met him, he was about to turn thirty-one years old, and had lived in East Africa, off and on, since 1911. Soon after the war began, he joined Cole's Scouts—a group of army irregulars, almost all Somali, put together by his closest friend in the colony, Berkeley Cole. Later he had been transferred to the King's African Rifles, where he was A.D.C. to Major-General Hoskins. This was a prestigious appointment, because Hoskins was for a time commander in chief of the East African campaign. Assisting the commandant had been a respectable way for Finch Hatton to fulfill his duty in the war effort.

In April 1918, Finch Hatton had just returned from a few months' home leave in England. When his commander in chief, Hoskins, was transferred to Mesopotamia, Denys had served there with him briefly. Now Denys was being reposted to Egypt, where he was to take a flying course. He had been in partnership in a farm near Naivasha with a man named Jack Pixley, but Pixley's death in a battle in France had forced Finch Hatton to reroute himself via B.E.A. (British East Africa) to make new arrangements for the farm.

When Karen first saw him, he was seated at a table with Monica Belfield, the daughter of the former governor of the colony. Cartwright introduced Karen to Finch Hatton; he and Denys were old friends who had grown up together in England. Denys was quite tall—six feet four—and handsome, even though his blond hair was thinning to baldness. There was something about the engaging look in his eyes, a twinkle of amusement, that held one's attention. He teased, but in a gentle way, and was so droll he kept everyone laughing throughout the meal. Those who had spoken to Karen about him had not exaggerated his gift of repartee, nor his unique good looks. He had a narrow face with an open expression, his lips were sensual, and his fair skin flushed as he talked.

Karen learned that he had gone to school at Eton, that elite bastion of scholarly influence attended by the most aristocratic boys in England. There he had begun his studies of Greek and Latin, absorbed the music of ages, and made lasting friendships. Indeed, he said his years at Eton had been among the happiest of his life.

He seemed to have memorized everything he had ever read. His conversation was full of asides and quotes of Shakespeare, of allusions to French and Greek writers, of clever phrases from great books, of jokes turned from the sentences of famous poets. He was extremely good at anecdotes; one might even say they were his forte. In "The Old Chevalier" a character behaving like him recites a tale about a monkey and "imitated the monkey in the funniest and most gracefully inspired manner that one can imagine" (*SGT*, 99).

Finch Hatton took a deprecating approach to army life and enlarged amusingly upon the foibles of his fellow soldiers. He had once been billeted in a tent with eight men of lower social rank, to whom he referred, with a roll of the eyes, as "such an eight" (DFH to KR 6-22-18). It was not for nothing that the Africans called him Makanyaga, "Master of the Put-Down"—although he was also known as Bedar, "the Bald One."

Karen felt remarkably comfortable with him. Finch Hatton had a way of listening appreciatively to what she said. Even if he did not agree, he might use her ideas as fodder for a joke, gently putting down life in general. He was completely unselfconscious, and although he made it clear he had little respect for the business of war, he seemed happy enough playing soldier until it was over. They talked of books, especially of the works of Shakespeare—and, as more wine was consumed, together they made spirited quotes. They shared their love of opera and the ballet, and their wish for the war to end so that they could return to Europe to enjoy themselves there. Karen had at her house a gramophone (*LFA*, 65) (if he gave her one later, as she says in *Out of Africa*, it was not her first), and she said he must visit the farm to listen to her records.

Although Karen had been shy about her English, she was more confident now in conversation, allowing her Danish accent and syntax to enhance her speech. She still wore her dark hair in a chignon, with curls around her face—in contrast to the short, bleached hair in fashion since the war. She had been losing weight since her return from Denmark—Bror actually worried that she was too thin. Chicly dressed in a Parisian design, she presented her most attractive self. Finch Hatton responded confidently. He appeared relaxed, in a cat-like, watchful way. He had no reputation as a womanizer, yet Karen found him very appealing.

She went home that night euphoric, as though she had taken strong coffee or drugs. So great an impression had Finch Hatton made on her that she had already decided if she ever had a son she would send him to Eton (*LFA*, 67). Remembering his skeptical yet appreciative smile, she was kept awake by fantasies of how she would see him again.

* 4 *

A hunt was arranged at the Karen Coffee Plantation for the second Sunday in May 1918, in honor of General Evan Llewellyn, then on leave in Nairobi. The party would consist of the general, Major Davis and his wife, Erik von Otter, Captain Gorringe, Johnnie van de Weyer—Karen's neighbor, one of the old settlers and also an officer in the colonial army—and Denys Finch Hatton.

When Bror had returned from Uasin Gishu toward the end of April, Karen was full of news about her new acquaintance, the charming Englishman; and she insisted Bror must meet him. Bror, still chafed by her friendship with Von Otter, was perhaps skeptical about meeting another competitor, but Karen insisted that Bror would enjoy Finch Hatton. However, Bror may have guessed that her plan for a hunt was little more than an excuse for her to see Finch Hatton again.

On the appointed day, the guests arrived before sunrise. There was heavy fog, so wet the air dripped. The fog contrasted to the dryness everywhere, for the plains too were suffering from drought. The hunters were dressed warmly, in boots and jackets, Somali scarves and felt hats. Bror provided horses for some; Johnnie van de Weyer brought the others. Several Africans went out ahead, barefoot, in red blanket cloaks, to scout for game. They carried spears, hoping to find lions. Karen, who had a memory for smells, noted the musky scent of the woods as her party rode through, and, when they came out on the plains, the change to the dry perfume of prairie grass. Mourning doves made their plaintive sing-song, and the soft hammer-and-anvil sound of waterbirds called for rain. Save for the snorting of the horses and occasional low consultations among the hunters about the direction to follow, they made as little noise as possible. With the lightness of day, the air became warmer, the fog began to lift, and they could see game. They came across several herds of impala, standing alert with all their delicate faces listening, the spiral horns of the one male among them protectively erect. Gunshots jarred the tableau; in all, the party killed thirty impala and sent their scouts to retrieve the caramel-colored hides. The hunters came upon two jackals slinking in the grass nearby and killed them as contemptible targets. But their greatest luck, difficult to come upon even in the best of times, was shooting a leopard. With this trophy the group rode back to the farm exultant, Karen marveling that the hunt had succeeded beyond her fantasies.

She had gone to some pains planning a cold luncheon to follow the hunt, and had had a fire laid in the dining room for the occasion. Her guests seemed impressed, and the meal was delicious. Finch Hatton certainly drew a laugh when he announced his plans to stay for dinner, and not to be outdone, Van de Weyer insisted he would join him (*LFA*, 67). Karen of course welcomed them, and Bror, puffed up by the success of her hospitality, would accept no refusal. The four of them—Bror and Karen, Finch Hatton and Van de Weyer—stayed up late talking and exchanging amusing stories, and Bror opened wine, until Finch Hatton, who had farther to go than Van de Weyer, was invited to spend the night.

If, the following morning, Karen served tea on the terrace, at two small tables there made from old millstones, Denys may have complimented her on her splendid view of the Ngong Hills. He was about to return to his lodgings at the Muthaiga Club, and, as it happened, Karen had some errands to do in Nairobi, so since Bror was busy with matters on the farm, Karen, who had recently learned to drive, went with Finch Hatton into town. She lingered there with him at the Muthaiga Club, sharing conversation over a long luncheon (*LFA*, 67). Later she may have lamented to Bror that they would not be seeing Finch Hatton again soon, since he was now to leave for his flight training in Egypt.

* 5 *

Everyone spoke well of Denys Finch Hatton, but few people knew him well. His closest friend was the Honourable Berkeley Cole, and it was with him that Denys spent his free time. Denys and Berkeley saw eye-to-eye on the humor in life, quoted poetry together, and maintained a camaraderie detached from the rest of society. They were Renaissance men—as Karen later put it, outcasts of another age. "It was not a society that had thrown them out, and not any place in the whole world either, but time had done it, they did not belong to their century" (*OA*, 222). Often seen together, Denys tall and languid beside Berkeley's small, wiry figure, the two made an interesting pair. Berkeley, brother to Galbraith, and to Lord Delamere's wife, Florence, owned a large cattle ranch in the highlands near Mt. Kenya. He usually came to Nairobi for business, entertained seldom, and had no wife or children; thus he lived a secluded life. The day Karen had spent luncheon with Denys at the Muthaiga Club, Berkeley happened to be in town to greet Galbraith and his new bride, Lady Eleanor Balfour, who had just arrived in East Africa after their wedding in England. Finch Hatton planned to travel with them to Lake Elmenteita, site of Galbraith's ranch; this trip would be the first short leg of Denys's journey to Egypt.

Passage by sea was difficult to obtain because ships were crowded with troops reassigned to Europe and the Mediterranean. Denys would travel to Lake Victoria by train and from there go along the Nile route, by boat and train to Butiaba on Lake Albert in northern

Uganda, then by steamer to Nimule in the Sudan, and by foot from Nimule to Rejaf. Between these towns, the river narrowed into a succession of cataracts impossible to negotiate by boat; but overland a caravan trail led through excellent safari country that harbored large herds of elephant, rumored to be lucrative for ivory. For this leg of the journey Denys would have to hire African porters to carry his luggage—including medical supplies, food and cooking materials, a camp bed with poles, and a mosquito net. At Rejaf, where the Nile widened and was calm, Denys would board a steamer for Khartoum and from there go by train to Wadi Halfa. The final stage of his trip would be a steamship ride to Assuan. This entire odyssey could take him as long as six weeks.

Finch Hatton was an infrequent letter writer who confined his correspondence to intimate friends and family; Karen did not hear anything from him. She learned only much later that he had arrived in Cairo on June 21, 1918, and that he had been forced to wait some weeks to begin flight training with a new batch of recruits. He wrote his friend Kermit Roosevelt, son of the former American president, Theodore, that he had brought with him to Egypt his Somal (Somali servant), Billea Issa, whom he said he had located after frantic wiring all over B.E.A., and intended to keep with him even though officers frowned upon the indulgence.

Karen had developed a romantic fascination for the details of Finch Hatton's life and was obsessed with possibilities about his adventures in Egypt. She wondered aloud where he was and what he was doing, and she finally exasperated Bror with her preoccupation. One of Karen's friends, named Mary Goschen, lived in Cairo, and the two had had some recent correspondence. Karen teased Bror that Mary had invited her to visit and that it would be fun to go. But Bror was not amused. He suggested that the only thing in the world she cared about anymore was Finch Hatton, and if she did not stop talking about him, going to Cairo was exactly what he preferred her to do (*LFA*, 70).

Bror had good reason to be on edge. The failure of the long rains meant there would be no coffee crop. He had written the shareholders of Karen Coffee to explain the situation, and they had not been sympathetic. There was talk, by return mail, of liquidating the corporation. The idea of selling out put Bror's back up; he was determined to resist. In his view, the drought was bad luck; it was only a matter of waiting for fortune to turn around. He was still convinced that there was a lot of money to be made from his African land. Gravely, he discussed with Karen how they should answer her relatives, and it pleased her that he needed her support. The result was that she fiercely took his side. Together they decided to oppose the corporation. In fact, they made up their minds to buy out the shareholders, and not be bossed any more in matters concerning the farm (*LFA*, 70).

But the plan was impetuous, a little whiff of smoke, with no fuel to keep it going, since they had no money, and capital was impossible to come by in wartime. Finally both sides backed down: the corporation agreed to wait, and Karen and Bror withdrew their threat to buy out. However, the incident allied Karen with her husband. She took up the staff of loyalty, and wrote to her mother, "he said that what counted for him was not the money, it was achieving something here and helping to shape the future of this country; and I am sure that he is going to do this . . . " (*LFA*, 69).

As the drought continued, Karen's main concern was not for their own assets, but for the Africans, who were already starving because the previous rainy season had failed. There was no maize to be ground for *posho*—the staple of the Kikuyu diet—and no grass for the cattle. Most of the wild game was inedible. Lord Delamere was killing all the zebra on his land to drive out a pestilence and sending the carcasses to Nairobi in hopes the meat would be eaten. But the taste was foul; Karen had tried it. For some weeks she ran a samaritan (a station giving out free meals) on the farm, and every day fed children from miles around. However, the Indian who brought maize-meal to her was soon unable to get supplies, because there were none to be had. She despaired at having to stop the food hand-outs and wished for more grain from America and Australia. But ships were not available, or could not get through because of the war, and she was anguished at seeing children swollen with malnutrition, carried to her door by their parents, who begged for food.

Toward the end of May 1918, it rained once or twice. People believed the drought had ended, but no more rain came. Karen wrote home, "Everything is enveloped in a deathly chill, clammy fog the whole morning, and the nights are really unpleasantly cold,—and at the same time everything in the ground is withering and dying from lack of water" (*LFA*, 74).

She met Lord Delamere a few times in Nairobi and urged him to think of a solution for feeding the Africans, and she also argued the problem with Dr. Burkitt, whom she considered a friend. She could not understand why there was not more of a general uproar among the whites to demand that something be done. Frustrated that people would not help, she told her mother, "Most of the whites take very little interest in their natives, regarding them partly as their natural enemies . . . " (*LFA*, 73).

Farah had just taken a new wife (in addition to another in Somaliland) and brought her to live on the farm. Karen had a hut built for her and welcomed her like a member of her own family. She invited the Somali women for tea and liked to see them enter rustling in their colorful silks and veils and bare feet. She gave the women a tour of her house and her treasures. They looked at everything with wonder and put out their hands to touch and stroke things they had never seen before. They had a musical way of laughing in unison. Karen said they were revered by their husbands, as perhaps the only thing of real value in life.

She had also made friends with two Scandinavian women who lived on the neighboring farm in her former house, Mbagathi. One of these women was Fru Holmberg, with whom she had had difficulties her first year in Africa. Her attitude had changed; now she was more tolerant of the white women of the country. She would sometimes ride over to Mbagathi for tea, and perhaps she felt, when visiting these quaint farm women, as if she were back in Denmark. Fru Windinge, with a lovely singing voice like Karen's sister Ea, had a child eighteen months old, an age which appealed to Karen.

Despite the drought, these were happy months for Karen. She was on good terms with her neighbors, her servants, her doctor, and Lord Delamere. She felt allied with her husband. Her health was only fair, and she was still losing weight, but, she told her mother, Bror was a marvelous nurse. She was still hoping to conceive a child, and he was as devoted to the idea as she was. She had written to her mother quite recently, "you may laugh at me if you like, but in these hard times I feel like Khadijah, the Prophet's wife,—and am certain that I have married a great man . . . " (*LFA*, 69).

* 6 *

Each successive dry day while waiting for rain, Bror drove into Nairobi or restlessly made the rounds of the neighboring farms. For three months the farmers had talked of drought, but by June 1918, they were avoiding the subject, because they knew the rainy season was over. Lacking the moisture to plant, they cultivated discussions about the future of the colony. There was still much good land to be settled, but the railroad needed to be extended, so that farmers at Uasin Gishu and beyond could get their crops to the coast. As soon as the war was over, ships would be freed up to carry their coffee and grain to Europe, and they envisioned enormous profits. However, everyone agreed that money would be needed to extend the railroad, and the colonial government was already complaining that the hut tax was not bringing in enough to cover the cost of running the protectorate. To enhance the colony financially more settlers were needed.

Since 1915 an idea for attracting new people to East Africa had been bandied about among the colonists, and this was the notion of offering land to soldiers when the war was over. But the farmers agreed that up until now there had been too much talk about a soldier settlement scheme without results. Bror seized the initiative and announced that he was going to Soysambu to enlist Delamere's support. Bringing in more settlers would open up the country; the government could make cheap land available to veterans. Bror thought he could recruit some Swedish money to help finance the project. His name was mentioned in the newspaper and for a few months the plan stirred much publicity, some good and some bad, while people debated the issue. Most agreed he had a good idea, but they were not sure they wanted the plan financed with money tainted by German-leaning Swedes.

When Bror struck out for Soysambu, Delamere's ranch near Lake Elmenteita, Karen went along. She was eager for a change of scene and did not want Bror to leave her all alone, but she was also intrigued by the chance to see the fascinating Delamere: short in

1918

stature, long-haired, volatile, and dynamic in his opinions. He accompanied Bror and Karen to dinner at Galbraith Cole's scenic highland farm. It was a pleasure for Karen to bring the conversation around to Denys Finch Hatton, about whom people were always willing to give amused and admiring impressions.

Karen brought up again the subject of famine among the tribes and pointed out to Delamere that Africans were dying not only of starvation, but of diseases like malaria and smallpox, made worse by malnutrition. Delamere thought it a pity that the natives would not eat zebra and wildebeest, since at least these animals were available in plenty, and they were a nuisance to him and the other cattle ranchers of the highlands. War, he said, made it difficult to be humanitarian. "People in uniform are not human beings," he commented (*LFA*, 77). Karen suggested that the same applied to the new English policy concerning the Native Pass. She was upset that the Somalis could no longer travel freely in the colony. Under this regulation they had been lumped together with "the Kikuyu and the other local natives, whom they call 'Ushesis,' i.e. slaves, and for whom they have a deep contempt," she said (*LFA*, 77). Delamere had always sided with the natives in such questions. He too thought it a disgrace that Somalis were no longer "allowed to reside in Nairobi unless they are in the service of a white man . . . " (*LFA*, 77).

He was voluble about his new scheme for growing wheat. His land in the highlands was ideal for it, and he had been urging the government to require farms to grow a certain number of acres of wheat, so that the Colony would be less dependent on imported foodstuffs (*WMC* II: 32–3). Some new land near Lake Naivasha was to be broken for wheat by a group of investors called Longonot, Ltd., and they planned to contract out the work.

Bror saw a chance to make some money. He wired the shareholders of Karen Coffee and received their permission to commit himself to plowing 2000 acres, the work to be completed over a period of eleven months. Karen encouraged the project; in fact, she may have masterminded it, for it gave her a chance to move temporarily to Naivasha, where she was delighted to be.

* 7 *

"I can't tell you how lovely it is to be out on the march again
... ," Karen wrote to her mother; "to me Naivasha is one of the most
heavenly places in the world..." (LFA, 83). It was one of only two blue,
freshwater lakes in the colony; all the others, including Elmenteita,
were sterile green soda lakes with no outlet. There were mountains
along Naivasha's horizon and grasslands up to the water's edge. The
lake hosted multitudes of exotic birds, since it lay in the great
migratory route from Europe. At times there were thousands of
colorful species—geese, egrets, plovers, cranes, blue and gold star-
lings, finches, herons, ibis, and storks. The setting made the spirit soar
like the winged creatures that abounded there.

Karen looked forward to a blissful period of intimacy with her
husband, turning over virgin land in this vast setting. They lived in a
makeshift shelter, made of "sheet iron of all possible shapes, age and
color" (LFA, 83). The interior of the hut—with floors of sand and walls
lined with papyrus—provided a cool and comfortable nest whose
shutters could be closed, making it completely dark and private. High
on a hill above the lake, they had beautiful views on all sides and, in the
early morning, could watch the wild game "coming down to the lake
to drink from several square miles around ... " (LFA, 83).

Karen did not mind the rustic surroundings. Living there
reminded her of her safari for the army; she liked the feeling of being
a wanderer. She and Bror had a little sailboat, The Flame, which they
used to sail across the lake to visit other white settlers. Karen had
brought two fourteen-year-old Africans along to help with the cooking
and the household chores, while Farah stayed at Ngong with his new
bride. One of the boys, from Aden, was a remarkable swimmer. She
took him with her on the lake in the afternoons, and he amused her by
diving in and disappearing, then coming up many yards from the boat.

She was content to have Bror to herself and hoped to conceive
the child she had talked of ever since coming back to Africa with him
in 1917. She thought of herself as his partner and support, and liked the
role. With pride, she wrote to her mother, "I think Bror enjoys being
up here dealing with oxen and plows" (LFA, 85).

1918

It was no small operation he was directing, and one must not imagine Bror walking in a furrow behind a plow. In all, there were nearly two hundred oxen, in teams of sixteen to a harness, and across the horizon plows and teams churned up the soil in clouds of dust, disturbing prairie that had never before known cultivation. Pacing the land in high boots and khaki shorts, and a broad-brimmed felt hat, Bror kept track of the teams and smoked a cigar as he surveyed their progress.

Karen spent her days exploring and hunting, and supervising the cooking and light work. She had brought her dog Banja with her, but he was nearly killed when a wild boar gored him. The experience shook her badly, for she had lost her beloved Dusk only recently, and had not yet gotten over the tragedy.

Dusk had been lost on their journey to Lake Elmenteita, under emotional circumstances. Karen blamed herself for the disaster, for she had brought Dusk to Africa, and had enjoyed his faithful friendship in times when even Bror had deserted her. In truth, Dusk, like her husband, had never been particularly manageable, and this failing was at the root of why he died. Karen and Bror's old car had broken down while they were on their way to have dinner with Lord Delamere. Fortunately, Bror's foreman, Von Huth, was following on his motorcycle and came to their rescue. While Bror and Karen continued ahead by motorcycle, Von Huth walked back to their camp, a few miles away. Karen had implored him to take care of Dusk, but Von Huth had more things to worry about than the baroness's dog. It was a long, hot march to find the camp, and Dusk had never been taught to behave. Eventually Von Huth grew disgusted with managing the leash, and turned the dog loose.

Dusk capitalized on his freedom to chase small fowl in the grass and soon lost Von Huth and the scent of his trail. Although Karen searched for him for three days, and Farah nearly as many more, he was dying when Farah found him. He had been injured by the kick of a zebra foal, and had starved to death. Farah's willingness to search for Dusk was testimony to his devotion to Karen, for Muslims believe dogs to be unclean and ordinarily will not touch them. Karen took the death as hard as if a child had died. She wrote to her mother, "My wonderful faithful Dusk. I miss him so much, and if I live to be seventy, I believe I will never think of him without weeping . . . " (*LFA*, 82).

So this holiday in Naivasha was a recuperation from grief, as much as a chance to be alone with Bror. However, Karen had been there only a week when she suffered another misfortune. She was out riding on a mule when it was startled by a jackal darting out from some bushes. The mule reared up, throwing Karen off violently against a boulder. At first she did not seem too badly hurt, but she had hit the rock with such force that her thigh was bruised along its entire length. She was thin and bruised easily, so it was not surprising that the injury was worse than it first appeared.

She wrote to her mother, "I am black as ink and badly grazed, but Bror can bandage like an angel and wraps me and Banja up like two mummies" (*LFA*, 84). She could not be outside as much as before, but hoped to stay at Naivasha with Bror. However, her bruise became dangerously infected, due to a collection of blood beneath the broken skin. She developed a high fever, and Bror was alarmed. He transported her by oxcart to the train at Naivasha and sent her to Nairobi, where she was taken directly to Dr. Burkitt's office. Burkitt put her to sleep fully clothed and opened the wound with a scalpel. She awakened groggy and in pain to discover stitches running the entire length of her thigh.

Burkitt was known for his drastic measures; Karen liked him, but she was never sure whether he exaggerated his methods. It seemed to her that the hideous wound was uncalled for; her once alluring leg was scarred from hip to knee. Dispirited, she attempted to recover her strength, first for two weeks in the Kenya Nursing Home, then at the McMillans' house nearby. During that time, Burkitt gave her chloroform two more times, opened the wound and cleaned out more infection. He tried to sew it shut, but the infection kept reappearing. Finally he left the incision open, with instructions to Karen to soak the wound several times a day with clean bandages wrung out in iodine solution. It would be months before the wound healed. Karen said she felt "like an old soldier." Upset by the look of her leg, she wept about it to Bror. He was solicitous, helping her into the bath and changing the dressings when he was there, and he said it did not matter to him how it looked. He teased her that he hoped not many people would see it (*LFA*, 89). Trying to be amused, Karen repeated his comment in a letter to Thomas. But surely she wondered what Finch Hatton might think of it.

* 8 *

Karen was thinking about Finch Hatton as she wrote to Thomas on November 7, 1918. She was still in bed nursing the leg she had wounded two months before. In the course of her fantasies, she had worked it out that Finch Hatton must have finished his flying course and was now flying for the Royal Air Corps in France. Perhaps, she wrote Thomas, he and Denys would run into each other there, since she had had news from home that Thomas was also thinking of training to be a pilot (*LFA*, 89).

Far from being in France at the moment Karen wrote her letter, Finch Hatton lay on his back in a hospital in Egypt, nursing a bad foot. The accident had occurred in early September 1918, in the same week as Karen's injury. He had tripped over some barbed wire in the dark, and the force of the fall had driven a piece of metal through his moccasin. (He was fond of soft shoes, in which he could tread softly like the Masai.) The metal had lodged in his foot and had to be cut out. When the foot flamed up and swelled, doctors had ordered it elevated to prevent blood poisoning.

The same week Karen asked Thomas to look for him in France, Denys had written a disgusted letter to Kermit Roosevelt. The war would soon be over and he had not even completed his classroom flight instruction. He realized he was never to see the inside of an airplane while in the army.

The armistice came on November 11, 1918. In Nairobi there was a series of wildly celebratory parties. Bror participated a little more than Karen could brook, treating friends to vast amounts of liquor and sponsoring lavish dinners in the local hotels. It was all part of the general euphoria over the ending of the war, but Karen was unamused and could not see how they were going to pay their bills.

Bror scoffed at her concern; now that the war was over he expected good prices for coffee, plenty of transport as ships were freed up, and the value of land to double or triple—all of which would soon make them wealthy. Even if, by chance, the crop was poor this season, now that money was available they could get a loan to tide them over.

However, Karen had begun to take a careful look at the farm accounts—something she had left to Bror in the past—and had lost her respect for his ability to manage money. Thousands of the British pounds they brought to East Africa in 1917 had been spent on projects like flax and cattle, which had so far not paid for themselves. In her opinion, Bror was squandering the money garnered from the Longonot, Ltd., contract and had nothing to fall back on. Had he no shame, spending frivolously the money invested in them by her relatives? She felt like an accomplice to a theft.

There were other problems between them. Karen had been an invalid for four months, able neither physically nor temperamentally to perform the duties of a wife. On the other hand, the giddy women of Nairobi were out in droves, in pumps and short skirts and cropped hair, sharing their exuberance over the armistice with sensual takers like Bror, who was an expert at appreciating them. He basked in his ability to win them over, and when he caught sight of a pretty woman, he bragged to his cronies how fast he could seduce her. Karen may have caught word of events, for in "Tales of Two Old Gentlemen," she describes her disgust at this sort of behavior; she was humiliated by it. When she came into a ballroom on his arm, she could feel all eyes on her, staring, as though they were wondering if she knew about his latest conquest (LT, 71–2). She evidently initiated a terrible argument with Bror over this and confronted him again with her concerns about the way he was spending money. Ordinarily Karen was slow to anger; she always questioned first whether she herself was at fault, and blamed herself for circumstances. But when she did get angry she made a scene, and ended with ultimatums. She did not believe she could influence Bror's sexual behavior—he had shown himself incorrigible in that regard—but she would not tolerate his spending more money until her family had been repaid. And she also made him understand that, if he could not be more discreet about the women he bedded, she would ask him to leave.

One may imagine there was a silence when she finished and Bror left the room on his heel, saying he would do as he pleased.

1919

By December 1918, Karen seems to have received word that Denys Finch Hatton was returning to East Africa. She wrote Thomas a lyrical letter, rhapsodizing on the glories of love, which she referred to as "the most divine of all the world's forces" (*LFA*, 93). Her purpose in writing was to congratulate Thomas on earning the Victoria Cross, Britain's highest honor for bravery in war. But she also described her view of the future for herself and Bror. She said they were trying to arrange their affairs so as to have their freedom. While this referred to freedom from interference in the farm's affairs by the shareholders of Karen Coffee, her thinking went further. She said, "We would manage the farm as before and naturally continue to live here, although I think that Bror would come to lead something of a roving life" (*LFA*, 93). This arrangement would perhaps allow her to encourage Finch Hatton's attentions, should he be inclined, and give her the freedom in relationships with the opposite sex that Bror had long ago assumed for himself.

She and Bror had devised a scheme with their neighbor, Johnnie van de Weyer, to lease the farm from the shareholders in return for turning over a percentage of the profits to them. In this way, she and Bror would have complete control over management, without being required to refer to the corporation for decisions. They suggested that they pay rent on the profits, increasing on a yearly basis— 7 ¹/2 percent the first year, 10 percent the second year, and so on, reaching 17 ¹/2 percent by the fifth year (*LFA*, 93). Lease aside, these profit percentages were already the same as established by the shareholders in 1916 as necessary for their continuing support. But Bror and Karen asked not to have to pay any interest on the investment for the previous two years, claiming bad luck due to the war and the drought. Karen hoped the shareholders might respect Van de Weyer's advice, since he was, after all, one of the old settlers. She was increasingly taking the farm's finances into her own hands. Her servants took note of the change, and were astonished at how toughly she spoke to her husband on the subject of money (*LFD*, 12–XIII).

She accepted Frank Greswolde-Williams's invitation, renewed from the previous year, to spend Christmas and New Year's 1919 on his farm at Kedong. Bror evidently did not accompany her. There was no mention of him when she wrote Thomas about her enjoyable holiday. Frank G.-W., as she called him, who prided himself on his attractiveness to charming, younger women, had taken Karen lion hunting.

She was proceeding with her own social life, regardless of Bror's activities, and meeting some rather enjoyable men—army officers drifting through Nairobi on their way to be demobilized. One of these was a childhood friend of Denys Finch Hatton, Geoffrey Buxton, whom she met at a dance. She established a rapport with him and, in the course of flirtatious remarks, agreed when he guessed her age to be only twenty-seven. She was actually thirty-three and cautioned Thomas, on pain of permanent estrangement, never to reveal her real age (*LFA*, 96).

Finch Hatton arrived in Nairobi the first week of February— in time to attend a gala Race Week in honor of the newly appointed governor, Sir Edward Northey. The balls and receptions, as well as horse races, brought out Nairobi society in fashionable dress. Karen was beside herself preparing for these occasions, and her clothes did not satisfy her at all, even though she had renewed her wardrobe in Europe only two years before. She wrote Thomas, "nothing,—be it illness, poverty or loneliness or other misfortunes, distresses me more than having nothing to wear!" (*LFA*, 97). She was the more concerned with her attire because she had been invited to sit next to the new governor himself at a banquet given on the race course by Lord Delamere, and her clothes would be on display. She accompanied Bror to the event; he and Delamere had conducted numerous dealings the previous year over the Soldier Settlement Scheme. (Such a plan had finally been implemented, but Bror's suggestion of financial backing by Swedish investors was rejected. Cheap land was being offered by the colonial government. To be eligible veterans were to be selected by lottery, and Karen hoped Thomas would qualify.)

She had been making discreet inquiries about Finch Hatton's sentimental interests and had not uncovered any. There were women among his close friends in England, but as far as anyone knew, they were not romantic attachments. A pretty older cousin named Kitty Lucas was thought to be happily married. She had lived with Denys's family for a time when Denys was twelve years old and Kitty was sixteen, the same age as Denys's sister Topsy. Kitty had named her second son after Denys, but this seems to have been done out of sisterly affection.

As for romantic interests in Kenya, Denys had none. But women loved him; they all said they would go to the ends of the earth for him, and this was because he was such fun to be with. He made them laugh and put them at ease, and he was always appreciative and a good listener. But he was not known to lavish time on women— unless perhaps on wives of friends, like Galbraith Cole's wife, Eleanor.

Denys and Berkeley Cole had been among the principal instigators behind the establishment of the Muthaiga Club. When it opened in January 1914, they had encouraged quality cooking and the serving of high-class wines. During the war, Denys had given up the lease on McMillan's Parklands mansion and arranged to share rent on a cottage at Muthaiga with Lord Delamere. Under most circumstances only one of them would be in Nairobi at any given time. However, for Race Week in February 1919, Delamere was using the cottage. So after Finch Hatton arrived in Nairobi, he made an appearance at the Blixens' farm at Ngong.

* 2 *

In the course of many rounds of drinks, much dancing, and a profusion of gay luncheons, the Blixens circulated among the elite of settler society during the February Race Week. Those who had not known them before quickly became aware of how charming life at the Blixens' farm could be. One devotee of their estate who had enjoyed the successful hunt of the previous year proposed that the baron and baroness should plan another shooting party. This they were quite happy to do on the weekend after the races. Twenty people were invited—all the cream of Nairobi society—including General Evan Llewellyn and his brother, Colonel Jack Llewellyn, Lord Delamere, Johnnie van de Weyer, and of course Denys Finch Hatton.

And for an entire month afterwards Denys Finch Hatton continued as houseguest at the Blixens' farm. He had had fever the day of the hunt, and Karen insisted afterwards that he stay. Nothing so aroused her maternal instincts as the opportunity to care for someone; it may have been this role that stimulated Denys to refer to her as "Tania." Bror called her Tanne, the name her family had used when she mispronounced Karen as a small girl. But she had never liked "Tanne." Denys announced he would call her Tania, after Titania (*T*, 69), queen of the fairies, in *A Midsummer Night's Dream*. By serving him, playing music for him, feeding him and otherwise caring for him, she was honoring an unworthy "ass." What she offered was too fine for the average dolt at her table; she provided nuts when he had anticipated only dried peas.

Deeply flattered that she had met someone who understood her vision of herself as a romantic heroine, she allowed Denys to call her Tania; and their mutual friends followed suit.

While Denys found Karen charming, he also enjoyed Bror. Blixen "had adopted in life"—as Karen describes a character like him in the tale "The Dreamers"—"the manner of a good, plain, outspoken fellow who is a little unpolished but easily forgiven on account of his open, simple mind" (*SGT*, 295). And although he could see that his wife preferred Finch Hatton's company to his own, Blixen tolerated Denys remarkably well. In fact, he seemed to enjoy Finch Hatton's stay as much as she did. He and Denys exchanged hunting stories and opinions on wine, and became fast friends over weeks while Denys recuperated from fever. They shared similar investments, since Finch Hatton held a financial interest in a farm at Uasin Gishu, near Blixen's. Denys also owned shares in the store at Sosiani, a town (now Eldoret) in the same district. Denys's property had been under siege during the war, when the Masai, egged into revolt against forced conscription into the army, had raided his *dukas*. He had mentioned this concern earlier in a letter to Kermit Roosevelt (DFH to KR 11-22-18), and he was eager to go there to check on the state of things. He was accustomed to traveling in Kenya on horseback, or on foot with porters, but he had told Kermit what wonderful coursing one could do in the colony by car (DFH to KR 6-22-18), a joy he had experienced for the first time when he bought an old Ford while on leave in 1918. He had eventually resold the jalopy for more than he paid for it, a move that he regretted because now he needed it.

The Blixens perhaps offered him the use of their car for a trip to Uasin Gishu. Karen would be delighted to go along; she had not visited their farm on the other side of the Rift Valley for two years. To accompany them, Bror would have to borrow his manager Von Huth's motorcycle, since their car was only a two-seater. It was not a good time to be traveling, because the rainy season had just begun, but they could take their vehicles on the train as far as Londiani and, with luck, motor the sixty-four miles from there to Sosiani.

It is known from a brief notation of the date in her diary (5.3.19.–14.3.19 *rundt om Kenya m. Denys*)(*SWS*, 148) that Karen traveled with Denys for two weeks at the beginning of March 1919, but there is no evidence to substantiate that they were hunting (or that they went alone). The rainy season had begun, and it was not customary to plan safaris for March. Indeed, Karen had written home at the end of February that the drought was at last ended. She said, "Now even the furthest, deepest valley is turning green,—it is something of a miracle how quickly everything here is transformed by the rain; the Ngong Hills and the Reserve, that were burned to the likeness of a doormat, are now brilliant with the finest, most glorious green and the whole shamba is flowering . . . I have a feeling that wherever I may be in the future, I will be wondering whether there is rain at Ngong" (*LFA*, 98). They struck off on their safari (the name given to any long trek over rough roads) on March 5, 1919, and were gone for ten days.

Karen still nursed a small open wound, less than the size of a match-box, on her thigh, but it was healing. She was taking some arsenic, and had told her mother that it was doing wonders for her (*LFA*, 97). Although she was not bothered anymore by her arthritis of the previous year, she was still dosing without prescription from an elixir of arsenic, a few drops in her bedtime tea, believing this would fend off a recurrence of syphilis. Remembering the ominous words of the specialist in Paris, she doubted that she had recovered, and so she attributed any new symptoms to syphilis. However, she had experienced one episode of illness during Race Week that she had blamed on sunstroke. The symptoms—sudden piercing pains in the head aggravated by bright stimuli and noise—may have been due to quinine taken for malaria, since an overdose can be toxic to the nerves.

Some have romantically assumed that Karen and Finch Hatton became lovers early in 1919, but reality probably differed. There is no evidence either way, but Karen's open leg wound and the angry scar attached to it were inhibiting. Karen's previous comments about him suggest that Bror, when he was home, satisfied her physical needs. She had so often said that there was less than a war's ration of intellectual interest in Africa; what she craved from Finch Hatton was his conversation. She told Thomas: "I have been so fortunate in my old age to meet my ideal realized in him . . . " (*LFA*, 89).

* 3 *

From the end of February to the middle of July 1919, Karen wrote no letters to her family, because she expected at any moment to board a ship and be on her way to see them. Like others restless to get back to Europe, she and Bror were forced to wait for cabin space. Lacking other transport, they talked of going down the Nile to Egypt with Denys; but disturbances had broken out there, and they had no guarantee of space on a ship out of Cairo. Besides, their difficult finances could not support an expensive safari via the Sudan. As a residual effect of the drought the year before, their coffee had failed to flower in the most recent rainy season. Money expected from home was delayed, and as they waited, the rate of exchange between the Kenya rupee and the English pound began to collapse, making the cost of everything in the colony twenty-five percent higher and causing astonishing losses of capital. The price of land had surged, so that a farm Karen wanted to buy for Thomas was already double the price it had been in 1917.

Karen and Bror made the best of the waiting period by cultivating new social contacts. The previous December when Thomas Dinesen was awarded the Victoria Cross, the news had been published in the Nairobi paper *The Leader*, and Karen had been exonerated of holding German sympathies. Bror, too, was respected by "everyone of account," as Karen put it (*LFA*, 90), and the invitations increased. She attributed some of their popularity to the beauty of their estate at the foot of the Ngong Hills and to its convenient location near Nairobi. In Denmark, Karen's socializing had been limited to family gatherings and quiet teas with close friends; now she was honing her skills as hostess on a grander scale.

It helped that introductions were being made for them by Denys Finch Hatton. He was prominent in their widening circle of friends. Conviviality drew them all together. The catalyst for such occasions was often Bror himself, especially when discussions of sport were involved. Talking about hunting was amusing and gave him a chance to brag about his prowess.

Secretly satisfied that she was spending time with Finch Hatton and that Bror was bringing them together, Karen at first welcomed these occasions. Comparing the two men may have been a source of diversion. Their complexions were similarly fair, ruddied by the sun. Denys's hair had at one time been dark blond and wavy like Bror's, but now Denys's receded severely. Bror's face was round and self-satisfied, like that of a boy, while Denys had the narrow face and classically defined nose of an aristocrat—his large mouth often distorting in some great mocking anecdote. Tall and graceful, Denys was, above all, languid; he moved with the litheness of a cat. Bror was so stocky the Africans had nicknamed him Wahoga, "the Wild Goose" (*AL*, xvii).

The two could converse endlessly about hunting, both remi-
niscing—Bror perhaps more than Denys—about memorable shoots at
home. Denys returned nearly every summer to hunt with friends in
Scotland. Bror had started hunting as a boy in Sweden and was
addicted to the sport. Although Finch Hatton had first come out to
Africa in 1911, a few years before Bror, he was frequently in England
and had had little more safari experience than Bror, so the two could
exchange hunting stories on an equal footing. Perhaps Bror's trophies
were distinguished more by their numbers, Finch Hatton's by their
quality—Bror talked of how many lions he had shot; Denys, of his
collection of fine manes. Bror's knowledge of livestock appealed to
Denys, who had never actually worked with animals although, of
necessity, he knew a little about horses. His success in hunting was due
to precision—for he had grown up in a social milieu where exactness
was a virtue. While both of them could react to a target uncommonly
well, Denys brought down his trophies through skillful grace, Bror
through physical prowess: Bror triumphed through energy; Denys,
through quick mental grasp of what was needed. In a sense, Bror
seduced his trophies; Denys courted them. Denys was less interested
in the prize than in the successful pursuit. For Bror the prize was
everything, the proof of his prowess. While Bror might exclaim over
the number and variety of zebra, antelope, rhino, and buffalo he had
slain on a given safari, Denys would elaborate upon his pursuit,
through many counterfeit encounters, of one old elephant with magnificent tusks. Hunting was their common language and, whatever
intellectual gap remained between them, it merely provided Karen
the opportunity to divert Finch Hatton's conversation to a higher
plane, talking of Shakespeare and Mozart.

Her talks with Denys were of an intellectual nature Karen
had not hitherto known in Africa. He brought her interesting books, far
superior to the poor novels she had been able to get in the colony. He
liked to read history and poetry. He was not keen on fiction, except for
novels of established merit, like those of Proust, but he loved poetry
and often quoted Homer, Shakespeare, Coleridge, and other great
masters. He was an expert on the classics. Karen knew nothing of
Greek or Latin, but had studied the philosophers. She surprised

Denys with her amusing approach to dogma: any great historical cause had something about it of the ridiculous.

When Bror interrupted, she wished him away, so annoyingly did he monopolize Denys. She was no longer content to bask in Denys's presence in her house, to serve him and listen to discussions about hunting. She wanted more exciting conversation and thought of Bror's talk as boorish—always keeping Denys, who might have appreciated better, to the same subject. Bror was not the kind to be distracted. If she attempted to turn the talk to more aesthetic issues, Bror brushed aside her remarks. If she pressed, Bror joked about her comments in a way to demean her. Discussions of literature and music necessarily excluded him; he was not content to listen. So, with jocular asides to Finch Hatton, he made her remarks seem ridiculous and therefore infuriated her.

In "The Old Chevalier" Karen vividly describes the situation that arises when lovers compete for the attention of a rival. The struggle between them is not a question of jealousy, as one might expect from husband or wife, but a *contest* (*SGT*, 87). Both she and Bror wished to win Finch Hatton's admiration, as two people might fight over a prized object. Karen attempted to separate Denys from Bror: to take him riding while Bror worked on the farm; to have lunch with Denys at Muthaiga while Bror was seeing about supplies; and to engage Denys in talk of books while Bror consulted with overseers. Taking note of her efforts Bror predictably redoubled his efforts to monopolize Denys.

It is not known whether Karen was sexually intimate with Denys at this early stage of their friendship, but such a relationship would have been awkward, since he was so much Bror's friend. In "The Old Chevalier" Karen's hero senses the rivalry between husband and wife and cannot decide whether she is fond of him or merely trying to make her husband jealous (*SGT*, 83). He says, " . . . I began to wonder what the relations between those two were really like, and what strange forces there might be in her or in him, to toss me about between them in this way . . . " (*SGT*, 83–4). Finch Hatton enjoyed both of the Blixens, and there is no indication that he considered his relationship with Karen more than a friendship. He spent as much, if not more, time with Bror than with her.

Like them, he was eager to get back to Europe, and by the end of July 1919 he had found passage on a ship to England. Karen and Bror had arranged with Denys to see him next in London. He was not mentioned in Karen's letters describing Race Week, which she and Bror spent at Government House, at the special request of the governor, Lord Northey. The governor's only other guests were General and Madam Polowtzoff, Russian aristocrats who had fled the revolution, and Lord Delamere. The Blixens were quite friendly with all these people, and after Race Week they went on safari with the Polowtzoffs, and visited Greswolde-Williams's farm at Kedong; and then they continued on to Naivasha with Delamere. Karen wrote to her mother that the Polowtzoffs had lost all their money when they left Russia and were living by pawning their jewels. The generous Bror could never say no to people, and liked to show off his largess. Too often, this meant he was signing chits he never intended to pay. In fact, the Muthaiga Club threatened to cancel his membership in a dispute over accounts.

Bror and Karen set aside social and financial interests in the colony on August 14, 1919, and boarded a ship for Europe. The only vessel available was going to England via Bombay. They were desperate enough to see their families to agree to this considerable detour.

* 4 *

Karen always said that the chief feature of Bror's personality was his sense of contest. His greatest amusement lay in outshining other people. Usually he succeeded, in pursuits that mattered to him: women, hunting, friendships, and money. But by the fall of 1919, in the cultural atmosphere of London, it was apparent that he was losing to his wife in the competition for Finch Hatton's admiration. Bror could not keep up with Karen's knowledge of the ballet and opera, the theater and literature. Karen openly teased that he did not know whether the Crusades came before or after the French Revolution (*IDKB*, 25–6). It was like Bror to laugh off the insult but to harbor thoughts of revenge.

Karen and Denys went off to the opera without him (*SWS*, 171). They must have made a handsome couple. Denys wore full evening dress with top hat; and, despite her meager budget, in the excitement of reaching civilization, Karen had bought in London one or two new gowns—in white, her favorite color.

Bror was left behind to be entertained by some other friends from Africa. Among these was Geoffrey Buxton, who bought tickets for a musical revue entitled "Chu-Chin-Chow," playing at His Majesty's Theatre in the Haymarket. There Bror met a small, attractive woman named Cockie Birkbeck, the daughter of a banker and wife of Ben Birkbeck, a cousin of Geoffrey Buxton. Her name, Cockie, was said to derive from her pert good looks and chirpy personality. Bror made an extremely poor impression that evening, acting bored and disinterested (*SWS*, 171).

His brooding attitude may have arisen from the conflicts increasingly evident between him and Karen. Both had reasons for annoyance. Bror could not stand to be upstaged by her in matters of friendship, and Karen found his careless spending intolerable. Whether the subject was money, or jealousy, in London a major battle seems finally to have occurred. Karen left England alone, on a ship Denys had arranged for, and it is said that Denys drove her to Newcastle to board it (*T*, 72). If so, he was not taking sides in the dispute. He remained detached—a friend to both.

One may imagine that Karen arrived in Denmark extremely upset at having to admit to her family to the crumbling state of her marriage and, with it, her good name.

1920

1

It was an age of reverence for symbols. What was done behind closed doors was not so important as the image portrayed in public. While many aristocrats lost their fortunes, they remained awe-inspiring by virtue of their names. Karen said later, "the name *was* the thing or the man" (*DOE*, 2). A name represented status and tradition. Like a piece of cloth that when fashioned into a flag represents the spirit of a nation, so a name might be regarded as a symbol of honor. Karen recoiled from the thought of divorce, as a threat to what she had achieved by marrying into a title. She viewed divorce as a fatal blemish on the plan of her life. It affronted her concept of the ideal, and it loomed as a failure that would set a precedent. She feared that, as a divorced woman, she would be rejected by society. Generally the wife was blamed for failing to maintain a harmonious house or for having made an injudicious choice of husband. Scandal was all the more serious in cases where divorce was instigated by the wife. It would not be unusual for accusations to arise that she had been unfaithful. No matter how much Bror had wronged her, and no matter how divisive their life together had been, she could not make up her mind to divorce.

Breaking with Bror would place her in an intolerable position. She would have to give up the farm and her life in Africa, for she could not envision returning there alone. Not only was she devoted to the exotic country, but life there was now suffused with her romantic interest in Finch Hatton, whom she would see again only if she went back. Moreover, she could not imagine a future for herself at home. What would she do with her life? Scorned as a divorcee, pitied by friends for failing at her vaunted scheme of living in Africa, smothered by a well-meaning family who had failed to educate her to earn a living, what course was she to take?

Although her family was aware of her soul-searching, there is no evidence that Bror, in Sweden with his own family, knew she was considering an end to the marriage. Worry about the farm eventually superseded her preoccupation with divorce, for she and Bror were receiving news of a growing crisis in East Africa. Since the war, inflation, due to the rising demand for land, and a precipitous fall in the world price of coffee were leading Karen and Bror to serious doubts about their enterprise in East Africa. She had to proffer a truce to him so that they could communicate about their growing financial problems.

Bror had enlisted Emil Holmberg to look after things on the coffee plantation while he was gone, so he could have undertaken a leisurely holiday, but, in contrast to Karen, who was delighted to be home, Bror had little interest in spending time in Europe. He visited his parents but stayed only à few months. Financial considerations were luring him back to the farm, since he was convinced a killing could be made on flax. Although profits on coffee had plummeted, the price of flax had shot to £ 300 per ton. Bror had interested a Swedish school chum, Gillis Lindstrom, in partaking in the windfall. In March 1920, while Lindstrom's wife and daughters made preparations to follow, Bror set sail for Africa with Gillis—collecting Farah, who had been on home leave in Somaliland, on the return voyage.

Even if Karen had intended to accompany them, she was unable to do so because she had come down with Spanish influenza. The epidemic was taking more victims than the Great War, although those whose health was feeble before the illness seemed for some reason to fare better. What with influenza, and another series of injections of Salvarsan in the hope of curing any residual syphilis,

Karen had spent five months in the hospital, and was in no way prepared to return to Africa in the spring of 1920.

She was on speaking terms with Bror again, but to her family she still talked of divorce. Only after heated discussions with him had she agreed to his returning to their farm alone. Bror's leaving her behind in Europe while she was ill seemed a repetition of myriad betrayals, none of which should have been so easily condoned, nor so blithely forgiven, and all of which pointed to the impossibility of carrying on with the marriage. Yet she despaired of the scandal associated with divorce, and of the failure it would represent to the eyes of the world. She railed about these difficulties, and about the possible loss of her title, to the member of her family in whom she placed the greatest trust, her brother Thomas.

Thomas was twenty-seven now, seven years younger than Karen. He had the narrow face of the Westenholzes but was better looking than his uncles; his eyes and his manner reflected some of the romantic qualities of the Dinesens. He had been Karen's confidant, a role her sisters had never fulfilled. When he and Karen were younger, she used to take him aside and recite the great Nordic poems to him. She had tried to instill in him her own idea of heroism, and to some extent she had succeeded, for he bore proudly his Victoria Cross. In the company of Thomas, Karen could experience a portion of the world of men. When Thomas was offered sailing lessons in Skaane in southern Sweden at the age of thirteen, Karen had insisted on accompanying him. It was with Thomas that Karen had joined the Rungsted Ice Hockey Club. She and Thomas had been skating and riding companions, and one winter they had vacationed in Norway and learned to ski together. Karen would have attempted none of these sports on her own, since she belonged to a family, and to a generation, that believed women dared attempt such exploits only in the company of men.

Karen could speak to Thomas knowing that he would not share her confidences with other members of the family. She had taken his side when he joined the army against their mother's wishes. She relied on his loyalty. Karen discussed with him the reasons that inclined her to divorce: Bror's involvements with other women, his unrestrained spending, his refusal to accept her directions and admonitions, his boorish competitiveness when it came to her friends. Yet, after citing these arguments, she declared she had come to the conclusion that none of these complaints—despite the emotional confrontations with Bror that had resulted—ought to carry weight when two people were working together for an ideal: in this case, the farm. Although she was exasperated with Bror, she had made up her mind to return to Africa, for, as she had said in the poem "Ex Africa," she had come to think of the colony as her "heart's land." Would not Thomas consent to travel out to Africa with her? Perhaps there he, too, would find his place in life.

Thomas had been directionless since the war. His days seemed bland after the excitement of battle; his life had reached its zenith when he received the Victoria Cross. He held a degree in civil engineering, like Uncle Aage, but raw materials like rubber in Malaya and cement in Bangkok did not excite him as they did Uncle Aage, whose generation was fascinated by development of new resources in the colonies. Thomas had come into a substantial annuity left to him by his father, so he was under no compunction to seek a profession. But the idea of investing in land in the colonies intrigued him. Karen may have used him as a model for Peter in the story "Peter and Rosa": He "was a good-natured creature and easy to dominate" (*WT*, 255). When Karen begged him to accompany her to Africa, he consented.

* 2 *

The trip they began in November 1920 was a trial from the outset. Karen's younger brother Anders, now twenty-six, took time out from the farm he managed in Jutland—the Leerbaek Estate, owned by his mother's sister, Lidda, and her husband, Uncle Gex—to accompany Karen and Thomas to London. Karen, Anders, and Thomas boarded a ship that was to take them from Denmark to England, but the crossing was so rough that the journey took thirty-six hours. Once in London, Anders irritated Karen with his inability to hear what was said to him without rambling off immediately on some associated idea of his own. Karen had booked passage on the *Garth Castle* and now learned that Prince Wilhelm and Sjögren would be sailing on it, too. Word had already spread that she and Bror were estranged; Karen was appalled at the thought of the effort it would take during the month's journey to maintain polite conversation. In addition, she and Bror had likely never cleared their debt with Sjögren since buying out Swedo Coffee in 1916, and seeing him daily would be an embarrassment. She and Thomas were due to board the ship at Marseilles; they passed through Paris en route, and there Karen contracted an illness involving vomiting and dizziness. When the ship departed on December 6, she was only just able to go aboard.

She had been tempted to send Thomas out ahead of her, and remain in Paris to await Geoffrey Buxton, now on his way to Europe from the colony. Bror had telegraphed that she should talk with Buxton about a much-needed loan. But Karen's horror of traveling alone prevented her from waiting behind. She wrote to her mother: "I am even afraid of being alone so long in Paris . . . " (*LFA*, 102).

What precipitated their need for this loan was a financial crisis that had occurred in the colony in February 1920. The rupee had been revalued by the British government, and the revaluation had resulted in more devastating consequences for the farm than had the combined effects of war and drought and Bror's mismanagement.

Ever since the war, the value of the English pound had been falling against the East African rupee. By February 1920, the rupee was worth two shillings-ninepence—compared with the pre-war exchange rate of one shilling-ninepence. Thus every pound coming from Europe was worth about half as much when exchanged for rupees in African banks.

Bror could not understand, any more than could other East African farmers, the forces that made the value of the pound and rupee vacillate. There were difficulties in the world economy following the war, since war-time levels of manufacturing were no longer needed. Returned soldiers could not find work, and their families had little money to buy goods. Business languished. England had bankrupted itself and could not back up its own currency.

The change in the value of the rupee caused an uproar. Farmers who sold coffee, sisal, and tea on the London exchange received payment in pounds. These profits, now reduced by nearly half when converted to rupees, must pay for wages and expenses in the colony. Furthermore, farmers held mortgages with East African banks that were to be paid in rupees. Thus the debt on the Karen Coffee Plantation, as on most other farms, had effectively doubled. Farmers demanded that the British government fix the value of the rupee so they would no longer be forced beyond their control into greater debt. They had hoped for, and sent Delamere to London to see to, getting the rupee's value set back by law to the pre-war equivalent, one shilling-ninepence. However, the English government approved a compromise—decried as favoring bankers—that stabilized the rupee at a value of two shillings. This decision was a disaster for Kenya farmers. (The Indian rupee, to which the value of the East African rupee was previously linked, was not stabilized in February 1920. Within six months natural economic change returned the Indian rupee to pre-war levels, where it remained. Thus if no action had been taken to stabilize the East African rupee, natural forces would have repaired the financial crisis in the colony [WMC].) Bror and others, now cemented in debt, saw little solution but to sell out.

Karen was indignant at the idea. She was willing to consider selling the farm at Uasin Gishu, and had entertained the notion of accepting Buxton's loan until such a deal could be struck, but she was not about to give Bror her consent to sell the Karen Coffee farm, and certainly not before she returned to Africa to evaluate the situation. She had never had much faith in Bror's business sense, and felt she herself could make a more considered judgment on what was to be done. Bror had written that the house and park at Ngong could be offered as collateral on Buxton's loan—a suggestion that made Karen furious. She wrote to her mother from Marseilles: "This is a truly fiendish idea,—undoubtedly hit upon by Bror himself, Buxton or Denys would never have suggested it—but Bror has never been able to appreciate the fact that I cared for my home out there" (LFA, 103).

Karen and Thomas arrived in Mombasa on December 30, 1920, where they were greeted onshore by the long faces of Bror, Farah, and the boy Abdullai. Thomas had to act as buffer between Karen and Bror because she was so angry. Her long-time neighbor Olga Holmberg happened to be in Mombasa, and she confided an earful of news of what Bror had been doing while Karen was gone. Olga claimed that there had been outrageous parties in Karen's house, and that Bror and his friends had been using her china for target practice. On one occasion they had taken the dining room furniture to the top of the Ngong hills for an exotic dinner party. While Olga was prone to exaggerate, Karen did not doubt that Bror had behaved inexcusably. He had already admitted to taking out a loan on her furniture, and this was not the first time. She wrote to her mother shrilly: "Well, God knows how it will turn out! All along I have been so afraid of fresh surprises, and doubtless this is not the last . . . " (*LFA*, 105).

1921

1

In January 1921, the British East African Protectorate became Crown Colony of Kenya, and the currency was changed from rupees to shillings. But these shillings remained based on the former rupee, so the problems surrounding the exchange rate continued.

When Bror had arrived in the Colony in April 1920, the flax market was booming because the crop normally supplied from Russia had failed. Kenya farmers were turning over as much land to flax as they could. Gillis Lindstrom, Bror's long-time friend, bought a few hundred acres from Geoffrey Buxton (*MWWL*, 61). This land in the Rift Valley was part of Delamere's original farm of 100,000 acres between the Molo River and Njoro (*WMC*, Vol I:104). Delamere had despaired of raising sheep there, and had moved to Soysambu ranch, near Lake Elmenteita, beginning in 1914. He had parceled out his land at Njoro and put in an elaborate water system so that the property could be sold to small farmers. Geoffrey Buxton, who seems to have speculated in rupees, bought up large chunks of Delamere's estate, watched as the price of land rose after the war, and by 1920 was making a healthy profit from selling off homesteading parcels.

Bror wished he had more land suitable for flax, and would have uprooted his coffee bushes to plant it, if he had not involved himself wholeheartedly in helping Gillis Lindstrom to settle, and in demonstrating to him the safari life. Throughout the latter half of the year 1920, in addition to luring Lindstrom into numerous hunting expeditions, Bror oversaw the planting of a few hundred acres of flax on Lindstrom's farm at Njoro, in exchange for a promise of a portion of the profits. Bror had hardly spent any time on his own farm at Ngong. He had given up on coffee and believed the Ngong farm would have to be sold.

Karen came back to fields overrun with weeds, and coffee bushes so neglected one could hardly decide where to start pruning. Nor did she have much idea what to do about it, because Bror had always had full responsibility for the farm. Bror stayed home after she arrived, buoyed by her refusal to sell out, and expanded on his intention to plant as many of their own acres as he could to flax, as soon as the rains came. Karen gave him her opinion of the irresponsible way he had cared for the farm in her absence. His neglect represented intolerable disrespect for her and her family, and she expected him to take immediate steps to improve the deplorable state of the coffee fields. But she was willing to go along with the flax scheme, if only it would rain.

A drought was in progress, "worse," she said, "than that in 1918" (*LFA*, 109). Not only did the flax scheme not materialize; the price of what was planted in the fields began to fall. In September 1920, a woman at Lumbwa, west of Njoro, had sold her flax crop for £590 per ton; but Russia was again growing flax, and the market for Kenya flax proved entirely ephemeral. By the early months of 1921, when Gillis Lindstrom was ready to harvest his blue and delicate crop at Njoro, it was not worth enough to bother picking it.

Bror had built up debts against his hopes for making money on flax. He had even been given an advance of 1,500 rupees (the equivalent of £15) by another optimistic farmer to whom he had promised seed harvested from his anticipated crop (*PA*, 17). He had been signing his name to chits all over Nairobi—to tailors and shop-keepers, hotel owners and bartenders. In Karen's view he had been living like a thief, gloating over his talent for obtaining credit, with no intention of paying. He had even taken out a loan of £ 5,000 on their furniture, so that Karen could no longer safely consider her home her own. Yet all this she could have forgiven him if she had not discovered, through Olga Holmberg, that Bror was having an affair with a married woman, Cockie Birkbeck. According to Olga, since Karen's return, Bror and Cockie had been sending notes back and forth concealed in the barrel of a rifle passed to Olga's husband Emil, currently foreman of Karen Coffee (*MWWL*, 59). Olga Holmberg had had some differences with her husband and was quite willing to be candid about his complicity in Bror Blixen's adultery.

These circumstances so infuriated Karen that she made a drastic decision: Bror must finally understand that she would not tolerate his spending and his betrayals. She ordered him off the farm, until such time as he could behave responsibly toward herself and the corporation.

So the farm teetered on the brink of bankruptcy, Bror was estranged from the farm, a drought prevailed, and Karen struggled, with Thomas's help, to bring order to the coffee plantation, despite pressure from money-lenders. In the midst of this state of affairs, in April 1921, the chairman of Karen Coffee Corporation, Uncle Aage Westenholz, arrived from Denmark, determined to understand the circumstances surrounding the farm and its finances.

* 2 *

Sharp-eyed and long-faced Uncle Aage had inherited the merchant wisdom of his forebears. His father had earned a fortune in the shipping trade, and Uncle Aage had built upon his inheritance by investing, as was the shrewd fashion of his generation, in overseas enterprises: rubber in Malaya, tea in Ceylon, cement in Bangkok, and coffee in East Africa.

But, despite much economic success, at age sixty-two Uncle Aage had reason to doubt his wisdom in having placed money in a pioneer farm in Kenya, where farming was at best experimental, and where the management consisted of his sister's daughter and her spendthrift Swedish husband. Uncle Aage had outlined his misgivings to the shareholders of Karen Coffee Corporation, the majority of whom were members of the family, including his sisters Ingeborg Dinesen and Mary Bess Westenholz, and Uncle Mogens and Aunt Fritze Frijs. It was evident that Bror Blixen had proved irresponsible with their capital, that the enterprise had proceeded without appropriate management, and that the time had come to salvage what they could from the unfortunate investment.

Uncle Aage was not prepared to lay all the blame at Bror's feet—nor would Karen have allowed it—for he recognized the impossibility of dealing with unexpected conditions like war and drought and the maddeningly hopeless state of the currency. Nor could Bror have anticipated the wide fluctuations in commodity prices, nor the difficulties with labor, nor the vagaries of coffee strains and requirements arising from pioneer crop-raising. Moreover, Bror had no way of knowing, when he bought what appeared to be an ideal farm, how the temperature and rainfall, the world demand and the return on his profit, the value of the rupee, and the affections of his in-laws would vary. But, in view of Bror's overwhelming personal debts, with which the shareholders simply refused further association, the time had come to discharge him from his duties as managing director of Karen Coffee, and either to sell out, or to appoint someone more responsible to oversee the farm.

Uncle Aage was inclined to favor the former alternative, until he arrived in Kenya and saw the blue Ngong Hills rising beyond 600 acres of glistening coffee bushes belonging to Karen Coffee Corporation. The highland air had an effect on him similar to that it had had on Karen seven years before: he fell in love with the investment. On a high pole in front of the house waved the red and white flag of Denmark. Beyond the roof line, the horizon was framed by distant mountains and the acacia trees of the wildlife reserve. Rows of coffee trees with shining leaves stretched to greet him; the bushes were now over five feet tall. In the park leading to the house, hundreds of Africans wearing leather aprons and the skins of colobus monkeys danced greetings, their beaded necklaces and copper anklets extending a glittering welcome.

Uncle Aage found the gray fieldstone house lavish by colonial standards. Its veranda, encompassing two sides of the house, was generously appointed with wicker chairs and settee. The three bed-rooms and the great room used as a dining room contained fine furniture, Persian rugs, and china and crystal that had survived Bror's entertaining. It seemed to Uncle Aage that the house was unnecessar-ily large for Karen's needs, and suggestive of a lifestyle more costly than was warranted for the manager of an African coffee farm. Karen pointed out that the house had been built by Sjögren as an example of quality Indian craftsmanship and the kind of comfort possible for early settlers. Its high-beamed ceilings and parquet floors may have ap-peared as luxurious as a palace compared to the homes of other farmers, but surely Uncle Aage would have to admit the house was less imposing, for example, than Rungstedlund. Uncle Aage maintained, nonetheless, that such a house violated the shareholders' intentions; Karen must convey to them her dedication to thrift; and she could best satisfy this impression by moving into a smaller house, more appropri-ate for a farm employee than a plantation owner. Furthermore, her present house could be a source of rental income to the corporation, for surely some wealthy businessman in Nairobi would find it a pleasant country home.

Uncle Aage initiated the building of a new "grass" house (as Karen ironically referred to it) for her on another portion of the estate. The floor was to be of cement, and the roof thatched. Meanwhile, he launched into efforts to sort out the convoluted debts left to Karen Coffee by Bror. What particularly appalled Uncle Aage was the loan Bror had taken out on Karen's furniture. He was shocked by the interest rate, fifteen percent, and by the enormous value of the furniture—clearly bought with investment funds contributed by the shareholders of Karen Coffee. He paid the debt by arranging to sell some of his own stock in Bangkok cement—a disgruntled sacrifice made out of affection for his niece and her mother.

Like his sister, Aunt Bess, he retained a great deal of critical fondness for Karen, and may have considered her his favorite niece, for she had more flair than her sisters. Moreover, he shared with her an ironic sense of humor that was lacking in the other members of the family. Also, Uncle Aage was not a man without passions. He had come under criticism only recently in the newspapers in Denmark for leading a successful campaign to raise money to send mercenaries into the Balkans against the Bolsheviks. Uncle Aage had fallen in love late in life, and he was devoted to his wife, Koosje, sixteen years younger than himself. The voyage to Kenya, grueling by any standards, had temporarily enfeebled him, but soon he was riding his bicycle the twelve miles into Nairobi—as an example of thrift to Karen. His one strict requirement was an afternoon nap, and it was only if Karen neglected to provide time for it that he became irritable.

He spoke gravely about the farm's financial problems, and pointed out that the coffee had not brought a profit in a single year. But Karen was vehemently against selling. She amazed him with her energy and her determination to create a success where, thus far, money had been swallowed up, as Uncle Aage said, "like the sand of the desert swallows water" (*PA*, 27). She accompanied him vigorously on rounds with solicitors and financiers, charming them with her attractiveness and composed conversation, and presenting herself in such a way as to expect and receive concessions. In Uncle Aage's estimation she had assumed the role of aristocrat with remarkable ease. Uncle Aage was not one to be awestruck by royalty, but he did note that, like the other members of the peerage who made up the bulk of her friends in the colony, she was deferred to, even when it came to the payment of debts.

On the basis of Karen's letters, Uncle Aage had come to Africa believing that, if he were to sell the farm on behalf of the shareholders, she had obtained enough assurances of financial backing to buy the farm herself. He wrote in his journal: "I came to the conclusion that we can establish so many guaranties that we can, after all, justify selling to Tanne." (He had been authorized to sell out at half the original value.) "Businesswise it is perhaps not the ideal solution, but most of 'the close ones' in the family will perhaps be willing to sacrifice a little, in money or risk, so that Tanne can obtain what she considers her life's goal" (*PA*, 16–17). But he soon discovered that Karen was in no way financially prepared to take on the purchase. So, under heavy persuasion from her, he agreed to postpone the sale.

It rained in May, breaking the severe drought, and, according to the usual farm schedule for the long rainy season, 250 additional acres of coffee trees were planted. Karen had agreed with Uncle Aage that Bror could no longer share responsibility for the investment, since he had conducted himself abominably. But—in a plan elaborately devised with the help of Thomas before Uncle Aage's arrival—she outlined to Uncle Aage that she herself was prepared to take over Bror's duties as managing director of the farm.

Uncle Aage spent days discussing the plan with Thomas. Finally, still expressing reservations, he agreed. He had no wish to excite Karen's volatile sentiments by refusing. But only the fact that she was Ingeborg's daughter allowed him to consent to a plan that intuition told him made poor business sense.

What gave Uncle Aage pause was the continued presence of Bror Blixen, if not actually on the farm, then nearby and legally able as Karen's husband to command the money and resources of the farm. Indeed, Bror made several visits during Uncle Aage's stay, and talked to him in a most congenial and helpful manner, revealing no disrespect for the farm and its finances. He seemed as concerned as the others about the viability of the enterprise, and humbly agreed with the decision that Karen take over his responsibilities. Uncle Aage wrote home, "Bror . . . is quite pleasant to talk with, always calm and amiable, full of good ideas; but one is, naturally, embarrassed to think about what he can come up with . . . " (PA, 16).

When Bror's Nairobi creditors realized that neither his wife, nor Uncle Aage, nor Karen Coffee Corporation would be further associated with his debts, they sent out writs for his arrest, and he had to flee into Masailand. Rumor maintained that, in an effort to spare Bror from legal action, Cockie Birkbeck had visited Bror's tailor offering to settle the debt with her pearls. Karen, too, spent one or two harried mornings in Nairobi, pleading on Bror's behalf. Uncle Aage wrote in his diary: "Tanne was angry because Thomas and I didn't appear to feel much for him—and she is right, we don't . . . " (PA, 18).

When Uncle Aage departed for Denmark on June 20, 1921, leaving Karen in full control of the farm, he held deep misgivings. Later he expressed to Thomas his suspicions that Bror would find a way to sabotage the investment. He said, "I believe as you do that Tanne has a burning desire to make KC succeed, but in front of Bror she is weak, truly weak 'as a woman' . . . " (PA, 22).

* 3 *

On an afternoon in the first week of July 1921, Karen and Thomas went out to hunt buffalo on the Orungi Plains. Thomas took aim from a distance of a hundred or more yards and shot a great dark bull with massive curving horns. The animal instantly disappeared from view near a clump of bushes, and they could not be sure whether he had dropped into the tall grass or was wounded and hidden. Searching for the buffalo represented the highest order of risk, for no other animal could so ferociously corner and gore a hunter. When the remainder of the herd stampeded, Karen and Thomas crept forward. The tall grass was wet from an afternoon drizzle, and they were soon drenched to the armpits. Carrying their guns at the ready and watching for a sign of attack, they suddenly stumbled over the dead buffalo, hidden in the grass (LFA, 107–8).

Such risky adventures attracted Thomas. Like many soldiers, he felt his life had met its apogee in the war; few activities satisfied him or held his interest. Karen took pains to keep him occupied, but she could not always entertain him, and he chafed at her efforts to plan occasions for him or to induce her friends to distract him. His original intention had been to buy a farm for himself in Africa, but Karen persuaded him to place his money in Karen Coffee, where it was more needed and where, she was convinced, he would eventually reap a healthy profit. She sought his advice when she could and searched for means to appeal to his skills, for his degree in civil engineering must be put to use. Eventually she hit upon the scheme of creating a dam to make a farm pond. This idea appealed to Thomas's practical sense; she was surprised at how seriously he undertook it. He gathered a team of Kikuyu, and together they carried soil and sank to their knees in mud to build a barrier over the stream that could hold back the water until, indeed, a pleasant pond formed. Their first efforts were not permanent; as soon as the rainy season came, the dam washed away, and a more clever construction had to be devised. But the final result was successful; a strong dam with a pond large enough to satisfy the farm oxen and sheep in time of drought. Karen and Thomas would stroll to the pond in the evenings, to smoke and watch zebra coming to drink.

Following Uncle Aage's departure, Karen's next great project for Thomas was the construction of a "factory," a building to house the various farm machinery used to prepare coffee for market. So far, the machines for soaking and pulping, hulling and drying the coffee beans had been ill-housed in scattered, makeshift buildings. Now she convinced Thomas they could save money by getting all the instruments of processing under one roof. Together they traveled around the colony looking at examples of factories on other farms; then Thomas drew up plans for a basic structure to be built upon a wooden skeleton, and roofed and sided with pieces of sheet metal of whatever size was available—usually old paraffin tins pounded flat. Thomas was assembling his crew and materials toward the end of July 1921 when Karen announced that she was leaving for a few days on her own, to visit the Lindstroms in Njoro.

She wrote her mother that her purpose in going was "to negotiate for oxen" (*LFA*, 108). However, a more important reason for her trip seems to have been that Bror had returned from Masailand and had sought refuge with the Lindstroms. Rumor had it that Gillis had redesigned the drive to his house to extend up a steep hill so that Bror's creditors would be discouraged from pursuing him. With a straight view from the house of anyone's approach, Bror could quickly escape into the bush.

Karen counted upon Bror's willingness to see her in hopes of a reconciliation. She had been unhappy since Bror left the farm. Although she had talked at home of divorce, since returning to Africa she had experienced a change of heart. She wrote to her mother, "During these six months I have come to realize that I am very, very reluctant to separate from Bror. There is so much here that binds us together, and it is impossible for me to stop believing in the good in him . . . " (*LFA*, 108).

When Karen had asked Bror to move off the farm, she did not mean to send him away permanently, but merely to teach him a lesson. Now that he had been humiliated by debt, she accused herself of having carried the punishment too far. Bror had been living in the wilderness without shoes. He was now sleeping in a round thatched hut on the Lindstrom farm, with no means of livelihood other than doing odd jobs for Gillis. She wanted him to come home. She could not pay his debts but she could support him on her salary from Karen Coffee.

When she made this proposal to Bror, he evidently lashed out at her. He said he had been unfairly treated. He had borrowed money believing that the corporation would support him, and she, his wife, had sabotaged his efforts. As managing director, he had made the decision to sell. The price of land had risen enough for them to make a healthy profit. Bror had paid the equivalent of fifty-three shillings per acre for the farm in 1913 (*SE*); now they could get at least eighty. A sale would mean a windfall for them, and he had depended upon it to pay his debts. By refusing to sell, she and her family had rendered him a fool and a fugitive. He had contributed his own savings toward buying the farm, and he deserved to regain what was due to him.

Karen could not understand his way of thinking but she stayed on a few days in Njoro. Ingrid Lindstrom seemed to encourage a compromise and gave Karen the impression that she was on her side. Ingrid thought highly of Bror, whom she found to be energetic, amusing, and kind. She shared these qualities with him, and Karen said later, "Therefore does the world love the Swedes, because in the midst of their woes they can draw it all to their bosom, and be so gallant that they shine a long way away" (*OA*, 218).

Despite his trials Bror retained a vigorous composure. His face was unlined and his blue eyes clear. Now thirty-five, he had grown more physically attractive with maturity. Karen had been alone for nearly six months. She was reluctant to abandon him. After her return she wrote to her mother that it was impossible "to think that his various inexplicably thoughtless and heartless outbursts are other than a kind of frenzy, that should surely subside. Perhaps it is simply that I care too much for him . . . " (*LFA*, 108).

1921

* 4 *

The revaluation of the rupee in 1920 had routed the old settlers. Many of Karen's friends from the early days who were dependent on pound currency had abandoned the colony and returned to England. Among these was Denys Finch Hatton, who had briefly returned to Africa in the latter half of 1920, but stayed only long enough to gather his belongings and settle his affairs. After spending a few weeks at Ngong with Bror, he had headed back to Europe. Karen was unaware that his ship had passed hers near Aden, as she came out to Africa. Six months later, in writing to her mother she dwelled upon this coincidence as a "tragedy" (*LFA*, 106). She had heard nothing more about his whereabouts; however, her difficulties with Bror preoccupied her.

She was dispirited by Bror's anger, and blamed herself for being a poor wife to him. While Thomas was engaged in building the factory, and the rest of the farm waited for rain—for the long rains earlier had not been enough—Karen brooded over her failings. She considered that she had an unreasonable desire to go home, to seek the safety and comfort of her mother, to escape the worries attendant in running a coffee farm. At the same time she blamed her family for her weakness. Her family had wrapped her in cotton wool, they had overprotected her, they had never taught her to manage for herself. Most men—and many women—in the colony, when they lost their farms or their spouses, or otherwise fell on hard times, were able to take up new livelihoods. They adopted hunting as a living, opened dress shops, bought land elsewhere, married more attractive partners, and survived without retreating to their families in Europe. She despised herself for seeing no way to manage her life, if the farm were sold, except to go home.

At the same time she blamed forces in her background that made her prone to discouragement. She wrote to her mother, "I think my greatest misfortune was Father's death" (*LFA*, 110). For some years Bror had replaced her father's image as the hero in her life. Now that he had deserted her, she searched for some means of moral support. Her thoughts turned for inspiration to the spirit of her father. She said, "Father understood me as I was, although I was so young, and loved me for myself" (*LFA*, 110).

When her mood was greatly depressed, she fancied that no one but he had ever really loved her. Her mother's family seemed to be assembled against her. She had received sharp letters from Uncle Aage and Aunt Bess, accusing her of leading an extravagant life and criticizing her weakness for Bror. It was true that she had not moved into the grass house Uncle Aage had directed to be built, but she said she had been unable to rent her own house at the 500 rupees a month specified by Uncle Aage. Truthfully, several interested parties had looked at the house, but Karen found the idea of moving to a thatched cottage appalling. Besides, she viewed the expenses of her present house as minimal. She was paying her staff only a few shillings per month.

Her sole extravagance consisted of inviting people to stay at her house. This they did frequently, rather than put up at Muthaiga, where the food was not as good, nor the view as spectacular. In September 1921 a young army veteran named Lord Doune spent a week in Karen's house. She had of course invited him with the idea of distracting Thomas, who like Doune, had performed well in the war and had plenty of money, yet felt he had little to live for. But Karen made the mistake of mentioning the houseguest in a letter to her mother, and the news was read by Aunt Bess, who was shocked that her savings, invested in Karen Coffee, were being spent to entertain "down-at-heel cavaliers" (*LFA*, 120).

Aunt Bess wrote Karen that those who had placed their money in a horse had the right to use "whip and spurs" to control their investment (*LFA*, 120). The members of the corporation were prepared to deal out ultimatums concerning Karen's behavior. Chief among their demands was that she divorce Bror, since Uncle Aage had been outspoken in his fear that Bror might find a way to spend more of Karen Coffee Corporation's money.

Karen was infuriated that her marriage was being discussed by the shareholders as casually and critically as the amount of tons of coffee harvested in 1921. To her mother she replied that the discussions by members of the corporation of her personal life must stop, and that it was outrageous that remote relatives were making pronouncements on a subject so personal and so little understood by them as the intimate aspects of her married life. In her exasperation, it seemed to Karen that such interference in her private affairs was characteristic of the Westenholz side of the family; the Dinesens would not have treated her this way. The Dinesen relatives had been accused in the past by her mother's family of being too superficial, of not regarding life with appropriate gravity. Karen threw this back at her mother now, saying that her actions would have been better accepted by her father's side of the family, that the Dinesens would have understood her. In fact, she proclaimed, nothing in life—not even being ill with syphilis—had been so awful as Sunday dinners at Folehave with Mama and the horribly staid Westenholz aunts and uncles (*LFA*, 114).

In regard to Aunt Bess's threat, Karen refused to be intimidated. She fired back: "I find it altogether degrading to be compared to a horse, especially one that needs whip and spurs, because that is a worthless horse . . . " (*LFA*, 120).

* 5 *

In the months since Uncle Aage's departure, Thomas's presence in Karen's house represented a return to the atmosphere at home: she had acquired an audience. As she had recited epics to him in his youth, she now began in the evenings to create stories for Thomas's amusement. She rejoiced in the challenge, since he had seen much in the war and would not be content with ordinary tales. She sought to arrest his attention with a tale of horror, a story different from his experience and intriguingly strange. The tale concerned a sister and brother who unwittingly marry and the terrible consequences of incestuous love.

Eventually written down, the story became known as "The Caryatids." It bore little resemblance to real life, but elements of it reflected her concerns at the time. The title, meaning "women of stone," seemed to represent her view of herself in Bror's eyes. She had been too upright with him, too inflexible. The tale reviewed the "extraordinary happiness" (*LT*, 119) of the first year of marriage, the early reluctance of the bride, who "had grieved as a child because she had not been born a boy" (*LT*, 122), the ecstatic, soaring honeymoon, and the following seven tender, if threatened, years of delight. The tale was filled with sweet and luscious memories, witches and charms, gypsies and flowers, rain and sunsets, and erotic longings—for lovers to meet, for children to suckle, for spouses to consummate love. The word "sweet," as a description of sexual love, appeared over and over. These agonized longings served to intensify the implication that the marriage between siblings must end disastrously.

She left Thomas to imagine the outcome. Later, in "The Dreamers," she says the storyteller loses the knack for telling horror stories when life itself becomes more frightening (*SGT*, 274).

* *

While letters from Uncle Aage, Aunt Bess, and her mother pressed for divorce, Karen worked for a reconciliation. Ingrid Lindstrom helped transmit messages from Karen to Bror. There were rumors that Cockie, the immediate cause of Karen and Bror's dispute, was about to divorce her husband. Ben Birkbeck had returned to England— ostensibly to raise money to buy land—without her. However, Bror had been involved with women in the past, and Karen did not think he intended any serious relationship with Mrs. Birkbeck. Karen shared too many tender memories with Bror that she did not believe he could set aside. They had joined their youth in pioneering a new land; the farm they had created, like a child, was a bond that must hold them together.

Her steady correspondence with Ingrid Lindstrom kept her in touch with Bror. When Gillis and Bror found a way to make money as safari guides for a Swedish photographer who had been assigned to make a wildlife documentary for his government, Karen invited Ingrid and her two daughters, Nina, age six, and Ulla, age four, to stay with her. Even Thomas was charmed by Ingrid. Not quite beautiful, she was small, blond and ruddy, with a separation between her front teeth; but she was full of energy and good nature. She teased Thomas that he should take her on safari in the sidecar of his motorcycle (*LFA*, 115).

Thomas sometimes shared the bike with Karen, for the old Ford box-body car Karen and Bror had bought in South Africa was on its last legs. Something was wrong with the electrical system; they could not get the lights to work. Thomas suspected the difficulty was with the battery but he could not be sure, and neither he nor Karen could afford to have it repaired.

Karen's only other means of transportation was a new horse named Rouge—a large russet Arabian of difficult temperament which she spent a great deal of time coaxing, since training animals had never been her forte. Friends had foisted upon her an old Irish pony named Poorbox, which made it possible for Thomas to ride with her, and these rides she enjoyed; the two of them had spent much time together on horseback as children. Karen kept a *syce*, an African who cared for the horses and saddled them, another extravagance Uncle Aage criticized in her lifestyle. No matter that the salary of the *syce* was only a few shillings per month. Uncle Aage would perhaps have preferred that she manage with a mule and a bicycle, and take care of them herself.

As for Thomas, Karen had begun to feel Africa was not the place for him. Truthfully, she was at odds with him, as with the rest of her family, over whether she should divorce Bror. Thomas had let them know that Karen was keeping in touch with Bror. In October 1921, her mother wrote an uncharacteristically opinionated letter saying that Karen "must choose between Thomas and Bror" (*LFA*, 113). Bror had been making occasional visits to the farm—visits that Thomas suspected were for the sake of obtaining money.

It was not unlike Bror to appear with some minor business to discuss with Karen, to stay for dinner, to agree to look at a sick animal with her, to offer her advice in a low voice, as soft as one would use with a child, to rub ointment on the animal and gently stroke it in a reassuring way. In these moments the hostility between Karen and Bror would fade into oneness. At thirty-six, Karen was, like other women, approaching her sexual prime. In "The Caryatids" she describes longing for physical love so strongly that it is like being pregnant; one grows heavier and heavier with it. Concerning the lovers in the story she writes: "Let them even separate our souls forever, if it be as they tell us. Our bodies they shall not separate at all" (*LT*, 126).

When, through Thomas, Uncle Aage realized what was transpiring between Karen and Bror, he took agitated measures to see that Bror should no longer influence the fate of the Karen Coffee farm. His solicitors drew up a pledge in which Karen must agree not to allow Bror to "appear at or reside within the borders of the company's premises" (*PA*, 24); otherwise she must forfeit her position as managing director. If Karen continued to treat Bror as her husband, she would be forced to leave the farm.

This document infuriated her against all her relatives. She threatened to stop writing to her mother for at least a year, and warned of her intention to send back the family's letters unopened. In regards to the pledge, she said, " . . . the entire mode of thinking here is to me so incomprehensible that I would really rather not have anyone know that my family has been capable of putting together such a document" (*PA*, 24).

A week before Christmas 1921, Karen was taken ill with severe abdominal pain. Thomas went with her to the hospital, where she feared she was going to die. Three doctors worried that perhaps this was so. They could not determine the source of her pain, although one doctor suggested that her appendix was inflamed (*LFA*, 122). The others overruled him. She might just as easily be suffering from a twisted ovary or intestinal obstruction. She had no fever and, believing surgery unwise, the doctors elected to observe her. Fortunately, after a few days the symptoms subsided. Following a week in the hospital she was discharged without a confirmed diagnosis and, still recuperating, spent Christmas in bed.

1922

Shortly after the New Year 1922, Thomas traveled to Njoro to see the Lindstroms. Karen told her mother he had gone "on behalf of the company in order to try to get contracts for maize and oxen" (*LFA*, 121). But farmers at Njoro were as hard up as people elsewhere. The Lindstroms' income was almost solely dependent on Ingrid's kitchen garden, from which she sent lettuce, flowers, and vegetables to Nairobi for sale at the market. Gillis, like Bror, was full of creative plans for earning money, none of which seemed to come to fruition. What with drought and the change in value of the rupee, the homesteaders on Delamere's former land lived a hard life, trying to meet the payments on their farms. So it would have been strange to find anyone at Njoro with money to pay for contracts on maize and oxen.

However, just before Thomas's trip, a rumor had begun to circulate in Nairobi that Bror planned to ask for a divorce to marry Cockie Birkbeck. Karen was unable to go to Njoro to investigate the truth behind the gossip because the symptoms that had taken her to the hospital, though they had abated, had made her a temporary invalid. But, as Thomas was soon to report, the alarming gossip about Bror and Cockie was true.

The affair had come about in a way typical of Bror. He had learned what a poor impression he made on Mrs. Birkbeck at their first meeting, in London in 1919, and had become determined to change her mind. She had arrived in Kenya with her husband in 1920, while Karen was in Denmark. Some time later, Bror discovered that Cockie had gone to the Nairobi races to avoid spending an afternoon with him because she thought he was such a boor. From that moment, Bror strove to change her mind, and he succeeded.

The affair had proceeded as Cockie's marriage to Birkbeck soured, until Karen discovered the romantic notes passed from Cockie to Bror in Holmberg's gunbarrel. While Karen treated the relationship as just another of Bror's dalliances, Cockie had decided she could not live without him. But the matter was complicated, because, to marry, both Cockie and Bror must divorce their spouses. Nairobi society watched with interest as the intriguing drama unfolded.

When Thomas returned from Njoro, Karen was stricken again with severe abdominal pains. Her doctors continued to be puzzled by her symptoms because they did not conform to a recognizable pattern. The physicians knew that Karen had once had syphilis, but did not find her symptoms characteristic of syphilis. It was too early to expect late complications; abdominal pain would not be expected for years, and not without other symptoms of *tabes dorsalis*, syphilis of the spine. Again her doctors observed and waited. When she recovered from her acute distress and was able to leave the hospital, among other instructions, they advised her to refrain for a time from riding her horse (*LFA*, 121–2).

She was still improving when, in the third week of January 1922, Bror came to her in his warmest, most engaging manner and asked for a divorce. Although she had been prepared for his request, she was nevertheless stunned. How could he wipe out of his consciousness what was, if nothing else, a most intimate companionship? How could he simply sweep aside the passionate moments they had shared, and all the years and difficult times binding them together (*LFA*, 122)?

He did not disagree; he had many good memories. But he had reached the decision that his best chance in life was to get a divorce (*LFA*, 125). She and her family had thrust him aside, left him penniless with no home.

She thought he must really be in some kind of frenzy to wish to do something as drastic as divorce. She would not oppose him; she could not. But she felt as though she were facing the loss of her soul, or the death of a child. For many years he had been the person closest to her in the world. She did not want to say yes (*LFA*, 122–3).

There was no bitter scene between them. In fact, Bror perhaps left her very tenderly indeed, for she wrote to her mother afterwards, "I feel for Bror now, and will until I die, the greatest friendship or the deepest tenderness that I am capable of feeling" (*LFA*, 123).

* *

As he left, he may have said, "It will be a consolation to me to remember that I have kissed you as often as you would let me. Will it be a consolation to you?" Later she recorded these words in the tale "The Pearls," describing the ending of a marriage very like her own (*WT*, 122).

When she wrote her mother that Bror had asked for a divorce, Karen did not blame him nor show any anger. She wished him only happiness, and the understanding of her family, who had borne so much grief because of his irresponsibility with their money. Much later she expressed what she felt to be her own guilt in the failure of the marriage. She seemed to be convinced that she had not been available enough to him sexually. "Many, many love affairs and marriages all through the ages have deteriorated and become embittered," she commented, through "whether, so to speak, she would or no . . . " (*OMM*, 81). She regarded the divorce as a profound personal failure, and was in such grief that she could see the future only with difficulty. She thought if the farm were also to fail, she could not live. She wrote to her mother, "if this has to be relinquished and come to nothing, no one must expect anything more from me in this life" (*LFA*, 123). What kept her from suicide was the thought of her responsibility to the shareholders, and to the Africans on the farm. She said the *totos* and Farah were depending on her, and this knowledge would steady her and bring out the best in her, despite her difficulties (*LFA*, 124).

One further matter prevented her from experiencing a spiritual collapse. She had received news that Denys Finch Hatton was returning to Kenya, some time in the month of April 1922. Karen told her mother she had had a letter from Denys (*LFA*, 126), but she may have said this for the sake of pride, for, since no letter survives, she likely learned the news in Nairobi. But his coming return had given her something to think about. A divorce from Bror might free her to pursue a greater goal. In an attempt to be philosophical about parting from Bror, she said to her mother, "I think I will come to feel it as a relief from many impossible situations" (*LFA*, 125).

* 2 *

The previous year there had been little word of Finch Hatton, and some thought he had taken up life permanently in England. No one would have blamed him for not coming back to Africa, considering the problems with the East African rupee, the new income tax enacted in 1920, and a rapidly escalating political conflict in the colony known as the "Indian question." What was being debated in England, by the British Secretary of State for the Colonies, Winston Churchill, and Delamere, and voices high in the British colonial administration was the future of the Kenya Colony: whether white settlers were to have sole power to govern, and whether unrestricted immigration would be continued—which many believed would soon convert the crown colony to a satellite of India. These controversial matters, highly publicized by the British papers, discouraged old Africa hands from returning. It was thought that Finch Hatton had had to sell his farms at Uasin Gishu and Naivasha at a loss. Some had been wondering whether, with the pound so low against the rupee, he had retained enough money to support himself in Kenya.

Finch Hatton's return represented hope to Karen in a time of great personal struggle. In an effort to sort out her thoughts and find meaning in her difficulties, she began to write a story entitled

"The Roads Round Pisa." In this story she reviews the reasons a husband leaves a wife and concludes that he is driven away by the wife's unrelenting jealousy. The husband says, "she is jealous of my friends, of my dogs, of the forests of Lindenburg, of my guns and books. She is jealous of the most absurd things . . . I am certain that it could not go on, and that I have been right in leaving her, for while I was with her it would have been the same thing always" (*SGT*, 166–7).

Karen's family, especially Thomas, had for years encouraged her to pursue her talent in writing, but she had taken little time to do so until the crisis of the divorce. Now, putting her thoughts on paper alleviated panic about her future. In the story she underscores the importance of *amitié sincère*—"sincere friendship"—as a substitute for bereavement (*SGT*, 168). One may wonder if she hoped Finch Hatton would be that substitute. "But," one of the characters says, "what will happen to me now? I do not know what to do with myself or my life" (*SGT*, 167).

Her belief that her entire future depended on the farm led to increased tensions with Thomas, who tried to convince her that the divorce presented an ideal excuse for selling out. To shore up the coffee farm, he had risked money intended for buying his own farm in Africa, and now he saw a chance to regain his investment. But Karen would hear none of his arguments, and accused him of simply not sharing her passion for farming and for Africa. She wrote to their mother, "I do not think you should assume that Thomas's future lies here . . . . Thomas is not suited to being out here" (*LFA*, 125).

It seemed that, no matter how philosophical the argument, whether on the religious aspects of morality, the writings of Sigrid Unset, or the implications of Einstein's relativity, she and Thomas could not agree. Karen attempted to hide her irritation from him, but she wrote guilty letters home, expressing her misgivings about trying to continue with Thomas on the farm. She was feeling it a burden, with the other difficulties on her mind, to encourage and advise him. He engaged her in interminable conversations of only meager interest to her; she was desperate for some quiet to think about her accounts and her oxen. By this it is clear that she had assimilated Bror's role as farm manager to a startling degree. Where once she had plied Bror to

distraction with impressions of Mohammedanism, now she was annoyed when Thomas interrupted her with theories about the New
Testament.

In March 1922, she was in bed with influenza for three weeks.
She said she had "Spanish flu" (*LFA*, 126), but she had already been
ill with that in Denmark in 1919, and one cannot get it twice. Whatever
it was, illness made her testy, and she wrote home again about her
concern that Thomas did not have the temperament to stay in Africa.
She thought he had a theoretical bent, which could be satisfied only by
his being an understudy of Einstein, or of H. G. Wells. She was serious;
she urged him to request to study with one of them for a year or two
(*LFA*, 126).

The theories of Einstein, the German who had been awarded
the Nobel Prize for physics in 1921, had already made an enormous
impression on the thinking of the time. He had proved that time and
space were relative, and the idea had captured the public imagination.
Suddenly there was widespread awareness of how everything was
linked, how actions occurred as a result of what had gone before and
exerted a profound influence on what was to come. Karen began to
question what colonization was doing to the Africans. She saw it as a
blinding light shining into the quiet primitiveness of African life and
she feared its effect on the Africans' future. She later wrote, "If for a
long enough time we continue in this way to dazzle and blind the
Africans, we may in the end bring upon them a longing for darkness"
(*SOTG*, 465). She also began to think in "dimensions," with space
containing three dimensions, and time the fourth, and she envisioned
the planet whirling through both space and time. It was in these talks
with Thomas that she came to understand the expression *Hier c'est
demain* ("Yesterday is tomorrow")—time is a continuum in which
people can move backward or forward, by means of memories (*LFA*,
133). She had incorporated Einstein's theory in her story for Thomas,
"The Caryatids," presenting by means of a magic mill-wheel a look
backward in time.

So she was stimulated by Thomas's ideas, and enthusiastic
over the notion that he might study with Einstein. She appears to be
thinking of Thomas when in "The Roads Round Pisa," she writes, "'I
want to study astronomy,' said the boy, 'because I can no longer stand

the thought of time'" (*SGT*, 182). So much at loose ends was Thomas that Karen felt a responsibility to help him find his future. She wished to sigh with satisfaction and say, "There he is, where he ought to be" (*OA*, 4). It was a characteristic of her family that its members must seek a niche in life, and not wander aimlessly enjoying their means. They must make a contribution, or miss their opportunity for greatness.

Such was not the case with Denys Finch Hatton. Denys had spent a year at home, golfing with friends, hunting for an occasional week in Scotland, attending the opera when he was in London, dining now and again with chums from Eton and Oxford—of which few had survived the Great War—and going to Haverholme from time to time to tease his mother and bask in her adoration, and to sing to her accompaniment at the piano for the entertainment of the rest of the family. His brother, Toby, and sister, Topsy, would visit, along with their children—eager for a chance to see Uncle Denys, the amusing and exciting uncle from Africa—and would join in the music. After a year of this lifestyle however, Finch Hatton had grown weary of the weather in England, and of the lack of purpose in post-war society, and had decided to return to Africa. To do so he would need to live frugally, since his father's estate suffered from the serious farming depression affecting England—as well as Europe, America, and Africa.

It was in the late spring of 1922, after an eighteen-month absence, that Finch Hatton returned to Kenya. Whatever his commitments, Karen apparently did not see him until June. She had been ill again in the Kenya nursing home for three weeks in May, and in June a family tragedy occurred that did not speed her recovery. In Denmark her sister Ea, after a difficult pregnancy, died giving birth to a still-born child. Karen, who maintained some faith in dreams, dreamed for two nights that Ea had died, and both mornings awakened in relief. But a telegram on the morning of June 19, 1922, confirmed her fears. Ea's death represented one more terrible happening in a terrible year, and at that moment she and Thomas were glad for each other.

Denys Finch Hatton was balder than when she had last seen him but otherwise as charming as Karen remembered. "His large mouth also had its old frankness and sweetness," she wrote of a character resembling Denys in "The Supper at Elsinore" (*SGT*, 253). Listening to his conversation, Karen was reminded of how much at ease she felt in his presence. She talked with him in a way she could not with other men. Like a character in "The Roads Round Pisa," Denys kept himself "away from the conventional accent of male and female conversation" (*SGT*, 184). The way in which he took "a friendly and confident interest" in her, without apparently giving any thought to what she thought of him, seemed fresh and "sweet" (*SGT*, 183).

He had heard about the divorce and was sorry, since he was fond of her and Bror. Karen and he held some sympathetic talks over lunch at Muthaiga, where she no doubt referred to Bror's demands for a settlement. Karen had the idea that Bror was going to make some difficult requests. He insisted that Karen and her family had unfairly pushed him out of the coffee company, and he was trying to make it look as though he, Bror, had been mistreated.

Denys was engaged with several other investors in setting up a land development company called Kiptiget, Ltd. In his spare time he was renewing his acquaintances with old settlers like Lord Delamere, occasionally socializing with the governor and his wife, Lord and Lady Northey, and getting to know some of the new people who had emigrated after the war. The colony had recently absorbed several hundred new settlers as a result of the Soldier Settlement Scheme, the desire for a new life and adventure, and the hope for quick fortunes. Most of these new colonists were living in mud and wattle bungalows, while trying to break their land in the highlands to the west, but from time to time those who could afford it came to Nairobi for supplies.

A legislative council of eleven members elected from various districts had been established in 1920 to advise the governor in colonial matters, with Lord Delamere as its most outspoken member. The council was currently considering several serious issues. Among these, most heatedly debated was the "Indian question": whether representation on the council should be extended to the members of the Indian population, who made up nearly three-fourths of the settlers in the colony.

This issue was one of the reasons Denys had waited so long to return to East Africa; its outcome meant the difference between investments rising or falling. The problem lay in the uneven numbers of immigrants in the colony. There were only 9800 white settlers and nearly 23,000 Indians. But, according to Delamere, it was white farmers who had made the country productive by turning what had been wild land into useful farmland, so whites should retain control of the council.

The colonial government had carried out a census in 1921: there were three-and-a-half million Africans—over twenty tribes. What would happen to them if Kenya became nothing more than a nation of spillover from India? Delamere thought Indian immigration should be stopped, and, furthermore, there should be a program to repatriate the Asians. It was too confusing for Africans to be exposed to two different civilizing influences, East and West. He believed the best spirit of the empire would be maintained by encouraging white colonization, with a view to turning over Asian jobs now held in civil service—such as government clerkships and railway positions—to Africans.

Karen was aware that Indians numbered among Kenya's earliest settlers. They had been brought in for the building of the railroad to Uganda at the turn of the century. The railroad had given England a foothold in East Africa, and many Indians had suffered and died for it. Those who survived malaria and drought, dysentery and man-eating lions had stayed to open small shops and import businesses, or to work for the government. Karen liked them; she counted the timber merchant Choleim Hussein among her friends and found that she could not climb with Delamere on his high horse. "I feel class differences so much more than racial," she said (LFA, 146).

In January 1922, Churchill had promised in a speech to Delamere and Lord Northey, among others, that the interests of white colonists would remain paramount. Churchill's words were taken as a guarantee by colonists like Denys who wavered about whether to return to East Africa. But in August 1922, the British government, having changed hands through an election, assumed a new attitude toward the situation in the colony. Lord Northey was recalled and a replacement sent: long-time Africa hand Lord Coryndon, recently governor of Tanganyika. (The former German territory had been conceded to British rule after the war.) Coryndon was both pro-Indian and pro-native—positions with which Karen identified. She held her stronger views quietly, however, for she did not wish to offend people of Delamere's caliber. She found his prejudices striking—he did cling to them beyond reasoning—but in other things Delamere was an interesting conversationalist, deeply versed in the ways of the Masai, and a defender of their way of life and customs. It was said that Delamere invited the Masai into his house in the evenings, where their elegantly greased and dung-painted bodies contrasted with Delamere's overstuffed divan and varnished English chairs. They talked with Delamere about their philosophy of life, and he often agreed with them.

Karen had never had much interest in politics, but she was obliged to pay attention because the future of her farm was at stake. Government debt brought about by the war had increased taxes and limited exports. The income tax had gone into effect in 1920 and been repealed in 1922. Large sums were being proposed to build a new leg of the railroad to Uasin Gishu, and the labor required would place a strain on the supply of farm workers. Such problems, plus the drought prevailing since mid-1922, had for a time kept settlers like Finch Hatton, who had to be cautious financially, away from Kenya. He had reason to wonder if he had made a mistake in coming back.

* 4 *

When Denys Finch Hatton stayed with Karen and Bror shortly after the war, he had admired her paintings. He asked her now what new work she had to show him. His interest inspired her to take up again the hobby she had not pursued since 1918. Between April and August 1922, she completed three portraits of Africans and showed them to Denys for his approval. Good paints and canvas could not be bought in Nairobi, so she offered her work to Aunt Bess as a bribe to get art supplies from Copenhagen. Out of cash, Karen sold her Paris-designed party dresses. Thomas, too, was short of funds; Karen told her mother he was considering pawning his rifle. They were still using his Harley motorcycle because they could not afford to get the car fixed. Karen treated her poverty as a joke, saying, "It is utterly unimportant whether one's elbows are sticking out of one's shirt and one's knees out of one's trousers—where the men are concerned, that is,—as long as the clothes stay in one piece sufficiently to stay on one ... " (*LFA*, 137–8). She had acquired a change of attitude since 1918, when she wrote Thomas that nothing was so important to her as her clothes.

Karen noted that Denys never bothered with the correctness of dress. He had his clothes made by a favorite Nairobi tailor and commissioned shoes in London with squared toes to keep his feet comfortable. He could seldom be bothered with convention; in England he had appeared in an old hunting coat as best man for a friend's wedding. At Eton he had sometimes walked about the lawns in bare feet and a maroon silk dressing gown. When it was cold in Nairobi he was unembarrassed to wear a Somali shawl around his shoulders. On hotter days, he wore his long sleeves folded to the elbow, a casualness characteristic of his approach to life.

Karen spent lunches at Muthaiga and teas on the veranda of the Norfolk Hotel with Denys. He came to the farm for dinner on occasion, and they talked. Mostly their conversation concerned music, books, the economy, and the prevailing atmosphere since the war. Times were hard for everyone, farmers in England and in America were struggling to hold on to their land, and taxes were destroying the wealth of the British aristocracy. In England it was difficult to get servants anymore because jobs at higher wages had become available. Those people who still had money behaved as though it came from an endless source and spent it on parties and nightclubs, dancing and drinking. Morality had collapsed, or rather the old concept of it; ideals like virginity and faithfulness, modesty and marital fidelity had become laughable. It appeared that a new definition of marriage would need to be fashioned if the current trend were to continue toward openly acknowledged sexual affairs by both partners.

Denys smoked a few cigarettes with Karen over the state of the Kenya economy, and they talked about Bror's demand that Karen sell the farm. Denys was gaining insight into the value of Kenya land from his newly formed corporation, Kiptiget, Ltd. He believed along with his partners that there was money to be made in buying up land during the current slump, since prices were sure to rise. He held Karen's view that she should either retain the farm for the corporation or buy out the shareholders, since the land was bound to increase in value. However, Denys was amused by Karen's attachment to the farm. While he appreciated the beauty of the house and view, he would not wish to be saddled with the headaches of a coffee plantation.

She encouraged him to stay at her house, as he had when Bror was there. The Ngong Hills had not changed; buffalo still hid among bushes on the high slopes, and lion visited the farm from the reserve across the river. Thomas was soon to go on safari for a few months; she would welcome Denys's company while he was gone, since she found it tedious to be alone on the farm.

She had socialized little during the previous year. The scandal surrounding her separation from Bror had forced her to seclude herself. Although the governor and his wife, Lord and Lady Northey, had each ridden out to the farm for tea to demonstrate their friendship, she was not invited to Government House for official occasions as she had been before. Because socializing did not interest Thomas, she lacked an escort.

When Thomas left on safari by himself toward the middle of August 1922, Karen succeeded in getting Denys Finch Hatton to spend a few days on the farm. They went riding in the Ngong Hills, hunted spurfowl and guinea hen, and in the evenings drove into the reserve to look for lions in the moonlight. On the third weekend of August 1922, Denys took her to visit the McMillans, whom she had not seen for some time, at the new estate they were building sixty miles north of Nairobi at Ol Donyo Sabuk—the "buffalo mountain." Denys had brought out with him from England an open Hudson touring car, which Karen admired. At his suggestion she took the wheel, doing well at managing the gears and negotiating the jarringly rough roads. She told her mother, "I am now a first-class driver, and I think one of the greatest pleasures in the world is driving an automobile . . . " (*LFA*, 134).

They made the return trip in a downpour over roads muddied by two inches of rain. The storm was unusual since the short rains were not expected for at least a month. In "The Old Chevalier" Karen describes a scene in which a couple comes inside thoroughly wet from the rain (*SGT*, 93). A fire burns in the fireplace, and the woman peels off her wet clothes in front of the man. The consummation of love that takes place is the first between them. Fragmentary comments upon Karen's first sexual encounter with Denys may have appeared in several tales. In "The Roads Round Pisa" she says she had foreseen that "this affair of spiritual seduction could not go on forever..." (*SGT*, 212). In "The Dreamers" she suggests that she was growing "bored" with his failure to take the initiative, and that she resolved to end his "dallying" in making love (*SGT*, 309). She identified the season as one when "there were a great many white lilies" (*SGT*, 310), and also told her mother in a letter from the late months of 1922: "I have such beautiful white lilies just now, bigger and whiter, I think, than those at home" (*LFA*, 138). If he "was nervous," she said in "The Roads Round Pisa," "this was deep down in him and showed itself only in a new softness and playfulness of manner" (*SGT*, 202). In "The Old Chevalier," as she often did in her fiction, she seems to transpose the sexual identities, giving herself the man's role. When, in a sudden gesture, the "man" embraces "his" lover's knees, "she" responds "with such a clear, severe, wild look, as I think that a hawk's eyes must have when they lift off his hood." But then "her" face changed and "lighted up with a kind of heroic gentleness" (*SGT*, 101).

In "The Roads Round Pisa," Karen relates the following conversation:

The woman says: "God, when he created Adam and Eve, arranged it so that man takes, in these matters, the part of a guest, and woman that of a hostess ... Now, tell me, what does a guest want?"

He thinks for a moment. "A guest," he replies, "wants first of all to be diverted ... Secondly the decent guest wants to shine, to expand himself and impress his own personality upon his surroundings ... What does a hostess want?"

She answers, "The hostess wants to be thanked" (*SGT*, 185).

In the seduction scene in "The Dreamers," set during the season of white lilies, Karen's story becomes more erotic as she implies the heroine's loss of virginity: "You are well worthy of coming in," she says to her lover, and he gasps, "Let me come in, then" (*SGT*, 311).

Sometime later, in a letter to Thomas, Karen described falling in love with Denys as a fierce sensation, like the strike of a hammer on an anvil:

> Eros struck out, like a smith with his hammer,
> so that the sparks flew from my defiance.
> He cooled my heart in tears and lamentations,
> like red-hot iron in a stream. (*LFA*, 225)

It appears that the experience was not physically comparable to the "yielding tenderness" she had felt with Bror (*LFA*, 225). Both Karen and Denys seem to have found the sexual encounter more of a challenge than a passionate interaction: perhaps Karen was broadening the scope of her hospitality, Finch Hatton responding to curiosity. In "The Dreamers," Karen relates the story of an affair that "began in the bed, helped on by wine and much noisy music . . . " (*SGT*, 284).

A day or so after their return from Ol Donyo Sabuk, Denys's stay at the farm ended. Events would soon indicate that their relationship had been consummated; but following his visit, whatever Karen's thoughts about Denys, she began to brood about Bror. On September 3, 1922, she wrote to her mother, "I do not know how to put it,—but I know that this *shaurie* [falling out] with Bror has been worse for me than Ea's death" (*LFA*, 132).

* 5 *

To gain a grip on herself after Bror's request for a divorce, Karen had begun to attend Sunday Mass at the French mission ten miles from her house. Her doctors had given her permission to ride again, since she had experienced no abdominal pains since early in the year; so she rode on Rouge to the church, along a road approaching the northwestern edge of Nairobi. The paintings in the church lent a festive, pagan atmosphere that appealed more to Karen's sense of humor than to her spiritual sense. She had been reared Unitarian

146

0

(her grandmother and aunts fervently believed in its precepts; Unitarianism had a strong following in Denmark, where an independent approach to dogma was fostered and Jesus Christ was regarded not as divine but as one of history's great religious teachers). Karen did not take any part of Catholicism seriously—but the warmth and the spiritual strength of the Fathers consoled her. Usually they invited her to drink a glass of wine with them after the service.

Thomas gained the impression that Karen was about to be converted to the "One True Church," but she laughed at the idea. She surely did believe in a Superior Force, but her concept of God was synonymous with Fate—less to be venerated than respected. In keeping with her Unitarian background she respected all great religions. Certainly the God of the Mohammedans was as admirable as that of the Christians, although of the Christian sects she preferred the Catholics, for their God was less personal; "God," she remarked, "likes us in the same way as we like our dogs..." (*SGT*, 198). She viewed the Catholic Church as "a remote and peaceful institution" where one could confide one's thoughts "freely without running the risk of interference in one's plans" (*LFA*, 208–9). Besides, in Nairobi the Catholic church was a good place to socialize because her friends Lord and Lady Northey, as well as others of their set, were Catholics.

Karen had long been fascinated by the literature of religion, and although she could not develop the same level of enthusiasm for the New Testament as Thomas did, parts of the Old Testament had sustained her when she grieved over the divorce. She was impressed by the story in Genesis of Jacob's struggle with the will of God, symbolized by his wrestling all night with the Divine Man. Karen applied this lesson to her relationship with Bror: "I will not let thee go before thou bless me" (*LFA*, 136–7). She was obsessed with discovering the good that might remain in her failed marriage. It was easier to accept Ea's death because she partook of no guilt in it. But she could not forgive herself for losing Bror.

* *

In mid September 1922, Denys Finch Hatton came to the farm, bringing with him new shoes and scarves for Karen's little *toto*,

Mahu, the apple of her eye (*LFA*, 133). Juma's little girl was now four years old, and Karen treated her like her own adopted daughter: she had bought pretty earrings for her, and taught her to make toast. Mahu curtsied to Denys, as though she were being presented to royalty. One may imagine that he laughed, flushing as he did when he was amused. However, Karen was never sure of his opinion of herself, since his comments remained impersonal. His attitude appears to have puzzled her. She wrote about such a relationship in "The Dreamers": since the love affair had begun "she" (a female character acting like Denys) had retained "the same earnest and sweet manner, and seemed to like me, but in our amorous *pas-de-deux* she was slow of movement. I, on my side, was patient." In the story she goes on to suggest that it was necessary to be cautious in proceeding with the affair because the friendship was being watched (*SGT*, 308). If Karen hinted at the truth, it is possible that she did not wish to lend credence to Bror's claim that she was the guilty party in the divorce. Even in these days a woman who asked her husband to leave, as Karen had done, was still judged culpable.

Karen had grown plump over the previous months. She felt anxious about maintaining her allure; just at this time her face was too full to be beautiful. Several months before when she increased her doses of arsenic due to illness, her hair had begun to fall out (*LFA*, 133). After accepting her mother's suggestion that she bob her naturally curly hair in the current fashion, she was still learning to manage the new hairdo. Yet, despite Karen's frustration with her looks, others noted a radiance that was difficult to explain.

* 6 *

The rains in September 1922 had been eccentric, and in October the grass on the plains was brown and dry. The Kikuyu living in the hills were accustomed to set fire to their *shambas* in this season to prepare them for the rains. The red laterite soil, subjected most of the year to drying heat, contained few nutrients. The ashes would fertilize the native maize and sweet potatoes. At night grass fires glowed beneath the stars, and the scent of smoke added romance to the night air.

Denys Finch Hatton had been making appearances at the farm, at first stopping by to keep Karen company while Thomas was gone, then after Thomas's return making more discreet visits. Karen's views of morality had been shaped by her family, and despite her show of rebellion from time to time, especially against the severe ideals of Aunt Bess, she retained a Victorian discomfort with sexual relationships outside marriage. But the years of marriage to Bror had forced her to take a somewhat more relaxed view of conventional morality, and discussions on the subject with Erik von Otter had convinced her that casual sexual liaisons were sometimes not only acceptable, but healthy (*LFA*, 190). She says of a character she wished to imitate in "The Dreamers" that these relationships had "assisted her to achieve a lightness in such things which was not hers by birth" (*SGT*, 337). As for her views on sexual promiscuity, her brother Thomas, pledged to the more liberal standards of the times, repeatedly accused her of being "reactionary" (*LFA*, 138). Perhaps because her conservative opinion about sex with Africans did not coincide with his, she gave Thomas his own cottage on a separate part of the estate .

She took pains to make her relationship with Denys appear to be just a friendship rather than a sexual liaison, and Finch Hatton seemed to fall in with the scheme. It would not do for him to be named in the divorce proceedings. Bror was capable of wielding her affair with Denys as a weapon to reach a settlement more favorable to himself. Besides, her sexual encounters with Finch Hatton seemed less the passionate coming together of two people who would die for each other than the culmination of a ritual of wine and music and long conversation. In the love scene in "The Old Chevalier," Karen wrote, "The wine helped us" (*SGT*, 100), and she said in a letter to Thomas, "As you know the sexual element,—physical as well as mental,—in a relationship between man and woman has never seemed the most important to me, there must be more . . . " (*LFA*, 293). The evenings Denys actually stayed at her house may have been few after Thomas's return. In the following months, in an essay on sexual morality she said love benefits from restraint, for in such a "cool atmosphere. . . goods keep well without much deterioration" (*OMM*, 74). Furthermore, a show of "violent" passion is unwise, she stated obliquely, because it can result in "total impotence" (*OMM*, 84).

But Denys did seem to enjoy her company. He often brought books she might like. Mostly he encouraged Karen to talk, while he listened with amusement. Karen says in *Out of Africa* that his ears brought him more pleasure than his other senses; he liked a story told. Karen was inspired to create tales for him, as she did for Thomas. Denys listened much as the sultan did to Scheherazade (*OA*, 235). He was not uncritical and would note when she mistakenly reintroduced a character who had already died. And there is a hint that she feared his fascination for her might cease when the story ended.

Denys had brought a guitar out from England and was teaching himself to play. Karen searched through her books until she found an old collection of German lieder for Denys to sing. These had been favorite songs of her sister Ea, and hearing them brought back nostalgic memories. From his mother Denys had inherited talent for singing and a natural feeling for music. He had performed in recitals while at Eton, and he preferred classical songs. Karen was charmed to hear his high, sweet voice.

An evening of song might lead to something more. But although Denys was gifted with a frank, sweet mouth, large and sensual, his embraces seem to have been diffident. (Nearly every later story by Karen contains the description of a kiss resisted.) However, while his sexual performance seems to have lacked the warmth of Bror's, she admired him and revered his attentions. And it was, apparently, in this way that sometime in the latter half of the year 1922 she became pregnant (*LFA*, 137).

* *

In her evaluation, fate was certainly sarcastic. She had longed for a child during her marriage to Bror and been unable to conceive. Now this pregnancy seemed a shocking joke. She was forced to assess the situation; her condition was likely to cause embarrassment, and she was unprepared financially or emotionally to go home. An abortion in Africa would be dangerous—really, out of the question, even if one could find someone to help with it. Moreover, she was elated to be pregnant. Bearing this child might even be socially acceptable: since she was still married to Bror, the child would carry his name.

However, possibly in late October 1922—before she was thoroughly accustomed to the idea of having a child—she miscarried. She was only several weeks pregnant when the disappointment occurred; she had as yet told no one about her condition, not even Thomas. She sent for him late in the night and, weeping hysterically, revealed she had lost the baby (*LFA*, 137).

Finch Hatton appears not to have learned of the incident, and Thomas could be relied upon to be discreet. Karen continued her friendship with Finch Hatton casually, as if one of the great hopes of her life had not been extinguished. Perhaps in an effort to accept the loss of the child, she ruminated upon the Bible verse: "I will not let thee go before thou bless me"—which, she told her mother in a melancholy letter on October 29, 1922, she had adopted as her "motto" in life (*LFA*, 136–7).

* 7 *

In Karen's garden the rains had brought masses of white lilies into bloom. Denys Finch Hatton had inherited from his mother an interest in photography, and he seems to have insisted upon taking some pictures of Karen and Thomas, and of the lilies. The pictures captured Karen looking disconcerted—perhaps not at all prepared to be photographed. She had changed into a flounced, white tea dress and matching shoes for the pictures, but seems to have given up trying to make her hair look presentable. At first she posed with a huge bouquet of lilies that hid her figure, but someone insisted upon taking a few snapshots of her and Thomas together without the flowers—in these pictures she was certainly plumper than she wished to record.

Karen and Thomas were preparing for the visit of relatives from Denmark for Christmas. Their brother-in-law, Viggo de Neergaard, who had not yet recovered emotionally from the death of Ea, was coming out to Africa for a change of air. He arrived, accompanied by a cousin, in the third week of December 1922.

Harvesting was under way. Africans were picking ripe berries from the tall coffee bushes and collecting them in closely woven baskets suspended by leather straps from their shoulders. Ox-wagons delivered loads of baskets to the new factory, built from Thomas's design. Inside was a large vat for soaking and pulping the beans, and another for fermenting them to remove their glutinous coat. The beans were dried, hulled, and graded, and then were loaded into gunny sacks and stacked, twelve to a ton, on heavy wagons. Teams of sixteen oxen pulled the wagons to Nairobi, from where they would be sent, first by train, then by ship, to the London market.

The week before Viggo's arrival an accident occurred on the farm that was bound to create a legal tangle. Although Karen had forbidden anyone to ride on the back of the delivery wagons, because the load was already great for the oxen, young Africans would jump on for a ride from the fields. So as not to be seen by Karen, it was their habit to leap off just as the wagons hove into sight of the house, but Karen had glimpsed the workers laughing at not getting caught. In the month of December 1922, a young Kikuyu girl named Wamboi fell as she jumped down, her body splaying under the bullock cart. The heavy wheel rumbled over her head.

The accident was viewed as a bad portent by the people of the farm. The Kikuyu would not approach the dead body, which lay with its skull in a pool of blood in the road near Karen's house. The people held an aversion to touching the dead, and left them to be salvaged by hyenas. Karen could recruit no one but Kamante, one of the house *totos*, and Dickens, her new overseer, to remove the corpse.

The girl's parents were determined to seek restitution, since they had lost the possibility of wealth from this girl's dowry. Expecting Karen to make good their loss, they camped for days on the lawn outside her house. But Karen would not give in because she had made plain her rule against riding on the wagons. Besides, she had no money to give to the parents. But, she told Viggo, the *shaurie*—which demonstrated the different thinking between whites and Africans—was likely to go on for months and years, to rise and fall, and to be raised again and again in the minds and conversation of the people of the farm.

And this was not the only subject of consternation on the farm because, only a few days before, Karen's old servant Esa had died—

poisoned, it was rumored, by his young wife. Karen had warned Esa against this May-December marriage, since he had a good, devoted old wife, but Esa was proud to take a nubile young woman as his own. When the new wife repeatedly ran away, Esa had forced her to come back, although she preferred to live as a prostitute in the shanty suburbs of Nairobi. Finally, it appeared, she had killed Esa for her freedom. But despite strong evidence against her, no charges were brought. Esa had been one of Karen's favorite servants, and she was indignant that nothing was to be done about his death; but Farah said a man must control his wife as he controls his horse, and if he does not, no one else should be blamed.

Viggo's appreciation of Africa extended little beyond the farm. He amused Karen with his Danish woolens and quaint shoes. He inspected the farm with interest, since he was a shareholder in Karen Coffee Corporation, but he did not care to take part in the safari life or in tours of Kenya. He and his cousin were staying in Thomas's cottage, and Karen invited them to dine at her house to celebrate Christmas. "Thomas and I tried to decorate with spruce and candles," she wrote to her mother, "and we had rice porridge, turkey and a kind of almond cake" (*LFA*, 141). But she did not try to take them along later to midnight Mass at the French mission or to the Christmas party that followed at the Northeys. Instead, she took with her Kamante, a little Kikuyu boy whom she had once treated for emaciation and leg ulcers. Now his legs were healed, and he was one of her favorite *totos* on the farm.

Kamante had always had a singular look about him: his head seemed a little too large for his body. He was small for his age, and shy, and his large eyes gave the impression that he withheld grave pronouncements. Karen felt that within this peculiarly formed body were talents the world might someday use. She employed him in her house in small tasks, and waited for him to reveal himself.

* *

What with business matters to resolve with Viggo, as representative of the shareholders of Karen Coffee Company, Karen saw little of Denys Finch Hatton during the holidays. She had not encountered him at the Northeys' after Midnight Mass, and it was, anyway, unlikely that he would attend, since he was reared in the Church of England and, beyond the poetry of the Bible, took little interest in religion.

However, on New Year's Eve 1922, long after Viggo and his cousin and Thomas had retired, and Karen had fallen asleep in bed reading, she was awakened by the sound of voices and laughter on the veranda outside her bedroom. The boy who slept there and acted as watchman brought a lantern to fetch her, announcing that *Bwana* Finch Hatton had arrived with friends. Karen's standard lounging attire included a white silk dressing gown trimmed with ostrich feathers, and high-heeled satin slippers with matching pompoms (these are casually apparent in a snapshot of her bedroom she sent home during these years). Denys had brought with him Lord Francis Scott, an attractive Englishman much respected in the colony, and his young niece, Lady Margaret Scott, for whom they were seeking a female chaperon for a party in Nairobi.

Karen agreed to accompany them to the Muthaiga Club, where glasses of champagne were being passed among a crowd wearing glittering gowns and tuxedos. As the night wore on, the hijinks in the Muthaiga Club escalated. The overstuffed chairs were skated over the floor in races, the more agile party-goers shinned the pillars and hung from the rafters, and people like Berkeley Cole, proclaiming they should all pretend they were bathing at Trouville, ended the evening by splashing bucketfuls of water across the dance floor (*OMS*, 170).

The party continued well into the next morning, and afterwards Karen invited a group of people to the farm for breakfast. One may imagine that Hassan, her cook, and Farah, under quiet orders from Karen to prepare the best possible table, were kept busy along the passage between the kitchen and the house, while the guests mingled on the veranda and terrace and admired the view of the Ngong Hills, the large lawn, and the cool woods surrounding the house. They stayed on until evening, some perhaps taking naps in the cushioned chairs in the sitting room, others resting on wicker furniture outside on the veranda. For lunch they had eaten the remaining food in Karen's larder, and when plans were made to return to Muthaiga for dinner, they insisted that she come too. So to start the New Year she spent a second gay evening in which Denys was the center of her attention, and she did not return to the farm until early on the morning of January 2, 1923.

1923

1

Denys Finch Hatton had grown in stature in Karen's mind, beyond
her initial good impression of him. He symbolized joy in her life.
Whenever she saw him, he made her laugh. He seemed never to take
anything seriously. He appreciated whatever she did, and he was adept
at drawing out her talents. She had nearly forgotten how good at
conversation she was; now she surprised herself at the ease with which
she entertained and impressed his friends. Around Denys she felt
happy and fearless of the future. Any pessimistic remark would draw a
joke from him. He gave the impression that no crisis could disturb him.

She wished to imitate his ease and confidence, and wrote to
her mother: "Here you can really move as a man's equal . . ." (*LFA*,
144). Her short hair was now "a lion's mane" (*LFA*, 144). It curled
naturally—this was never so evident until she cut it; she could arrange
it to her satisfaction with a simple combing, just like a man. She was
thinking of taking up the new fashion of wearing trousers, and would
have liked to wear shorts, too, but said sadly, "I do not have the legs"

(*LFA*, 144). In "The Roads Round Pisa" she remarks, "In Denmark everybody has thick ankles . . . " (*SGT*, 181).

Finch Hatton's inspiration was essential to her at this moment, because Thomas had announced his intention to return to Denmark with Viggo and his cousin, to pursue a way of life other than farming. His decision was made firmer by a misfortune that occurred on the night of January 24, 1923, when he was alerted out of bed by shouts from the boys that the coffee factory had caught fire. In the dark, they hitched oxen to the wagons to bring water from the pond, but the fire went out of control before they could save either the building or the machinery. This best example of Thomas's work in Africa had been destroyed, as well as his further interest in continuing with the task of coffee farming.

It was a consoling irony that Viggo, one of Karen Coffee's most agriculturally astute shareholders, was on hand for the factory fire. Having suffered similar losses in farming, and possessing good business sense, he encouraged a philosophical attitude: the insurance money could provide capital for improvements on the farm, since the factory would not have to be rebuilt immediately (*LFA*, 145). Relieved by his optimism, Karen mentioned the fire almost casually in a letter to her mother.

She followed the news of the misfortune by telling her mother a gay story about how she dressed up her overseer Dickens for a party "as a Dutchman,—he looks just like one, small and stocky with a round ruddy face. I helped him to make his costume, with clogs and a fur cap, to which I sewed my false curls, and was rewarded by his getting first prize . . . " (*LFA*, 145). But her gayness disguised fright at the thought that Thomas was leaving. Despite her complaints about him in the past, he had been a support to her since Bror left. After the burning of the factory—a measure of the unaccountability of fate—the idea of running the farm alone filled her with dread.

1923

* 2 *

The departure of Thomas ignited in Karen an anxiety she could not shake off. She began to imagine herself as the central figure in an unfolding tragedy and could not escape the premonition that she had been left alone to preside over the failure of the farm. Her intuition insisted that she would receive all the blame, yet she must follow through to the dénouement. Soon after Thomas left, she wrote to her mother, "If my marriage had turned out differently, or if I had had children, I probably would not have felt this sort of terror hanging over me . . . " (*LFA*, 149).

She understood that solitude had created her anxiety. Yet merely living alone should not have worried her. She saw many examples in Kenya of women living as independently as men. The colony was famous for its pioneer women running farms by themselves. Some, like Karen, exasperated with impetuous schemes for getting rich, had given husbands their freedom. Others, like Ingrid Lindstrom, forged ahead despite husbands who, always searching for the golden fleece, were never home. While men investigated gold mines in Tanganyika, pursued ivory in Uganda, and collected horses and cattle in Somaliland, women supervised planting, made decisions about livestock, and oversaw work of Africans on their Kenya farms.

Karen was ashamed of her fear and attempted to distract herself from obsessive thoughts of failing by writing letters home. These letters, however one-sided, represented conversation, for which she was desperate. She had never lived alone before in her life. Some member of her family had always been within reach. When Bror had gone for long periods on safari, during the war and on business in Uasin Gishu, she had experienced distress; it felt unnatural to her to be alone.

Her letters to her mother betrayed her loneliness on the farm, but she insisted that she was not really alone. She had her "boys and dogs and white people," she said (*LFA*, 149). However, her business relationship with her overseers prevented her from confiding her intimate feelings to them, and she could not find adequate comfort in speaking to the Africans on the farm. Their culture isolated her from them; they did not see things in the same way. It was long conversation that she needed, the kind of interaction from which she might gain perspective, and none of the Africans on the farm was fluent enough in English, or well-enough read, to act as her sounding board. She commented on the frustration of discourse with individuals who could not give her back an echo, who could not respond to what she said.

She was not sleeping well. Unsure of her ability to save the farm, she often lay awake reviewing the alternatives. Thomas had advised her to sell out, but she could not believe the finances of the farm were bleak enough to give up hope. In the dark she could not imagine her way through, but when the sun rose she thought she had exaggerated the difficulties. It was characteristic of her, she told Thomas, to "rise very slowly to the surface again," despite agonized misgivings (*LFA*, 223).

On her horse Rouge, she would ride out in the morning to inspect the farm. A slight mist softened the sunlight over the coffee fields. Smoke rose from cooking fires in squatter huts. Occasionally she caught sight of a woman bent over, sweeping the ground at the entrance of her hut with a handful of long grass. They raised a hand to each other. These people had faith that she could bring the farm through.

She would confer with her white foreman Dickens, a South African hired since Bror's departure. His cottage and that of Thaxton, an American brought in to supervise rebuilding and running a new coffee factory, lay through the woods less than a mile from her house. Farther up the track lived Pooran Singh, manager of her smithy and mill. As yet, she had no idea how she would find money for this season's wages; other debts, such as the insurance and the mortgage, were already greater than she could pay.

After she held her morning clinic for the sick on the terrace outside her dining room, Farah would drive her to Nairobi for consultations with the land office or her solicitors, about debts and, more recently, fines that she must pay for not attending to planting regulations on the Uasin Gishu farm.

She had calculated the farm expenses over and over for the next six months, and the results were always the same: there was not enough money to make the payments due on April 1, 1923. By August she would be £1600 in arrears. The corporation had already indicated its unwillingness to help. They had authorized Uncle Aage to express their disappointment in the investment and their growing wish "to be free of the whole enterprise" (*LFA*, 158). Karen found it hard to accept that ten years of her life must be written off as wasted. Selling the farm, she was convinced, would render the past meaningless. More importantly, she saw no future for herself if she sold out. In keeping with her belief that yesterday is tomorrow, she envisioned that afterwards her life line would stretch to eternity as "*Failure, failure, failure*" (*LFA*, 149). In her mind, success with the farm had become her only hope of salvation.

She feared that Thomas might side against her with the shareholders, and sent him a letter, which he would receive at home as he stepped off the boat, to beg him to consider the alternatives. Perhaps he would be willing to help her with his own money, or he and Viggo could borrow the money for her, or they could find friends to help, or together they could offer to buy out the shareholders at whatever price a forced sale would bring. The current value of the farm she guessed to be no more than £ 20,000 (*LFA*, 148).

To raise money she had written to a real estate agent in Eldoret about selling the Uasin Gishu property, but he answered that absolutely no buyers could be interested until the Indian question was settled. She had also looked into selling the Mbagathi house, where she and Bror had first lived, on the basis that it would make an excellent country house for someone with business in Nairobi. She visited investors in town, including Milligan of the landholding and export business, to propose that, in exchange for a percent of the profits, he back her purchase of the farm from the shareholders. The economic slump had led to a proliferation of unctuous and refined, portly and shrewd land sharks—men whose vision went beyond the depression to a time when profits would soar. They twirled their mustaches and made loans on bad debts that could garner a fortune in interest and, when payments failed, make them owners instead of lenders. But Karen could undertake no loan or sale without consent of the corporation, and it was this continuing, disapproving supervision from Denmark that would decide the future of the farm and her own future.

By April 1, 1923, despite frantic letters to Thomas, Karen had received no word from the shareholders about the funds she needed to continue her operations. With no money to make payments on the mortgages, she was desperate for a course of action. If she was not yet convinced that doom had arrived, she nevertheless envisioned exhausting negotiations with creditors in a struggle to keep the farm. On Wednesday morning, April 4, she directed Farah to drive her to the office of her solicitor, W. C. Hunter, who, she expected, would declare that the farm be sold.

* 3 *

The office of W. C. Hunter, like those of other Nairobi businesses, was located on a dusty street in a block of stuccoed buildings with pillared overhangs. Since the year before, when Uncle Aage had set up a bank account for Karen Coffee Corporation and authorized withdrawals by her solicitor only, Karen had remained uninformed about deposits from Denmark until she consulted Hunter. On this particular day Hunter's greeting to her was, as ever, gracious. But his response to her concern about the payment of debts was strangely off-hand: of course he had received money from Denmark; it had been in the farm's account for several days. Her uncle had sent money for her to continue through August.

Karen wished to have received word about this sooner. She was infuriated that no one had cared to let her know. It seemed to her that the corporation's lack of concern for her feelings gave ample reason why she should break free from their oppressive control.

Her day might have been completely spoiled by bitterness about this affair, if she had not encountered in town another of Hunter's clients, Denys Finch Hatton (*LFA*, 150). He had been on safari, and Karen had seen almost nothing of him since the New Year. He invited her to lunch with him at Muthaiga, and she was quite willing to accept. His remarks consoled her; he offered to help her borrow money to buy out the corporation. Perhaps Geoffrey Buxton would put up the funds. It was not in Denys's nature to worry about the future; he had taken in life the role of a satisfied man, a cat dozing in the sunlight. She said later, "it was as if he could draw upon forces unknown to us if he wanted to" (*OA*, 356).

Bror and Karen—the honeymoon. *(Bror Blixen: The Africa Letters)*

Bror. *(The Life and Destiny of Isak Dinesen.)*

Denys. *(The Life and Destiny of Isak Dinesen.)*

Karen—August, 1928. *(Century Publishing Co. Ltd.)*

Denys on safari—June, 1927. *(Silence Will Speak.)*

Rungstedlund. *(© Linda Donelson 1995.)*

Mbogani house (east façade). *(© Linda Donelson 1995.)*

The millstone tables (west façade). *(© Linda Donelson 1995.)*

Mbogani house (east foyer). *(© Linda Donelson 1995.)*

Mbogani house (south veranda and Ngong Hills). *(© Linda Donelson 1995.)*

Ngong Hills. *(© Linda Donelson 1995.)*

Karen Blixen's World

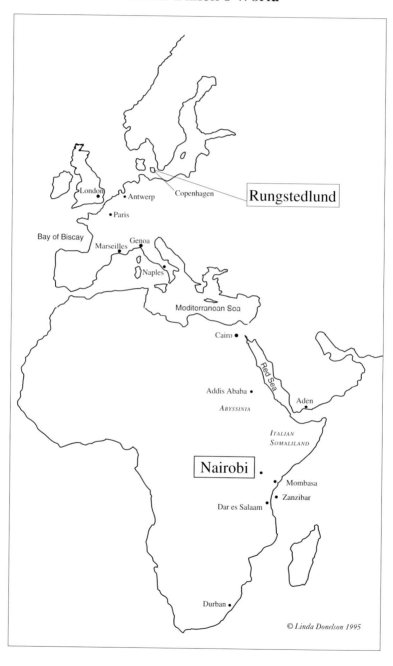

London
Antwerp
Copenhagen
Rungstedlund
Paris
Bay of Biscay
Genoa
Marseilles
Naples
Mediterranean Sea
Cairo
Red Sea
Addis Ababa
Aden
Abyssinia
Italian Somaliland
Nairobi
Mombasa
Zanzibar
Dar es Salaam
Durban

Karen Blixen's Journeys to Africa

1913—from Naples via the Red Sea—*Admiral*

1916—from England via Durban—R. M. S. *Balmoral Castle*

1920—from Marseilles via the Red Sea—*Garth Castle*

1925—from Antwerp via the Red Sea—*Springfontein*

1929—from Genoa via the Red Sea—S. S. *Tanganyika*

Family

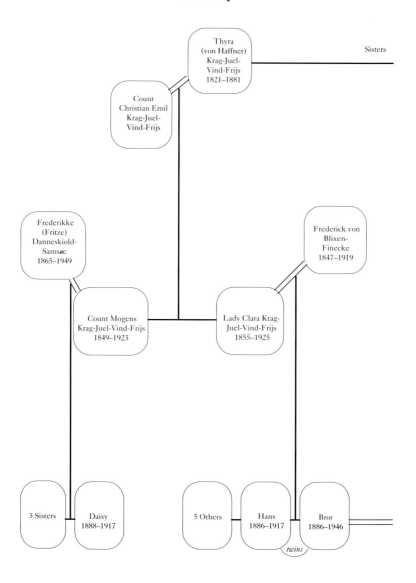

Thyra
(von Haffner)
Krag-Juel-
Vind-Frijs
1821–1881

Sisters

Count
Christian Emil
Krag-Juel-
Vind-Frijs

Frederikke
(Fritze)
Danneskiold-
Samsøe
1865–1949

Frederick von
Blixen-
Finecke
1847–1919

Count Mogens
Krag-Juel-Vind-Frijs
1849–1923

Lady Clara Krag-
Juel-Vind-Frijs
1855–1925

3 Sisters

Daisy
1888–1917

5 Others

Hans
1886–1917

Bror
1886–1946

twins

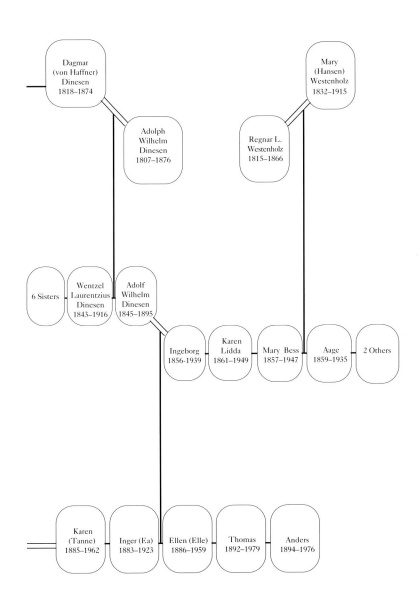

The Years In Africa

Key: Seeing Denys, but not living with him:
Denys living at the farm:
Karen away in Europe:

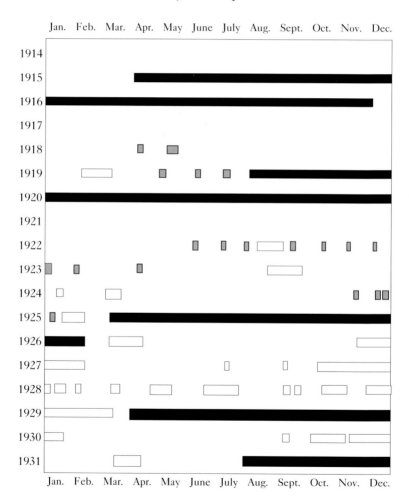

She hoped she would now see more of him, but it was not to be. Finch Hatton's family was expecting his yearly visit, and he had already booked passage for Europe. His freedom to leave contrasted with Karen's ties to the farm. Not only was she needed as manager, but she could not think of going away until the divorce was settled. The news that he was leaving made her so dispirited that she felt ill. She began to brood that she had not really felt well for some time (*LFA*, 154).

* 4 *

Karen had never been so anxious about her future, and the terror was escalating. For a period in her youth, when Hans Blixen decided to marry someone else, she had experienced a kind of panic over her future—an anxiety that threw her "completely off balance" (*LFA*, 208); then her family and Daisy had helped her to regain her perspective. Now that she was alone, the inner voice echoing the words "*Failure, failure, failure*" (*LFA*, 149) revived old symptoms of despair.

She had experienced moments of panic in earlier years, but never so frequent as in 1923. These attacks were similar to those she had suffered during the war when she was suspected of being a German sympathizer. Later she said, "Whenever I was ill in Africa, or much worried, I suffered from a special kind of compulsive idea. It seemed to me then that all my surroundings were in danger or distress, and that in the midst of this disaster I myself was somehow on the wrong side . . . ." She described the sensation as like walking in a "nightmare" while being fully awake (*OA*, 361). At such moments she would feel she was going to suffocate.

Shortly after Thomas's departure an illness of some kind had sent her to the hospital. She did not elaborate on her symptoms, nor even reveal the incident to her family except to let it slip that she had been talking to an old Scottish nurse (*LFA*, 150–1). But in a letter to Thomas, she said, "I think that being left alone suddenly sent me slightly mad" (*LFA*, 148). The old nurse had advised her to see more of her neighbors.

In early May 1923, Karen consulted a young doctor in Nairobi named Anderson. She told her family, "I am not ill, but so tired—I don't feel like doing anything" (*LFA*, 154). Her symptoms were serious enough to interfere with her ability to manage the farm. Perhaps fearing some drastic cure like that which had scarred her leg in 1918, she did not "dare," she wrote, to see Burkitt, although she said she liked him; they were, after all, old friends. Doctor Anderson may not have been so shrewd, however, at diagnosing depression. He examined a sample of her blood and, finding her anemic, said she must be suffering from chronic malaria. She reported, "He gave me some revolting stuff to take for it" (*LFA*, 154).

When her symptoms continued despite this regimen, she resigned herself to consulting Burkitt, who rightly judged she was suffering from depressive anxiety. Her episodes of suffocation and her panic in the face of rather ordinary difficulties were attributable to depression at being left alone with the responsibility of the farm. He had seen her stricken before by attacks of anxiety, and he may have known the story of her father's suicide—a dangerous precedent. As a long-time friend, Burkitt could not be optimistic about her living by herself. His advice to her—that she should go home to Denmark—was the drastic cure she had feared.

He realized she was not going to take his advice, and so afterwards he wrote her a letter, emphasizing in a kindly manner that she "must and should go home" (*LFA*, 165). Her mother, too, understood that she was under psychological strain. She insisted that Karen needed "peace and quiet" (*LFA*, 149) and implored her to come back to Rungstedlund.

Believing that her anxiety was nothing more than "nerves" and that with self-discipline she would overcome these feelings, Karen ignored their pleas. She made up her mind that her physical symptoms must be due to syphilis, for which she could treat herself—with arsenic. She said, "actually I think it is one of the easiest diseases to deal with if one keeps a watch on it" (*LFA*, 151). She concentrated her energy on saving the farm and tried to create pastimes that would assuage her loneliness until Finch Hatton returned sometime in early fall.

1923

* 5 *

In 1923 the long rainy season from February to May was unusually wet. There were nine inches of rain in March, sixteen in April, and over ten in May. This rainfall should have meant a good coffee crop, and there was abundant bloom. The branches of the coffee bushes were covered with thick clusters of tiny, star-shaped flowers, and new ones kept appearing; flower buds and blooms brushed against developing green and red berries on adjacent branches. But the actual number of mature berries was disappointing—not nearly so many berries as blooms.

The coffee bushes, some nine years old, were now taller than Karen as she walked through the rows. She had hired Emil Holmberg to give the trees a pruning before the rains; the bushes should have been trimmed when they reached three and a half feet, again at four feet, and at five and a half feet. Cutting the top growth encouraged side-branching.

But, despite the pruning, the crop was frustratingly small. Karen could not understand this, and asked Trench, an agricultural expert from the land survey department, to inspect the fields with her. His assessment was that it might take the coffee a year to "pick up" (*LFA*, 155). The farm had been neglected, he said, and wanted better weeding and plowing between the rows of coffee. He suggested manuring the rows and planting shade trees. There was still some debate among coffee growers about the merits of shading. Some people said shade trees robbed the coffee of moisture; others insisted that coffee fruited poorly in harsh sunlight. But Trench thought that, because of the altitude of Karen's farm, she would benefit from shade trees anyway; they would protect the coffee from frost.

Karen followed Trench's advice, and she bought a tractor and learned to plow with it herself. Dressed in khaki trousers, a smock and clogs, and a double *terai* (soft, wide-brimmed hat), she picked coffee in the fields beside African women with shaved heads and aprons made from skins. She would not have felt obliged to join in their work except that the activity and the association with other human beings helped her to maintain her mental balance. Living just a mile or two through the woods—as had her grandmother and her aunts Bess and Lidda during her childhood at Rungstedlund—the Africans were now her family, her human support on the farm.

* 6 *

Now that Thomas had gone, Karen relied on Farah. His English had improved through the years, as had Karen's, so they could converse. She would speak to him about what she was reading. He knew the stories in *The Thousand and One Nights* and liked them because they concurred with his Muslim sense of justice. But of other books— *Kristin Lavransdatter*, the writings of Cellini, and the works of Shakespeare, for example—Farah was scornful. She related to him the story of *The Merchant of Venice*. He was much intrigued by the plot, but when she told him the outcome, he fairly spat, for he thought the woman should have been forced, in fairness to a promise made, to yield her pound of flesh.

Karen sometimes gathered the *totos* loitering about her lawn to listen to stories. Their sheep mingled among them, punctuating Karen's recitations with bleats. The children understood only part of what she was saying, but were fascinated by her voice. She found that she could delight them by repeating certain melodious phrases. They liked her stories better for hearing them three or four times over.

In the evenings when the silence of the farm was broken only by crickets and hyenas, Karen wrote the stories down. She worked near the fireplace in the great room used as a dining room, from which she could step out onto the terrace and see the stars, and wonder if they were also shining on Finch Hatton's home in England. Denys had encouraged her to write and to paint, and she hoped to finish something she could be proud to show him when he came back. The story "The Roads Round Pisa" exhibits themes that parallel thoughts in her letters in 1923: visits to the Catholic Fathers, an essay for Thomas dealing with the nature of "Truth" and searching analysis of a failed marriage. Her style of writing imitated *The Thousand and One Nights*, in that the stories were staged in an older era and contained stories within stories. These tales were inspired, it appears, by others Karen had read;

she added new twists and creative insight. Much of the framework for the stories came from her surroundings and experiences. She says in "The Deluge at Norderney," "The story, correct or not, was a symbol, a dressed-up image of what she had in reality gone through . . . " (*SGT*, 46). The stories were inspired, it seems, by events in her life, symbolized so as to achieve perspective. She described her house and grounds at Ngong in more than one of them, and often used her friends and family as models for the characters. In creating a story she mulled over a paradox and attempted to understand its inconsistencies by taking each role herself. Every character represented a different facet of her own thinking.

Writing kept her mind off loneliness; and by romanticizing her problems she trivialized them, transforming anxiety into poetry. To achieve serenity she placed herself at a distance from what really happened—like a member of the audience at a drama studying the action while free of its implications. So, in writing "The Roads Round Pisa," she says of marriage, "I do not cling to it, for I know enough about it to realize that whatever you cling to will either patronize you or get tired of you" (*SGT*, 171).

Writing tales allowed her to consolidate her philosophy. She preferred to do this in conversation with someone she trusted, but Thomas's departure had forced her to seek an echo on the printed page. She had found little time to write while Bror or Thomas was with her; now loneliness made her a writer.

From the beginning she considered writing a significant exercise, not merely a hobby. The divorce had made it necessary to re-evaluate the direction of her life. Without a child she must seek another avenue to immortality. The characters in her stories might live longer than children—maybe forever.

She espouses the theory in a youthful story, "The de Cats Family," that one cannot escape one's destiny. In "The Roads Round Pisa," she develops this theory further, imagining her life as a drama on a stage in which she has only to play her role. Such an idea might free her from agonizing about her future—her overwhelming preoccupation since Bror left. She wrote, "Perhaps in a hundred years people will be reading about me, and about my sadness tonight, and think it only entertaining . . . " (*SGT*, 168).

Living in an era when appearances were vitally important, she had often evaluated herself from afar; so it came naturally to create her stories as allegories for actual experiences. The duel brought about by a misunderstanding, which forms the central theme in "The Roads Round Pisa," becomes a symbol for her struggle with Bror. She believed she should have forgiven Bror's infidelities, in exchange for the greater pleasure of continuing to live with him. At the end of the story the heroine frees herself from grief by forgiving. Karen concluded that Bror would forever idealize her, and this was consolation.

As artist, she could narrate the story, but she had no power to change the outcome; only her view of events might change. She composed the story over months, incorporating characters and events as one finds them in dreams, in a jumbled and intriguing refashioning of experience: "The Roads Round Pisa" taking place in 1823 (not 1923), beginning at sunset near Pisa (Ngong), Count Augustus von Schimmelmann (modeled, in physical appearance, after her somewhat overweight friend Hugh Martin from the land office—or perhaps herself) writing a letter on a table made out of a millstone, to Karl in Germany (Thomas in Denmark) about his separation from his spouse. Other details include a bonnet with curls sewn inside like the one she made for Dickens, a fear of child-bearing (arising from Ea's death), a wife escaping her husband (like Esa's), an enormously fat hero, Prince Pozentiani (Sir Northrup McMillan), and a Dionysian figure with pantherine grace (Denys Finch Hatton). No element of the story is without symbolism, even to the wrongful consummation of love between strangers—an ironic view of her entire marriage to Bror.

As she wrote, Farah stood nearby, his white robe silhouetted against the paneled wall. Since first Bror, and then Thomas, had gone, she had been saying to herself, "It is good that I still have Farah" (*LFA*, 158). He had always run her household, for which she was grateful, since she had embarked upon housekeeping with no training. He supervised the houseboys and kitchen *totos*, acted as butler, advised her on matters of decorum in dealing with the Africans, and interpreted for her in Swahili. He looked after her personal welfare, brought her morning tea, nursed her when she was unwell, and made deferential suggestions for how the house might be better run. Although he was respectful, he conducted his duties in the manner of a prince who is used to having things done his way. He spoke to the houseboys with an economy of words, and they took care not to disappoint him, nodding to his directions and doing his bidding wide-eyed.

On Sundays, when work outside halted, Karen painted, with Farah standing by to fetch what she needed or to interpret her wishes to Africans who sat for portraits. Karen's patience was short, for she was painting to distract herself from loneliness. She grew irritated by her subjects' wiggling and sulking, since the Africans hated to pose. One day she became so frustrated that she threw down her brush and paints, and shouted to Farah to burn them. Her behavior was all too familiar to Farah, who had soothed her in other difficult situations. He merely collected the paints and said, "Try one more day, then I think that God shall help you and it shall be very good" (*LFA*, 156). In the memoir *Shadows on the Grass* she describes an acquaintance having a "nervous breakdown" that resembles remarkably her own state of mind during this time. When agitated, she could never feel sure she was doing what she ought to do. "When I was painting a picture," she quotes the acquaintance in the memoir, "I felt that I ought to make up my bank account. When I was making up my bank account, I felt that I ought to go for a walk. And when, in a long walk, I had got five miles away from home, I realized that I ought to be, at this very moment, in front of my easel. I was constantly in flight, an exile everywhere" (*SOTG*, 427).

Farah was now her chauffeur for trips to Nairobi, for he was in love with the car. Karen had subjugated her own delight in driving to Farah's obvious preference for taking the wheel. Sometimes she asked him to drive her into town at night to attend parties that began long after dark. These midnight rides seemed to her more pleasurable than other trips in the car. The plains lay in intriguing darkness, the night air was scented with mystery, crickets sang a secret song, spring hares and owls materialized in the headlights upon the road, and overhead shone the Southern Cross. In contrast to trips to Nairobi for business *shauries*, these rides were undertaken in a spirit of anticipation, since she was escaping the silence and foreboding of the farm, to exercise her best talents: charm, and conversation in the wider world.

IN AFRICA

Among her friends in Nairobi were the Northeys, the
McMillans, and a number of other mutual friends of her and Denys
Finch Hatton. They noted her need to talk and her escapes from the
farm in search of reassuring company. They knew that the farm's
finances were in a sad state—like those of so many farms during this
period of agricultural slump—and that, since her husband's request for
a divorce and her brother's return to Denmark, the baroness was
managing with difficulty. Some of those who took the kindliest
interest in her privately commented that she would do better not to
live alone. So when the opportunity arose, they recommended she
take in as house guest a young woman in need of refuge, a troubled
young wife named Beryl Purves.

It was well known in Nairobi that Beryl, the daughter of
Charles Clutterbuck, one-time horse trainer to Lord Delamere, had
been married at the age of sixteen to Jock Purves, a twenty-five-year-
old farmer. Gossips commented that she was a lovely girl with little
concept of what it meant to be a wife, for her mother had abandoned
her when she was four years old, and her father had allowed her to grow
up with few influences other than the African children on the farm.
Beryl treated the concept of wifely fidelity as nonexistent; it was said
her husband drove a nail in the pillar of his veranda for each new man
she slept with. His drunken rages and beatings had made little
impression upon her behavior, until now that Beryl had finally left him.

Since her father's emigration to South America shortly after
her marriage, Beryl had no one to turn to. She had taken up training
horses, a skill learned from her father, and was looking for a place to live
as well as somewhere to stable her horse. Karen willingly invited her
to stay at Mbogani, and accepted the task of interacting with a woman
who at age twenty was like "a child" (*SOTM*, 54). We "will have some fun
together," Karen said, approaching the task diplomatically (*SOTM*, 53).

However, the girl's brief visit—for she soon went back to her
husband—did little to alleviate Karen's anxiety over the farm. She had
developed a fear of open spaces and avoided going hunting by herself
on the plains. Outdoors she seems to have felt as she describes a figure
in "The Monkey," "terribly and absurdly small, exposed and unsafe"
(*SGT*, 133). Nearly five months had passed since Thomas's departure

170

when she wrote to him in June 1923: "I have not been able to prevail upon myself to go shooting at Orungi one single time" (*LFA*, 158).

At night fearful thoughts about losing the farm menaced her. Her difficulties seemed to grow in proportion to the lateness of the hour. In the dark she could not get her perspective, and she came to think of her most trivial mistakes—some as far in the past as her childhood—as omens of life-long failure.

Such was the case one night in July 1923, when her ruminations about the events of the previous day brought to surface the memory of a disturbing incident. During an otherwise typical drive to Nairobi to see about the insurance on the farm, she had been preoccupied by a number of matters, including how to pay the fine of five thousand shillings assessed against the Uasin Gishu farm. She had received news a few days before of the death of Uncle Mogens Frijs, which left her in a melancholy mood. To her mother she had written, "it seems as if a whole age has disappeared with his passing" (*LFA*, 160). And she continued to dwell on the problem of buying the farm, for which the corporation had not yet given an answer.

As Farah drove her toward town, she barely noticed some African boys leaning into the road and wildly waving to get her attention. They were grinning and holding high something they hoped to sell. It was a bushbuck, a tiny antelope for the *Msabu's* dinner. As the car passed, neither Karen nor Farah acknowledged them.

Late in the afternoon, as Karen and Farah motored home, they found the boys still there, gesturing for them to stop. They had tied the little bushbuck upside down by its hooves on a string stretched between two sticks, so as to display him better. Karen felt vaguely sorry that the boys had spent all day without a customer but, tired from conversations with bankers and government officials, and wishing to arrive home as soon as possible, she directed Farah to drive on.

It was the thought, later that night, of the plight of the bushbuck that drove Karen to panic. How could she have ignored the poor animal? How could she have left it to its fate in the hands of boys? In the dark her callousness seemed to symbolize every wrong decision she had made in her life. In *Out of Africa* she says that "a great feeling of terror . . . as if someone had been trying to choke me" startled her out of bed, and made her shout for the houseboys (*OA*, 70). They came running, perhaps believing from her distress that a snake had got into the house, only to find that *Memsahib* wished them to go out into the night to search for the boys with the little antelope.

She might have wondered why they complied so unquestion-ingly, if she had not noted that Africans liked being out in the night, as much as if they were in league with it (*OA*, 93). From her veranda in the evenings, she had often seen them passing in the distance, in groups of two or three, silhouetted between the trees. Unafraid of leopards or lions, they sang or laughed, comfortable in the dark. They had no trouble locating the hut of the boys in the Kikuyu village, where people slept around the embers of fires laid on the ground. The hut was smoky inside, a deterrent to insects; beside the sleepers dozed goats and dogs. The little antelope was tethered there. When they brought the bushbuck to Karen, she gathered it in her arms as if it were a child and called it "Lulu."

Over the years she had gathered the impression that wild animals were comfortable with her because she gave them free rein in her house: owls would perch on the top of her china cupboard, birds wandered in and out of the doors to the veranda, and Lulu now ruled the sitting room; her favorite sleeping place was under Karen's writing desk.

Karen regarded the little antelope as a symbol of herself. Lulu, whose haughtiness intimidated even the dogs, would tap-tap over the polished wooden floor as though she owned the house. She was out of place indoors, but made the most of her security, and for a long time did not realize she belonged elsewhere, in the woods where she was born. When she was dispirited, she became temperamental, and was not afraid to throw tantrums for the benefit of Karen's horse Rouge. Like Karen in Africa, she was a woman in a foreign land, afraid to go home, unsure of her moods, and terrified of being independent.

* *

Attempting to submerge loneliness in gracious entertaining, Karen turned her house into a guest station for friends traveling through Nairobi. Ingrid Lindstrom stayed with her when she came to town, and one or two young friends of Thomas, such as the Norwegian

Gustav Mohr, came to talk. Big-nosed and large-hearted, young Mohr was manager of a six-thousand-acre sisal plantation near Limuru, ten miles west of Nairobi; and because his responsibilities precluded his staying for long periods at Karen's farm, he established a rendezvous with her on Monday afternoons, for a vermouth on the veranda of the New Stanley Hotel (*OA*, 276). He exchanged books with her, discussed philosophy, and advised her on farming matters—since, in addition to sisal, he supervised five hundred acres of coffee plantation. He kept abreast of Karen's moods. When she was depressed, he intervened—either by coming to stay at the farm or by finding another of her friends who would.

In the middle of August 1923, Karen persuaded Hugh Martin, head of the land department, his wife, Flo, and their five-year-old daughter, Betty, to spend a week with her. Before his marriage to Lord Northey's daughter, Hugh had been stationed in the Orient, and Karen noted that Hugh in his portliness resembled a Chinese idol (*OA*, 216). Laconic and thoughtful, his manner was worlds different from that of his no-nonsense, energetic wife. Betty was the same age as Juma's little girl, Mahu, whom Karen regarded as tenderly as a daughter. Recently the festival of Ramadan, which Karen considered to be the Mohammedan "Christmas," had been held in Nairobi, and Karen had dressed Mahu winningly for the occasion, in silks and a shawl (*LFA*, 161). While Karen was delighted that Betty and Mahu could play together, she harbored a more compelling goal for inviting the Martins to visit: she wanted Hugh to use his influence to get the fine deferred on the Uasin Gishu farm, until she received payment for the next harvest.

Karen arranged for a big *ngoma* (evening of dance) to be held on the farm in honor of the Martins' visit, and directed that an easy chair be brought out on the lawn especially for Betty, who was enchanted by the bonfires and the dancing. The warriors wore necklaces of lion's teeth and headdresses simulating a lion's mane. They painted their faces and legs in intricate patterns of ochre. The women, wearing leather aprons and stacks of copper necklets and anklets, chanted to the music of drums and pipes and, with the young men, took turns at jumping inside the large circle of clapping dancers.

Later, Martin listened to Karen's sad story and agreed—for only a few more months—to defer payment of the fines. Perhaps Denys Finch Hatton had also put in a word with Martin, a friend from Oxford. In an August 1923 letter to her sister Elle, Karen rhapsodized on the "natural unselfishness" of the English—an opinion markedly different from her views of them in earlier years. Referring to Denys—although she did not mention him by name—she said, "In my opinion they have such great calm features in their temperament... I think that living with the best of them is like getting up into clearer air..." (*LFA*, 162)—a description of Denys she later used often.

Martin had learned that Denys was due to return to Africa unusually early. Generally he stayed in England until fall, but this year he was expected back in Nairobi toward the end of August. Commenting to Elle on the subject of feminism—as though mulling over her immediate future—Karen remarked, "I think that there is a really fine time ahead for women" (*LFA*, 163). She spoke as though she were confident of learning to be independent—in the same way as, after some difficulties, she had learned to drive a car. She went on to tell her sister hopefully, "it is reasonable enough for the woman's movement to vacillate a good deal before finding its,—more or less,—real answers ..." (*LFA*, 163).

Over the previous year, she had relied for support more than she cared to admit on her friendship with Denys. Her regard for him seems to have become a kind of hero-worship. When he was away he occupied her thoughts. When she faced a crisis, she asked herself, "What would Denys do? What would make him proud of me?" When she experienced a happy event, she longed for Denys to share it. Over the previous year he had replaced her father as imaginary overseer of her happiness. She worked herself into a frenzy of excitement at the imminence of his arrival, writing to Thomas in the middle of August 1923, "I am expecting Denys, perhaps today, anyway this week, and so you will know that:

Death is nothing, winter is nothing . . . " (*LFA*, 167).

* 7 *

When Finch Hatton did make his appearance, he brought along with him from Nairobi his friend Berkeley Cole. Karen insisted they both stay at her house rather than take a cottage at Muthaiga. Denys gave her several works of George Bernard Shaw that he thought she would enjoy. Perhaps she avoided telling him about two books she had requested from her mother in his absence: Herman Wildenvey's *Love Poems* and an anthology entitled *Danish Love Poems* (*LFA*, 155).

Berkeley had recently taken a seat on the legislative council, as representative from his district at Nyeri, near Mt. Kenya. Although a shy, introverted settler, Berkeley was glad for some escape from his farm in these days of agricultural crisis. He established immediate rapport with Karen, by means of wry remarks concerning mortgages. He too was having great difficulty meeting his farm payments.

Berkeley's ample, burnished mustache contrasted with the paleness of his skin. There was something more than the fairness of a redhead in his complexion; his skin bore the color of a man with a bad heart. Although he was slight in stature, he carried himself erect and had the gestures and speech of a once energetic man. He charmed by exaggeration, extravagantly complimenting Karen's meals, her conversation and her hospitality. He and Denys praised her furniture and cooking, her china and her view of the Ngong Hills, and proclaimed her house the most civilized in the colony. They created a raucous atmosphere at dinner, and, perhaps teasing that her glassware could reach even greater heights, they built a tower with her crystal (*OA*, 221).

Later Berkeley talked of politics, in which he was reactionary. On the subject of the Indian question, he would climb on his high horse, which greatly amused Karen, although she barely took an interest in politics. The Indian question had been settled in July 1923, when a "white paper," or declaration of policy, was sent to Kenya from the British Colonial Office. In it "Asians" were declared to share communal rights with white settlers and were given five seats on the legislative council. European settlers retained the majority, eleven seats on the council, but segregation of Asians was outlawed in all Kenya communities. Europeans were allowed to continue their monopoly over farming in the highlands, but the white paper had eliminated consideration of their demand for exclusive rule in Kenya. The Indian community still remained up in arms over the settlement. So far, they refused to fill their allotted seats on the council, feeling they were unfairly represented.

Listening to him side heatedly with Delamere's position, Karen judged Berkeley to be a "fundee," or expert, on only a few issues. Later she listed these to her mother as "wine, hunting," and "a certain kind of love with sincere understanding . . . " (*LFA*, 219). On racial matters Karen could not sympathize with his views. She said, "I personally have so little racial feeling that I find it hard to understand them" (*LFA*, 146).

In the middle of September 1923, while Denys stayed on with her after Berkeley's departure, Karen received a disappointing letter from Uncle Aage, putting an end to her talk of buying out the shareholders. Terribly upset, she wrote to Thomas—exaggerating, as it were, the need for an immediate decision about what to do with her life, threatening to give up the farm and leave Africa, and asking Thomas what to do. She flung out the idea that she might be willing to run "a small hotel for colored people in Djibouti or Marseilles" rather than live at home (*LFA*, 169).

Her letter clearly represented a crisis in thinking, and perhaps her agitation was due to something more than Uncle Aage's letter. Someone, possibly Jack Llewellyn, had hinted that he would be happy to marry her; she said, "I could make a very good marriage as things are at present; but I have become absolutely convinced that I would not marry except for love . . . " (*LFA*, 169). One wonders why she entertained this idea at all, unless she had been disappointed by Finch Hatton's intentions. As usual, he had been kind and amusing; he had sung Schubert's lieder; he had read aloud from Walt Whitman; he had appreciated her storytelling and her cooking; and he had gone riding with her and been affectionate. But marriage to her did not appear to be in his plans. Still, no matter how desperate her talk of leaving Africa and starting a new life (away from Denys), she ended her disturbing letter to Thomas by insisting: "I have been really completely happy, indeed, so happy that it is worth having lived and suffered, been ill, and had all the shauries, to have lived for this week . . . " (*LFA*, 169).

8

When Denys played football (soccer) with the *totos*, he would start the game indolently, as though hardly a challenge to his opponents, then, with lightning quickness, he would send the ball into the goal. When he was at school, an article in the Eton *Chronicle* had read, "The Hon. D. C. Finch Hatton, when not charged is apt to be careless, uses the left side of his foot as if his leg were a golf club and kicks short. When charged, he rises to the occasion and is very hard to get past" (*SWS*, 32). Watching the *totos* play, Karen learned the meaning of "goals" and "offsides." She wrote her mother that Kamante was "big and strong" and playing well (*LFA*, 181).

During this visit, Denys stayed at the farm for over a month. Toward the end of September 1923, in a letter to Thomas, Karen referred to Denys in rapturous terms, as though his appreciation of her hospitality had gone beyond admiration. "That such a person as Denys does exist—," she said, "something I have indeed guessed at before, but hardly dared to believe,—and that I have been lucky enough to meet him in this life and been so close to him,—even though there have been long periods of missing him in between,—compensates for everything else in the world, and other things cease to have any significance" (*LFA*, 171).

Yet in front of Denys she maintained a casual attitude toward their relationship—one to match his own. Denys, like a character in "The Dreamers," seems to have had a way of talking about love and making it seem "like a pastime in a kindergarten" (*SGT*, 308). His conversation remained neutral, as though what happened between them was as pleasurable yet as impersonal as events in the stories she invented or the poetry they read together. Perhaps fearing she would frighten him off with talk of love, Karen wrote to Thomas: "if I should die and you should happen to meet him afterward, you must never let him know that I have written to you like this about him . . ." (*LFA*, 171). When he finally left, all she could say about the future was, "I hope he will be coming back . . . " (*LFA*, 170–1).

* 9 *

In the late months of 1923 there were unusual sightings of lions and leopards in the town of Nairobi and the surrounding farms. Ordinarily the big cats kept to the open plains, but this year they were more sociable. Some said they were a sign of portentous events.

A leopard had climbed onto the veranda of Mr. Hemsted, the D.C. (District Commissioner) at Dagoretti, and stolen his pet bushbuck. This incident, not far from Karen's farm, alarmed her into asking her manager Dickens to set up a gun trap. First they tried using a freshly killed animal to lure a leopard inside, but lacking success, their trap now contained a live goat, with a gun set to go off when the leopard entered. While danger lurked, Karen kept Lulu shut inside the house.

Berkeley Cole, also noted for his unusual pets—other settlers joked that sheep and chickens had the run of his house (*OMS*, 240), sympathized with Karen's agitation over leopards. In Nairobi people were talking about the recent incident of a lion's being shot in the botanical gardens, just outside Government House. Lord Delamere was about to give a banquet for Sir Geoffrey Archer, governor of Uganda, and for the new Kenya governor Lord Coryndon, and people wondered what danger there might be to the crowd arriving at Muthaiga after dark. Berkeley had invited Karen to be his companion for the affair. She would sit at table directly opposite Sir Geoffrey, with Coryndon on her left and Berkeley on her right.

Berkeley now stayed frequently at the farm when the legislative council was in session. Knowing Karen had little money, he brought vegetables and oranges from his farm, and kept her table supplied with wine. He convinced her to let him use her best crystal to drink champagne in the forest—a game, like many others, in which she was happy to humor him. Berkeley had developed a fantasy that his true calling should have been captaincy of a large merchant ship. Karen suggested that someday they might ply the waters of the Indian Ocean together, sailing dhows laden with spices and fine Persian silks on winds from the east. Aunt Lidda had given her some red and green lanterns, relics of the Danish shipping trade, and these she hung at the entrance to her house, so that Berkeley, returning to the farm from a day of politics, could imagine himself being welcomed aboard ship.

She enjoyed being alone with Berkeley for the opportunity to talk about Denys. She could ask Berkeley's view of why Finch Hatton had not married and inquire, in a casual manner, if there were a great love in Finch Hatton's past. One may imagine that Berkeley was amused by her queries and gave her his own view: as far as he knew, Finch Hatton had never known a woman more charming than herself. He may have replied wickedly that he wished she were as interested in his own romantic life. Karen began to suspect he was not entirely teasing. In a letter to Thomas she indicated that she thought Berkeley might like to marry her (*LFA*, 223). Berkeley's appreciation of the comforts of her house made her think he would, indeed, enjoy a wife's care, and in this short time she had grown fond of him. Sitting beside the fire in her house, he reminded her of a cat, comforting her by his very presence. She was delighted to entertain him, the more because he was Denys's friend. As long as Berkeley visited, she could count on Denys to return.

However, when Berkeley went back to his farm, loneliness closed in upon her, and she begged Thomas, who had been gone less than seven months, to return. "You really should not let the fact that we have perhaps been too optimistic this year convince you that this is a hopeless undertaking . . . " (*LFA*, 172), she said. One day she dared to go riding on the plains alone. She was due to regret the experiment because Rouge stumbled into a hole, fell, and threw her off. The experience, which validated her forebodings, inspired in her a horror bordering on the surreal. "I felt as though I was lying at the bottom of a grave, and saw Rouge's back balanced over me . . . " (*LFA*, 172), she wrote to her mother. She had fallen in soft grass and was not injured, yet she burst into tears of despair, certain that the horse would abandon her and be eaten by lions and that she would drown in the high grass or faint with the heat while trying to walk home. If Bror had been with her when this incident occurred, perhaps she would have marched home beside him in the expectation of receiving accolades for her courage. As it was, Rouge calmly stood by until she had composed herself; then they rode home.

She continued to paint but had little patience for it. Once, when her subject, a young Kikuyu, would not sit still, she threatened him with a pistol for the remainder of the sitting. But although she was under mental strain, she was not physically ill until the third week of October 1923, when she experienced an attack of dizziness while picking coffee. She went to bed feeling as if she were "in a real storm on the Red Sea," as seasick as she had ever been, with "head-,tooth-, and earache" and "the most horrific pains in every limb" (*LFA*, 176). She herself diagnosed the illness as "*sunstroke*." She had had it before, notably in February 1919, and Thomas too had experienced the symptoms. "Ask Thomas if this isn't right," she declared to her mother (*LFA*, 176). Many of the settlers complained of sunstroke, and no one, least of all the local doctors, seemed to entertain a better diagnosis, since it was accepted that the white man poorly tolerated the tropical sun. Even wearing a sturdy hat and draping the body in a way to cover the skin did not always avert the illness. But these attacks seemed prevalent in the rainy season: the rains, although torrential, were intermittent, and during the hiatuses people went out in the sun. Karen was beyond correlating Thomas's and her "sunstroke" with the malaria season, but the symptoms she described—pain in the ears, headache, nausea, and irritation of the nerves—are typical of what doctors now recognize as "cinchonism," the syndrome which occurs after an overdose of quinine.

* 10 *

It had been nearly a year since Lord Coryndon, early in his term, made a special visit to the farm to urge Karen to start a school. Karen had been at pains to charm her overseer Dickens into the idea, since he was certain that once Africans learned to read they would scorn farm work. But since the government had commandeered Africans to help build the new leg of the railroad to Eldoret, there was a shortage of ready workers. A school on the farm might entice workers—or so Karen persuaded him. She had in mind a certain outbuilding, next to the stables, that could be used for the school, and classes would be held only in the evening, so as not to disrupt the work of the farm.

Educating the Africans had become a popular issue in the colony since the arrival of Coryndon, since he espoused the theory that

production and exports could be improved, and so increase tax rev-
enues, by sending Africans to elementary schools followed by trade
schools, and teaching them crafts and skills.

Early in 1923, Catholic Fathers began touring the neighboring estates, saying Mass, and encouraging the hiring of teachers trained
in their missions. The opportunity for proselytizing proved equally
irresistible to representatives of the Protestant mission, and soon there
developed a competition for placement of teachers. Karen had not
decided which religion to encourage, since she found the competition
odious, but she said, "I think that every large farm ought to have a
school; there is no point in saying that natives are more happy in their
primitive state; besides that being very questionable in itself, it is
impossible to keep them there and by making no attempt to educate
them, all that results is that they get hold of all the worst aspects of
civilization . . . " (LFA, 177).

She was collecting these plans more firmly in her mind one
evening near Christmas 1923 when she stepped out on the veranda to
smoke while Farah prepared her bath. Suddenly she heard the sound
of a single shot, followed by silence. She thought it odd to hear the
sound of a rifle, since it was dark, and a hunter would not be able to see.
She had turned to go in to her bath, when she heard the sound of a
motorcycle coming from the direction of the woods. Shortly after, the
foreman of her coffee mill, the American, Thaxton ("Belknap" in *Out
of Africa*), arrived in a state of wild agitation, gasping for help. It seemed
that he kept his shotgun loaded to scare predators away from his
chickens, and while he was outside, a curious *toto* working in his house
had picked up the gun and playfully pointed it at his companions. He
had accidentally pulled the trigger, and several boys had been wounded.

As she ran through the woods to Thaxton's cottage, Karen
could hear moans and screams from the children. She took a lantern
from Farah and entered the blood-spattered kitchen, finding one boy
near death, and another with his jaw shot away. The boy who fired the
gun had disappeared. Karen dispatched Farah to prepare the car, now
extremely unreliable and lacking tail lights. The boy with the missing
jaw screamed until she took his head in her hands and said, "Calm
down. I have come to help you" (LFA, 178). She bandaged him to

staunch the bleeding; then she and Thaxton and Farah loaded the wounded boys into the car. The men had to push to get the car started. Karen later said that the drive to Nairobi seemed longer than a voyage to Denmark (*OA*, 99). One boy died at the hospital as they lifted him out of the car. The other, Wanjangiri, the boy with the wounded jaw, was taken inside, where doctors noted that Karen's bandaging had saved his life.

* 11 *

What with spending much of the remainder of the night in the police station with Thaxton—because keeping a loaded shotgun was against the law—and wearing only a light coat and no boots against the chilly night air, Karen incurred a severe cold. The next morning, after consulting her solicitor in Nairobi about the consequences of the shooting, she took herself in a sad state to Chiromo, the home of Lord and Lady McMillan.

When Sir Northrup McMillan, now weighing nearly four hundred pounds, was elected to the colonial legislative council, he had leased a mansion in town, to avoid having to cart himself back and forth eighty kilometers between his estate at Ol Donyo Sabuk and Nairobi. The gray fieldstone mansion, called Chiromo, had been built in 1905 by another esteemed early settler, Edward Grogan. It was situated on a hill overlooking Nairobi to the south and the Athi plains to the southwest. The gravel drive approached the palatial house through trees and elaborate gardens. By damming the Nairobi River, Grogan had been able to include in the garden streams, waterfalls, and an artificial lake. His wife, Gertrude, an enthusiastic horticulturalist, had established large beds of roses, cannas, and madonna lilies. Purple and rose bougainvillea cascaded over the veranda. The mansion boasted leaded windows, high-arched ceilings, and parquet floors made of Canadian pine. After Grogan and his wife separated, the McMillans had taken over the house and crammed it with expensive carpets, comfortable furniture, and relics of their travels.

Karen often fled to the McMillans' when anxiety got the best of her because they were kind and supportive. She related to them the story of the shooting. Sir Northrup had a way of listening and nodding, and giving out little wheezes of understanding; Mr. Bulpett could not resist invoking a number of similar incidents he could recall; and Lady McMillan believed it was certainly courageous of Karen, a woman alone, to manage a coffee plantation in Africa, in an atmosphere of such shocking tragedies.

Chiromo lay on a hill on the northwestern edge of Nairobi, very near the hospital, and after luncheon Karen paid a visit to Wanjangiri. The boy was alive but unable to speak. When she took his hand, he would not let her go, obviously desiring her to stay beside him. In the hospital they were giving him milk, and the doctor was making plans to operate, but his lower jaw and teeth had been shot away.

Karen had gone to town to collect money to pay the salaries of the Africans before Christmas. As soon as she returned to the farm, she went to bed, ill and discouraged. The shooting accident had added to her already melancholy mood, since she was due to be alone for Christmas—the first time in her life she would spend Christmas without family. Some time earlier she had invited Finch Hatton to celebrate the holiday with her, but although he was evidently pleased at the invitation, he had remained vague about his plans.

Mr. Bulpett, concerned about her illness, made a special visit to the farm to see her and to insist that she spend Christmas with him and the McMillans; but she could not make up her mind whether to go. She was planning a treat for her African family on Christmas day. She and Farah would hand out gifts of sugar, cigarettes, or snuff to each (*LFA*, 180). Berkeley Cole had sent her a cat as a Christmas present, but she would rather have his cat-like presence in her house—along with his friend, Denys Finch Hatton.

* 12 *

Shortly after Christmas 1923, while in Nairobi on errands, Karen encountered Bror. She had not expected to see him, since she believed him to be hunting in the Congo. The meeting was upsetting. Clinging to his arm was Cockie Birkbeck—pert, dark-curled, and vampish. She was nearly ten years younger than Karen. Perhaps Karen recognized insolence in her gaze; she wrote to her mother, "there is always some conflict as long as Bror is in this country, and as long as his friends and he himself feel that he has been unjustly treated and thrown out by the company and the whole of my family . . . " (*LFA*, 182–3).

She may have been overly sensitive to the incident, for it was not Bror's nature to be vindictive. But there was some truth to her suspicion that Bror had been painting himself as victim. Thomas, who was seldom ruffled, had written angrily to Uncle Aage about Bror's attitude in August 1922: "That Bror, by his vicious lies, has made my position here in this country all but impossible is not so important, since I don't intend to stay here, but as far as I can see he does everything he can to ruin Tanne's position. It suits him for the moment to appear as a martyr who has been treated disgracefully by Tanne and her family, and more and more he gets his own and Tanne's acquaintances to see things from this point of view" (*PA*, 25).

Bror had written to Karen from the Congo, where rumors reached him that she was seeking a loan to buy out the corporation. He offered to procure the money she needed "from home" (*LFA*, 153). Karen could not imagine what he meant, although she had heard that Cockie Birkbeck's father, a banker in England, was wealthy. Karen was suspicious of the conditions Bror was offering. He still owed money to the corporation and perhaps was hoping to be forgiven these debts in exchange for the loan. She had rejected his offer, and was later aghast when Cockie Birkbeck appeared at the farm alone to negotiate on Bror's behalf. Karen had no intention of doing business with her.

Now that divorce was inevitable, Karen wished to expedite it. She attempted to arrange meetings between her lawyers and Bror's, but Bror, still ducking creditors, did not cooperate. Suspicious that Bror had learned of her sexual relationship with Finch Hatton and was planning to enlarge upon it in the divorce proceedings, Karen elaborated to her family a scheme to prevent herself from being "branded as the 'guilty' party" (*LFA*, 183). She explained that, by English law, if the woman does not ask for "*maintenance*," she is automatically assumed to be at fault in the divorce. Karen desired that her lawyer, Repsdorph, specify in the settlement that she was to receive a small maintenance from Bror. She intended to refuse the maintenance on a yearly basis, thereby proving her generosity toward Bror and making it difficult for him to insist he had been mistreated.

Encounters with Bror continued to disturb her. In late December 1923 she wrote her mother, "I am really still very attached to Bror . . . " (*LFA*, 183). Her longing for him was complicated by her not having seen Finch Hatton on intimate terms for some months and, apparently, by more than a little irritation that Finch Hatton had forsaken her during the holidays.

1924

1

Denys materialized the second week in January 1924. It was like him to show up wearing a Somali shawl draped like a cape around his shoulders. Perhaps he looked thin to her, for when Karen was annoyed with the English she noted their tendency to thinness. "The mere fact that the English are always so skinny shows their uncongeniality," she complained (*LFA*, 409). Probably she did not interrogate him about his holidays, but she may have suspected that he had spent Christmas in the region of Mt. Kenya with Berkeley Cole.

He had shown up, humbly presuming upon her hospitality for a week or two, while he outfitted himself for another safari. The previous two years, while difficult for farmers, had been exhausting to his own financial assets. He had been hunting more seriously, hoping to expand his income by trading in ivory. His investment in Kiptiget, Ltd., a land development corporation, had left him with little capital and was, so far, bringing in few profits. For the moment he was thinking of pursuing elephant in the southern Masai country, near the Tanganyika border.

He was interested to see the paintings Karen had completed, and after she showed him what she had achieved he suggested that she send them to Europe to be exhibited. She said she felt she was not experienced enough to paint really well; what she needed was further training. When she was in Europe she would take an art course. She intended to spend time in Paris on her next trip to Europe.

Although Finch Hatton was evidently preoccupied with safari arrangements, every day just after sunrise they hunted pigeons. She wrote to her mother, "It is wonderfully beautiful here in the early morning when the sun is shining on the Ngong Hills and making them quite copper colored, while the woods as you wade through the soaking grass are still shadowy" (*LFA*, 185). In "The Dreamers" Karen says of a female character resembling Denys, "She was extraordinarily alive to all impressions. Whenever we went together she would observe many more things than I did, though I have been a good sportsman all my life" (*SGT*, 285). Denys had an eye and an ear for the things of nature. Karen says in *Out of Africa* that, better than any other white man, he understood Africa's "soil and seasons, the vegetation and the wild animals, the winds and smells" (*OA*, 369). As they hunted, he made observations about the dew, the weather, the clouds, the late moon and the morning stars. (Did she reflect that people interested him less?) These expeditions with Denys were reminiscent of hunting with her father. However, she seemed to enjoy them less this time. Watching the pigeons fly, she felt oddly homesick. She wrote to her mother, "the yearning is almost strong enough to make me a suit of feathers so that I could go flying home . . . " (*LFA*, 184).

Perhaps Denys's unpredictable visit disappointed her. By not coming for Christmas he had disturbed her faith in their friendship. She may have drawn the conclusion that he was taking advantage of her hospitality without offering enough in return. In a letter to her sister Elle during the second week of January, she dwelled significantly upon the importance in a relationship of "reciprocity" (*LFA*, 185).

When, on Saturday, January 12, Colonel Jack Llewellyn called at the farm, she insisted that he too stay on. She made a fuss over him and announced she was going to plan a "big tea-party" in his honor (*LFA*, 185). Amid the preparations, Finch Hatton, who had visited less than a week, pleaded other commitments and departed.

1924

* 2 *

The houseboys at Mbogani house regarded tea parties as solemn undertakings. These were occasions on which the name of the house might be established, or lost. China was taken from Karen's lacquered cupboard. Farah held the keys, as he did for all the house. He supervised the laying of the table to ensure that no plates or crystal were broken. Cakes, pastries, biscuits, and tea were carried carefully from the kitchen into the house and through the hall to the dining room. Depending on the number of guests, tea might be served on a small table in the drawing room, along with delicate sandwiches of egg and cress, pâté and cucumber, tomato and finely grated cheese. Tea was poured with hot milk, or brewed in the Asian fashion with milk, honey, and cardamom. Depending on the guest, Karen might offer tangerines, Chinese ginger, or crystallized fruit.

Recently she had spent time teaching her cook, Hassan, to make such things as "croustades" and "puff-pastry pretzels" (*LFA*, 185). She could not afford to entertain on a grander scale, but in her teacups and pastries she found the opportunity to fulfill a larger mission than her guests suspected. In this way she felt able to disseminate her attitudes toward Africa and Africans. She did not hold forth, on these issues; she merely allowed her example to take its effect. Karomenya, a deaf and dumb boy for whom Karen had puzzled out a useful role on the farm, might shyly enter the room to collect the dogs. Mahu, Juma's precocious five-year-old daughter, might be presented to the guests, to curtsy as Karen had taught her. Karen might introduce and boast of the school exploits of Abdullahi, a young relative of Farah, for whose education she was paying. She spoke with enthusiasm of the new school begun on the farm and of her efforts to establish a private *kiama* (native court) to handle personal quarrels—such as disputes over wives—for which the Kikuju chief Kinanjui lacked interest.

Jack Llewellyn, always charming—she knew he admired her—listened with amusement, but she could see he did not have the love of Africa and Africans that she detected in more aristocratic settlers like Denys and Berkeley. It was a pity. He was remarkably eligible as a marriage prospect—well-to-do, with a good position, and Karen's age, thirty-seven. But she told Thomas that the idea of such a marriage was no more significant to her than marrying her dog Banja (*LFA*, 223).

Still, if Denys felt no loyalty to spend the Christmas holidays with her, she need not restrict her companionship to him. She outlined in a letter to her mother the limits of a woman's duties in such a relationship: "both partners consider that one should not take or give, risk or enjoy, or as a whole put more into it, —than the other" (*LFA*, 188).

She had recently been infuriated by a letter from Bror's mother, Clara von Blixen, who defended Bror by excusing the philandering of men as helpless submission to "great temptations." Karen commented tartly, "Perhaps Aunt Clara has never had any of these 'temptations,' and I think that women like this do their own sex much harm by positing their own case as the norm, which is naturally gladly accepted by many men" (*LFA*, 192). She was prepared to maintain that an "erotic" (*LFA*, 187) friendship need not place any more constraints on the behavior of the woman than of the man.

* *

Undaunted by her fall from Rouge in October 1923, Karen rode her horse around the farm, surveying the effects of diligent weeding and pruning. Coffee picked in the preceding weeks was being processed in the factory—pulped and fermented, hulled and graded. She took Thaxton's place supervising the factory's operation, while he attended to the legalities following the shooting at his house. Wanjangiri, jawless, had lived. Kabero, the boy who had pulled the trigger, had disappeared, perhaps to seek refuge with the Masai.

* 3 *

On the 27th of January 1924, as Karen wrote her usual Sunday letter to her mother, a car drove up with an unexpected visitor. Behind the wheel was an unfamiliar farmer from the neighboring region of

Kiambu. As a kindness he had brought to Karen's house an old, nearly blind Dane named Aarup (Old Knudsen in *Out of Africa*), who had heard that a Danish woman lived there. Karen could see that he was destitute, and his purple cheeks and bleary eyes revealed that he was a drinker. But she had not heard a Danish accent since Thomas left, and, reluctantly charmed by the sound of his voice, she invited the old man inside.

Aarup wanted her to lend him a cottage where he could, without bothering anyone, live and pursue his small craft, making *kibokos* (leather whips) for driving oxen. He was an amusing old man with a quaint outlook and rather too many stories about the old days in Denmark. Karen knew of an empty hut on the premises, one she had originally planned to use for the school; she turned it over to Aarup, cautioning him that he must not create trouble for her workmen, Dickens and Thaxton, because they would not tolerate it.

Throughout the months of February and March 1924, in the evenings the old man would stumble up the path to Karen's house, ensconce himself in a chair on the veranda, and pour out his view of the world. He elaborated a number of plans certain to make her rich, the most prominent of which was turning her pond into a resort for the people of Nairobi, by building a restaurant near the water's edge and stocking the pond with fish. Initially Karen joined in this fantasy—a game similar to the one she played with Berkeley about sailing with him in a dhow. But when she realized he was taking it seriously, she had to point out that the scheme was impractical. At this he turned on her, berating her as though she were one of a species known as women, meant for maligning. She had the impression that a wife had once given him much to feel bitter about.

Something about Aarup's attitude reminded her of her relationship with Bror. In *Out of Africa* she credits Old Knudsen with Bror's failed plan to make charcoal, among other things. She had not been able to keep her sense of humor with Bror; eventually she had lost her ability to encourage his fantasies. With him she had been the stern disciplinarian, as impatient with unrealistic schemes as, in her immediate family, Aunt Bess had been. Indeed, if any of the Dinesen children sometimes resembled Aunt Bess in her stern approach to life, it was Karen, who had taken Bror to task on numerous occasions in the same manner as she had been lectured in the nursery by her well-meaning aunt. In "The Pearls," she discusses such a relationship: "the young and the old maid had many qualities in common" (*WT*, 107). She recalled Bror's wild ideas—the abortive plan to make charcoal symbolized them all—and regretted railing against him. She thought of herself wryly as the one who, like "Madam Knudsen," "stopped all enterprises," who "snatched away the man's glass of gin from the table before him," and who "washed the faces of boys" (*OA*, 200). She should have been more playful with Bror, it seemed to her.

During the previous few months she had been writing an essay on "Marriage"—a task she said would help her to "exercise my mind a little on such things and also see whether I can still write in Danish" (*LFA*, 191). She was, in part, placing her marriage in perspective to see where she had gone wrong. Moreover, in light of Finch Hatton's seeming lack of interest in marriage, she was reflecting on how to deal with a different type of relationship with a man—one in which producing children played no role. She had developed the idea that a love affair must be more of a "game," that it depended on the playfulness of the participants. She could not succeed with Denys by being a "Madam Knudsen."

* 4 *

Feeling as usual unsure whether she would see Finch Hatton again, one day she seized a box of cigars Denys had left behind and grandly bestowed them on old Aarup (*LFA*, 191). In truth, she hated cigar smoke, but dispensing with Denys's cigars represented indeed a stroke of courage. These were of an extraordinarily expensive variety, selected and given to Denys by his brother, Toby, who meted out the supply, keeping track in a ledger of how many remained (*SWS*, 208). Blithely giving away anything belonging to Denys, considering his attachment to his own things, was flirting with danger. Perhaps she was convinced he would not be back.

In a turbulent letter to Thomas toward the end of February 1924, Karen railed about "the generally insecure feeling I have with regard to the future . . . " (*LFA*, 195). The coffee crop was not the focus of this complaint, for in the same letter she said, "the farm is now in a completely different state from when I took it over . . . everything is prospering . . . our bad name is beginning to be a thing of the past . . . " (*LFA*, 194).

As in previous years, when circumstances went beyond her control, her health suffered. She did not list her symptoms, but claimed, "I am not well . . . I must go home next year; I seriously think that I will die if I do not . . . . Of course it is not certain that I am going to die; but it is a good deal more likely than anyone at home believes" (*LFA*, 194–5).

The long rains began on time, in mid March 1924, dropping onto the house sheets of water that overflowed the eaves of the tiled roof. At times it rained so hard that the house seemed to be draped in flowing robes of water. These cloudbursts were short-lived, however, and the sun came out gloriously after an hour or two. After one of these rains—perhaps while water still trickled from the gutters and dripped from the trees—Denys Finch Hatton drove up to the house in the open-topped Hudson he had brought out from England in 1922. Karen indicated in a letter to Thomas that she was overcome with rapture at his arrival (*LFA*, 196).

Denys had spent two enjoyable months in the Masai country of Tanganyika, where he had investigated what he referred to as a gold "scare" (DFH to KR 3-21-24). He had not been impressed with what he found. While in Tanganyika, he had arranged for a license to shoot twenty-five elephants. He planned to spend the months of June and July 1924, collecting ivory, which would provide some welcome income, but he would not go out on safari until the end of the long rains.

The idea that he might stay for several weeks placed Karen in a state of ecstasy, but she concealed this from Denys. Letters home made it clear that she confined her conversation with Denys to the usual anecdotes and teasing (*LFA*, 196). They discussed colony news and current scandals. Soon a new branch of the railway would reach from Nakuru to the Uasin Gishu plateau and connect with the line to Lake Victoria. Now that the Indian question had been temporarily settled, and her western land had been made more attractive by the new trains, Karen would be able to sell off her Uasin Gishu farm and use the money to pay some of her debts. Farmers envisioned an end

to the shortage of field hands caused when the government commandeered workers for building the railway. A few settlers complained that
Lord Delamere had used his influence to have the rail line routed near
his land, but Denys had it on good authority that Delamere had long
since sold nearly all of his 100,000 acres in the region.

Delamere was just then the subject of sympathy because he
had been severely injured in an assault in December 1923. Jock
Purves, Beryl's husband, had descended upon him in a drunken rage,
accusing Delamere of allowing his son Tom and his manager, Boy
Long, to sleep with Beryl. Delamere was rumored to have incurred a
broken neck in the altercation, and would be confined to bed for at
least six months. Beryl had left Purves—some said, for good—and had
gone to England, where she was seeking an abortion (*SOTM*, 362). No
one knew who the father of the child was. Karen wrote to her mother,
"I think it would be better if Beryl stayed away . . . I don't think she
has the slightest idea that in some ways people are blaming her . . . "
(*SOTM*, 55).

Denys himself was not feeling particularly well, and this
surprised Karen. She was used to the impression that he lived above
worry; it was as though he lived in another, clearer dimension. But now
she began to realize, as she says of a character resembling Denys in
"The Dreamers," that the "extraordinary impression of great strength
was somehow false after all"; he had not all the strength that he showed
(*SGT*, 283). For some time he had not been able to tolerate winter in
Europe. In 1918, when he had entered flight training in Egypt, he
failed to pass the physical for combat in a northern climate, and the air
corps limited his service to the tropics (DFH to KR 7-?-18). On this
occasion Denys did not go into detail with Karen about his ailments;
but much later he speculated that his heart was bad (*LFA*, 328).
Perhaps his association with Berkeley Cole, who had a bad heart, had
given him cause to worry about his own. Denys's father suffered from
heart trouble, and his favorite uncle, Harold Finch Hatton, had died of
a heart attack at the age of forty-eight. At the moment Denys's stomach
was bothering him, and his discomfort seems to have appeared simulta-
neously with news from England that his mother was unwell. He was
moping, as only a close friend such as Karen could have noted (*SWS*, 44).

Karen made an observation in the many-chaptered essay she was still writing on "Marriage": "Truth cannot be fully achieved before people know all about each other's childhood love affairs and toothaches in detail" (*OMM*, 72). One may imagine that she crooned over him, made him comfortable, played soothing music on the gramophone, directed Hassan to prepare soups and soft custards for him, and created an atmosphere of refuge from his trials. Perhaps she forgave him for not coming at Christmas, and for not explaining why. A few weeks later she elucidated a grand conclusion in a letter to Aunt Bess: "I do not think there can ever be justification in *demanding* confidences, any more than love. Nor can there be a demand for reciprocity . . . " (*LFA*, 207–8). However, Denys's intimate visit provided the "reciprocity" for which she had earlier yearned.

In her essay on marriage and sexuality, Karen emphasized the importance of playfulness in maintaining a healthy love affair. She refers to word games in various writings—conjuring up voyages by dhow with Berkeley, fictional characters imagining themselves in far-away lands and times, Denys listening to her invent stories. Her tales and her correspondence suggest that she and Denys also practiced an intimate game that he may have learned at school. Late at night, in an atmosphere of wine and high feelings, perhaps they amused them-selves with tricks of conversation in which ordinary descriptions held erotic meaning. Imitating in stories the kinds of seductions cleverly written in code in classical poetry, and in the Bible, one of Denys's favorite works, Karen often hid sexual descriptions in symbolism. In "The Cloak," the passionate man knocks at the window of his lady's chamber and pleads, "Open to me, my sister . . . for my head is filled with dew . . . " (*LT*, 31). And in *Out of Africa* the farmer receives the passionately desired rain: "Give me enough and more than enough. My heart is bared to thee now, and I will not let thee go except thou bless me. Drown me if you like, but kill me not with caprices. No *coitus interruptus*, heaven, heaven!" (*OA*, 286).

Referring to the potential of games to enhance the relation-ship between lovers, Karen said, "Much is demanded of those who are to be really proficient at play. Courage and imagination, humor and intelligence, but in particular that blend of unselfishness, generosity,

self-control and courtesy that is called *gentilezza*" (*OMM*, 83). These
qualities describe perfectly her view of Denys's character.

Karen wrote to Aunt Bess, "There are many aspects of life that
are so intimate that no one can be expected to reveal information about
them . . . " (*LFA*, 206). But Denys seems to have begun opening
himself to her. In a letter to Thomas, she said, "I will not write any more
now; I can't collect my thoughts. Denys is staying here at present and
I have never been as happy, nor half as happy, in my life as I am now.
You, who have known what it means really to care for someone, —and
not because of reasons of circumstance and habit and so on, as seems
to be the case in most marriages and love affairs that I have known, but
solely because one has met with the most wonderful being on earth, —
you can understand what it means to be happy in this way, and how it
occupies all one's thought and all one's being . . . " (*LFA*, 196).

But she sensed there was still much about Denys she did
not know. She mentioned to Aunt Bess the "deceptions" that
people who are "forced by society to live at close range mutually
pay each other" (*LFA*, 205). Karen was in no way ready to make
Denys aware of her own thoughts. She repeated to Thomas her
caution of the previous year, "Nor if, for instance, I should die, and
you should later meet Denys, must you ever let him know that I
have written or spoken of him to you . . . " (*LFA*, 196).

* 5 *

Denys's visit was, as usual, an exhausting period for Karen,
since his normal sleeping and waking hours were the reverse of hers:
he preferred to be up at dawn and in bed early, while she was able to
carry on projects well into the night, provided she could rest later.
Trying to keep pace with Denys, she arose early to go shooting with
him, to take walks, or to ride in the reserve. At night their wine and talk
aroused her, and, once he had gone to bed, she was often awake for
hours, so that, overall, when he was in her house, she hardly slept at all.
Intensely stimulated by his presence, she kept going on nervous
energy—and occasionally, as she hints in "The Dreamers," by chew-
ing *miraa*, an amphetamine-like plant easily obtained in East Africa
(*SWS*, 191).

While Denys stayed with her, Karen extracted as much as she could from each day he spent with her, but she was already looking ahead with dread to the moment of his departure. Later she admitted to Thomas, "it has become a kind of habit or fixed idea with me to be continually anticipating like this and calculating how much is left of anything . . ." (*LFA*, 280). She attributed this compulsion to years of seesawing between happiness and great difficulties. The thought of his leaving was nearly enough to spoil the pleasure she took in his company. So it was devastating to her when, on March 16, 1924, after barely a week at her house, Denys received two urgent letters from home, one from his father and one from his brother reporting that his mother had suffered a stroke. Taking time only to pack a bag, and leaving most of his gear behind, he left for Mombasa. Karen held a faint hope that his passage would be delayed, but soon, on a torn scrap of paper, she received the following note:

> Dear Tania,
>   Goodbye—I settled after all I ought to go home and I have managed to squeeze into the *Llanstephan*.
>   Goodbye and thank you for so many pleas- ant days when I was so bad tempered. Denys. (DFH to KB 3-19-24?: *KO*, 18)

Perhaps she found this hasty and inelegant note touching. He was not in the habit of writing to her. She saved it, for it was worth fondling from time to time. Then, overwhelmed that he had gone, she collapsed.

For two weeks she did not get out of bed. She wrote her mother that she was ill but did not say what was wrong. Whatever her symptoms, she seemed to be suffering from anxiety, and it was not the farm that troubled her but her romantic life. The price of coffee was up, land values were increasing, farmers in the colony had regained their optimism, and as for her own farm, Karen had told Thomas everything was prospering (*LFA*, 194). But she added, "in a way the more happy and satisfied one feels at the moment the more nerve-racking it is" (*LFA*, 195). The uncertainty of her relationship with Denys had become nearly intolerable. She wrote to Thomas: "I know you can understand that there is a good deal of anxiety bound up in this shaurie; for me it has come to be more and more the only thing that matters in my life, and how will it end? . . . the very fact of possessing something or having possessed something that is of such immense value to one, brings its own terror with it . . . " (*LFA*, 196).

The last week in April 1924, she was aroused by a letter from Bror saying he had fallen ill while hunting in Uganda. A friend sent a note confirming that Bror appeared to be dying. He was suffering from sores, inflamed joints, fever, and "a kind of paralysis." Karen was convinced it was his "old illness," syphilis (*LFA*, 214).

She made an impassioned decision: she would offer Bror a place in her house again, where he could recuperate or spend his last days. Since this was against the agreement she had signed with Uncle Aage in 1922, she told Thomas she accepted freely the risk of being dismissed as managing director of the farm. But Bror proved more resilient than expected. In his robust manner, he recovered—long before he could decline her offer.

She had to console herself with having taken in Old Aarup. This charitable effort had ended on April 7, 1924, when, after living on the farm only two months, the old man died of a heart attack while walking up the road to her house. Kamante and Dickens helped Karen carry the body back to Aarup's cottage; later, when the police came in a blinding rain to collect the corpse for burial in Nairobi, the road was a river. The bearers were drenched loading the dead man into the police lorry, which afterwards fairly floated away to town. Karen thought Aarup would have approved of the drama surrounding his departure from the farm.

That same day, Rose Cartwright, sister of Geoffrey Buxton, Denys's friend from childhood, had looked in on Karen. Rose, who had married Algy Cartwright and was eight months pregnant in April 1924, had come to Nairobi for supplies. She and her husband ran a farm in the Rift Valley, near Gilgil.

Karen felt some nervous excitement when Rose visited, for Rose was a link to Denys, and a source of information about him. But it is likely that Karen approached the subject with caution. It would not do for Denys to believe she had been interrogating his friends. She orchestrated her talks with Rose, one may imagine, with a measured intensity that left her nearly trembling from the effort of guiding the conversation subtly to Denys. Rose was soft-spoken and unemotional; she responded to Karen's probes in an uncomplicated way, as though unaware of the importance placed on her answers. She was surely sorry to hear that Denys's mother was ill; their families had been friends for years, and she knew that Denys was devoted to his mother. Nan Finch Hatton had been particularly lovely as a young woman, and Denys had been her favorite child. The family doted on Denys. He had a marvelous sense of humor. He was full of pranks—kind ones, received with laughter—and he had a gift for mimicry even when he was small. Karen was not surprised, since she herself had sometimes been the target of his imitations. When she worried aloud to Denys about some trivial exasperation on the farm, he would mock her by drawing himself to attention in the Somali attitude of despair, his arms draped with theatrical helplessness at his sides. As for his playing football with Kamante, Rose could testify that Denys had always been athletically gifted. At Eton he had been captain of his football team, and he was quite good, too, at golf and cricket.

Rose was adapting to living in a crude bungalow on her farm. Her husband was gone a great deal, and she often ran the farm by herself. She seemed to accept her lot complacently; Karen may have envied her lack of anxiety. She herself had finally recovered from whatever had sent her to bed after Denys left. She had wanted to go on home leave, but wrote to her mother during the second week of May 1924, "I am actually somewhat better now and I think I can hold on until next spring...." (*LFA*, 217) By then she would have seen Denys again, and perhaps would be invited to travel on the same boat with him when he made his yearly trip to Europe.

* 6 *

In the middle of May 1924, Berkeley Cole arrived at the farm to spend the weekend. The visit had a special purpose: he had been given the responsibility of distributing medals of valor to twelve Masai chiefs living in the reserve across the river from Karen's estate. Berkeley, who along with his brother Galbraith, had lived in the Kenya highlands since at least 1907, spoke fluent Masai. Like Lord Delamere, he and Galbraith found the Masai to be the colony's noblest tribe. They studied their customs because they desired to be on social terms with them—in Karen's view, in the way people of a certain class seek others at their level.

Karen regarded Berkeley and Delamere, as well as Denys, as Englishmen who represented the old, genuine aristocracy. She said they were noblemen "of a certain class and period" (*LFA*, 219), more reminiscent of the Elizabethan age than of Victorian or Edwardian England. She had difficulty putting her finger on what she meant by this, but felt that a nobleman was able to adopt a unique attitude toward his future. He had already achieved what ordinary men were striving for; he was at the pinnacle of his social milieu. So he approached the future gracefully, without the struggle to achieve status that occupied the middle class.

Karen was impressed by the way Denys ignored the future, content to live day to day, unhaunted by goals. He had never felt the necessity to achieve. Children with titles came into the world with laurels already in place. Karen wrote an essay to Aunt Bess in which she described the character of the "English"—a euphemism for Denys, Berkeley, Delamere, and her other titled friends. Without realizing it, she distinguished in the essay between the aristocratic and the middle-class temperaments. The "English" temperament—and she stressed that she meant the English aristocracy prior to Victorian times—resembled a "park." In contrast to a classical garden of the French variety, wherein the paths were linear, the bushes sculpted along regular lines, and the flowers arranged in rigid ensembles, the English park was a random creation, with mixtures of flowers and trees, broad, expansive lawns, and walkways flowing in various directions according to the choice of the wanderer. To her such a park represented freedom, and this was the essential element in the character of Englishmen such as Denys and Berkeley. They had no need to present a façade to society, nor to work to make something of their lives; they could wander and enjoy life.

In stressing to Aunt Bess that her view of the English excluded the Victorians, Karen delineated the difference between the middle class and the aristocracy. Queen Victoria and her husband, Prince Albert, represented values that had become irrevocably tied to the concept of middle-class character: strict moral rectitude, strong family ties, hard work, and belief that material progress led to salvation. The Victorians justified to themselves spreading their empire around the world through the certainty that they were bestowing the benefits of industrial civilization on savages. When Karen said she "hated morality," she was referring to middle-class, essentially Victorian, self-righteousness. The Westenholz side of her family, especially Aunt Bess, embodied this spirit of morality, while the Dinesens and their aristocratic kin, the Frijses, she believed, were free of it.

Karen had always sought to distance herself from her middle-class upbringing, but her striving for success on the farm represented the essence of the middle class ethic. Periodically she spoke out against conventional morality, but she was not free of its constraints. She feared being named the guilty party in her divorce because of the accepted conviction that the woman must hold the family together. Men were thought to be morally inferior to women, thus they could be forgiven for infidelity; but a woman who asked her husband to leave, as Karen had, failed in her duty to be forgiving and supportive of her husband, no matter what his indiscretions.

Paradoxically, Karen was never more strikingly bourgeois than when compared to Cockie Birkbeck. Karen's manner of dress, staid and tweed, contrasted with Cockie's bow-emblazoned, carefree frocks. Cockie was a person who took on risks, plunged into the future. She did not tie herself to one husband, nor to a way of life like farming that might constrict her options. Karen's approach to the future was filled with angst, related to the responsibility for her fate, well described by Søren Kierkegaard, the Danish philosopher who was currently in vogue among the European bourgeoisie. Karen referred to him at times in her letters—although not so frequently as she referred to Einstein. She felt panic when she thought she had not carried out her responsibility to her destiny.

By contrast, Berkeley and Denys had grown up unconcerned about fate. Educated at a time when religion had gone out of favor at

British universities, they treated piety and clerics with amusement and skepticism. Although Denys had been taught to respect the Bible as literature, he was unaffected by its exhortations to serve. Men of his class and generation were content to seek a happy life. Bored by their parents' preoccupation with saving the world, they exaggerated their disinterest in causes, a middle-class preoccupation.

This attitude had left Britain precariously unprepared for the Great War, for war required organization, and few in England understood how to meet the challenge. As Karen said, "the Germans . . . had their affairs impeccably well-organized, calculated for every eventuality, while the English waged war by muddling through" (*LFA*, 234). In her view, Denys and Delamere lived their lives in this manner, "only able to practice this system because of the enormous capital resources they have to fall back upon . . . so that miscalculations and setbacks have no material effect on them . . . " (*LFA*, 234).

* *

Berkeley, who had been given medals to hand out to the Masai in appreciation for bravery during the war, arrived at Karen's house without any plan for how to do this. It was going to be difficult to pin medals on naked men. Moreover, the Masai might be confounded by their design and purpose, let alone the reason for receiving them, some six years following the end of the war.

Berkeley sensed that the presentation required some ceremony. He therefore drove out to the *manyattas*, villages of oblong houses made from earth and dung surrounded by thorn *bomas*, to ask the chiefs to appear at such and such a time on the lawn in front of Karen's house. When they had assembled the following day, he made them wait a long while to impress upon them the importance of the occasion. Karen had directed that an easy chair be placed on a rise in the lawn to give the impression that a visiting potentate was about to present a history-making speech.

The Masai, wearing ochre-red blankets fastened over one shoulder like togas, were otherwise unclothed. Every aspect of their bodies, from legs to cheekbones, was long and graceful. They listened to Berkeley's oration and accepted the medals solemnly, stretching out their hands to meet Berkeley's. They had acted as scouts during the war and had refused to be used as bearers for the carrier corps. Europeans had been unsuccessful in drafting them to work on farms. Like other nobility, they felt no obligation to work. They pursued a life as wanderers, retaining the freedom to move their flocks at will to other pastures. They were not surprised to be honored by His Majesty's government, for life itself had honored them. The medals were a display of admiration of which they were tolerant. They turned them curiously in their hands and carried them away in the same serious manner with which Berkeley returned to the house.

* 7 *

During the months of Denys's absence, the farm prospered. Karen picked coffee along with the Africans in the month of June, scouring the rows with a striped Kikuyu basket strung from her shoulder. The berries were smaller than she would have wished, but abundant. The rainy season continued well into the month of June. Mornings were overcast and cold enough to warrant wearing two cardigans and good shoes while working in the fields.

Karen was experiencing, and trying to ignore, a kind of "lumbago" similar to the "arthritis" she had felt in 1918. She described shooting pains in her heels, hands, and ears that were driving her mad, "like a toothache" (*LFA*, 221). The weather was too cloudy for her to call it sunstroke; she was perhaps afflicted again with cinchonism, or may have compounded her misery by taking aspirin, too much of which leads to the same kind of pain. "I think there is something the matter with my nerves," she said (*LFA*, 221), and this was correct, for such shooting pains reflect a poisoning of the nervous system.

Once the rains ended, her symptoms subsided. However, elsewhere on the farm there was sickness. She was called to the Kikuyu village to examine children suffering from bubonic plague. Relatively few deaths resulted, but she directed her workers to put out rat poison, warning them to hide it from the dogs and children. She was particularly anxious that there be no illness in the coming months, for a great event was soon to occur: the arrival in Africa, after many years of

Karen's pleas, of her mother, Ingeborg Dinesen. Farah had given Juma and Hassan three months' furlough, so that they would request no leave during the important visit. Karen was intent upon presenting a well-kept house.

The voyage of a sixty-eight-year-old woman to Africa was no light undertaking. Karen wondered if her mother could be happily entertained by what Africa offered. How was her mother to spend her days? Would she stroll among the flowers, as she did at home? Or sew? Would she approve of the staff? Karen worried that her mother had few interests or hobbies other than her family. Was Karen to be her companion throughout all the waking hours? The burden of entertaining grew in her mind, so that she actually began to dread her mother's arrival—that same arrival for which she had so long yearned. It relieved her to learn that Thomas was to accompany Ingeborg Dinesen to Africa. It was decided they would sail for Africa in the month of October, on the French liner, S. S. *Chambord*. This meant they would arrive during the season of short rains. They could expect some glorious weather at Christmas time, and they would see the country green and blooming, and the coffee blossoming in the fields.

One aspect of these plans, however, created further anxiety. Perhaps from gossip in Nairobi, Karen learned that Denys Finch Hatton was due to return in October. It was said that he too was coming out on a French ship. Denys might travel with her family. She was mortified at the thought that her mother or Thomas might reveal how she had rhapsodized about him. She wrote Thomas a hasty note cautioning him, "it would be best if you ask Mother to appear as if she has never heard of him" (*LFA*, 226).

* 8 *

The arrival on November 5, 1924, of Karen's mother and brother was the subject of enormous anticipation by the people of the farm. They gathered on the lawn to greet the mother of the *Msabu* and her brother, whom they remembered with affection. Farah had been sent to Mombasa to greet them, for Karen always avoided the uncomfortable trip to the coast. But Thomas was familiar with the arrangements and itinerary to Nairobi—the least stifling coastal hotel, the late afternoon train that coursed first across the desert, then mounted the uplands during the night, arriving about dawn in the Athi Plains, and finally reached the Nairobi depot toward ten o'clock in the morning. Karen was at the station to meet them. When Denys Finch Hatton stepped down from the train, Karen may have been slightly unsettled; she felt her attention divided. However, Denys withdrew to see about lodgings at Muthaiga.

Thomas and their mother had arrived in time to see the jacaranda trees in bloom. The delicate blue flowers towered over the surrounding woods and lined the drives of some estates in a way to amaze visitors. The veranda of Karen's house was drenched in the fuchsia and orange of bougainvillea and frangipani. Inside were bouquets of roses and lilies, carnations and pink pyrethrum. The parquet floors had been polished, the rugs and leopard skins shaken and aired, the bedrooms laid with freshly ironed linen, and the paraffin lamps shined and filled with scented oil. Juma greeted them in his fez and embroidered waistcoat, and the houseboys lined up to bow to the guests.

Ingeborg Dinesen, dressed in the style of Edwardian widows, all in black with her hemline reaching to the tops of her high black shoes, returned their greetings graciously, shaking hands with the servants and speaking their names. She was smaller than Karen, her thick white hair drawn into a bun, her eyes dark but smaller than those of the *Memsahib*.

It was Thomas's intention to put on boots and khakis and ride into the reserve. Aboard ship he had held conversations with Finch Hatton about the quality of the game; both agreed that the numbers were decreasing alarmingly. Thomas established rapport with Denys on the journey. He beat Denys in chess—which he suspected with amusement had displeased Finch Hatton (*MSID*, 101). As prearranged with Karen, he did not mention to Denys that he had once driven her car over the dam on the farm. Denys had attempted the trick just before leaving in April 1924, and was extremely pleased with himself for doing it. Karen had warned Thomas not to spoil Denys's sense of achievement by bragging that he had done it, too. She told Thomas: "I do not wish to deprive him of his game" (*LFA*, 215).

While Finch Hatton was in England, his mother had died, and he himself had not been well. He had had his appendix removed in May 1924; however, he was now recuperated. He had returned to Africa to see about earning "an honest penny" (DFH to KR 3-21-24). He had not been able to make enough money from his annuities—from the Anglo-Baltic Timber Company in Norway and Kiptiget, Ltd., in Kenya. His assets too were suffering from the world-wide slump in land prices and agricultural goods. He was disappointed that his hunting trip to Tanganyika had fallen through, since he had thought to recoup his losses somewhat in ivory, but now he was planning to take wealthy customers out on safari. The thought of Denys's having to hunt from necessity disturbed Karen; she had always thought that, as a true aristocrat, he lived above economic considerations, and hunted merely to amuse himself. He was now adopting the same livelihood pursued in desperation by Bror.

In the midst of preparing his safari gear for more formal undertakings, Denys took time to call at the farm during the visit of Karen's mother. Karen was glad that Denys had met her. Although both Ingeborg Dinesen and Thomas had a certain Danish provincialness that Denys perhaps found quaint—Karen had before remarked, "I do think Danish conviviality is frightful!" (LFA, 193)—their demeanor was aristocratic by virtue of wealth, and Karen believed they would survive a comparison to Denys's own, titled family.

Finch Hatton seemed to enjoy spending time with the Dinesens. He accompanied them on a picnic in the Ngong Hills, and on another occasion drove with them in his own car—since Karen's old car could not withstand the rough terrain—into the game reserve. To reach the reserve they had only to cross the river that formed the southwestern boundary of the farm and drive out across the plains. Toward Christmas the trail could be negotiated without encountering much mud, and the grass was short enough to see wildlife. On a good day they sighted families of warthogs hightailing through the grass, giraffes grazing in the ravines among the acacia trees, herds of zebra and wildebeest mingling together against the horizon, a pride or two of lions dozing on a sandy outcrop, families of ostriches strutting in line, rhinos in groups of two or three bumbling across the road, and the occasional cheetah streaking after its prey.

Despite these gorgeous attractions, Karen's mother made plans to leave for Denmark on January 14, 1925, after a stay in Africa of only two months. She seemed pleased with the farm and content to keep her investment in Karen Coffee Corporation, but she wanted to return to her granddaughter Mitten (Karen), without a mother since Ea's death. Karen and Thomas were unhappy with her decision, because she would arrive in Europe before winter had ended; the seas would be rough, and traveling alone would be inconvenient and uncomfortable for her. Thomas wanted to stay in Africa until spring; he had persuaded Farah to lead him on safari in Somaliland. Karen herself had made plans to go home, but not until March. She could not leave the farm until the coffee crop was ready for market, and the harvest had only just got under way. She would have liked to keep her mother until March, for she hated traveling alone. But Ingeborg Dinesen was firm. Her children thought she had become somewhat unreasonable since the death of Ea, whose loss she had not accepted well.

The day her mother left, Karen received a telegram from her Danish solicitor, Repsdorph, announcing that her divorce from Bror was final. "Strange," she said, "that it should have been on the eleventh anniversary of my marriage" (*LFA*, 229). In a notebook she jotted down a poem entitled "Au Revoir," in which she compared her marriage to a duel, honorably engaged and justifiably ended, testifying to the honor of their peculiar love (*ID*, 201).

Denys planned to rehearse his new occupation as safari guide during the month of January 1925. He had lined up a wealthy client named McLean and would begin by camping with him in the Ngong Hills, where he hoped to find impressive numbers of bushbuck and observe the large herd of Cape buffalo. Karen, who had been introduced to McLean, desired to accompany them; she had for some time been hosting, as it were, people wishing to visit the Ngong Hills and felt almost as if the hills were part of her farm. Denys and McLean proposed to carry out their brief safari during the full moon of the last week of January 1925. With them they would take the Kikuyu boy Kamante, whom Karen was now training to cook.

1925

Karen had begun to train Kamante in the kitchen during the three-month furlough of her cook, Hassan, in 1924. Following the illness that had brought Kamante to Karen's attention in 1921, he had worked in Karen's house, first as a house *toto*—looking after the dogs and doing small errands—and then as a kitchen boy, peeling vegetables, fetching water, feeding the charcoal oven, and otherwise doing Hassan's bidding. When Karen came into the dim little outbuilding to discuss new recipes with Hassan, Kamante would be sitting quietly in a corner preparing vegetables. He listened to Karen give Hassan directions for rolling and dicing, blending and whipping, arranging and serving a variety of delicacies. Sometimes after Karen left the kitchen, Hassan would murmur over the recipe, unable to keep clear the sequence. Then Kamante, as though humming the refrain of a song, would repeat the instructions. Karen would come upon them as Kamante's slender hands demonstrated to Hassan her methods for cooking.

Kamante's fascination with cooking struck Karen as the sign of a kindred spirit; she was herself learning to cook and made him part of her endeavor, and he proved a worthy partner. In Hassan's absence, he began to master poaching and kneading, pastry and soups. She foresaw a great career for him in the kitchen, one that would add to the name of her house and table. Although he was a neophyte, Karen thought he could handle the responsibilities of a cook on safari, where the meals would be game, vegetables from tins, bread, and fruit.

To begin the adventure, Karen, Denys, and McLean set out for the Ngong Hills on horses; their gear was carried on the heads of twenty-five porters. The Africans trod the dusty paths barefoot, in single file, singing a rhythmic chant. Accompanying them were Kamau, a Kikuyu from the farm whom Denys had hired, Nduetti, one of Karen's houseboys, and Farah and Kamante. The track to the summit wound through low forest, then crossed the tree line, above which the vegetation was interrupted only by low bushes and buffalo paths. A variety of wildflowers blooming after the rains colored the slopes violet, yellow, white, and pink. A path along the summits linked the hills together, rising and falling a few hundred feet between peaks, so that the hunters could walk along the ridge from hill to hill without descending into foothills; indeed the hills were really one extended mountain with its summit gracefully scooped out into a row of rounded prominences. Near the top the riders dismounted and directed the porters to pitch their tents. From their campsite they could see Karen's farm at the foot of the hills and, far to the east, Nairobi. To the west, on the other side of the ridge, the hills fell two thousand feet to the Rift Valley. The hunters camped two nights while the moon was full. Their only trophies were bushbuck, because regulations forbade shooting female buffalo and their calves; and the bulls wisely stayed away. However, during the full moon of February, Denys was due to take McLean and his wife and sister on another, more ambitious safari in the Masai Reserve; there they would find a large variety of game.

Denys spent the intervening few weeks at Karen's house, preferring the farm to Muthaiga, where he was increasingly loathe to leave his belongings. There had been thefts at Muthaiga; the African staff was under suspicion; and Denys did not want to lose his expensive books and guns, his safari gear, his clothes, and the shoes made to his own design by a bootier in England. Karen, who saw the chance for which she had dreamed, assured him her own servants were trustworthy and offered him the use of her house and space to store his possessions for as long as he wished. She designated permanently for him the room he had always used, and directed her carpenter, Pooran Singh, to mount an extra row of hooks for Denys's hats. His books, many of which she had already read—including, most recently, the works of George Bernard Shaw—she shelved beside her own in a bookcase in the sitting room.

It was agreed between Denys and Karen that, when he returned from his safari with McLean, Denys would stay in her house, although she herself would have already left for Europe. She did not contemplate returning in less than eight months. She had stayed in Africa too long without going home, and her health had suffered. The contracts of civil servants in Kenya stipulated six months' home leave every three years; salaried farm workers like herself were generally granted a holiday at least every four years for health reasons, but Karen had spent five continuous years in Africa. However, she had no intention of traveling directly to Denmark. She still regarded her divorce as a failure and was embarrassed to confront the pity of her family and friends. She hoped to vacation in Paris, perhaps take some art classes, and then proceed to a resort on the Riviera when the weather was warm. Sir Northrup and Lady McMillan would rendezvous with her at Nice.

Denys was planning to make his usual spring trip to England but was vague about when he would sail. They did not arrange to meet in Europe but, as long as he had accepted the use of Karen's house, she might still hear something from him while she was in Denmark.

* 2 *

For nearly two years, whenever the legislative council sat, Berkeley Cole had made his appearance at the farm. Karen liked to see him almost as much as she liked seeing Denys. The engine of his old car made a characteristic clatter as it came up the drive. At the sound, her deerhounds barked joyfully. Berkeley would step down from his car with energy amusing in such a small man, mount the steps of the veranda, rumple the dogs, and sweep into the house with exaggerated compliments for the hostess and some joking criticism revealing his fondness for Karen and her house. Once he saw a rat as he came up the road, and this led him into a rousing discourse, before he had had a chance to sit down, on the importance of cats on a farm. Berkeley had a way of holding himself stiffly when declaiming, with his head cocked to one side as though his shoulders were crooked. He fairly hopped as he held forth on a topic important to him—which nearly all his topics were—his slender arms in sleeves rolled to the elbow, delicate fingers gesturing in the air. Karen was amused at the limits of his subject matter, for he could discuss wine, politics, the Masai, domestic animals, poetry, and love without marriage; yet on other subjects which she liked to propose—religion, modern literature, and Denys Finch Hatton, for example—he was blank, uncomfortable and, ultimately, bored. Having once proclaimed his views on the topics preoccupying him, he would sink exhaustedly in his chair and lapse into silence.

Berkeley was Karen's best friend in Kenya; she was comfortable with him in a way she could not be with Denys, toward whom she must always maintain a façade of casual friendship. However, despite her fondness for Berkeley, and the soothing comfort he brought to her house, she could not talk to him about everything. She told Aunt Bess she had known only three people in her life to whom she could entrust all confidences—Thomas, Farah, and a long-time family friend named Ellen Wanscher (*LFA*, 208). Not even Berkeley was privy to her true feelings about Denys.

Berkeley, whose long-standing heart condition required that injections of medication be given to him by his Somali servant, worried his friends with fainting spells in their houses. His family was prone to rheumatic conditions. His sister, Florence, wife of Lord Delamere, had died at the age of 36—possibly from the long effects of rheumatic fever—and his brother, Galbraith, suffered from rheumatoid arthritis, which had made him an old man in his early forties. In March 1925, as Karen prepared to leave for Europe, she received word from Berkeley that he was coming to Nairobi. She knew he was not well and wired him: "Will you not come and stay at Ngong for the sitting of the council bring bottles." He wired back, "Your telegram straight from heaven arriving with bottles" (*OA*, 232).

Berkeley's appearance alarmed her. He was thinner and paler than she had ever seen him; his ankles were swollen, and he was painfully breathless. He who had always complimented her cooking would now barely taste the food she prepared. He sat limply at the table, talking little. She asked what the doctor had advised him to do. He said that he had been told to go to bed and stay there for not less than a month. She insisted that he remain with her and she would care for him. She would put off her trip to Europe until he was better. After some silence, he answered, "My dear, I could not do it. If I did it to please you, what should I be afterwards?" (*OA*, 232)

What should she do with friends when they would not accept her help? With a heavy heart, Karen set sail for Europe on March 5, 1925. Thomas and Farah sailed with her as far as Aden and then left for their tour of Somaliland. When Karen arrived in Paris on March 28, she learned that Berkeley had died. At the age of forty-three, as he descended from his car at his own farm, his heart had stopped.

* 3 *

In the spring of 1925 Paris was cold and damp. The warmth of its music and paintings, for which Karen had longed over the previous five years, failed to soften her impression of the frightful chill in the museums and halls, where the heat had been turned off, according to the yearly schedule, on April 1. Karen found herself miserably reluctant to leave the room she had taken in a little boarding house on the rue St. Honoré. Here she passed her fortieth birthday alone, unable to motivate herself to begin the painting lessons she had mentioned so consistently in her letters from the farm.

The white stone buildings of Paris seemed bleak—gray in the misty weather, and streaked with black soot. Her walks in the city did not inspire her, for she was painfully chilled. Her clothes, designed for cool Nairobi evenings, did not protect her from the unrelenting damp wind and cold. Besides, her dresses were frayed and faded after years of being scrubbed by servants in Africa. She must buy herself something new; she wrote to her mother: "I have been looking so ill groomed, with holes in my shoes and my clothes more or less in rags . . . " (*LFA*, 232).

Studying art in Paris and then traveling alone to the Riviera had begun to seem impractical. Anemic, after five years of African diseases and dosing herself with arsenic, Karen was unable to cope with such an itinerary. More importantly, her self-confidence had suffered from years of fear of failure on the farm, and from her divorce. Although her attacks of panic had receded, being alone put her into a state of anxiety that worsened when she thought of going on alone to a resort on the Riviera.

In Paris her social outings involved friends she had known in Africa. She went to tea at the Polowtzoffs', with whom she and Bror had spent time in 1919, but she had few other contacts in the city. She was holding out for her anticipated rendezvous with the McMillans, when she received news that Sir Northrup, aged fifty-three, had collapsed and died in Nice. A man who had spent his life overweight, by any standards, could be expected to meet a premature death, but to Karen the loss represented a demoralizing shock. Despite previous avowals that she could not go home while her divorce *shaurie* was fresh, all she wanted after three weeks in Paris was to see her mother. On April 22, 1925, she fled Paris on the train and traveled, via Hamburg, back to Denmark.

* 4 *

The centuries-old farmhouse at Rungstedlund was so quiet one could hear the clock ticking almost any time of day. In contrast to Karen's house in Africa, the doors were not left open in fine weather so that *totos* could steal in to watch the cuckoo. But Karen enjoyed being back in Denmark more than she had thought possible. It was a relief to be free of the problems, uncertainty, and difficulties of the farm. She was invigorated by the view of the sea from her mother's house, and walked in the woods and meadows of the estate. The apple trees were blooming and lilacs budding; daffodils, tulips, and hyacinths spiked colorfully in the garden. Her long-held yearning to scent the fragrances of Denmark was assuaged.

One of her first tasks at home was to consult Dr. Rasch about the symptoms she had experienced over the previous five years. He examined her, took a sample of her spinal fluid, and tested her blood. The Wasserman test was negative, and he found no signs that she still had syphilis. He was not surprised, for the experience of physicians over the previous fifteen years was that arsenic injections such as she had undergone in 1915 were indeed effective in arresting the disease. She was anemic, and this might be due to a number of causes; tropical illnesses such as malaria and dysentery were notorious for causing chronic symptoms and stealthily undermining one's health. Although as a physician Rasch was unusually perspicacious, perhaps he did not know that she continued to dose herself with elixir of arsenic whenever she had symptoms of any kind. In keeping with her role as healer on the farm, she maintained a supply of medicines that she administered to herself upon her own advice. From reading about the great poets and philosophers, like Nietzsche, rumored to have suffered from syphilis, she may have become convinced that her disease would not be cured. She numbered herself among the tragically romantic victims, and possibly felt a greater association with her father because of it. She had not forgotten the words of the French physician who in 1915 had doubted she could be healed. Rasch sent her home with advice about recuperating from anemia and assured her that the Danish air and careful nutrition would go a long way toward improving her health. He expected that she would not need his expertise again in the matter of syphilis, and there is no evidence that she was seen by him again.

Karen envisioned taking some classes in *haute cuisine* at the royal kitchens during her stay in Denmark. She was also going to ask her former painting instructor, Bertha Dorph, to critique the portraits she had done in Africa. And Aunt Bess, who had always believed in and insisted upon Karen's talent for writing, had kindly made arrangements for her to meet the greatest Danish literary figure of the day, Georg Brandes.

Aunt Bess's efforts to arrange an introduction to Georg Brandes were the result of a letter she had received from Karen early in 1924, in which Karen blamed Aunt Bess for a great disappointment of her youth. Brandes had been one of Karen's heroes from an early age. As a literary critic, he had promoted the careers of Danish writers, including her father, for several decades; his renown extended across literary Europe. The newspapers, for whom Brandes's life was irresistibly titillating, kept a running account of his activities and opinions. His views shocked the staid, conservative public. He had been one of the first figures in Denmark to espouse atheism, his sexual liaisons were notorious, and his views supporting a modern approach to literature and philosophy fascinated students. In a burst of youthful adoration, Karen had once sent flowers to Brandes while he was in the hospital. She may have relied upon him to recognize the Dinesen name on the card, but she was also aware that Brandes, who maintained a legendary interest in the female sex, would be intrigued at receiving a gift signed by a young woman. After he had recuperated, he corresponded with her briefly, and she thought that she might meet him—until her family found out about her gift and reacted with shock. Aunt Bess said that Karen had behaved shamefully, and she was forbidden to continue the correspondence.

Karen still blamed Aunt Bess for this incident, over twenty years later; she said, "it is the only time in my life when there has been a possibility for personal contact with one of the great minds of Denmark, and I believe that Brandes might have made a writer or artist of me, as he did with so many . . . " (*LFA*, 210).

The meeting with Brandes that Aunt Bess arranged for Karen in the summer of 1925 was a great success. Karen was inspired to salvage and dust off a play she had written in her teens called "The Revenge of Truth." She revised it and submitted it to the Danish literary magazine *Tilskueren*, where it was accepted for publication. This triumph encouraged her to consider the alternatives to a life in farming. She had begun to dread, with a kind of horror, the prospect of returning to Africa (*LFA*, 271).

* 5 *

The summer in Denmark had been particularly beautiful. The air was warm but fresh from the sea, and Karen had found life at home unusually serene. She dined with old friends and relatives, who did not ask embarrassing questions about her divorce. She walked the familiar streets of Copenhagen and marveled at the goods not available in Africa. She went to museums and the ballet with her mother and sister; and they engaged her in pleasant conversations and encouraged her plan to be a writer. She noted "with how much harmony and beauty people there,—without reservation!—directed their whole lives toward being happy and content . . . . To walk through the woods from Rungsted to Folehave, to make a cup of tea and some toast, to plant a new row of hyacinths,—that gives meaning to life, that is worth doing, because one enjoys it, feels contentment in doing it, is happy in it" (*LFA*, 279). Her friendship with Georg Brandes perhaps imbued the idea of living in Denmark with a grandness it had never held before. She weighed the contrast between her happiness at home and her dread of returning to Africa.

Along with the problems, *shauries*, and trials of the farm, which she felt almost beyond facing again, she was demoralized by the death of Berkeley Cole. His warm friendship, his commiseration with her about the problems of farming, and his strong ties to Denys had made her life bearable over the previous two years. Added to this loss was the death of the fatherly Sir Northrup McMillan. But perhaps her greatest disappointment was Denys Finch Hatton, who had not written to her during her months in Denmark nor attempted to see her in Europe. This relationship was the greatest of a host of uncertainties associated with returning to Africa, and she was weary of them all.

Where Denys was concerned, she may have been genuinely angry. In March 1925, referring to some difficulties Thomas had encountered in passing through British customs in Somaliland, Karen wrote to her mother, "sometimes I get so furious with the English that I think I will never have anything to do with them again!" (*LFA*, 230). It was predictable that there were no letters from Denys—she had noted before that he was hopeless at writing (*LFA*, 215). But he might at least have given her some word of the farm while he was staying there.

She could not discuss Denys with her mother and sister, and certainly not with Aunt Bess. But she alarmed Thomas with her despair at the idea of going back to Africa. What about the money Thomas had invested in the farm? Who was to oversee the farm's sale? Thomas had just announced his engagement to Jonna Lindhardt, the daughter of a clergyman; he was no longer free to help Karen. She must grapple with this matter of the farm herself. Their conversation led to her desperate outburst: "I hate it there! I will not go back!" (*LFA*, 241).

As a final gesture, Thomas agreed to accompany her on a three-day holiday to Sweden, where they could discuss in private what was to be done about the farm. It was clear to them both that Karen, at age forty, was experiencing a crisis of confidence. She simply must make something of her life, but now she felt too old to start a profession, and she was untrained to do any work besides farming.

Thomas pointed out that she had a responsibility to the shareholders to decide the fate of the farm, and that in Africa she could more easily find the freedom and experiences needed for a writing career. By the time they returned from Sweden, he had convinced her that there was no future for her in Denmark. But she held a foreboding about going back, and later blamed Thomas for what seemed to her one of the worst decisions of her life.

1926

1

Thomas consented to go with Karen as far as Antwerp. She had booked passage on a Belgian ship, the *Springfontein*, and they set out by train on Christmas Day 1925. Karen wished to appease her mother, who could not part with her before the holiday, but she wanted to escape the Danish winter. She boarded the ship with a new Scottish deerhound, named Heather. Except for part of the journey in 1925, between Aden and Marseilles, she had not sailed unaccompanied since 1913. Then she had taken with her the dog Dusk. (Even now she did not sail entirely alone, for Ette Fjaestad, Ingrid Lindstrom's sister, was on board [*MWWL*, 97].)

Karen did not anticipate the difficulties created by a storm in the Bay of Biscay, where, somewhere between France and Spain, she had to risk her life to save Heather. Agitated by the great pitching of the ship, the dog broke her leash and nearly leaped overboard before Karen could regain hold of her.

Seasickness added symptoms to a respiratory infection Karen had caught in Antwerp. Eventually she was incapacitated with fever and vomiting, and had not recovered when the ship docked in Mombasa. Farah was there to meet her, and it was a lucky thing, since she could not have negotiated the train ride to Nairobi without him.

When she arrived at the farm on February 1, 1926, her sinuses were deeply infected—Karen referred to the illness as "a kind of inflammation of the brain" (*LFA*, 238)—and she had to keep towels beside her to blot her dripping nose. Unable to greet her on the lawn as was their custom, the people of the farm filed through her bedroom to thank her for returning. Her room lay to the left of the front sitting room and contained another entrance from the hall, so that the Africans could move through, past her bed, and out by way of the dining room. The men were naked except for earrings and leather tunics; the women wore leather aprons and had babies tied on their backs. The old women, bent from years of carrying firewood, bobbed as they gave greetings; taking her hand in both of theirs, they puckered and crooned to her, punctuating their talk with meaningful nods. Their hands were cool and dry and their faces as wrinkled as walnuts. They called her Jerie—in Kikuyu a tender sobriquet meaning someone who cares for you—and emphasized their remarks by saying, "mm-*hmm*," with little bows. One old woman who had lost both feet to leprosy shuffled into the room on her knees, weeping with happiness at seeing Karen, whom she had not expected to return (*LFA*, 238).

As soon as she was well enough to be out of bed, Karen inspected the farm. Proceeds from the crop harvested in January 1926 could tide them over until the next season, although there were still heavy debts. The white foremen had not been paid their salaries for some time; Dickens had married, and Karen would lose him if she could not guarantee prompter wages. In the years of the slump, 1921 to 1924, Dickens, Thaxton, and Pooran Singh had been content to weather hard times as long as they had a place to live. Like the squatters, they had survived with *shambas* (garden plots), and a few cows and chickens. But times were better, other farmers offered higher salaries, and Mrs. Dickens had brought to her husband's life a new factor: ambition. He would no longer tolerate lateness in wages.

Karen went to Nairobi to consult Hunter, her solicitor, about obtaining operating funds. While in town she visited the widowed Lady McMillan, who, she wrote to her mother, "looked terrible"

(*LFA*, 238). Karen encountered a number of people, members of what she termed the Nairobi smart set, who said they had visited the farm in her absence, at Denys's invitation. Something about their conversation annoyed her. She did not like the thought of "his friends"—as she described them in a letter to Thomas—in the house when she was not there, nor was she amused to learn about the dinners from someone other than Denys. She told Thomas, "at least they have the politeness to say that it 'was always you we came out to dine with,—but it was ghastly without you, like a haunted house" (*LFA*, 240). Karen learned that Denys, who had returned from England in October 1925, was on safari with a client. He was expected back in March before the long rains.

* 2 *

She wrote to Thomas a few weeks after her arrival that she had had "a couple" of letters from Finch Hatton (*LFA*, 240), but no letters survive. She had heard that Denys would be leaving soon for England. It was his custom to go home in the spring—but this time he must surely go, for his father had had a heart attack, and the family expected him.

The news was not what Karen had hoped for—that he might stay on with her for a few months. Still in the grip of her terrible cold, she began to brood. She wrote to Thomas, "it is seldom that I have felt so devoid of energy for work and life as I do now . . . just now I feel that I will never have the strength to walk down to the dam again . . . " (*LFA*, 240).

For weeks after her return she suffered continually from headaches and draining sinuses. Africans came to her terrace for medicine, but she herself was more appropriately the patient. It was difficult for her to concentrate on their ailments. They would gesture at their aching bellies, their skin sores, their mattered eyes, or their feverish children; and, with her own head throbbing, Karen found it an effort to come to an appropriate decision for each of them.

The weather had grown cold and damp, and it was raining when she awakened in the mornings. There was a peculiar musty scent that comes with rain in Africa, like an essence of ground and leaves. She directed Juma to lay a fire for breakfast in the dining room, since there would be a chill in the house until mid-day when the rain stopped.

Karen was annoyed that some valuables were missing, including a set of antique shirt buttons she had meant to give Thomas. She told Thomas that all signs indicated a house thief—no doubt her chief house boy, Juma. She made a scene with Juma about it since, after all, he had been in charge, even if he had not taken the lost items himself. And it was not the first time things had disappeared. But Karen could not resist mentioning to Thomas that Denys or his friends might have borrowed the missing valuables (*LFA*, 239). It was unsettling to her that others had used her personal things.

Just who Denys's friends were, Karen did not say. Up to this time, one of his virtues had been that he always shared his friends with her—Berkeley Cole, Hugh Martin, Lord Delamere, Lady Colville, the Belfields, Jack Llewellyn, and others—and some new names do appear in her letters the following year, members of a notorious social set that was to inspire the standing joke of the decade: "Are you married?—Or do you live in Kenya?"

The group centered on a flamboyant couple, Lord and Lady Kilmarnock, better known as Joss and Idina Errol. Josslyn Hay, heir of the Earl of Errol, had eloped with Lady Idina Gordon in 1923. She was eight years his senior, and had been married twice before. Idina was already well known to Kenya society, since she had lived there with her previous husband, Charles Gordon.

When they came to Kenya in 1924, Joss was twenty-three and Idina thirty-one. They bought property along the wooded slopes of the Aberdare Mountains, but later they moved to a thatched mansion called Clouds in the Wanjohi Valley—a region soon known as Happy Valley, because of the frequently changing sexual liaisons between the Errols and their friends. Men and women alike, including Joss Errol's former schoolmates at Eton, spoke lyrically of his good looks. He was tall, blue-eyed, and blond. His wife was witty, pretty, and vivacious, and her size-three feet matched her small, perfect figure. If she did not invent free love, she played a major role in promoting it among the new, young, smart set of Kenya. She held parties where the theme was sexual promiscuity. Her guests were invited into her spacious bathroom to watch her bathe and dress; afterwards they assembled around a table to play a game of blowing a feather back and forth over the top of a sheet to determine who was to sleep with whom (*WM*, 31).

The group provided a model for the characters in Karen's tale "Carnival," where she said of jealousy, "the chic thing about it is to provoke its abortion" (*CEPT*, 77).

Idina and Joss were not interested in farming; they had come to Kenya for the good life. They and their friends spent their time inventing diversions to keep from getting bored. When they were not hunting or playing polo or experimenting with hashish and opium, they came into Nairobi. Denys found them eating luncheon at Muthaiga or having drinks on the veranda of the Norfolk or New Stanley hotels.

It was not like Denys to participate in party games. He hated dances too, and preferred to spend evenings at home (*LFA*, 384). But interesting conversation never failed to intrigue him, and Berkeley Cole's death had left him without a close companion. Suspicions arose in Karen's mind, as they had in her early days in Kenya, when she was certain everyone was against her. In 1914, she had shown a striking dislike for the white women of Kenya, and found no friends among them. At that time she had also been exceptionally critical of the English, and could not mention a single one who met her standards. She always associated these antagonistic feelings with the accusations by the English that she was a German sympathizer. But she had complained about the English long before the War; and in May 1914, at a time when she was perhaps suspicious of Bror's activities, she had remarked that there were not more than ten decent women in all of Kenya (*LFA*, 10). It was usually jealousy that inspired this attitude in her, and now the old feelings rose again.

Her letter to Thomas in late February 1926 was full of criticism of the English. Strangely, she dwelled on some of the same themes as she had in 1914. The hut tax had just been raised, which was a disgrace. The highest wage an African could earn was 150 shillings a year. How could he continue his time-honored custom of having more than one wife, when twenty shillings' tax per year must be paid on each wife's hut? Karen said, "The ladies here are quite capable of asking, when they hear that the natives cannot get *posho* [maizemeal], why they do not eat wheat or rice instead, just like Marie Antoinette, who asked why the poor did not eat cake if they could not get bread" (*LFA*, 240). Yet, still sensitive about being an outsider, Karen feared openly stating her views. She wrote to Thomas, "I dare not talk to any of the

English, I think my influence here as a woman and a foreigner must be strictly confined to being an example . . . " (*LFA*, 240).

The governor had ordered construction of a new Government House, due to cost £ 80,000. Karen was disgusted that this opulent display of colonial power was being financed by taxing the Africans. She went so far as to include her old friend Lord Delamere in her critical harangue. Shortly after her return to Kenya, Race Week had been held in Nairobi—that holiday when, twice a year, the settlers abandoned their plows and tools, and came to Nairobi for a week of festivities. They brought their best mounts and entered them in competition at the Nairobi race course, and spent long days playing polo, toasting old friends, engaging in good-natured rivalries, and cramming themselves into the cottages at Muthaiga and into the Norfolk Hotel and all the other available hostelries in Nairobi. There were balls, athletic events, banquets, and receptions.

This year, as in other years, Delamere, who promoted the colonists' cause against that of the Indians or the Africans, gave a dinner to honor the governors of the Sudan, Kenya and Uganda, and Tanganyika. He had invited 250 guests, who consumed 600 bottles of champagne. Karen said, "they are really completely without shame" (*LFA*, 240). She herself had not attended the banquet. The invitations perhaps went out before her return; surely her absence from the list was an oversight. In fact she was not really up to attending, and she did not have an escort. But it insulted her to be left out, and recreated for her the old feeling of being somehow on the wrong side.

* 3 *

Berkeley Cole had been Denys Finch Hatton's greatest friend, and now that Berkeley was gone, Karen was uncertain who would replace him. Would he ally himself with young English people with whom she had little in common? Even their styles were repulsive to her: she had no desire to bleach her hair or to wear short, fringed chemises. In truth, she did not have the legs for it, and, anyway, there was the scar on her thigh. But she was also too poor to travel and entertain as the smart set did. She repeatedly told Thomas how empty-handed she felt before Denys (*LFA*, 241), adding "It is not that I want to 'put on airs' in front of him or butter him up like some aging mistress who has to ply him with delicacies and comfort in order to make an impression; but when I feel that, as I wrote in my previous letter, I sometimes come to him empty-handed, it is largely due to the fact that I have no money" (*LFA*, 286).

She had accepted her return to Africa with great difficulty. Her problems and uncertainty had not eased, and she continued to long for the relative serenity of Denmark. But, despite these preoccupations, the beauty of Africa offered solace, and she had convinced herself that she preferred living there. One evening, after several days of a new fever and throat infection, she left her bed and went outside to sit on the veranda, from where she could see rows of coffee stretching to the east. There she began a letter to Thomas: "It is blowing from over the Athi Plains, and the hyenas are howling quite close by. Everywhere is green after the rains and the woods and maize fields are fragrant. The moon is rising from behind the coffee, the whole sky is filled with great white clouds,—I am sure you can remember this African night" (*LFA*, 242). She had made up her mind: "*I could not stand another transplanting now* . . . .When my heart has once more been firmly rooted here it cannot be pulled up again" (*LFA*, 241).

* 4 *

As her health improved, Karen went riding and caught glimpses of lions on the plains; the newly green grass offered food for wildebeest, and there were herds of zebra too for the lions to prey upon. The giraffes who had been seen among the acacia trees at the river in the dry season had moved on, with ostriches and antelope, to a wider, wetter territory. The safari season ended when the rains began: dry stream beds were flash-flooded, and tents and vehicles could not withstand repeated drenchings. The appearance of a Masai, waiting, as was the custom, on one leg, outside Karen's door, signaled Denys's imminent arrival. This red-cloaked messenger brought news that she must make ready for the visit of Bedar. Denys came on March 5, 1926, and he must have been glad to see her; two days later she wrote to her mother that she was so happy she had "nothing more to ask of life" (*LFA*, 242).

At Karen's house Denys could stretch out in soft chairs, read in peace without being attacked by mosquitoes and chiggers, and eat elegant meals in civilized surroundings. He could ease his long legs onto the wicker divan on the veranda, enjoy the sunset over the Ngong Hills, and express his discouragements—much like a husband finally at home. Denys had been leading safaris for little more than a year, and he poked fun at himself for trying to earn an honest penny. Ever after this time, Karen associated Denys's beginning to work with Berkeley's death. She said: "Up till his death the country had been the Happy Hunting Grounds, now it was slowly changing and turning into a business proposition" (*OA*, 233).

She alone could appreciate how deeply Denys had felt the loss of Berkeley, and it was obvious to her now that she had, as a result of Berkeley's leaving, become Denys's most intimate friend in Kenya. One may imagine that she gathered up the responsibility with a sense of grave exaltation. But she wanted to know about the friends he had invited to the farm while she was away. Had they enjoyed themselves in her house? Was he thinking of inviting them again? He perhaps described the dinner parties in his usual, entertaining way, not placing much importance on them. He had a way of creating caricatures of people that made her feel she was part of a secret joke. Generally they agreed upon their opinions of people, for their tastes were the same. They played at comparing people to different kinds of wine: claret, champagne, or port. But this time Karen was not amused. Whether because of her conversations with Denys, or as a result of some unusual event, something transpired while Denys stayed with her that shattered Karen in the extreme, and rendered her so agitated that on March 31, 1926, she drafted—but did not send—a telegram to Thomas: "*Will you help me to get to Europe, I shall die if remaining here*" (*LFA*, 243).

1926

* 5 *

Why was she desperate to get away from Kenya? Only a month before, she had written to Thomas that she could not stand another transplanting. She now said, "You must imagine me as if you saw me lying in darkness with the weight of the earth on my breast, and forgive me for this screaming" (*LFA*, 244).

She checked herself from telegraphing Thomas when she realized he was still on his honeymoon. But, passionately trying to unburden herself, she wrote him a letter. She raved for page after page, interrupted herself, then continued two days later, again page after page. She said she was in the midst of great difficulties, without hope, and should never have been born. She called herself Lucifer's child, implying that she would never fit in, and that whatever she undertook in life was bound to end badly. She railed, "I have constantly pondered upon *when* it actually was that I first got on to the wrong track that led me to the point where I am now, that is, at the end of my resources . . . was it when I got engaged to Bror?—when we decided to come out here?—at some point out here? As I look at it now I can see that it was at none of these points in my life, but much earlier, I could almost say at my entry into this world" (*LFA*, 244).

Only on the second day of writing did she become specific about what was bothering her: Denys was there, but he would soon be leaving, and, as usual, his visit had left her in a "state of quite perfect bliss, mixed with a state of quite perfect despair" at the thought that she might "possibly never see him again." (*LFA*, 248) She could not bear the thought of his going away again and putting her "on the shelf" for another six months until he came back—if he came back at all.

But was this uncertainty enough to make her threaten suicide? Why would she never see him again? Why should she never have come back to Africa, but should have given up the farm to stay in Europe "and bought newspapers to sell on the street" (*LFA*, 251)? Whatever had triggered this immense agitation, it was not the news that Denys was leaving again soon; she had known about his leaving a month before he came. She said she was "forced to silence," and must write Thomas because she had no one else to turn to (*LFA*, 244).

Despite the length of her letter, she never explained what instigated it. Perhaps the circumstances were too humiliating to discuss. The essence of her letter was not what had happened, but what she might do to escape from it, and her ranting and raving was a cry of despair that she had no training or talents to find work other than running the farm. She blamed herself, she blamed her family, she finally blamed her luck to have been born under influences that allowed her to reach the age of forty-one without any money-making talents or skills.

She begged Thomas to help her find a way out. She told him desperately, "I would be happy to go into the white slave trade if I saw an *opening* for me there" (*LFA*, 251).

That is where the issue ended, for she never finished the letter. And it is in the very abruptness with which she abandoned it that a clue lies to what happened next. It is as though she had meant to say more but lost the necessity for it.

* 6 *

For four years Karen had entertained and seduced Denys but had always hidden that she was in love with him. In the meantime, she had openly flirted with Berkeley Cole, Geoff Buxton, and Jack Llewellyn. Denys knew they had stayed at the farm, and he may have thought he was only one among her many intimate companions. Her goal had been to pretend she did not think of marrying him.

In their conversations Karen had said she thought of sexual relationships as private *shauries* (affairs), "where everything is *all right*, providing no partner *loses his temper* or in any way pretends to take it seriously" (*LFA*, 323). But the subject of her letter to Thomas was what to do about a situation she found intolerable. She wrote in "Carnival"—a tale begun only a few months later—that men expected to serve themselves at the buffet: they could love whom they wanted, and they never worried about waking up at night with "a heart that screamed" (*CEPT*, 73).

At the same time, she expressed her concern to Thomas that her relationship with Denys might evolve into nothing more than "a purely physical hunger and its satisfaction, and I will not allow that to happen; and anyway it would never last only in that manner, it would burn out *in no time*" (*LFA*, 248). In "Carnival" she describes a woman's frustration at never being content with her lover's attentions. It is as if, once she has eaten, he does not expect her to be hungry again (*CEPT*, 72).

It was difficult to break the pattern of eight years in which she had avoided discussing her intimate feelings with Denys, but portions of Karen's letters in the weeks surrounding Denys's departure resemble excerpts from a tirade; she ranted to her family in a way she may have repeated to Denys. In "The Dreamers" one of the characters says, "I am slow to get angry... When I really become so, it is a great relief to me" (*SGT*, 314). She wrote to her family, "I will not and cannot continue to go on living in this way... It is an intolerable situation and I find it impossible to allow my immediate future to take the form of six months of utter desolation, emptiness and darkness, with the hope of seeing him again in the autumn, then being lifted up to the same unqualified happiness, only to be cast back into desolation and darkness—and so on and so on for infinity" (*LFA*, 248). It was like lying "in a perfumed bath and listening to the loveliest music in the world for six hours," and then being "put on the rack for the next six" (*LFA*, 248). "When one goes to a fine concert one is not in a state of utter despair when it comes to an end and one gets up to go, and when one has eaten a really delicious meal one can see the coffee arriving without pain; but where certain things in life are concerned one's whole being rebels at the idea of an ending, and there is a built-in instinct that demands endlessness and will not accept compromise!" (*LFA*, 242).

She outlined her expectations for the relationship later in an essay to Thomas: "To what degree does one take it upon oneself to be faithful when one embarks upon a love affair? ... I am quite aware that no one, whether he holds views in either one or the other direction, can work miracles or change human nature. But some ideal or other can be set up and striven for. Where it is a matter of a relationship, where therefore it is a matter of more than one person's happiness or well-being there must be a certain clarity, a certain understanding;

otherwise you may find yourself playing football with a partner who does not know what it means to be *offside*. Either a 'sexual relationship' means something in itself and carries a certain weight, a significance outside itself… or it exists entirely for the pleasure of the participants, and is entered upon and dissolved *in accordance*" (*LFA*, 324–5).

* 7 *

Subsequent events suggest that Denys's attitude toward Karen changed in connection with this highly emotional period outlined in her letters.

In *Out of Africa* Karen says of Denys that the farm "knew, in him, a quality of which the world besides was not aware, a humility" (*OA*, 234). It is possible that his humility arose about this time. In the subsequent months of 1926, Karen wrote to her family repeatedly about a subject that had never appeared before in her letters, homosexuality. She gave Aunt Bess a laundered definition: "sincere friendship, understanding, delight shared by two equal, 'parallel moving' beings" (*LFA*, 264). Karen was studying the writing of Aldous Huxley to understand the type of relationship where two people might love each other but not marry. She said,

> Aldous Huxley has an expression: "*The love of the parallels*," which he uses in a somewhat tragic context, it is true, but which I must surely be permitted to construe as I like,—which to a certain extent expresses what I mean by this: one does not "become part of," become "devoted to," the other; perhaps one is not as close to the other as in those partnerships that are able to encompass such merging, and there is no question of each being the aim and goal of the other's life, but while one is oneself and striving for one's own distant aim one finds joy in the knowledge of being on parallel courses for all eternity. (*LFA*, 271)

She seemed transfixed by the tragic but noble idea that two people could live in tandem, pursuing similar ideals, yet never combining their ideals into one. She told Aunt Bess that this appealed to her because a woman need not devote her life to serving a man. But in "Carnival" she hints at her true attitude to such an idea: "He wants me to run parallel with him in life . . . how sorry one ought to feel for all parallel lines which want to intersect as badly as I do" (*CEPT*, 65).

In a story called "The Monkey" Karen writes about the dilemma of a young man whose homosexuality has recently been exposed: "During the last month clouds of strange and sinister nature had been gathering over the heads of that very regiment and circle of friends to which the boy belonged . . . His name had been brought up . . . as one of the corrupters of youth . . ." (*SGT*, 111). His loss of reputation is intimately connected with "those romantic and sacred shores of ancient Greece which they had till now held in high esteem" (*SGT*, 149). (Karen's letter to Aunt Bess on May 23, 1926, also alludes to the relationships between men and youths in ancient Greece [*LFA*, 264].)

In "The Monkey," an old woman, a prioress, exchanges her soul with that of a demon. This magic emphasizes the power of sexual obsession to transform one's personality into something less than human. While the monkey has control of her spirit, the prioress plots to obtain consummation of the sexual act between her nephew, the homosexual, and a young woman. The monkey's appearances, as Karen describes them, bear a striking resemblance to Denys's visits to the farm: " . . . the Prioress's monkey would feel the call of a freer life and would disappear for a few weeks or a month, to come back of its own accord when the night frosts set in" (*SGT*, 110).

In the tale Karen speaks of a "terribly agitated week, and a row of wild scenes" caused by "love and jealousy." In a physical battle, in which one of two lovers is determined to marry and the other violently refuses, the conflict is resolved in a manner that, however unsatisfactory to each of them, nevertheless binds the fate of the two: "from now, between on the one side, her and him, who had been present together at the happenings of the last minutes, and, on the other side, the rest of the world, which had not been there, an insurmountable line would be forever drawn" (*SGT*, 161–2).

Near the end of the tale, a goblet is broken, staining the white tablecloth with red wine—a symbol for the loss of innocence. If this story, like others Karen wrote, was an allegory for what she had actually gone through, a new understanding may have been established between Denys and her prior to his departure for England in April 1926. A few weeks later Karen wrote to her sister, "Now I have to go around putting on a good face after Denys has gone and the scent faded from the roses and the light from the full moon,—but everything in this world must be paid for, even having one's own way" (LFA, 257).

* 8 *

When Denys left, he turned over to Karen the keys of his car. He wished her to make full use of it, since her own car, the one she and Bror had bought in South Africa, was in so poor condition.

Denys more or less bequeathed his Hudson to Karen, because he intended to bring back a new car. In Kenya, where it was preferable to travel at night to avoid mid-day heat, the nights were cool, making driving in an open car unpleasant. Denys, who was sensitive to the cold, had learned that the new Hudson sedan was enclosed, with windows that would keep out the wind.

From Mombasa, he sent Karen a series of instructions that perhaps he had had no time to offer in the hurry of leaving. The tone, much different from that of his previous—and only other—note to her, was direct, like a note from Thomas or Bror:

> Don't drive fast when the car is cold: The red should
> be up to the lower edge of the white circle in the
> thermometer.... Don't force your gears in if you miss
> them: start again. . . . Be very careful not to go into
> reverse from 1st speed—it is right opposite and can
> *easily be done* especially if the 1st gear sticks as you
> come out of it. You may find it difficult to get into first
> gear when you start. If so get into neutral and let the
> clutch in and accelerate slightly and try again. . . . I
> will write again more about the car, but I send this in
> haste about the gears: they are so important if you

want the car to run nicely and not get *strained* by forcing gears.

He advised her, if she had difficulty, to consult Flo Martin, Hugh's wife, who he said was "very good with gears" (DFH to KB 4-12-26: KO, 20). Flo had publicized her decision to become the first woman to drive the round trip from Nairobi to Mombasa. She planned to make good her challenge in September 1926, before the beginning of the rains.

Denys also said in the note that he had proposed Karen for membership in the Muthaiga Club. She had been technically excluded when the divorce became final in January 1925, having been a member previously only through her marriage to Bror. Denys assured her that there would now be no obstacle to her membership as a single woman.

* *

In his latest visit, Denys had stayed with Karen, with small interruptions, for about a month. Her health had been good then, but during the weeks after he left for England she experienced a growing fatigue that made no sense to her. It did not resemble depression, nor was it similar to any illness she had had. She told her mother, "I cannot say that I am actually ill, but so immensely tired, and not fit for anything at all. I have never felt anything like it before, it is as if it's too much trouble to live, and I can't tell how it is going to develop"(*LFA*, 252–3).

Minor discouragements became pronounced in the face of her continuing fatigue. During the second week of May 1926, Karen heard a rumor in Nairobi about the impending landing, after a two-hour flight from Lake Victoria, of the first airplanes ever to reach Kenya. Hurrying to Dagoretti Junction, not far from her farm, to watch the four aircraft descend toward the ground, she declared them "*beautiful* when they came rushing past" (*LFA*, 256). She had kind words for the English, who brought as many Africans to the event as they could cram into their cars. But she was disappointed in herself for not having time to go back for the *totos* from her farm.

She frequently blamed herself when events went wrong, and her attitude often led to fatigue. However, six weeks after Denys's departure, she began to understand that her tiredness was not due to discouragement, but to pregnancy.

* 9 *

Since 1923, Karen had been making general comments to Thomas and her mother about the importance of birth control. In *Out of Africa* she mentions *coitus interruptus*—withdrawing at the moment of ejaculation. She told her mother that such precautions were aesthetically distasteful (*LFA*, 176) but essential to the emancipation of women. When Thomas sent her his own essay on birth control, she suggested that the practice was so widely accepted that only naïve people would bother to read his tract (*LFA*, 290–3).

It appears that Karen and Denys had worked out a codeword for an imaginary child: "Daniel." Once, in a letter, an African had in confusion addressed Karen not as "Baroness" but as "Lioness." As the child of a "lioness" and a lion hunter, any son of Denys and her must be, like the biblical Daniel, fearless of lions. He would be "a chosen youth—a young man of royal family—a strong, healthy, good-looking lad—who would be taught language and literature, who would be widely read in many fields, well-informed, alert and sensible, and have enough poise to look good around the palace" (Daniel 1:3–4, *LB*, 675).

Denys admired the Bible as literature and frequently quoted it. The custom of using keywords such as "Daniel" arose naturally in Africa, where confidential communications often passed through the hands and ears of intermediaries. Referring to the Hudson he had left in Karen's charge, Denys had written to her: "Keyword *Denys* (also for spare lock inside tool box)" (DFH to KB 4-12-26: KO, 20). Servants were often asked to deliver messages orally so that the sender did not worry about a note's being lost or falling into the wrong hands. Speaking in code was also a delicate way to negotiate the network of functionaries monitoring the telegraph service. So Karen made Denys aware that she was pregnant via a telegram that contained words to this effect: "I understand that Daniel is on his way."

His response to her telegram appears to have been noncommittal. (One account has it that Denys's reply was, "Strongly suggest you cancel Daniel's visit." However, no such telegram exists in the Blixen archives [KO, 20–21].) Karen wired him again, imploring advice. His answering telegram, sent on May 21, 1926, said: "Reference your cable and my reply please do as you like about Daniel as I should welcome him if I could offer partnership but this is impossible—stop—you will I know consider your mother's views. Denys" (DFH to KB 5-21-26:KO, 21). It seemed obvious to her that he thought she had played him the proverbial dirty trick: getting pregnant deliberately to trap him (*LFA*, 324). Her draft of a return telegram exists: "Thanks cables never meant ask assistance permission—consent only. Tania" (KB to DFH undated:KO, 21). It is not certain whether she sent this telegram, but subsequent events indicate that she had determined to teach Denys a lesson.

* 10 *

These exchanges concerning the baby caused Karen great emotional turmoil later described at length in a letter to Thomas (*LFA*, 277). But the "unpleasantness," as she called it, ended abruptly, near the end of May 1926, when she apparently lost the baby. She claimed that she might even have been mistaken about being pregnant. "I do not know for certain if it was really so, and will never know . . . ," she told Thomas. But earlier in the same letter she had said, "Surely there must always be one moment in life when there is still a possibility of *two* courses,—and another, a next moment, where there is only the possibility of a single one. Now I am fully aware of this: this time I have burned my ships" (*LFA*, 271).

She had made up her mind that she "did not want to have a child" (*LFA*, 277). She had thought the matter over carefully, had taken stock of her life, and had decided she did not have the money to support a child. She could not bring into the world a child dependent on the earnings of "a remote coffee farm whose future continues to be extremely dubious!" (*LFA*, 279). Moreover, she had analyzed her motivation for wanting a child and decided the idea of "living in one's children" (*LFA*, 277), as her mother had done, was unworthy. She must strive for her own greatness.

Her soul-searching stood her in good stead, for she did not seem seriously dispirited by the loss of the child. Her letters recorded no panic or weeping spells. Throughout the months of June and July 1926, she went about the business of the farm. She directed the servants to plow up the lawn behind the house and plant corn, since the grass needed to be reseeded, an expense she could justify if corn were harvested first. She planted cinerarias in her garden, taught herself and Kamante to make chocolate eclairs, and continued writing two "marionette comedies" (*LFA*, 257). One of these appears to have become "The Monkey," the tale touching upon the unpleasant consequences of bearing a bastard child, as well as the themes of homosexuality and aversion to marriage. The Denys-like female character, Athena, "surely feels no reluctance toward this alliance in particular, but she tells me that she will never marry, and that it is even impossible for her to consider the question at all" (*SGT*, 135). In the story Karen treats ironically the unfulfilled sexual passions of older women.

The setting for the other tale, eventually called "Carnival," is a dinner party in Copenhagen in 1925, but the characters are based upon Denys's friends among the Nairobi smart set and the background is really Karen's house at Ngong. The story concerns hidden motives and how people disguise them. In the narration Karen gives generous rein to erotic fantasies, describing, in blank verse, slim legs like "a golden tuning fork, / God's favorite implement, powerfully turning / life's dissonances into harmony" (*CEPT*, 69). She also says, "If women were as intemperate in regard to food as they are sexually, a supper party would become entirely repulsive" (*CEPT*, 72).

She did not tell Denys her pregnancy had ended, nor did she write to him at all. Soon she wrote a long letter to Aunt Bess on the subject of feminism, wherein she outlined her impatience with the view that the life of a woman must revolve around a man. She pointed out that in the past "no work, no talent, no form of productivity could pay women anything nearly so much as pleasing, or making themselves necessary to a man" (*LFA*, 261). She was out of sorts with this philosophy, and so she was not particularly receptive when she received a note from Denys, written in June 1926, saying he was depressed and wished he were back at Ngong. With the note he sent some photographs. He seemed annoyed that she had not written to him. "I want your news," he said. "What of Daniel? I would have liked it but I saw it being very difficult for you" (DFH to KB 6-15-26:KO, 21).

At least his note suggested that he was holding no grudge. She forgave him for implying she had played him a dirty trick, and shortly after hearing from him, she wrote to Thomas, "my great devotion to Denys fills my whole life with indescribable sweetness, in spite of constantly missing him. If things can continue as they are now I will never wish for greater happiness" (*LFA*, 270). These lofty thoughts aside, she did not respond to Denys's note, nor write to thank him for the photographs.

* 11 *

When Karen went to Europe in 1919, she had taken with her a young Somali servant named Abdullai. Dressed in a silk robe and turban, he had followed a few steps behind her on outings in London and Copenhagen. Karen envisioned this procession as her gift to the staid people of the north: for some it would be their only glimpse of the exotic East. Furthermore, she had been intensely curious to observe how an African would react to the civilized world. Would he be enthralled and yearn to stay? Or would he scornfully long for home? The boy had remained at Rungstedlund for several months, but he had finally chosen to return to Africa with Bror.

In August 1926, Abdullai succumbed to blackwater fever during an epidemic of malaria on the farm. Many Africans were dying, especially the old. Karen mourned the death of Abdullai and drove to visit his mother in the Somali quarter of Nairobi. Inside a tent filled with rich rugs and the scent of incense, she drank mint tea with Abdullai's mother. Karen was agonized to hear that eleven of the mother's children had died—most of them from tuberculosis.

She then visited the Kikuyu villages with quinine for malaria. Dusty children besieged by flies stared at her and smiled shyly. Women prepared food in front of their huts in gourds set on the hard packed ground; the elderly lay on mats inside. The Kikuyu naturally distrusted modern medicine. They received Karen graciously, but preferred their witch doctor's medical treatment. In Karen's view their instincts, in some respects, were right. About their custom of putting their dead out for the hyenas instead of burying them, she said, "I am *in sympathy* with the Kikuyu on this point and would rather like my own transition to a skeleton,—which takes such a short time out here with the aid of sun and wind and animals and birds,—to take place in the dry grass and the open air and under the stars . . . " (*LFA*, 269).

In early August Karen received from Denys a framed picture of himself—looking ingenuous at the age of 19 or 20, with lots of wavy blond hair. There was also a book about Egypt—which he had inserted into the parcel to keep the glass from breaking—and a piece of music he said was the background for a pretty lesbian ballet he had seen in London. He told her suggestively that the ballet raised "many recollections" (DFH to KB 7-?-26:KO, 23). But, although Karen embraced the gifts, she did not answer his letter.

Just then she was taking great interest in her African school. It had been set up in a shed adjoining Rouge's stall, and she had hired a teacher from the Protestant mission. Sometimes she walked to the stables in the evening to listen to the hymn singing. The sound was a kind of "bleating," she said, and the titles of the hymns—"There is life in a look at the Crucified One"—seemed ironic to her (*LFA*, 266). The songs were punctuated from time to time by Rouge's giving the wall a kick. But she thought the new teacher was an improvement. African teachers were trained in mission schools, either Catholic or Protestant, where they acquired values passed on to their students. Frequently their attitudes were hostile to the other Christian sects. Karen thought spoon-feeding foreign prejudices and religion to Africans was irresponsible and confused "the really good, healthy, well-balanced native disposition" (*LFA*, 266). She hoped the new teacher would prove less dogmatic.

During the third week of August 1926, Karen received a book from Denys entitled *China Under the Empress Dowager*. She enjoyed it and recommended it to her mother. But she did not keep the note he sent with it, nor did she answer it. At that time she was more concerned about an infuriating incident: her servants had allowed Heather, her new deerhound to copulate with a *shenzie* (mongrel) dog. She had given the servants strict orders to keep Heather, who was in heat, in her pen while Farah and she went to Nairobi on errands, for she had planned to mate the dog with a purebred deerhound belonging to friends upcountry. But while she was gone the *shenzie* dog had come slinking around the kennel and somehow found his way inside. Karen came home from Nairobi to find the loving pair together, and threw a screaming tantrum such as the houseboys had seldom seen.

She fired her entire staff. But within a few hours—after soothing remarks from Farah, who was bound to say, "God is great"— she hired them back, since she could not do without them. However, she did not soon forget the disgusting event, and she was illtempered with the household for some days afterwards.

* 12 *

The prolific blossoming of the coffee bushes in May had amounted to nothing, and this did not improve Karen's mood. Almost no berries were coming to fruit. Eventually she consulted Taylor of the survey department, who examined the rows with her and declared that such a stunted crop was not unusual the year after a drought. At this altitude the bushes did not have the strength to pick up again quickly. Something similar had happened to the crop in 1922 (*LFA*, 272).

Karen's discouragement over the crop's failure brought back some of her old anxiety. She had no one to turn to, since she had been short-tempered with Farah, who lapsed into one of his sulky moods (*LFA*, 158). Her overseer, Dickens, was also out of sorts with her. Incited by Mrs. Dickens, he saw in the failed crop more delays in his salary. Karen felt as though everyone were against her and often went outside in the hope of seeing some of the *totos* run by, for at least they would sing out "*Jambo*, Memsahib!" (Hello, Mistress!).

Attempting to vent her anxiety, as she had done often in such times, she furiously typed a letter to Thomas nearly as long as a book. She reviewed all the old issues: her divorce from Bror; her failure to develop her talents; her decision to come back to the farm, and the justification for why she must now stay there; her emotional dependence on Denys; her despair at being poor; and her determination to continue living in Africa to the end of her days. She reviewed the alternatives: If she had had money, like Denys or Thomas, she would have lived a roving life and not worried about failure. If she had had the strength and verve of Bror, she would have wandered without money and happily lived on other people's assets. But a longing for satisfaction impelled her to save the farm. She clung to the hope that she might end her days in Africa, with Denys her trusted friend, successors to her dogs Pjuske and Heather, and Farah's son as her faithful servant. However, a strange dread tormented her. She told Thomas desperately, "If only those who have been through something similar to my experience would tell me really honestly how it ended!" (*LFA*, 289).

* 13 *

Toward the end of September 1926, Karen received from Denys a long letter accompanied by some daffodil and crocus bulbs. This time he sent the letter in care of their mutual solicitor, W. C. Hunter. He explained why, in a kind of lover's exasperation: "The reason is that I cannot remember whether your box is 223 or 332: I think 223 but as you have never answered any of the letters which I have sent you I may be wrong" (DFH to KB 9-12-26:KO, 22–23).

He seems to have realized that he had seriously offended her, and set out to right whatever wrong he had done. He waxed amorous, and resorted to writing endearments of which, under other circumstances, he might have preferred to leave no record. She could appreciate his code and be swayed by his evocation of their sensual word play. He crooned to her,

> I believe I could happily die looking up at
> the hills, with all their lovely colors fading out above
> the darkening belt of the near forest. Soon they will
> be velvet black against the silver fading sky—black
> as the buffaloes which now come pushing softly out
> of the bush high up under the breasts of the hills to
> feed with sweet breath unafraid upon the open grass
> of the night.

I am much looking forward to seeing you again, Tania.

He coaxed her with thoughts of further delights. He had decided to buy some property at the coast, he said, where they could get away, just the two of them. "Do not tell of this," he added conspiratorially, using a Shakespearean voice.

He ended the letter with a whine, perhaps hoping for pity: "You ought to have given me something of your news—nothing—no word even of Daniel—"

His tender farewell, "Goodnight, Goodnight," sounding like he was ready to prostrate himself for her forgiveness, could have made her laugh; it was so uncharacteristic of him.

As it turned out, Karen had finally written to Denys only a week before, and their letters crossed in the mail. When Denys heard from her, he responded quickly, thanking her for the charming letter. He was already packing his things for returning to Africa. He teased her about some music she had requested. They could never agree on composers, so he referred to the Rubinstein (recordings of Chopin by Artur Rubinstein, or music by the Russian composer Anton Rubinstein) as "muck" (DFH to KB 9-23-26:KO, 24). But his teasing was affectionate. He was very much looking forward to seeing her near the end of October 1926.

* 14 *

Karen was piqued with Farah, whom she had called sulky in a letter to Thomas early in September. He would disappear for days at a time, on business. He owned a *duka* (native shop) at Thika—an hour's drive north of Nairobi—and would often leave to see to his affairs. While Karen teetered on the brink of bankruptcy, Farah was prospering. He had amassed enough money to buy himself a Chevrolet truck, so that chauffeuring Karen had lost its mystique for him. Karen was irritated by his unusual wealth, as well as by the dwindling amount of time he spent carrying out tasks for her. She gave him an ultimatum (*LFA*, 289). If he insisted on continuing his outside business, he must buy a duka closer to Ngong. Otherwise she would have to ask him to leave her service. One may imagine that Farah pondered her words while staring straight beyond her; beneath the voluminous red turban, his brow and lips betrayed no emotion, but his eyes were haughty.

Karen would regret this conversation with Farah, since it was to have long-reaching effects. Her suggestion that Farah find a different duka led to a feud among the Somalis in her household: Farah, evidently with Karen's blessing and perhaps in payment for a debt, assumed ownership of a duka nearby that had previously belonged to Karen's cook Hassan. Since Hassan belonged to a different Somali clan, Farah's heavy-handedness ignited a dispute that would rage with flashes of intensity for years to come. Both sides were able to recruit supporters from Nairobi's crowded Somali quarter, and attacks with firearms and knives were considered fair play under the Somali rules for settling arguments. Karen tried to make the best of the situation. Since Farah had, for some time, had a free hand with the grocery budget, anyway, it was convenient that she could now buy all her "stores and meat" from Farah, perhaps at a discount (*LFA*, 289).

The short rains arrived on time, calming Karen's distress over the poor crop of the previous rainy season. By mid November 1926 she wrote to her mother, "We have more blossom on the trees now than we have ever had before during the short rains, and I think I can say than we have ever had at all" (*LFA*, 296). But she could concentrate little on the farm or the Somali vendettas while Denys's return beckoned. She spent her time perfecting an essay for Thomas on sexual morality (*LFA*, 290). Obviously referring to the social set spearheaded by Joss and Idina Errol, she commented to Thomas: "when I observe the situation out here and see how people with the greatest equanimity and social success conduct themselves—I am certain that the old, negative 'sexual morality' has long since had its day" (*LFA*, 290).

She mentioned to Thomas, in a veiled manner, several concerns. She reminded him about a discussion during which he had told her "that the abstention from women practiced by the young men at Oxford often led to more or less erotic relationships among themselves . . . " (*LFA*, 292). Homosexuality was discouraged by law in England, and Karen did not mention it further, but she did say that she and Denys had talked about the social freedoms in Denmark denied by other countries. Denys had remarked that he considered the Danes "very advanced in all kinds of social problems" (*LFA*, 290). On the subject of birth control, still debated in the Danish press, he was astonished that a country so broadminded in some areas was still so prudish in that particular aspect.

Karen's erotic writing in "Carnival" suggests that her physical desire remained strong during the months Denys was gone, and she may have been unsure of how to deal with her emotions when she saw him. In "The Monkey" she writes about certain attractive women, "To all of them it had been a fundamental article of faith that woman's loveliness and charm, which they themselves represented in their own sphere and according to their gifts, must constitute the highest inspiration and prize of life. . . . Had they known that it might ever be called into question, all these lives . . . might have looked very different" (*SGT*, 112). However, toward the end of her letter to Thomas Karen remarked idealistically, "I myself am inclined to think that in future sexuality as a whole,—for a time,—will come to have less importance when its rights and freedom have finally come to be established and confirmed; this is, after all, what has happened to many forces that have been fettered . . . " (*LFA*, 293). She insisted to Thomas that the sexual element in any relationship should not play a central role; there were more important considerations.

In diminishing her interest in the sexual element, she was perhaps deceiving herself. But it may not have mattered, since by the time he returned, Denys appears to have been willing to satisfy her longings.

* 15 *

Denys's letters indicate that a change had occurred in his attitude toward her over the previous months. The tone of his writing to her—brusque at first—had become persuasive and endearing. Whatever the cause for this difference, the transformation of his thinking was certainly influenced by elements of his current situation in life.

Denys's mother, to whom he had been devoted, had now been dead two years. Nan Finch Hatton had admitted to some that

Denys was her favorite child, and Denys had written an emotional tribute for her gravestone: "No effigy would do justice to the beauties of her person nor any epitaph express the beauties of her mind, therefore neither is attempted here. But those to whom she left the world a void live in the humble hope that through the mercy of God it may be given to him when their time of departure comes, to be with her where she is" (*SWS*, 207). Ironically, in 1924, soon after his own mother's death, Denys had boarded a ship to East Africa with Karen's mother. The meeting brought new light to Denys's view of Karen. Ingeborg Dinesen's serene character was in some ways very like that of Nan Finch Hatton.

Denys had felt more deeply the loss of his mother because he had always lacked rapport with his father. Upon hearing about the Earl of Winchilsea's illness in the spring of 1926, Denys had sailed to England, only to find his father indifferent to his presence. He had written to Karen, "I came back here to see if I could be of any use to my father who is now moving out of his home. But I find that in spite of his being very unwell he insists upon doing everything himself as long as he can stagger around: so that all I can do is to stand around like the French clown at a circus."

In 1926 the family was undergoing an additional disturbing change. Denys's boyhood home, the estate at Haverholme Priory, was being prepared for sale. Financial worry had contributed to the Earl of Winchilsea's ill health. Denys said, "The atmosphere here is very depressing and I shall be glad to get away from it" (DFH to KB 9-12-26:KO, 23).

Denys had written to Karen in June 1926 and again in September that he was depressed. His family's situation was changing radically, and Berkeley Cole's death had deprived him of his closest friend. When Karen refused to write to him, he must have sensed the risk in losing his best remaining contact in Kenya, and the only home he knew there, the farm at Ngong.

Karen may not have understood all that was represented by his change in attitude, but she accepted sincerely what seemed to be a new order in their relationship. She was overjoyed when he wrote to her from Mombasa: "*Homeward bound I feel that I am, for now Ngong has got more of the feeling of Home to me than England*" (*LFA*, 297).

What, then, occurred when he arrived? In a series of letters to her family before the beginning of the New Year, 1927, Karen revealed obliquely that she wanted to be alone with him, and that Denys seemed to agree. Since June 1926, there had been talk of Ingeborg Dinesen's making another visit to Kenya. In a letter to Aunt Bess on July 4, Karen had stated emphatically that she did not intend to leave Africa until the spring of 1928, and that, if money for travel were to be spent, Ingeborg Dinesen should come to Africa. Karen was persuasive, pointing out that although "this great wild plan" might be difficult for a woman almost seventy years old, still it would be worth the adventure (*LFA*, 267).

But despite having strongly stated this view, by the end of October 1926—after Denys had made his sentiments clear—Karen cabled "a definite cancellation," and emphasized her reasons in a letter to her mother on November 14: "besides the problems of your health and strength, the circumstances you are leaving behind at home and the difficulties of your journey, there is also to be considered the question of the circumstances you will be coming to meet with here . . . ." One can only guess at what circumstances in Kenya she was referring to, since she said in the same letter, "The farm itself is looking better than I have ever seen it" (*LFA*, 295). Karen was at that moment expecting Denys any day, and his letter to her from Mombasa had implied that he would be exceptionally glad to see her. She would prefer to be alone with him.

Did Denys share this view? It appears that he did, for later Karen wrote to Thomas: "at Christmas I telegraphed you: '*prospects doubtful*' and later at New Year to Mother herself: '*prospects very uncertain.*' Denys, who was staying here and saw all my telegrams, said: '*Your people must be quite mad if they let your Mother start after this*'" (*LFA*, 299).

In *Out of Africa*, Karen describes the wonder of the Africans, while Denys visited the farm, at seeing the glow from her house, lighted until all hours as she and Denys sat in animated conversation. She says the Masai must have thought of her and Denys in the same way the peasants of Umbria thought of Saint Francis and Saint Clare and must have believed she and Denys were "entertaining one another upon theology" (*OA*, 165). One may imagine she and Denys formulated this comparison as an intimate joke, for their conversation was hardly the chaste talk of the saints. Evidence already indicated that, like many women at age forty-one, Karen was at the height of her sexual interest, and her delight at seeing Denys again certainly involved more than the chance to discuss philosophy. Perhaps his willingness to provide the intimate companionship she wished can be explained less on the basis of his sexual desire than on his friendship and admiration for her.

Later Karen told Thomas that Denys had gone ashore in Somaliland during his trip out to Africa in November 1926 (*LFA*, 316). She was possibly confused in remembering, since he was not to visit Italian Somaliland, as well as Abyssinia, until the following June. Her confusion may have occurred because Denys had bought her during his recent journey the ring of Abyssinian gold, described in *Out of Africa*, designed to adjust to the wearer's finger. In a photograph taken in front of her house a few months later, she was wearing such a ring. With her in the picture were Mahu, now ten years old, Tumbo, age five, and Ingeborg Dinesen.

1927

1

 Fru Dinesen had indeed arrived, at the end of January 1927. However, this time Denys did not go off to stay at Muthaiga, as he had when she visited in 1924; he remained at the farm.

Having at last achieved what she had dreamed of for nine years, a devoted relationship with Denys, Karen was wild with dismay at news of her mother's imminent arrival. In order to spend a few more precious days alone with him, she sent Farah to Mombasa to meet her mother's ship, along with a note saying, "I hope you will not mind that Denys is staying here at present. He has been very ill with dysentery and fever, and is just getting over it, so I am reluctant to send him away to Nairobi, where sickness and death are lurking. He has offered to take himself away when you come, but I said that I did not think you would have any objection to his being here; he is so much looking forward to seeing you again . . . " (*LFA*, 298).

A week after her mother's arrival at the farm, however, Karen wrote Thomas an exasperated letter blaming him for allowing Ingeborg Dinesen to come to Africa. "If you had given any thought at all to *my* point of view wouldn't you have realized that there must be a reason for this standpoint, probably that I was afraid that the situation here would prove too difficult?" (*LFA*, 299). Not only did she prefer to be alone with Denys; she was now faced with the embarrassment of her mother's guessing that she and Denys were engaged in a sexual relationship—behavior that could not be condoned by Ingeborg Dinesen's Victorian upbringing.

To underline her frustration with the family's decision to send her mother, Karen listed for Thomas the letters and cables she had sent discouraging the visit. These dated from the end of October 1926 (when she had received Denys's erotic letter concerning the "black buffaloes"). Forestalling Thomas's obvious objection that she should have made her feelings known earlier, she said, "The reason for my not being able to say anything more definite earlier was that circumstances have a habit of changing so much from one day to another, something that you, who are familiar with them, can surely understand." She concluded the letter with a nearly audible sigh of resignation: "I do believe that you have all done your very best to arrive at the best decision; now you must believe that I will do my very best to make the best of it" (*LFA*, 299).

The house at Ngong contained three bedrooms; two on the south, beside the veranda, and a third on the northwest with its own bath, separated from the other two by the great room with a fireplace that Karen used as a dining room. So there was privacy for those sleeping on either side of the house. Denys stayed on until the end of February 1927, when he returned to England. He began his trip home earlier than usual because he had lined up a rich American client for a safari in June. He envisioned a brief stay, merely time to take care of a few things related to the sale of Haverholme and to buy a truck especially outfitted for safaris.

It was almost surely when he said good-bye this time that he gave Karen a wooden seal engraved with the motto: *Je responderay* (*DOE*, 6–7). The motto inscribed on the Finch Hatton coat-of-arms, in the archaic French of Norman times, meant "I will answer." He would write to her while he was away, and did not want her to ignore his letters as she had the summer before. She asked him to let her adopt his family motto, but his gift made it seem as though he had already begun to think of her as one of his family.

* 2 *

Karen's mother still wore black—proper nineteenth-century attire for a widow. Her dresses were designed to discreetly cover her ankles. All her life she had worn her hair pulled tightly into a chignon; only her family knew how wavy and luxurious her hair was, even in old age.

She had married Wilhelm Dinesen when she was twenty-five, he thirty-six. Like Karen she was the first in her family to marry, and like Karen she had nearly resigned herself to being an old maid. Like Karen, she seemed to have been swept off her feet by the force of erotic attraction. And like Karen, she had had little in common with her husband. She was a quiet woman whose deepest interests lay with her family. She loved to read, discuss philosophy, sit by the fire. While she was interested in gardening and loved horses and dogs, she could not share, nor was allowed to share, Wilhelm Dinesen's passion for hunting and fishing and all outdoor sports. He came from an aristocratic, if untitled, family of landed gentry; she came from the bourgeois class. He had inherited old money, while the Westenholzes were nouveau riche, having earned their money in trade. Wilhelm Dinesen would not inherit a fortune; therefore it was in his best interests, as it had been in Bror's, to marry into wealth.

Three generations of wives in Karen's family had followed a similar pattern: marriage to men with whom they had little in common, yet to whom they were devoted. Karen's grandmother, Mary Hansen, whose mother was English, had married Regnar Westenholz, a Danish corn merchant twice her age. Before she was widowed at age thirty-four, she had borne him six children. Ingeborg Dinesen, widowed at thirty-nine, had five children and had enjoyed, she always said, a blissful family life with Wilhelm Dinesen, before the illness that led to his suicide (*LFA*, 427).

Karen and her sisters, Ea and Elle, all adored their husbands, although they married late. There seemed to be two forces leading to contentment. One was their inherited passion for being part of an intimate family. The other was the "erotic element" (a common Victorian euphemism for sexual interest) acknowledged by Mama Westenholz (*B*, 101)—their simple enjoyment of sexual fulfillment. Karen herself described this feeling: "I think one can go so far as to say that the majority of happily married people find happiness in marriage because *they enjoy being married*, much more than because they like their particular spouse, and because marriage or the marital relationship attracts them, even though he may not always do so. They are blissfully happy in his arms because they like to be fondled and paid court to,— and this happiness makes them care for and feel deep affection for the person who pays court to them and caresses them" (*LFA*, 321).

Ingeborg Dinesen once wrote of her husband: "How he could ever have come to choose me, and during all the years we lived together show me,—and feel, as I know that he did,—the greatest love and understanding, has always been a riddle to me.... I have no doubt that he was happy here in his home,—happier than Tanne has ever been" (*LFA*, 427). Karen's mother, who clung outwardly to Victorian traditions, was inwardly the same woman who had ignored her family's admonitions and her own misgivings to marry in pursuit of an erotic element. So when she guessed, as she surely did, that Karen and Denys were not living together platonically, she seems to have remained imperturbed.

In March 1927 Karen wrote Thomas, "Denys and Mother took a great deal of pleasure in each other's company while both were staying here for the first month of her visit. Technically I have not been entirely honest in this situation, although I have often thought of being so,—mostly for the following reasons: first I thought that Mother would get a more *really* true impression if she apprehends the relationship between Denys and me as friendship, because then she will see it as a joy for me, while otherwise, given Mother's background and philosophy of life, it would be difficult for her... For that matter it may very well happen that I will manage to confide the situation to Mother before her departure, and it is possible that it will not make the slightest impression on her" (*LFA*, 300). And indeed several months later she confided to Elle, "Mother knows all about this relationship, you know, and so does everyone else out here, naturally . . . " (*LFA*, 338).

1927

* 3 *

As early as 1917, Karen had explained her philosophy for coping with frustrating difficulties. She said she was always reminded of the stork—the surprise at the end of a tale in a volume of children's stories at home: A man woke up in the night to hear the sound of water leaking from his farm pond. He flung himself out of bed, put on his boots, and began rushing around the pond to discover the source of the leak. In the darkness he could not see where he was going, nor could he discover where the water was getting out. After many falls and trials he at last found the leak and stopped it by making a little dam. Then he went back to bed and slept peacefully, but when he awakened in the morning, he saw that while he had been rushing and falling in the darkness his footprints in the mud had created a beautiful image—a stork. Concerning this story, in June 1917, Karen had written her mother, "I often still find the answers to life's problems in it. . . . Just when one feels one is floundering in the deepest despair . . . is when one is perfecting the work of art of one's life. . . . I have experienced this in my own life, and the greatest moments have been those when I have been able to glimpse the stork . . . " (*LFA*, 49).

On November 7, 1926, she had told her mother:

Something has happened to me that I can only call a miracle in miniature. You know that I have often enlarged upon and taken comfort in my theory of the stork:—that is to say that it happens to one in life as it did to the man in your old illustrated story, who heard the water rushing out of the lake and ran to stop it, fell into a ditch and so on—and next day discovered—the most unexpected result of all: a stork! The day before yesterday, precisely as I was sitting outside by the stone table and thinking . . . over this philosophy of life, I looked up, and there was a stork!—one of the real European or Danish kind, exactly as if it had come down from a roof at Ølholm or out of H. C. Andersen's fairy tales. It is completely tame, walks

251

about on the veranda and comes when it is called, and
makes no attempt at all to go away. I do not know
where it can have come from; it gives the impression
of being familiar with human beings. I am feeding it
on frogs, which the totos bring in buckets for 3 cents
a piece, and rats caught in the store, it is amusing to
watch it eating; it does everything with great dignity.
At this moment it is standing on the lawn just outside
looking at me gravely. (*LFA*, 293–4)

And when Denys left for England in February 1927, the stork
was still at the farm. Karen wrote Thomas in March to say that she was
sure it was making the acquaintance of his family "before setting off to
the north to deliver" Thomas's first child (*LFA*, 300). She may have
guessed that the stork's arrival was a sign of the end of her years of trials
on the farm and the beginning of years of joy. She had several reasons
for optimism: The weather and the season had been favorable to the
coffee. Her mother was impressed at how healthy the farm looked.
Contrary to Karen's fears before her arrival, Ingeborg Dinesen showed
no intention of suggesting it was time to abandon the investment.
Moreover, her serene acceptance of Karen's relationship with Denys
had the effect of consecrating it. Some months later Karen wrote a
letter to her saying: "I am so happy that I can write to you about Denys,
and it is beautiful and generous-hearted of you; I know you understand
how far I am from having any feeling of bad conscience over the
matter,—but it is of course a little outside the bounds of the law."
(*LFA*, 319)

One may imagine Karen's triumphant satisfaction that Denys
allowed Kenya society to know the truth about their sexual liaison and
agreed to let her mother know about it.

While Ingeborg Dinesen was in Kenya, Karen ushered her to
the homes of various friends for tea. Among their notable hosts was
Charles Gordon, first husband of Idina Errol. But, despite her mother's
demonstrated openmindedness, Karen was cautious about explaining
to her the full complement of sexual vagaries in Nairobi society. She
wrote Thomas in March 1927, "when we invite ourselves to tea with
Charles and Honour Gordon and then hear that Idina and her current

husband are staying there I am obliged to try to recall my civilized way of thinking and out of consideration for the dignity of an elderly, distinguished Danish lady, to postpone the visit" (*LFA*, 300).

Several times she attempted to persuade her mother to remain until September, but Thomas and Jonna's first child was due. To prolong the leave-taking, in the first week of May 1927, Karen accompanied her mother to Mombasa, where they spent a few days with Ali bin Salim. He entertained them with palm-filled views from his seaside villa. Karen and her mother took walks along the white beaches; and Ali later drove Karen along the coast to explore Denys's property, with its shuttered cottage overlooking the sea. There were some Moorish ruins nearby, moss-covered and crumbling, overtaken by mangrove trees and vines. After this visit, Karen's overriding memory of Denys's property was of the oppressive heat and the uncomfortably humid setting.

After seeing her mother off, Karen returned to Nairobi on the train, getting in about noon, and felt too weary to lunch in town. She should have waited there until after the lunch interval when the banks reopened at two o'clock, since she was late in paying wages; but instead she picked up her mail and went straight home.

She told her mother that there had been several letters from Denys. She said he had written, "I bless you whenever I think of you, which is very often" (*LFA*, 302). But the letters she claimed to have received do not survive; and her report of receiving them may have been to mollify her mother, since in the Dinesen family it was customary to write every week, and it would be difficult for her mother to understand how Denys could be so lax about writing. (Another possibility for the absence of the letters is that they were too intimate to be kept. Denys had requested of his sister and of certain friends that they destroy his letters after reading them [*SWS*, xiv], and perhaps he had made the same request of Karen. Indeed, the only letters to Karen that survive are written in a businesslike tone or in the kind of code represented by the black buffaloes.)

Whether or not he really wrote several letters to her in the four months he was gone, Karen's conviction that Denys thought of her often and blessed her appeared to be genuine. Her letters overflowed with new-found happiness and confidence.

* 4 *

On May 23, 1927, Charles Lindbergh made his pioneer crossing of the Atlantic by air, but news of the great event went unnoticed by Karen, whose thoughts were occupied with the deaths that week of two of her favorite deerhounds, Banja and Pjuske. She still had Heather, but the dog caused her some trouble that week. Karen had never been particularly successful at training animals. She insisted that Heather accompany her on a ride with Rouge, and since Rouge was perennially difficult to manage and Heather would not obey, Karen might have expected the outing to be a disaster, and it surely was. Karen had put Heather on a lead to force her to follow. The lead became tangled in the reins, and Karen was dragged off her horse. She struck the ground head first, which "highly amused some totos who happened to be up by the house" (*LFA*, 302).

In Denys's absence, the Africans of the farm drew closer, as was their custom when she was alone, since then she belonged to them exclusively, and for a while was not distracted as when she was "with the white people" (*OA*, 143). When she was ill, the Kikuyu women would come gently into her bedroom, their heads shaved, their breasts pendulous, their necks encased in stacks of copper rings. Their copper armbands, the copper rings around their ankles, and their beaded earrings complimented their dark, rich skin. They exchanged nods and song-like greetings with her, and went away smiling. The Somali women came in colorful veils and shawls, looking, Karen said, "like a great bouquet of flowers" (*LFA*, 301), wafting the incense of the East. Their hair and bodies were perfumed, and they carried the scent of spices on their hands—a thousand and one nights recreated in Karen's bedroom.

Karen had had little cause to complain about her health for nearly a year. But in June 1927 she experienced another serious sinus infection, with fever, headache, purulent drainage from her nose, and pain in her ears. She called it "pneumonia" (*LFA*, 303), and went to bed until the fever came down.

Archie Ritchie, chief game warden of Kenya, who in the third week of June stopped at the farm, found Karen ill. He had come calling in his Rolls-Royce with the rhino horn mounted on the hood, and he gave Karen a little gossip concerning the game situation. There had been a serious development affecting the Masai. Since the Masai had been forbidden to kill lions or to carry spears in the game reserve, the population of lions had grown out of proportion, and the lions were coming at night to the *bomas* to feed on the Masai and their cattle. In Ritchie's opinion regulations were to blame. He was going to ask Denys to join with some twenty other hunters to help in killing lions.

After only two months in England, Denys was out hunting with a client named Patterson, an American vending machine tycoon. Patterson later wrote an account of the safari in which he gave his impression of Denys, heightened by the romance of getting off the train at midnight, at Voi—elephant country 225 miles south of Nairobi: "The next moment I was shaking hands with Finch Hatton . . . He loomed tall in the darkness. He is six feet three inches tall. In the dark he seemed eight feet. The grip of his muscular fist reassured me" (*SWS*, 233).

By this time, Denys's safari regalia included a Dodge car, two Chevrolet trucks, a hundred African porters, three tents—two for sleeping and one for dining—and a bevy of assorted cooks, trackers, and gun bearers, including Billea Issa, Denys's Somali second-in-command. Patterson's particular interest was photography. In addition to a host of other photographic equipment, he had brought with him two Bell & Howell movie cameras. Denys set off with him, first to pursue elephant, and later to make his way westward into the Serengeti Plains. By June 29, 1927, they had set up camp in sight of Mt. Kilimanjaro, where Archie Ritchie gave Denys news about Karen's illness.

From the nearest telegraph office, at Taveta, Denys wired Karen: "Very sorry to hear you have been ill. How are you—telegraph. Denys." But his anxiety was unnecessary, since, once the fever had abated, she was not confined to bed. He came home for a few days in mid July, while his safari party rested in Nairobi, and he found her cheerful and energetic despite her symptoms.

Prospects for farmers were much better than in the difficult early 1920s, so Karen's financial worries had eased. However, two serious *shauries* did concern her. One was the resignation of the American, Thaxton, who had been running the coffee factory. She had to rely heavily on her overseers, and with Thaxton gone, she would be even more dependent on the South African, Dickens, whom she admired. "If we pull through," she said, "I will not forget Dickens and how he has kept up his hopes and spirits during these *trying* months. Running a farm under such conditions is probably like leading an army in retreat, and I have been thinking a lot about Napoleon on the retreat from Moscow; he has my heartiest sympathy" (*LFA*, 318).

The second problem was that a drought had overtaken them, the third in the farm's brief history. She was beginning to see in the weather a pattern of which early settlers had been ignorant. Indeed, she had learned why there had been so much apparently unused land when she and Bror first came to East Africa. Drought and disease before the turn of the century had killed three-quarters of the native population. The abundant rainfall in the region of Nairobi when Bror had first selected this land had been an aberration of climate; the average rainfall between 1900 and 1910 was thirty nine inches per year, yet there were three separate years between 1918 and 1927 when as little as twenty inches of rain fell. A difference of a few miles could mean a change in climate, and the Ngong farm lay adjacent to the plains, where it was drier than at coffee plantations like St. Austin's Mission north of Nairobi or at Kiambu, in the Kikuyu hills.

In the third week of August 1927, despite pain in her "head, nose, and ears practically the whole time" and eyes "running continually" (*LFA*, 309), Karen felt well enough to plan a picnic in the Ngong Hills with Nils Fjaestad, his wife, Ette, and Ingrid Lindstrom's two girls, Ulla and Nina. Along the ridge at the summit she got out and ran alongside the car. She said, "I wanted to try and see if I could run as fast as the car; it is no strain at all to run when one is up there, but when I came to a stop I could hear my heart beating so loudly they must have been able to hear it down in Nairobi . . . " (*LFA*, 311).

Plagued by her continuing infection, she consulted Dr. Sorabjee, a specialist in Nairobi, who diagnosed "frontal sinusitis" (*LFA*, 309). He examined her rigorously, inserting needles into the tear ducts. Karen, dazed as she emerged from his office, felt the pain intensify on the way home. She was driving Denys's Hudson and swerved off the road into a ditch. She broke the windows, smashed the fenders and bent the steering gear. In earlier years she might have become hysterical. However, she was not hurt, and after determining that her passenger—an invalid named René Bent, whom she had found at the hospital and invited to the farm for a few days—was unharmed, she burst out laughing, to have done "such an idiotic thing on a good, straight road" (*LFA*, 309).

Sorabjee had advised her to undergo an operation that could be performed in his office, but Karen put him off until after Beryl Purves's wedding on September 3. After shocking the Nairobi community by living for a time with Frank Greswolde-Williams and canceling a brief engagement with another suitor, Beryl had consented to marry Mansfield Markham, the son of a wealthy English peer. The only virtue Karen could see in the choice was that, in contrast to Beryl's first husband, who had been fifteen years older, Markham was three years younger than Beryl.

Through the years Karen had followed Beryl's adventures with sympathy, commenting in letters to her mother how she counseled the "naive and confused" girl (*SOTM*, 56). When Beryl agreed to marry Mansfield Markham, Karen said, "I do hope they will be happy, and won't express any more of my well-known doubts about marriage—but this one seems more of a lottery than usual!" (*SOTM*, 68–9).

Although Beryl's mother had returned to Kenya in 1923, Karen played the role of mother of the bride in preparations for the wedding. She supplied lilies and carnations, lent her house for the honeymoon, and at the wedding dinner was placed at table next to the groom, while Beryl's mother was seated several chairs away. Wearing a stylish dark straw hat and elaborate make-up, and still thin from her recent illness, Karen looked particularly chic. Later she joked to her mother that everyone must have thought her especially moved by the ceremony: infection had clogged her tear ducts and she could not help weeping through the entire celebration (*SOTM*, 69–70).

On September 6, 1927, she went through with her sinus surgery, emerging with a bandage around her eyes. What neither she nor Dr. Sorabjee noted was the probable reason for her trouble: chronic small doses of arsenic causing persistent sinusitis. After healing had begun, she wrote to her mother optimistically: "When you are thinking about me, you must not dwell on my loneliness and my difficulties, but on this lovely country, my dear natives, my horses and dogs, on the feeling I have of being in the right place for me, of being able to achieve something, and then on the great joy I have of being with someone here whom I really do love" (*LFA*, 314).

* 5 *

When the Patterson safari ended toward the middle of October 1927, Denys returned to the farm exhausted and hypochondriacal. He told Karen he thought there was something wrong with his heart, and she did not disagree with him, for she had heard her sister Elle mention that her husband, Knud, had similar symptoms (*LFA*, 328). It is not certain whether she knew that Denys's father had died while he was on safari, but she did recognize in him symptoms of depression. Karen said he "was subject to a special kind of moods and forebodings, and under their influence at times he became silent for days or for a week, though he did not know of it himself and was surprised when I asked him what was the matter with him" (*OA*, 359). He was "absent-minded, as if sunk in contemplation," and his cigarettes would burn half-way down their length without his noticing. When she spoke about it, he would laugh, but he admitted that he thought he was "a deserter" and that he had run "away from a duty" (*OA*, 222–3).

Just before Christmas 1927, a little Kikuyu girl was found strangled in the maize field. This was the second murder of its kind on the farm that year, and a most unusual crime in Africa. The murder sent fear over the entire farm, and police swarmed the coffee fields. This aspect of the tragedy Karen disliked most, for she had an inherent anxiety about dealing with British officials, whose actions never seemed predictable or reasonable.

Denys shared Karen's discomfort with legal entanglements and preferred to keep himself distant from police matters. In this uneasy atmosphere, on New Year's Eve 1927, it occurred to him that he might be in for trouble. Lending a gun to people going on safari, he had forgotten to show them the safety mechanism. The safari had already left Nairobi, but only the day before. Denys suggested to

Karen that they pursue the party by car and give the hunters proper safety instructions.

On the following morning of New Year's Day 1928, while driving on the plains, Denys shot two lions for Karen at dawn. In *Shadows on the Grass* she says they each shot a lion. This is partly for the effect of the story, for she wishes to make the lion hunt a symbol of the sexual surrender of woman to man. She describes the seductive animal growling in anticipation of the hunt, "Praise be to thee, Lord, for my sister of Europe, who is young, and has come out to me on the plain in the night" (*SOTG*, 442). In an erotic fantasy, she imagines herself receiving Denys's rifle: "it was too heavy and in particular too long for me . . . ," but "the shot, here before daybreak, was in reality a declaration of love—and ought not then the weapon to be of the very first quality?" (*SOTG*, 439). Truthfully, Denys's gun was too heavy for her, and she let Denys shoot both animals.

When Karen and Denys had first sighted them, silhouetted against the sunrise, the lions were standing upon the carcass of a dead giraffe. She and Denys were afterwards blamed for killing the giraffe, and there was a court case over it—an incident which increased their contempt for British officialdom. Despite this, shooting two superb lions in such a magnificent setting constituted the most rapturous hunt Karen had ever experienced. After the trophies were skinned, she and Denys sat in the cool grass and celebrated with almonds, raisins, and wine. She had never been so happy. Later she said, "I knew then, without reflecting, that I was up at great height upon the roof of the world . . . I did not know that I was at the height and upon the roof of my own life" (*SOTG*, 444).

1928

1

In "The Supper at Elsinore" Karen describes "a left-handed marriage" unsanctified by "legitimate union" (*SGT*, 222). Her relationship with Denys resembled marriage in some ways, although she had no contract: she wore his ring, she maintained a home for him, and—judging from her lack of anxious crises since his return from England in 1926—there were no other women. She was now comfortable enough with her life and emotions to discuss the subject of angst casually, even humorously, with her friend Gustav Mohr. She said, "I think that I myself have come to the conclusion in life that all fear in reality is nervous, because *there is nothing to be afraid of* . . . All terror is more or less terror of the dark; bring light, and it must of necessity pass . . . " (*LFA*, 339). The panic she had experienced in previous years, which could "raise its head on the most unreasonable occasions" (*LFA*, 339), seemed to disappear as she became secure in her relationship with Denys.

She had all the companionship one might expect from a traveling husband, without having to contend with the arbitrary demands of a spouse. "The English have an expression: '*to call your soul your own,'"* she said, "which fits this situation very well; this is exactly what those people who want to give their soul to others and can be satisfied with nothing less in return will not allow one, and in this, for me and other ordinary people, there is something utterly unbearable and intolerable . . . " (*LFA*, 348). She insisted that her relationship with Denys was superior to conventional marriage. "In spite of all the privations I am happier here than I ever believed it possible to be," she wrote to her mother. "For after all I am free. . . . And, you know, my relationship with Denys makes me very happy" (*LFA*, 314).

She said she was grateful that he did not hang over her and adore her: "I do not in the least like being caressed; I just can't stand being called by pet names and *made a fuss about*" (*LFA*, 321). Bror's continual affectionate demands had made her feel guilty when she did not comply. Even Denys's more cerebral attentions could be annoying when she was trying to concentrate on something else: she apologized to Thomas one day, "This letter is far from being what it should be, partly because I have been interrupted the whole time by Denys, who has now driven off to Nairobi, thank God" (*LFA*, 326).

Sometimes when Denys left on safari, she seemed relieved. She confided to her mother, "I think that it is true of an exceedingly large number of married people . . . that they would be extremely surprised . . . if they were suddenly told, or suddenly realized with certainty that they themselves are not 'more to'—their spouse than she or he is to themselves" (*LFA*, 373). In Denys's absence she could turn her attention to the affairs of the farm. The weather was still dry despite rain before Christmas. The grass in the park in front of the house was turning brown, and Karen had to chase away the *totos* who liked to graze their sheep there. Kamante had traded his cattle and sheep to marry "a big blooming ndito [young woman]" (*LFA*, 310), and it was a good thing, because at that moment the farm did not have enough pasture for his livestock.

Karen had never brought herself to sell Mbagathi, the house where she had first lived with Bror; now she was looking for tenants. A number of people came to look at the cottage, and she spent much time riding and walking over that portion of the farm. She was reminded that, although much had changed in fourteen years, one thing had not: she called it "my passion for my black brother." When she referred to the Africans as "my people," she was using the same language one used for one's kin. For some months she had been brooding over a story from Denys about atrocities in Italian Somaliland, where he had gone ashore in May 1927 on his way back to East Africa. There, he said, he found "labour very badly organized: families split up and sent to work 150 miles from their homes. The inevitable insurrection was suppressed with army brutality: women and children butchered in cold blood after the men had been rounded up and flattened out with machine guns . . . " (DFH to KR 6-3-27). Karen wondered why Denys did not bring up the matter with influential people at home, but he said that the British were reluctant to antagonize the Italians; Britain would not want Italy interfering with the running of Britain's colonies. Upon Karen's insistence that someone must carry the banner for the Somalis, he merely suggested that France might take up the matter "since the French hate the Italians and resent them getting more of Somaliland . . . " (*LFA*, 316).

Denys was not one to involve himself in humanitarian issues. A few causes interested him—game conservation, for instance, since he was dependent on hunting for his livelihood. In 1927 he had written a series of letters to the *London Times* to protest the slaughter of game resulting from illegal "Hunting from Cars" (*SWS*, 273–9). But in general, he did not immerse himself in causes. Like many others of his age, Denys believed that one contributes to the world by being happy oneself. As a reaction to the endless rules developed by Victorian society, the cult of the individual had overtaken thought in art, music, and politics. Denys's attitude concurred with that of his generation: the avant-garde strove for freedom. In works by contemporary composers such as Stravinsky and Debussy, melody and rhythm were secondary to mood and personal expression. Karen understood the philosophy; "I also think," she said, "that the person who can be said to have created something beautiful and harmonious has given the world something of value, even if this is apparently only to be found and is effective in his own sphere" (*LFA*, 371).

Denys believed that to interfere in the political sphere was neither polite nor appropriate. He gave Karen to understand this: "Because of the far-reaching effects that may be caused by the political action of a member of a great nation, in general their politics must be left in the hands of those elected to be responsible for them" (*LFA*, 316). But Karen came from a line of activists. Members of her family, in a tradition more compatible with that of the Victorian middle class than of the contemporary aristocracy, worried about how their lives might be of some value to the rest of humanity (*LFA*, 369–74). Karen's mother had been the first woman elected to her parish council; Aunt Bess had once made a spectacular (and inappropriate) intrusion into the Danish House of Parliament to protest national war policy; Uncle Aage had arranged public support for mercenaries fighting against Bolshevism in the Balkans; and Karen's sister Elle was at that moment running a hostel for the homeless in Denmark (*LFA*, 335). Karen had no intention of abandoning—for someone else to worry about—the matter of atrocities in Somaliland. Although her knowledge of them was not first-hand, she resolved to take up the issue with influential people in every possible way. She begged Thomas to assume an interest, she made plans herself to alert the English Parliament, she considered studying Italian in preparation for a verbal assault upon the governor of Somaliland, and, one afternoon in March 1928, she took aside old Lord John Islington to give him an earful of the subject, when he and his wife came to the farm for tea.

Lord Islington—formerly governor of New Zealand—a gracious, elderly flirt, and father of the new Kenya governor's wife, Lady Grigg, listened sympathetically to Karen's arguments about Italian colonial brutality. When she finished, he said, "My dear, when you are in England I shall be happy to introduce you to the appropriate people in Parliament" (*LFA*, 343). From this detached remark she understood that the subject was closed.

* 2 *

During the safari months of January and February 1928, Denys was away hunting with a client. But when the moon was dark or when he needed supplies from Nairobi, he would stop at the farm for a night or two.

Often he arrived without warning. Karen would be out in the *shamba* (coffee field), or at the coffee factory—for January was one of

264

two principal months, the other being July, in which coffee was harvested and processed for the London market—and as Karen's horse approached the house, she would be greeted by strains of music. Inside she would find Denys reclining in an easy chair beside the gramophone. The sight of him created in her a kind of ecstasy: she bloomed, she says in *Out of Africa*, like the coffee "dripping wet, a cloud of chalk" flowers with the first sudden rain (*OA*, 234). When he came back to the farm, she gave out what was in her and felt her truest desires fulfilled.

* *

A recent advance in the electric recording process had improved the quality of the gramophone records. Karen had ordered some new ones from Denmark. But her taste in music did not coincide with that of Denys; she preferred the earlier classics, while Denys loved modern music, like *Pelleas et Melisande* and *Petrouchka*. He also appreciated the work of Picasso, who was gaining attention in Paris for a new style called cubism. Inside the flyleaf of a copy of *The Rime of the Ancient Mariner*, Denys drew a sketch of a rhinoceros, with its muscles delineated in geometrical designs. He expressed much of the ferocity of the animal in his drawing of the feet. Karen wrote to her mother, "he has a great talent . . . but cannot be bothered to do anything about it" (*LFA*, 139).

After their lion hunt on New Year's Day, Karen had written to her mother, "If 1928 continues to be so enjoyably exciting there will be a lot to look forward to" (*LFA*, 333). An earthquake occurred on January 6, doing little damage, but portending other interesting events. A few weeks later a rumor arose that bandits had taken refuge on the farm. Karen was unable to confirm the rumor and was not threatened by the bandits but, "if I knew where they were and that they would not kill me," she said, "I would really like to meet them; there is always something fascinating about people who are absolutely desperate . . . " (*LFA*, 334).

Associating with fugitives was like reading the great epics; she imagined herself playing a role in the adventure. So she was intrigued when, in February 1928, a disheveled Swede named Casparson

(Emmanuelson in *Out of Africa*) appeared at her door. Casparson had been maître d'hôtel at the Norfolk, but he had not held the job long. Recognized as a homosexual, he was considered an unsavory character. He had once been an actor but was now out of a job and in trouble with the law. Karen helped him to flee to Tanganyika, and later he sent back the money he had borrowed from her. It might have amused Denys more, when she related the incident to him, if she had not sent Casparson off, in a great gesture, with two bottles of Chambertin 1906, a burgundy of rare vintage left behind by Berkeley Cole (*OA*, 207, 211). (The gesture was typical of her, although she later declared in a letter that she gave him beer, not wine [*LFA*, 341].)

Karen included a character modeled after Casparson, and also mentioned the earthquake, in "The Deluge at Norderney," a highspirited tale filled with humorous philosophical observations, which bore some resemblance to a series of dinner conversations recorded over months. This tale—in contrast to those written previously, which revealed more of herself than she wished him to know—might have been created for Denys's amusement. Although no draft of "The Deluge at Norderney" survives in her African notebooks, the tone matches Karen's carefree attitude of 1928. (The vivid unveiling, or unbandaging, at the end derives from a similar dramatic event on the farm in August 1927, when the Somali child Halima tricked Karen with a false bandage on her leg.) The stories within the story seem to analyze the evolution of her spiritual and sexual philosophy. In one, the tale of a young man who learns he cannot escape his destiny, she alludes to her youth in Copenhagen among the Frijsenborg set. In another she evaluates the change in attitude of a young woman toward sexuality, from repugnance to willing surrender. In a third she makes fun of the passions of an aging woman. In the character Kasparson— she changed the spelling—the consummate actor seeking a life of dramatically changing roles, she proposes an approach to dealing with tragedy: "I have lived long enough, by now, to have learned, when the devil grins at me, to grin back" (*SGT*, 77). However, in relating the tale of Barabbas, freed so that Christ might be crucified, she pursues a disturbing dilemma: how can you find meaning in life once you have completed your greatest role?

Denys was about to leave for the Sudan on an elephant hunt, and Lady McMillan had invited Karen to go on safari in Uganda while he was away, but Karen declined, telling Lady McMillan that she did not have enough money for the trip. However, to her mother she said, "I do not want to go away when Denys is coming back. Of course, this sounds pretty stupid, I see him often enough, but I am so much happier with him . . . " (*LFA*, 353).

Farah had married a new wife—Karen was obliged to pantomime in order to communicate with her, for the bride spoke no Swahili—and Kamante was now married. Observing these new unions gave her reason to evaluate her freedom. In 1926 she had written to her mother, "I think I have quite a gift with wild animals,—do you remember how tame the owl became, too, in quite a short time? It must be the same ability I have for getting on with the natives,—and the same which gives me my aversion to marriage, if you understand what I mean! I have no desire to capture and shut in and appropriate them, and they can feel that" (*LFA*, 294). The tame stork—tall and gangly, like Denys—still strolled gracefully in the environs of the house (*LFA*, 368). He had brought harmony into her life, and she had no wish to disturb his freedom, nor to have her own disturbed. She analyzed why she was so happy, and decided, "I think that here it comes naturally to me to be myself, to be what I believe that 'God meant when he made me'. . . . particularly with Denys, I believe that I am '*myself as the whole man, the true.* . . ." (*LFA*, 376).

* 3 *

Nineteen twenty-eight was the first year since 1918 that Denys did not go to England. By early April, when the rains began, he was back from safari at Ngong. Together he and Karen celebrated her birthday on April 17; she was forty-three years old. She had never looked more healthy, cheerful, and lovely. In contrast to the tweeds, boots, and heavy suits of the years with Bror, she now wore soft cotton print dresses that barely covered her knees. Her face was full and radiant, her eyes soft and a little dreamy. She wore scarves knotted fashionably at the neck, and a round, soft hat that crowded the curls around her face. Lady Islington was fascinated by Karen's allure. She teased her husband that he was in love with Karen, and he answered, "Yes, you're quite right, it has been my greatest experience out here" (*LFA*, 343).

Apart from her skill in conversation, her wit, and her sense of humor, Karen was at once charming, gracious, and sensual. A friend, the Russian general Polowtzoff, had remarked in 1919 that he had never known anyone so "sensual and so little sexual" (*LFA*, 321). But nine years later Polowtzoff would have assessed her differently, for she was assuredly sexual now. She was experiencing the "force of erotic feeling" (*LFA*, 321) enough to write Thomas a discourse on the subject, in which she said, "Say what you will, these are dangerous circumstances. (And grow still more so through the much discussed children whose only means of getting into the world to date is through these circumstances.)" (*LFA*, 322)

Denys had talked to his safari client, Patterson, about what it might be like to have children (*SWS*, 236). By this time, however, Karen had given up the idea and had taken to referring to herself as an "old aunt." Preventing conception was more her concern than conceiving. She said, "There is actually not a little to be said for the sensible views of the old folk, who tried to protect themselves in every way they could and equip themselves with both safety valves and fireproof walls; this perilous power was necessary to life, but no one should be permitted to set it free, play with it without being under control or run around with it by themselves" (*LFA*, 322–3).

There were certainly moments when she received the attentions she yearned for from Denys. On November 19, 1927, she had written to Thomas: "The lover groans in the beloved's arms: 'I have never loved anyone but you. I will die for you. *You wonderful woman, I want nothing in life but you.*'" She interrupted her writing in Danish to phrase these last words in English. Yet she went on to say, "Does he mean it?—Yes. Must he make good his utterances and be held to account for them the next day?—In no way. He was not compos mentis, and his greatest confusion of ideas was the error of mistaking an individual for one of the strongest forces of life" (*LFA*, 322).

She was not sure Denys would die for her, and she was certainly not all he wanted in life, but in their relationship each was comfortable in his role. Describing the situation as similar to marriage, she said, "the men come in, tired out after their safaris . . . and place quite a different value on a comfortable living room, flowers, conversation . . . , and take us out hunting or driving on trips that we could not undertake by ourselves, not even I, who do not consider myself to be naturally timid" (*LFA*, 358).

* *

In the last part of April 1928, there arose on the farm an undertaking that required a man's courage. On the eve of Denys's birthday, April 24—a week after Karen's—a lion invaded the cattle *boma* and killed one of the farm's oxen. The overseer Dickens, inflamed by the hysterics of his wife, came puffing and red-faced to Karen's house to demand that the lion be killed. He insisted on using poison, since to lie in wait to shoot it would mean risking his life, and his wife forbade him to do so. He said that once a man had children his life was worth too much to be risked in this way.

Karen, who thought poisoning a mean-spirited method of killing a lion, said to Denys, "Come now and let us go and risk our lives unnecessarily" (*OA*, 242). People like Mrs. Dickens—and even, of late, Aunt Bess, who had recently bemoaned the fact that she had never devoted herself to a mythical "Mr. Petersen"—seemed to Karen to value only the lives of married people.

Denys had been melancholy, thinking about how little he had to show for his life as he turned forty-one (*OA*, 243), and Karen wanted some special excitement for his birthday. She describes in *Out of Africa* how they transformed the lion hunt into a game, marking the coffee row, like Hansel and Gretel, with strips of white paper, so as to find their way to the bait in the moonlight. The coffee field—shadowed by drifting clouds—was a stage for tragedy, and Karen's torch (flashlight) the spotlight, as Denys raised his weapon and fired on a lion, then, startled by the growl of a second lion, spun around, and killed it too. The children at the school holding night class were shouted outside to witness the triumphant display of two dead lions. They showered the hunters with cheers. In *Out of Africa* the rapturous hunt becomes a

symbol for passionate intercourse—the rain beginning soon afterwards—and the feelings shared later, over a glass of wine, an expression of the strength of Karen's relationship with Denys. She says, "We
did not speak one word. In our hunt we had been a unity and we had
nothing to say to one another" (*OA*, 247).

* 4 *

While Denys stayed on, they drove into the Ngong Hills and
picnicked on a high slope with Mr. Charles Bulpett in honor of his
seventy-seventh birthday. The drive took them along a dirt track past
native *shambas*, conical huts, and patches of woods, upward to the
grassy hills, where dik-dik (miniature antelope) were plentiful. Above
the first ridge, just inside the game reserve and a short hike from the
road, they found a slope with a particularly beautiful view. From here
they could see the rounded snowy heights of Mt. Kilimanjaro to the
south and Mt. Kenya, a silver spear, in the north. To the right were
plains where wildlife roamed all the way to the Serengeti. On the left
they could discern among trees the tiled roof of Karen's house, a red
speck in the distance. Karen announced she would like to be buried in
this spot. In *Out of Africa* she says that "Denys remarked that then he
would like to be buried there himself as well." Afterwards, when they
considered an outing, he would often suggest, "Let us drive as far as
our graves" (*OA*, 365).

Toward the end of May 1928, Denys said he was going for a
holiday to his coast property. Karen ought to go along; they could spend
time at his cottage by the sea, and he would take her sailing along the
coral reef to observe the colorful fish. There were hundreds of yellow
weaver birds in the trees around his house; their nests dangled prettily
like miniature hives. The birds would serenade her, with the sound of
the waves as accompaniment. Would she not like to see the moon over
the ocean, the dhows in from India, the old Moorish ruins, and the
people of the coast? Together they could drink milk from fresh
coconuts, smell the sea, and at night, lie in the sand and view the stars.

After waiting a few days as if she meant to consent, she
remembered some obligations that could not be shirked. She seems to

have been unwilling to tell him that she detested the heat at the coast. Her excuses were that she had already promised to go to Lord Delamere's wedding—he was marrying for the second time, his first wife having died in 1914—and she did not dare miss a banquet for the royal visitor from Schleswig-Holstein, Princess Marie Louise (*LFA*, 361).

Having retained the title baroness despite her divorce, she was still in demand for Nairobi social affairs. Lord Francis Scott was her partner one evening for bridge; they trounced the governor and Tom Cholmondeley, Lord Delamere's son. In an essay to Elle, Karen said she was glad not to be married: "If one limits oneself in this way so as to concern oneself only with those to whom one is nearest, surely the result must be that not only does one cut oneself off from much in life, but one becomes terribly dependent on those people, and when they become occupied with other things one feels deserted" (*LFA*, 349).

* *

On June 1, 1928, Choleim Hussein, the Indian timber mer-chant, drove up to her house. He sometimes brought the women of his family—his wife and her mother, their daughters and a sister—on Sunday afternoon excursions to see her. Dressed in billowing saris, Karen said they looked "like a huge bed of colorful flowers" (*LFA*, 397). Knowing how repressed by custom these women were, she teased Choleim Hussein that he must now teach his wife to drive. "I don't think he could have been more horrified if I had said that I thought it was time that his wife boiled him up for soup," Karen wrote to her mother (*LFA*, 397).

On this occasion, however, he had come to the farm with an unctuous request to make of Karen. The high priest of India was making a tour of Kenya, and Choleim Hussein desired that Karen entertain the high priest with a view of her farm and the Ngong Hills. Would she be kind enough to receive them for tea on a specified afternoon of the following week? He himself would take care of the preparations. He would bring cakes and fruit blessed for the occasion, and she would present the high priest with a gift provided by him.

On the appointed day, she was "quite overwhelmed to see eight cars driving up, with altogether seventeen high priests accompanied by Jevanjee and others from among the Indian elite of Nairobi" (*LFA*, 363). The high priest, a small man dressed in a white cashmere robe, spoke no English. He sat beside Karen at the millstone table and beamed with good will at the farm, the Ngong Hills, and his hostess. He presented her with some earrings, and in a sudden great gesture—in addition to giving him Choleim Hussein's gift—she bestowed upon him the lion skin earned during her adventure in the coffee field with Denys. When Denys returned from the coast after an absence of less than two weeks and she related the incident to him—playing the roles of all the grand characters, as Denys himself would do—he certainly found the tale amusing but did not understand why she had given to a stranger the superb lion skin he had shot for her with so much trouble.

From Mombasa he had brought her a camera and several rolls of film, and now announced that he would teach her photography. But although Karen allowed Denys to show her how to hold the camera and frame the pictures, she could not develop enthusiasm for the sport. It was not like shooting animals, when within seconds the trophy was yours. The long delays in developing the film negated the triumph of capturing the images.

In late June 1928, she was ill with influenza for over two weeks. Afterwards, for a change of air, she thought about going on safari with Denys in the direction of Tanganyika, for two weeks of photographing lions. But the trip seems to have been abandoned, since still at home several days later, in July, she and Denys routed goats from the maize field (*LFA*, 374). Together they agreed against punishing the little African girl who should have been watching the flock. It was a season of singular rapport between Karen and Denys. She describes such a relationship in the story "The Old Chevalier": "I have never in any other love affair—if this can be called a love affair—had the same feeling of freedom and security . . . I believe that this feeling of safety and perfect freedom must be what happily married people mean when they talk about the two being one" (*SGT*, 99). Before Denys left again in August 1928 on safari with a client, he had spent nearly four months on the farm.

Despite her recent bout with influenza, Karen was plump and, becoming concerned about her weight, wrote to her mother in September 1928, "I must not get fat . . . " (*LFA*, 381). Once in her youth in a moment of panic over losing her figure, she had flung her lunch out the window of a train. She particularly wished to look chic in the late months of 1928 because a social event of the first order was about to take place in the colony: the Prince of Wales was to arrive on a tour of East Africa.

Karen had written to Thomas in 1926, "If it did not sound so beastly I might say that, the world being as it is, it was worth having syphilis in order to become a 'Baroness' . . . " (*LFA*, 281). Despite the troubles resulting from a life in Africa, she had been constantly solaced by her role as aristocrat. She was able to participate in the very highest level of settler society and to avoid associating with civil servants, white farm employees, and non-titled settlers, whom she found generally boring, peevish, small-minded, and lacking imagination. Her attitude was typified by a remark she made about some "undoubtedly very good, nice people": "For my sins I was dragged off to a dinner and dance with the Steeles last week, horribly *trying* and they are the sort of people I find completely uncongenial . . . life does become simpler as one gradually comes to understand oneself and so avoids wasting time trying to combine what *cannot* be combined . . . " (*LFA*, 318).

On the fourth of August 1928, Karen's title, and therefore her position in society, came into question: she received a letter from Bror to say he was at last to marry Cockie Birkbeck. He could not have chosen a more inconvenient time, just as the Prince of Wales was to grace Kenya society; Karen was now confounded about whether she could still call herself Baroness Blixen. How was she to be presented to the prince?

Fortunately, Bror had chosen to live with his new bride in Tanganyika. During the prince's visit Karen would be spared the embarrassment of the presence in Nairobi of another Baroness Blixen. Her aristocratic friends supported her; when she broached Lady Colville about dealing with the delicate situation, Lady Colville—now a little senile—responded, "Nonsense, my dear. You will soon be the Honourable Mrs. Denys Finch Hatton" (*SWS*, 182). Such foolish talk was not reassuring.

As though to counteract the dilemma, her friends the governor and his wife, Lord and Lady Grigg, invited Karen to stay at Government House during the royal visit. It was fitting that she do so, for Denys, her accepted consort, had been requested as official hunter for the prince's safari. Karen was amazed at his reaction to the news. She wrote to her mother: "Denys is in absolute despair because he has been asked to take the Prince of Wales, who is coming out here in October, out on safari. I laughed at him for taking it so hard, but he says that I don't know what English royalties are like, or the '*fuss*' that is made about them" (*LFA*, 361).

In the middle of August 1928 Karen arranged to visit the Lindstroms in Njoro. She could rely on Gillis and Ingrid to know the details about Bror's marriage to Cockie Birkbeck; Gillis had probably been best man at the wedding. Karen used Denys's new Hudson for the trip. She put the car on the train for the ride down the escarpment into the Rift Valley, past old volcanoes and grassy plains dotted with zebra and wildebeest, beyond Lake Naivasha and Lake Nakuru, and finally to Njoro, on the upland side of the valley, where the landscape resembled the English countryside and the car was off-loaded for her visit to the Lindstrom's farm.

Ingrid had not planned for guests. There was no sugar or milk in the house, and she served tea on a table made from a packing crate (*LFA*, 377–8). Although she herself could never entertain so informally, Karen saw Ingrid's "broad bold insinuating joviality" (*OA*, 218) reflected in herself, for were they not both examples of the sensuous Scandinavian woman? "I think this is why the English like us, because they think we are poetic, in contrast to their own practical females, who have to get something out of everything" (*LFA*, 377), Karen told her mother.

They discussed the elaborate preparations being carried out for the visit of the Prince of Wales: the roads in Nairobi were being repaired, the governor had called for £ 7500 for the building of a ballroom at Government House, and every colonial woman within miles was consumed with thoughts of what she was going to wear.

Karen was trying to lose weight before the royal visit, and she showed Ingrid the "Marienbad pills" that, taken with meals, she said, acted as a kind of laxative.

Back at Ngong, in a letter to her mother Karen rhapsodized: "I love Ingrid,—she is . . . the kindest and jolliest sort, and something really poetical . . . they are the happiest family I have seen out here. It is all due to Ingrid, . . . I think that Gillis and the children all adore her" (*LFA*, 377–8).

Denys, who stopped overnight at the farm on two quick visits during the month of September, was on safari with a client named Phipps, looking for a rare species of waterbuck called sitatunga. He hoped the prince might not have time for shooting. He was ferrying his client to the Sudan for a few weeks and dreaded returning to the royal fanfare.

* 6 *

Edward, Prince of Wales, arrived in Kenya the first week of October 1928. The heir to the throne was a small, handsome man, thirty-four years old, with blond hair and beguiling features. Women everywhere were said to be in love with him. After his travels around the world, to India, the United States, South America and the Islands, Kenya settlers were dazzled that he had seen fit to pay a visit to Africa.

Among the entourage debarking from the royal ship were the prince's brother Henry, Duke of Gloucester, and Audrey Coates, rumored to have had a dalliance with the prince on the voyage to Africa. After the welcoming ceremonies, the prince was taken to the new dairy farm of Lord Delamere at Naivasha, an inspection of which, white settlers hoped, would persuade him of their superior contribution to the success of the colony.

Denys was still away on safari during the first week of the prince's visit, but when he returned, an airplane was sent to take him to speak with the prince at Delamere's farm. Denys later described in lyrical terms the flight over the extinct crater of Mt. Longonot and across Lake Naivasha. The prince was indeed planning time for a safari, and now it was up to Denys to prepare for it. The royal entourage would include the prince's secretary—Denys's school chum—Tommy Lascelles, and the prince's aide-de-camp, Piers Legh. Prince Henry, whose interests inclined more to exploring the mountains, would safari separately.

While Denys made ready, the festivities surrounding the prince's visit continued in Nairobi. Karen stayed overnight at Government House, where a banquet and ball were held, and a few nights later she persuaded Denys to accompany her to a dance for the prince at the Muthaiga Club. He did so under duress, for parties bored him. He did not like to dance, nor was he amused by drunken excessiveness. At one party for the prince, someone began sailing gramophone records out the window and smashing them on the drive below. One by one others joined in the hilarious game, including the prince. At another party, which Denys had declined to attend, Lady Delamere began a bread fight at the table, aiming one particularly ferocious throw at the prince. It missed him and hit Karen, seated beside the prince, hard enough to give her a black eye. Lady Delamere, Karen said, "finished up by rushing at him, overturning his chair and rolling him around on the floor. I do not find that kind of thing in the least amusing . . . " (LFA, 387).

Denys was having difficulties lining up someone at the last minute to help him hunt with the prince. He approached several hunters with the proposal, including his friend, J. A. Hunter; however, Hunter was occupied with an American client, who was outraged at the suggestion he delay his safari in deference to royalty. Meanwhile Denys kept his base at Karen's farm and avoided interactions with the prince.

On November 6, 1928, Karen was invited to plan an *ngoma*— an evening of African dance—at her farm. The invitation, offered by the prince himself, was to take place four days hence. Karen felt the weight of a challenge because, as part of the festivities associated with the *ngoma*, she would naturally prepare a gourmet supper for the prince. The reputation of her table had become known to him, and he had commented upon it. The prince would bring along to dinner his aides, Tommy Lascelles and Piers Legh, and Karen must find ladies to fill out the table. She managed to persuade an old friend of Denys's, Vivienne de Watteville—a striking brunette—to accept at short notice. Vivienne, then touring and writing about Kenya, was Swiss, and cousin to Denys's cousin Kitty Lucas. Also available was a newly sophisticated and stunning Beryl Markham, who was acting as hostess for Prince Henry's safari. In honor of the royal visitors, special races had been held, for which Beryl's husband, Mansfield Markham, who now ran a stud farm in the highlands, had supplied mounts for the Prince of Wales and his brother. After a long honeymoon in Europe, Beryl was training horses again. She had been married to Mansfield Markham only a year, but rumor had it that the marriage had already gone sour. However, the money of Mansfield Markham had transformed Beryl into a sophisticated woman. She had returned to Kenya with bleached hair and exquisite clothes, and Karen considered her an excellent foil for her royal dinner party. It was no secret that, during the weeks of the royal visit, Prince Henry had developed a more than casual interest in Beryl. (Kamante says in *Longing for Darkness* that "the Prince and the Duke" came to dinner [*LFD*, Ch. 11].)

Karen's silver and china, her table and cuisine, indeed her own social graces, were about to reach the zenith of her career. She planned the festivities in a way to make the future king's visit indelible in his memory, so that when he succeeded to the throne he would remember "the cause of the Natives, in the matter of their taxation . . ." (*SOTG*, 430). She ordered bonfires prepared for the *ngoma* and easy chairs installed on the lawn for the chiefs and the royal visitors. She directed that sugar and snuff, tobacco and *tembo* (millet beer) be readied for the dancers and their families, and she planned a ceremony for introducing the Prince of Wales to his African subjects.

In the seating arrangement for her dinner she placed Denys opposite her at the head of the table. The prince's visit to her house might never have occurred if not for her position as Denys's consort. She wrote to Aunt Bess, "I have the most heartfelt belief in reciprocity, where two people who understand each other can achieve things that would be quite impossible for either of them alone" (*LFA*, 393).

* 7 *

Karen had worried that attendance at the *ngoma* would be sparse, but large numbers of Africans arrived, some coming in groups of two and three, others bringing their entire clan, the young warriors and the pubescent girls gathering in their respective throngs, and even the old men and women making a good showing. All were eager to entertain the "son of a king."

Karen directed her people to light bonfires along the approach to her park, and throughout the dancing area—a large grassy clearing in front of her veranda. Never had there been such a festive evening at Ngong. Three thousand Africans gathered on the lawn, dressed in the style of ages: chalk stripes, leather aprons and bare, painted breasts, heads shaven or hair plaited intricately with red clay and dung, necklaces of lions' teeth and rows of colored beads, ostrich plumes, copper necklets, bracelets and anklets, capes made from lion and leopard pelts, earlobes sculptured and stretched almost to the shoulders with earrings of elaborate design, and ruffs and anklets made from the black and white fur of colobus monkeys.

The Prince of Wales greeted the people of Karen's farm with words of Swahili learned for the occasion. He spoke with the chiefs, visited their huts, and took *tembo* with them: The gray, vinegar-tasting brew was served in bowls made from decorated gourds; decorum required that these be tipped to the raised mouth with two hands, and drained in one motion. Later the prince entered the circle of dancers; their clapping and voices rose to ululations at his participation. They danced in circles around the lighted fires, chanting and clapping in time to the drums, groups of two or more coming into the circle to display their agility, hopping from side to side or back and forth on two feet, bending their heads and knees with the rhythm. From time to time smoking branches were rubbed over the drums to tighten their skins; the smell of smoke added incense to the festivity.

Karen had hoped to talk to the prince about the needs of the people. If he could see to changing the policies concerning the hut tax and the *passe partout* (the government permit required for an African to travel away from his place of work), if he could persuade the British to spend more money on education for Africans, then improvement in colonial police and justice, working conditions and medical care would follow. As he mingled with the humblest subjects of the empire, she was ready to believe he could right all the ills of the kingdom. Karen could not anticipate that the Prince of Wales's unorthodox interests would lead him to abdicate the throne and marry a commoner. Later she said, "He walked with me into the huts of the squatters and made inquiries as to what they possessed in the way of cattle and goats, what they might earn by working on the farm and what they paid in taxes, writing down the figures. It was to me later on . . . a heart-breaking thing that my Prince of Wales should be King of England for only six months" (*SOTG*, 430–1).

* 8 *

In a letter to her mother Karen drew the seating plan for the dinner. The chart showed herself and Denys at either end of the table, with the Prince of Wales on Karen's right, and the prince's A.D.C., Piers Legh, on her left, while in the other chairs, or so she indicated, were seated the prince's secretary, Tommy Lascelles, Vivienne de Watteville, and Beryl Markham. It was odd for Beryl Markham to be available to dine with the royal party when she had been married only a year, and odder still that her husband, who had provided horses for the races held in honor of the princes' visit, was not invited to join his wife at Karen's home.

Karen told her mother that Beryl happened to be in Nairobi on her way to England. She said that Beryl, seated next to Denys at dinner, looked "ravishing" (*LFA*, 387). Indeed, there was a reason for Beryl's special glow: she was five months pregnant. Gossips said Beryl's husband had expressed doubts that the child was his, but he was sending her to his family in England for the birth.

While the other women wore the little cylinder dresses typical of the late twenties, Karen had designed and commissioned from a tailor a longer dress fashioned from silver brocade, with a dropped waist and a full skirt that covered the scar above her knee. (She says in *Shadows on the Grass* [*SOTG*, 434] that she ordered the dress from Paris, but in fact she did not really have the money to do this.) The neckline of the dress enhanced what she considered to be one of her best assets: her shoulders. She had decorated the dress with a tiny bouquet of flowers and perhaps wore the same flowers in her hair—which was naturally curly in the short style first cut for her in 1923. She had written to her mother that hair styles were longer now—smoothly waved to a chignon at the nape of the neck—but in her own hair style she felt "free." "I should like to give all young women two pieces of advice," she had said: "to have their hair cut short and to learn to drive a car" (*LFA*, 144).

The conversation at dinner did not disappoint her, although Vivienne de Watteville was a "giggler," as Denys put it privately to Karen (DFH to KB 11-5-30: KO, 37), and Beryl's conversation was not scintillating. Beryl contributed occasionally to the facts of the discussion, but she lacked feeling; people remarked on how emotionless she seemed. Denys, as always, looked and behaved like the aristocrat he was; servants of others who did not know Denys actually thought he was the prince. Describing a character modeled after him in "The Supper at Elsinore," Karen wrote, "He would have looked a gentleman on the gallows."

On the previous day Karen had experienced a brief doubt about using a former "dog toto" (*LFA*, 386) as chef to the son of a king. Suspicious and even scornful of the white man's food, Kamante would seldom taste what he prepared. Yet he exhibited a preternatural ability to prepare European dishes, in ways to surprise and delight even an epicure like the Prince of Wales. Karen described the menu later in a letter to her mother: "clear soup with marrow,—fish from Mombasa, a kind of turbot, with sauce hollandaise,—ham, that Denys had given me, with Cumberland sauce, spinach, and glazed onions,—partridges with peas, lettuce, tomatoes with macaroni salad and cream sauce with truffles,—croustades with mushrooms, a kind of savarin and fruit,—strawberries and grenadillas" (*LFA*, 386). Afterwards the Prince of Wales told Karen he had not had a better meal in Kenya. Denys said he himself had never had a better meal in his life (*LFA*, 387).

* 9 *

In the following days, while Karen basked in the success of her royal dinner party, Denys was preoccupied with ensuring the prince an enjoyable safari. He was under pressure to flush out impressive game, although he warned the prince in advance, "Africa does not wear her heart upon her sleeve" (*SWS*, 264). The arrangements for the safari had been hastily made, leaving Denys embarrassed at having no hunter to help him, for the party was too large for one safari guide. In addition, the weather was inappropriate for a safari. The short rains had begun and would probably not end until mid December. After consultations between Denys, the prince and his large entourage, including Delamere and a few other prominent settlers, it was decided to begin the hunt in Tanganyika, where perhaps they could escape the rains. But the downpour on November 14, the day chosen for starting, made proceeding by motor vehicle out of the question. With the help of the governor, the party commandeered several railroad freight cars for hauling trucks and equipment by train to the region of Arusha, a border town near the Serengeti Plains.

The town had been alerted to the arrival of the prince, and a great welcoming celebration was prepared. A throng of settlers eager for a sight of the prince had poured into Arusha and, due to limited hotel space, had set up safari tents along the outskirts of the frontier town. Among the celebrants were Bror and Cockie Blixen; Bror had taken a job as manager of a farm at Babati and had driven 115 miles over a dirt track to attend the festivities. Denys spied Bror and Cockie among the crowd at the hotel bar and approached Bror about helping him with the royal safari. When later the Prince of Wales paid a visit to Bror's tent to repeat the invitation, Bror suggested that the territory surrounding his own farm was rich in lions, and in this region they were likely to find plenty of game.

The royal safari was conducted in a manner somewhat elevated from the usual. Hunting was interrupted for sorties to the homes of prominent settlers for lunch or tea, and the Prince of Wales often dined graciously under the roof of a wealthy settler in the neighborhood of Denys's camp. The Prince of Wales was accustomed to sharing his royal company with people who were wildly eager to meet him and would contort themselves to provide their best hospitality. However, the prince encountered an interesting contrast when Bror introduced him to his own house and wife. Home for the newlyweds Baron and Baroness Blixen was a cottage made of mud and wattle with a thatched roof. The prince was so shocked by the cottage's mud floor, and by the thatched ceiling inhabited by lizards, that he would not allow Bror to leave her there alone and invited the new Baroness Blixen to participate in the royal safari.

The future king, it was noted, had an eye for attractive women. When he had met a particularly interesting lady in the neighborhood, he was known to disappear discreetly in the evening after the hunt. Although his interest in Cockie was platonic, she made a refreshing addition to the company of men, for she bubbled and flirted and praised their shooting, and they were amused by her inept efforts at using a gun. The Prince of Wales noted that "the guinea-fowl beat her every time" (*SWS*, 267).

The prince himself had come to Africa ill-prepared for serious hunting. He was using guns lent to him by Denys and Bror, and had borrowed a camera from Governor Grigg. The prince had brought with him some special equipment that served well on safari, including a paraffin stove for heating water for tea and an ice-making machine. These he took with him wherever he traveled. He had not planned to spend many days in the bush, but the plains and the great herds of animals, the high African air, and the feeling of freedom in being out in the open excited him more than he had anticipated. On one exhilarating day he was chased by an elephant while trying to photograph it; on another, Bror shooed a lion within the range of his gun; it was a fine specimen with a mane he was proud to take back to England. This last prize made him eager to shoot Cape buffalo before going home.

When the prince communicated his desire to hunt beyond the week planned, Denys was forced to requisition more supplies. He sent out a truck to Nairobi with an African driver, but the lorry was swept away in a flash flood—minus its driver who had leaped to safety. On the first day out, Denys's Hudson had encountered a rock that cracked the gas tank, so the car had been towed back to Nairobi. Nine days after the party set out, on November 27, 1928, there was more bad luck. The Prince of Wales received an urgent telegram in code. The hunters had to abandon their safari and travel to Dodoma, near the railroad, to find a cipher. The king was gravely ill and the prince was ordered to leave for England immediately.

Denys was left to disperse the elaborate safari. Lord Delamere had lent his car, which he had driven himself, but several other cars and trucks had been hastily bought at government expense and now had to be resold. The prince and his aide, Piers Legh, suggested pawning them off on the Aga Kahn, then on safari in Kenya. Denys had to take care of the matter, along with recovering and repairing his own safari equipment, devastated by the rains. The prince had personally offered to cover any expenses not paid by a grant from the Kenya Government for the safari, but he told Denys he thought the government would reimburse him for the damage to his Hudson (*SWS*, 269). The effort—and embarrassment—of asking the governor for the money was left to Denys.

Exhausted and discouraged, on borrowed transport, Denys arrived at the farm to spend Christmas at Ngong. He was greeted by a ferocious Karen—in a rage at the news that he had taken Bror and Cockie along on the prince's safari.

1929

By associating with Bror and Cockie, Denys had offended Karen, perhaps beyond forgiveness. It was intolerable to her that the other Baroness Blixen should be invited to participate in the royal safari, while she was excluded. Denys had betrayed her, he had humiliated her, he had placed her again somehow on the wrong side. She was as aghast at Denys's alignment with Bror as she had been when people sided against her during the war. However much Denys needed help with the prince's safari, he had not gone far enough, nor tried hard enough, to avoid a conflict of friendship; surely he must realize that, by making it possible for the other Baroness Blixen to attend the safari, he had compromised his relationship with Karen.

In "The Old Chevalier" Karen describes a severe scolding given with the sort of moral indignation members of her family, especially Aunt Bess, were uniquely capable of dishing out—behaving, she says, like werewolves, capable of outbursts of snarling and getting down on all fours (*SGT*, 84). But Denys did not apologize. Bror had performed well as second hunter; if it had not been for him, the prince might not have shot a lion. Karen had been divorced from Bror for four years, and it was not Denys but the prince who had invited Cockie to accompany them. Denys himself would not have wished it, for Cockie had no interest in hunting.

Afterwards Karen analyzed what it was about Denys's association with Bror that galled her. She reviewed the early years, when she had been obliged to compete with Bror for Denys's friendship. Dismayed that, after all this time, she was forced back into the competition, she wondered if Denys had always preferred Bror. This situation was very like the one presented in "The Old Chevalier": "She was jealous of him as if he had been another young woman of fashion, her rival, or as if she herself had been a young man who envied him his triumphs" (*SGT*, 87).

For the three-month period after the prince's safari, she wrote almost nothing to her family. Finally, in mid March 1929, Karen told her mother: "as a rule women will not acknowledge to themselves how much more, on the whole, it means to them than to men to be loved and admired, to have someone who *makes a fuss about* them and is grateful to them and cannot do without them, etc.; when it comes to the crunch they can't really renounce that . . . " (*LFA*, 399–400). And so she did not ask Denys to leave, but a deep rift remained in their understanding.

* 2 *

An airfield had been laid out along the southern outskirts of Nairobi on land adjacent to the game reserve. Flying had become a source of recreation for those who could afford it. The airplanes, with their two-tiered wings, delicate struts, and open cockpits, were now a common attraction over Nairobi. As a pilot circled for landing, he—or she, for women too were taking up the sport—would see herds of zebra and gazelle, and sometimes giraffe and rhino, scatter in the airplane's shadow.

The year before, Denys had been fascinated, when he flew to Naivasha to meet the prince, by his view of Africa from the air. A handful of people in Kenya now owned their own planes. One of them, John Carbery, had lost his wife in a crash in March 1928. There was talk of erecting a monument to Maia Carbery, a "Pioneer Aviator," although Karen said she thought it was silly for the mother of a three-year-old child to risk her life in such a way (*LFA*, 365). Denys frequently drove out to the airfield, looking for someone to take him up for a spin. In early March 1929, he took some photographs of Karen's house from the air, and presented the photos to her—possibly as a peace offering. The house looked liked a toy in the pictures; she and the dogs and Ali, and some of the *totos*, who had watched the plane fly over, all could be seen outside (*LFA*, 398).

After several rides in the air, Denys had decided to take flying lessons. Nairobi had a flight instructor named Tom Campbell Black, veteran of several air exploits, a hero with a mustache. Black had recently rescued a war flying ace who had crashed in the Sudan; and he had established an air record for the trip to Cairo and back, which increased his fame and gained him financial backing to start a commercial mail service in East Africa. Denys began learning to fly, with a view to taking the licensing examination during his coming summer in England. Meanwhile, Karen, who, in late March 1929, had not foreseen her own departure for Europe, received a telegram that her mother was gravely ill, and made hasty arrangements to return home.

She arrived at Rungstedlund on May 18, 1929, and found that her mother, who had suffered for weeks from fever, had now recovered. Karen was under no obligation to stay a long while, since she was not so exhausted with *shauries* as she had been in 1925; but she needed to settle her financial affairs. Although large debts lingered, chances were good for a profit from the farm in 1929. Interest rates were coming down, and Karen hoped to renegotiate the loans on her farm. Lenders, optimistic thanks to the state of the stock market, were willing to assume new risks.

Karen Coffee Corporation had always carried out its financial affairs through London solicitors, since its coffee was sold for pound currency on the London market. In early October 1929, Karen traveled to England. Denys, who had spent the summer there, had agreed to lend her money to refinance the corporation's loans—£ 10,000, an amount equal to half the total worth of the farm as estimated by Karen in 1923 (*LFA*, 148). She had not told her family that Denys was to be the lender. Indeed, they did not know she was going to see Denys at all.

In London, after nearly a decade of economic slump, the stock market was booming and the atmosphere was ebullient. People whose fortunes had languished for many years were investing again with enthusiasm. The American stock market was especially lucrative; Winston Churchill, the bombastic former member of parliament who had been defeated in the recent election, had traveled to America to keep a closer watch on his stocks; he as well as hundreds of other Englishman had bought heavily into the American market.

Denys, too, had evidently made money. Karen had first written to him concerning a loan in August 1929, and he had managed to obtain £ 10,000 on short notice. In London he and Karen went to the office of his solicitor, Wykes, where this money was offered to her through Denys's Kenya corporation, Kiptiget, Ltd. Karen wrote to Knudtzon, her attorney in Copenhagen: "Finch Hatton in the middle of our negotiations received a telegram from Hunter in Nairobi which distinctly advised him against lending KC this money, since he anticipated a poor harvest in the season 29–30" (*PA*, 32). But Denys ignored the warning, since the contract was to stipulate that Kiptiget receive the first debenture; so he would get his money back even if the farm were sold (*PA*, 31). The loan was to earn nine percent interest— less than he could make in the stock market—but he perhaps had been advised to invest in safer holdings.

Although Karen was persuaded that the terms of Denys's loan were acceptable, she could not act without permission from the shareholders of Karen Coffee. It would take a week or two before confirmation arrived from Copenhagen. Denys's solicitor wrote a memorandum to Karen on October 8, 1929: "It is essential that I should know definitely by the end of next week as to proceeding, not merely from the point of view of getting the work done in Nairobi, but because Mr. Finch Hatton must know without further delay whether the money which is available is to be used for this investment or not, as he is not prepared to wait indefinitely before investing this money" (*KO*, 28). In fact, this was Wykes's opinion, since Denys was with Karen in London on the date of the memorandum and could have communicated this information to her himself, had he wished to do so. Indeed, she had been staying with him for the previous five days at Buckfield, the home of his brother Toby, Lord Winchilsea (*SWS*, 281–2).

1929

Denys saw Karen off to Denmark on October 8, urging her to return to the farm as soon as possible. His solicitor wrote to her:

> Mr. Finch Hatton makes it a stipulation, that if his company is to complete the advance, you should undertake to return to East Africa not later than the end of this year, to manage and supervise the estate during the term of the debenture, as he feels that the well-being of the estate depends very largely on your being on the spot to manage and develop it. (*PA*, 31)

She finally left for Kenya in late December, sailing from Genoa on the S.S. *Tanganyika*. So great was her confidence that she was taking with her to Africa new furniture bought during her stay in Denmark (*LFA*, 401). But the American stock market had crashed on October 29, 1929, setting off, as she was soon to realize, a world-wide economic maelstrom.

1930

1

Karen arrived in Mombasa on Monday, January 13, 1930. She was in the habit of staying at the villa of Ali bin Salim, the only tolerable accommodation at the coast. But the ship docked too late in the day for her to descend upon Ali. Lady Colville came aboard to greet her and persuaded Karen to accept a room in her hotel for the night. The room proved to be the standard colonial fare: a starkly furnished space with a cement floor, one window covered with a slatted wooden shutter that provided no breeze but encouraged mosquitoes, and a bed with a shabby mosquito net. It was not the most serene setting for listening to the news that Farah had brought from Nairobi.

The coffee harvested during the months of December 1929 and January 1930 had yielded only forty tons per acre. This figure was far below the sixty tons Uncle Aage had specified would be needed to retain the farm. The drought beginning in 1927 had never completely abated. Locusts were appearing on the land in increasing numbers. Many farmers were selling out.

Farah's news of a poor crop confirmed what Karen had dreaded: that Hunter's pessimistic estimate of the anticipated coffee yield, cabled to Denys during their negotiations over the proposed loan, was correct. She could no longer see how the loan could go through. But she soon found good reason not to want Denys's money, because the news awaiting her arrival in Kenya was that Bror and Cockie Blixen had been invited, along with Denys, to join, in March 1930, a second safari for the Prince of Wales.

Karen had not even gone ashore in Mombasa before hearing about the arrangements for the pending royal tour. Now she flew into a bitter rage. Karen, the "other" Baroness Blixen, could not, of course, be included, even though the prince congenially accepted the fact that she was Denys's consort. The prince had written to Denys in late 1929 to say that he had enjoyed meeting Karen's brother Thomas at a dinner to honor winners of the Victoria Cross, and to pass along the news that Karen would soon be coming back to Kenya. Yet protocol eliminated the possibility that two Baronesses Blixen might join the royal safari. Karen blamed the awkward situation on Denys, whose continuing friendship with Bror was, as she decried to him in a note, "a law against nature." She was sure that Denys would not condone anyone's treating his sister or a close friend in that manner (*SWS*, 271).

The paperwork for Denys's promised loan of £ 10,000 was never completed, since the harvest of only forty tons per acre of coffee made the loan prohibitively unsafe. Dismayed, and angered by what she regarded as his collusion with Bror, Karen adopted the view that Denys had let her down in every important way. In a letter to Uncle Aage on February 19, 1930, she said, "With respect to the loan, I must also bear the blame for having raised and maintained a false hope and for having such unreliable friends. For my own part, I generously pass along all reproaches to them" (*PA*, 33). She had Denys's things moved out of her house and taken to the Mbagathi house on the other farm (he sent for them later) (DFH to KB, undated:KO, 36)—although she kept the books, possibly because the roof there was known to leak.

For the first two weeks of his second visit to Kenya, the Prince of Wales disdained public ceremonies in favor of trekking through the Serengeti with Denys and Bror, who arranged for him to shoot a wide range of trophies, including two lions, a buffalo, a leopard, three rhinos, and a variety of antelope. More than anything, he wanted an elephant, and Bror and Denys struggled to produce the opportunity. On foot they followed the spoor of one old bull for four days, over a distance of forty-two miles, until Bror's shoes gave out and the prince's blistered feet prevented him from going any further. Exhausted, they all returned to Nairobi to recuperate.

But people were clamoring to see the prince; the usual fanfare could not be postponed. Speeches and ceremonies, receptions and banquets had again been planned weeks in advance. Although most were sponsored by her friends, Governor Edward Grigg and his wife Joanie, Karen was not included and had to read about the festivities in the newspaper. The parades and gay parties were duly chronicled by Nairobi's paper, the *Standard*, which described the attire of the governor's wife, Lady Grigg, and that of Baroness Blixen, without specifying *which* Baroness Blixen.

On Sunday morning, the third of March 1930, Denys made a hasty appearance at the farm to inform Karen she was about to receive a visit from the Prince of Wales. He did not linger; Karen was so angry with him that polite conversation in the presence of the prince would have been impossible.

People might have dismissed this visit made by the Prince of Wales to Karen's farm as a thoughtful gesture, if they had not been aware that the prince was not inherently considerate. He was notorious for snubbing people when he found it inconvenient to keep his appointments. He had no obligation nor even arrangements to come, so his visit to the Ngong farm on March 3, 1930, was unusual.

Karen, who was aware of the prince's affection for Fort Belvedere, his country house, had extended to him, through his aides, an invitation to use her home as headquarters for the official visit. Although the prince assured her that he was delighted by the suggestion, he had been obliged to decline; he must stay at Government House to avoid offending the governor. The prince held fond memories of the special *ngoma* Karen had arranged for him in 1928. He wished they could have seen more of each other during the present visit. Denys was being a very great help to him. He had enjoyed being introduced to her brother and his charming wife in England the previous year.

In 1928 Karen had felt particularly confident when she met the prince; slim, chic, and brightly conversational, she had made a charming impression. Her contentment with life then had showed. Now perhaps the prince was disappointed at the change in her. She had lost her radiance and begun to age.

While in Nairobi, Denys was staying at Government House, along with Bror, Cockie, and the Prince of Wales. When he could escape, it seems he came out to the farm one evening for a dinner of fresh trout given to Karen earlier in the day by Gustav Mohr. But the meal was rancorous. Karen later told her mother she made a scene (*LFA*, 407). Not once, but twice, Denys had compromised their friendship by including Bror in a royal safari. This second time, however, he had gone ahead, knowing how deeply it would affect her.

In an undated note, Denys wrote to her from Government House:

> Your talk disturbed me very much last night. Do not think that I do not see your point of view: I do absolutely. But I feel that just now you are looking on the very darkest side of things. I would like to see you before I go off and shall try to get out later. I am sending Kamau to collect a box of papers and a Jaeger dressing gown from the other farm (DFH to KB undated:KO, 33–6).

The prince's party was now due to travel south of Nairobi, a day's drive to the Masai Reserve near Mt. Kilimanjaro. There they were to witness a tourist attraction of the first order, the spectacle of Masai *moran* (warriors) stalking and killing a lion. The prince hoped to take motion pictures of the amassed *moran*, their hair plaited elaborately with red earth and dung, their faces and limbs painted with stripes, their spears and shields decorated in red, white, and black geometrical designs, readied for the ritual of the hunt. Unfortunately, the expedition was cut short when both the Prince of Wales and Bror came down with malaria and were obliged to return to Nairobi to recuperate.

Arrangements had been made for the royal hunters to leave Nairobi on March 9, 1930, to continue their safari into Uganda and the Sudan. Bror and Cockie would not accompany them, but Denys continued as leader of the safari and had been invited to fly to England afterwards in the prince's entourage, leaving Khartoum on April 13. Having earned his pilot's license the summer before, this year Denys planned to go home to buy an airplane.

Denys was not called Makanyaga, "Master of the Put-Down," for nothing: over dinner he had related the safari's progress to Karen in humorous detail, taking care to deprecate every aspect of the royal hunting expedition: the prince's special primus for tea—a ritual so sacred that they must abandon the hunt at the stroke of four PM, oblivious to whether a superb male lion stood growling nearby—Cockie's taking aim on a guinea fowl and accidentally shooting a giraffe, Bror creeping through the high grass and waving his arms shouting, "Shoo! Shoo!" to drive a lion in the prince's direction (*SWS*, 267). Karen, although still bitter about Denys's safari, wrote to her mother, "I made a scene of the first water [highest rank] because he had taken on Bror as *second white hunter* for the Prince of Wales, and even that ended up with my laughing . . ." (*LFA*, 407). So when Denys left for England with the prince, Karen said good-bye to him on good terms. But she had not really forgiven him.

* 2 *

In the midst of profound disappointments with Denys—over his friendship with Bror, his failure to supply the loan she needed, and his allowing her exclusion from the events surrounding the prince's second visit—Karen was meeting staggering problems on the farm. The coffee crop had failed to bring the desired yield, and to make matters worse, on February 26, 1930, Dickens, Karen's manager of ten years, resigned. Not only did he foresee the end of his usefulness to Karen Coffee farm, but a recent incident had sealed his determination to leave. A few nights before Karen's return, the Africans had held an illegal *ngoma* on the farm without Dickens's knowledge. Spontaneous *ngomas*—those not associated with a harvest celebration—were forbidden because the government had concluded that disturbances were being caused by Africans drinking too much *tembo* along with the dancing. The reasoning for the law was underscored by the conviction that *ngomas* were a heathen practice unworthy of encouragement by His Majesty's government; people like Mrs. Dickens were terribly agitated by the thought of drunken natives dancing in the environs of their homes. The *ngoma* held in January 1930 did not celebrate the harvest; it was an extemporaneous undertaking. Unfortunately, the fears of the Mrs. Dickenses of Kenya were realized when a fight broke out and a man was killed. In the eyes of the police, the responsibility fell on Dickens, for his failure to maintain order on the farm. Police again scoured the premises, interrupting the coffee harvest at its height and arresting twenty-five young African men, among the strongest of Karen's workers, as well as Kamante—although, Karen assured her mother, Kamante had merely been taken for questioning. Faced with this crisis, and having borne more crises than might have been expected of an overseer in the course of ten years on the farm, Dickens quit.

Desperately negotiating, Karen could only persuade him to stay until July 1, 1930. As for finding someone new, Taylor from the land office came out to the farm to enter into the discussions. Karen also called upon her friend Gustav Mohr to advise her. He took leave from his work on the farm he managed to walk around Karen's farm and give his opinion of what she should do. Karen had been reading the stories of Charles Dickens and envisioned herself as a victimized waif in an unfolding tragedy. Mohr, she said, "has been the only one in this Dickensian dilemma who has 'acted and not talked,' and I will not forget what he has done . . . " (*LFA*, 404).

In comparing Mohr to a savior in a novel by Dickens, perhaps Karen clung to the belief that her difficulties too might in the end be happily resolved.

* 3 *

Knowing how she liked to fulfill a role, Denys had asked Karen before he left for Europe if she would consent to store some of his valuable things. Soon eighteen large crates arrived from England containing two collections important to Denys. First there was an array of vintage port—enough to fill twelve crates—which he had bought as an investment upon the advice of his brother Toby. Denys had written to Kermit Roosevelt in 1924, "My brother and I have taken to investing in a pipe of port between us in vintage years and I have often found it a pleasant thought out in Africa to remember those silent rows of black virgins steadfastly awaiting me in England, ready or getting ready, preparing in fact to pour out their life's blood for me and my friends anytime after about 1938" (*SWS*, 214). Something had made him decide to bring this wine to Africa.

Six other crates contained a collection of rare books left to Denys as part of the inheritance from his mother. Why he would choose to send such valuable things to Africa is not clear, unless the Ngong farm had become more a home to Denys than England.

In May 1930, Karen sold the smaller bookcase that housed the books she shared with Denys—the complete works of Shakespeare, Hans Christian Andersen, the writings of the romantic poets, the Greek and Latin classics, *Kristin Lavransdatter*, Danish love poems, Kant, Proust, *The Forsyte Saga*, *The Man-Eaters of Tsavo*, and the poems of Walt Whitman—to name only a few of them. For the first time in many years, she invited carpenters into Mbogani house; and the sound of hammering joined the smell of sawdust as a new set of bookshelves was fashioned, as she told her mother, "along the whole of one wall" (*LFA*, 406).

Among the crates that Karen fetched from the railway office was "a first edition of Voltaire's 'Dictionnaire Philosophique' in sixteen volumes, and a very beautiful edition of Racine" (*LFA*, 409). She was less enthusiastic about the port: "I don't myself drink port, so I wish it were something else . . . " (*LFA*, 406).

When the Indian carpenters had completed their work, Karen asked them to make small brass markers for the edges of the shelves, and to engrave them with the letters D.F.H. Denys had agreed to pay the cost of building the shelves, for she had no money for it (*LFA*, 406). Since the failure of their agreement on a loan, he should have been fully aware that the farm might soon be sold. However, the new bookcase symbolized Karen's belief that a miracle would prevent her from having to sell out.

* 4 *

Denys wrote to Karen near the end of April 1930 within two weeks of his arrival in England. It was a wet spring, not the best sort of weather for testing airplanes. Denys's holiday was being taken up by the Prince of Wales, who insisted on learning to play golf. He began the letter to Karen by saying, "This is a cursed country . . . everyone sallies out in the rain and plays golf and apparently likes it . . . ." He said he had played "rather well," in spite of being disgruntled by the weather and the prince's less-than-expert performance. Denys expressed concern for Karen's health and frame of mind: "I hope that you have paid a visit to my coast property: I feel it would do you a lot of good to get away from Ngong for a little."

He said he hoped to bring a Gypsy Moth airplane back to Africa with him, but he was doubtful that production of the new planes was equal to popular demand for them. Still, he already envisioned landing on the lawn behind Karen's house. He had bought new records, including *Die Meistersinger* and said "I shall be quite ready to start back for East Africa . . . and hear it with you at Ngong."

Over the eight pages of this letter, Denys struggled to think of news that would interest Karen. His witty recall of dialogue, his mimicry of expressions and gestures, his brilliant use of comparisons, his insight into personal foibles—little of these came out in his letters. He did describe England's economic state. Since the crash, the young aristocracy were carrying on as if nothing had happened, buying Rolls Royces, stashing money in Swiss bank accounts, continuing the roaring parties characteristic of the previous decade. Denys said, "The trouble is that the *land* which cannot escape is taxed to death, and English agriculture is at its last gasp. Australia is bankrupt! Germany full of unemployed; America ruled by gangs of gunmen. . . ." (DFH to KB 5-11-30:KO, 37–8).

* *

Amid world-wide chaos, Karen's farm teetered on the brink of insolvency. Although bankruptcy could not be attributed to her own personal failure, if she were to sell the farm she would, as she told her mother, lose "the only thing that I have produced in my life" (*LFA*, 406).

A larger shame was that she would be letting down the Africans; they would surely be forced to move if the land were bought by a developer. She said, "The great trust that all the black people place in me, and in my ability to arrange everything for the best for them, and my own awareness of the appallingly insecure basis of it, uses up all my mental powers . . . " (*LFA*, 407). Her greatest solace at that moment were the children of her servants—especially Tumbo, and Farah's little boy, Saufe, now two years old, whose "chief interest in life," she told her mother, was joining in the dancing at *ngomas* (*LFA*, 409). Farah's wife, Fathima, had recently given birth to a new child: a tiny girl upon whose sober face had been painted, in the Somali custom, blue eyebrows—which, Karen said, made her look like an Algerian doll her sister Elle had once owned. In May 1930, Karen wrote to her mother, " . . . it is clear to me *by now* that *my black brother* here in Africa has become the great passion of my life, and that this cannot be changed. Even Denys, although he makes me tremendously happy, *carries no weight* in comparison" (*LFA*, 407).

Throughout the course of June through August 1930, it became increasingly apparent that the farm could not survive. Torrential rains in April and May had promised a good crop, but soon afterwards the buds were killed by frost. Still unwilling to set a date for a sale, Karen was beyond making reasonable decisions. Her letters to her mother were as scarce as the cherry on the coffee bushes. She apologized, saying "It is this truly frightful tension that I constantly live under and that affects my whole future that makes it difficult to concentrate on producing anything like an interesting and entertaining letter from here" (*LFA*, 406).

She did not write back to Denys, and hearing nothing from her, he sent no more letters.

In the first week in August 1930, the governor's wife, Joanie Grigg, invited her to see a motion picture at Government House. Karen had been to the pictures before; as early 1918, during the Great

War, silent films had occasionally been shown in Nairobi. On this evening, Karen viewed the Hollywood version of *Beau Geste*. The action included Arabian horses, the French Foreign Legion, and sheiks of the northern Sahara Desert. In a telling reaction to the movie, she wrote to her mother: "there was no love element, which is a blessing . . . " (*LFA*, 408).

* 5 *

The feud begun in 1923 between Karen's former cook, Hassan, and Farah had become a war between clans. Farah had recently survived three attempts on his life. One evening he was jumped and stabbed in Nairobi while waiting for Karen outside a Somali hotel. Intruders repeatedly threatened his family at night, and Karen gave him a gun to protect himself. Farah's wife Fathima seemed entertained by the situation, but Karen desired that no ill come to the apple of her eye, Farah's two-year-old son, Saufe.

In addition to her worries on the farm, Karen was allowing herself to be annoyed by a petty aggravation with her brother Thomas, to whom she was at the moment loath to write. Thomas had been given instructions to deliver to the King of Denmark's palace the lion skin shot on New Year's Day 1928 and recently cured by the respected firm of Rowland-Ward of London. This great gesture—the attempt to gain the attention of a popular figure—was reminiscent of her youthful gift of flowers to Georg Brandes. Karen's family was embarrassed about the gift. What would the king do with it? "He will have some attic at Christiansborg or Amalienborg where he can put it away," answered Karen sarcastically (*SOTG*, 445).

She had prepared a letter to be sent to the king with the lion skin and wrote her mother in June 1930 that it was not particularly nice of Tommy "to be in possession of a lion that he had not shot himself" (*LFA*, 408). Within a few months, Karen received a letter from the king, thanking her for the trophy. Shortly after she received it, Denys Finch Hatton returned from Europe.

1930

* 6 *

Karen had for some time understood the essentials of Denys's temperament. As early as 1925, in an essay to Aunt Bess, she had outlined the "English character." The foibles she attributed to the English were clearly lifted from her observations of Denys: "miscalculations and setbacks have no material effect on them and in some ways they lack the ability to grieve or be chagrined over an error or a miscalculation" (*LFA*, 234).

There were no signs that Denys had agonized or brooded over having upset her earlier in the year. He behaved, as Karen had noted earlier, as though there were situations in life "where no rules are enforced, where everything is permissible and where nothing matters provided it be lively, amusing, in some way or other free and delightfully human." One cannot help loving people like this, Karen told Aunt Bess, for such people uplift by virtue of their spirit (*LFA*, 235).

She seems to have assumed throughout Denys's absence that her great anger had ended their relationship. Perhaps she had avoided thinking of "love interests" because of her belief that the friendship was over. She did not imagine such bitter feelings could be ignored. Yet, ignore them Denys did. Upon his return he behaved with her as if nothing had changed. He teased her in the old manner, said nothing about their dispute, and proceeded as though there were nothing whatever dividing them or hanging over them.

She followed his example. They discussed little about the state of the farm, about the possibility of selling out, or about Karen's leaving Africa. She kept her worries over her debts to herself, in the same way Denys reserved talk about his own financial affairs. As to the reasons they did not communicate about matters so vital to Karen's immediate future, Karen later said, "most of the time when we were together, we talked and acted as if the future did not exist; it had never been his way to worry about it, for it was as if he knew that he could draw upon forces unknown to us if he wanted to. He fell in naturally with my scheme of leaving things to themselves, and other people to think and say what they liked" (*OA*, 355–6).

She had developed the idea that Denys would not give up the home he had made in her house; she believed that he preferred to live at Ngong, and that, if she should have to sell, he would at least buy the house and the surrounding park. This conviction allowed her to resume her friendship with Denys and to carry on with the farm throughout the last months of the year 1930—a time during which Denys introduced her to the most transporting pleasure of her stay in Africa.

* 7 *

By ship Denys had brought with him a Gypsy Moth airplane, painted green and gold. It could land in a field a mile from Karen's house; Denys had directed some of Karen's farm workers to clear the ground. The Africans were fascinated by its lightweight propeller, its open cockpit, its fragile wings, its delicate struts and wheels. The way it suddenly appeared in the sky, its whirring sound, its swooping motion, its gliding landings and hopping stops reminded the Africans of the locusts of the months before; they christened the airplane *Nzige*—the Grasshopper. Karen was as fascinated as the Africans, although she was afraid of the plane. Denys reassured her with flattery: "He says he has brought this machine out here for my sake"(*LFA*, 411), she wrote to her mother.

She took her first ride in it on Saturday, September 20, 1930. Any terror she had held of the dangers of flying faded in the face of exhilaration at being in the air with Denys. She had always said that being near Denys was like getting into clearer air; the experience of flying embodied what she had always known to be true. She wrote to Elle: "flying suits Denys so perfectly. I have always felt that he has so particularly much of the element of air in his makeup . . . There is a good deal of heartlessness in this temperament . . . but so pure, compared with the earthly beings . . . clear, honest, without reservation, transparent . . . " (*LFA*, 413).

His heartlessness was reflected in his seeming indifference to the imminent sale of the farm. He had once written to Kermit Roosevelt: "I am never sure of Africa as a place for women" (DFH to KR 1-27-19). He spoke as if she would be better off without the farm, not as if he were concerned at the loss of what had been his home for the past six years. Karen's love for the land—a frankly romantic preoccupation—self-defined her as a person with heart. "A garden and a cornfield can be so full of heart," she told Elle (*LFA*, 413).

Denys was to have been on safari from the end of September 1930, until November, but he was released early. He returned to Nairobi in October, after only a few weeks' hunting. On October 7, he met with his solicitor to make out a will. In it he specified that £ 8000 was to go to his sister, Topsy, and the remainder of his estate, along with his safari gear and his guns, should go to his brother, Toby. His collection of port—a considerable investment—and his mother's legacy of valuable books, were still in Karen's house.

In making a new will Denys seemed to be mulling over the dangers in flying. Only a few months before, in England, he had experienced an embarrassing accident: while taking off from his brother's estate, he had underestimated the height of trees at the end of the field. His airplane was damaged by branches and his pride injured in front of family members who had rescued him from the tangle.

During the first weeks after his return from safari, he spent much time with other fliers. He was reviewing the elements of flying in Africa, taking short flights with experienced pilots, listening to suggestions about wind currents and landing areas in Kenya, and familiarizing himself with the colony's landmarks. But nearly every afternoon he flew to Ngong, landed on the farm, and took off with Karen as passenger. In *Out of Africa* she says she felt as though Denys were a genie taking her on a ride on a flying carpet. They glided over the Ngong Hills; chased buffalo with the plane's shadow; swooped over clusters of round thatched huts, long rows of coffee bushes, and quilted *shambas* of maize and sweet potatoes; and flew across the forest near the dam and pond on the farm, and over the roof and park of Karen's own house.

Denys operated the airplane with a kind of joyful reckless-ness. Karen described the rides to her sister Elle:

> It is the most divine *game* imaginable; you cannot
> prevent yourself from laughing when you streak

down from on high and chase, quite low down above
the plain, a flock of madly galloping zebra, and see
your own shadow over them and the grass, in this
light, light air,—when you steel yourself against the
strong daylight, cut through the air, occasionally
make just a couple of brisk, quick turns, fling yourself headlong down, lurching, turning, climbing,
beating down like a dragon caught by the wind
almost to the earth,—spinning, rushing, writhing
through the turns! (*LFA*, 413)

In November 1930, Denys invited Karen to go to the coast
with him, and for the first time she accepted. They may have landed
at Mombasa and slept in his house above the beach at Takaunga. She
describes such a visit in *Out of Africa*, although her letters do not. She
recalls the moonlit nights and the sand blowing in from the sea.
According to her diary, they flew to Lamu Island, off the coast of
Kenya, a romantic Arab enclave of white houses and minarets, before
circling and returning to Nairobi.

* 8 *

Denys offered rides in his airplane to many people, in fact to
anyone he could persuade to fly with him. One day he invited Lady
Delamere to go up with him, while she visited Karen for tea. But Lady
Delamere did not go in for flying.

One person who showed considerable interest, and was enthusiastic to go for rides, was Beryl Markham. Beryl had recently
returned from England in the wake of scandal, since after the birth of
her child, a son, Beryl had continued the love affair begun during the
royal safari in 1928 with Prince Henry, Duke of Gloucester. When the
king and queen learned about the affair, they took measures to end it.
Certain legal negotiations with Beryl's husband resulted in the ultimatum that Beryl must leave England. She was offered a pension by the
royal family, on condition that she stay away from the prince. The
Markham family disowned her, for their reputation was at stake, and

insisted that she relinquish her son. Since her return to Kenya, Beryl had been living at the Muthaiga Club because her father had remarried, and she did not like his new wife.

Herself a storyteller, Beryl wrote much later that she had flown frequently with Denys. People gathered from this that she had been involved in a romantic relationship with him. Karen's tale "The Poet," containing many references to flying, to the sea, and to a developing tragedy (symbolizing loss of the farm), centers around a young protégée, fifteen years younger than the narrator (Beryl Markham was seventeen years younger than Karen), who reappears after some lapse of time (*SGT*, 379). A young woman is sent to the country to recover from a disappointment in love (*SGT*, 365). This lively girl gives the impression that she can fly (*SGT*, 375). When a husband goes off for a walk with her, his wife becomes jealous. She has "no reason to be jealous" but that does not cure her of "watchfulness and distrust . . . " (*SGT*, 381). Karen observes that "together those two might fly, nobody could tell where to . . . " (*SGT*, 377).

In her previous tale about jealousy, "The Roads Round Pisa," Karen features the same character, Count Augustus von Schimmelmann. But Denys gave airplane rides to virtually anyone willing to accompany him, and Beryl herself relished a good story. Seemingly indifferent to outrageous rumors, she had never denied gossip that her son had been fathered by Prince Henry—although this was impossible, since she was five months pregnant when she first met the prince. Karen had invited Beryl to stay at Ngong again and sympathized with her difficulties. Karen said, "In spite of all her experience she is still the greatest baby I have known but there is more in her than in most of the people who pretend to be so shocked at her now" (*SOTM*, 92). Yet Karen had always thought that Beryl's perceptions were not the same as others'; after she heard Beryl's account of how her husband had sent her away and kept their child, Karen wrote skeptically to her mother in February 1930, "I can hardly believe that everything is as she describes . . . " (*SOTM*, 92).

In later years Beryl would not admit to having had a romantic relationship with Denys, although she greatly admired him. She said he "was something you would not like" (*SOTM*, 365), meaning homosexual. She said she doubted that even Karen's relationship with him had been consummated (WBM), perhaps because her own had not been.

1931

During the last months of 1930, while Denys was introducing Karen to the joys of flying, the creditors of Karen Coffee Corporation prepared an ultimatum. They informed its chairman, Aage Westenholz, that no further moratorium on payment would be tolerated. Unwilling to assume the blame for telling Karen to sell, Uncle Aage resigned his chairmanship, turning over the seat to Viggo de Neergaard. He was under the impression that Karen would try to buy the farm at the liquidation. He wrote to her at Christmas 1930, "The best we can wish for you, presuming you will be in good health, is the buying of KC at a low price and a good year following that" (*PA*, 35).

Karen needed time to find the money. Denys had been on safari since shortly after New Year's Day 1931 with Marshall Fields. When the bank threatened to foreclose, Karen sent him first a telegram, then a letter, alerting him to the emergency. She was ill and unable to cope with the problem under the circumstances. Would he not agree to lend money so that she would not have to sell before he returned? She had devised a plan for forestalling a sell-out. Could not Denys buy the first mortgage on the farm, and so take the matter of a

sale out of the bank's hands? For a certain fee, plus the balance owed
of £ 10,000, Denys would hold the first mortgage, the payments and
interest would be due to him rather than the bank, he himself would
decide the date of sale, and given this eventuality he would keep the
house and grounds if he wished. Had she not interpreted correctly that
he wanted to retain the Ngong house as his home? The fee for taking
over the mortgage would amount to £ 2000.

He answered her:

Dear Tania,

Your letter and telegram I found on getting
in this morning from chasing an elephant.

They leave me a little uncertain as to the
situation. I gather that the bank will sell their 1st
mortgage for £ 2000 and that your company want an
extra £ 500 to keep the place going until a more
favourable moment for a sale arrives in three
months' time.

You say that if I "bought for £ 2500 the farm
would be going on till you come back from safari and
I would need £ 500 on top of the purchase price. I
take it you might keep the house and grounds and
sell the remaining land." But I should not be *buying
the farm*, merely buying a 1st mortgage, which would
only mean that I have a right to recover my money out
of the proceeds of the sale—*not* retain the house and
sell the rest.

If I wanted to buy the house and grounds I
should have to come in for it at the sale as any other
would-be buyer, and should be in no better position
by holding the 1st mortgage.

I have not the necessary sum available myself to buy the mortgage. But I am prepared to buy
the 1st mortgage for £ 2000 on behalf of Kiptiget Ltd.
if Hunter [the solicitor] agrees on behalf of the other
shareholders. I am perfectly willing to do this, as I
cannot see that Kiptiget will stand to lose anything

1931

when the sale comes even if they have to buy in to get their money. But I am unwilling to put up the further £ 500 for manning the place for another 3 months. Surely the company will do that in their own interests if they have reduced the Bank debt at one fell swoop by some 12,000 pounds! So that they may sell better in the end.

I am writing Hunter to this effect.

I am sorry I cannot do more to help. I have not the money myself and must consider Kiptiget shareholders' interests primarily. I am very sorry to hear you are so seedy. In haste for the post.

Denys

I will do anything I can to prevent your house and grounds going over to the enemy [a buyer].

You are having a bad time, poor thing. I wish I could help more—will not your brother find the £ 500 wanted? (DFH to KB undated:KO, 31)

To say she was feeling seedy was putting it mildly. The imminent sale of the farm had placed her on the verge of nervous collapse. She could neither eat nor sleep nor think clearly. Late in January 1931, she consulted Dr. King in Nairobi. His examination revealed some disturbing findings: the reflexes in her extremities were decreased—the result of some insult to her peripheral nerves (KBS, 1978). He could not understand what would cause it. She showed no other signs of *tabes dorsalis*—late syphilis. Deterioration of the peripheral nerves in *tabes dorsalis* is accompanied by weakness in the legs, and early signs of urinary incontinence, but she did not have these symptoms. He brushed aside the idea that syphilis was the cause of her nerve damage and told her she might be suffering from pernicious anemia—a deficiency of vitamin B_{12} (*LFA*, 415). Although a tendency to this disease (fatal in 1931) is sometimes hereditary in Scandinavians, Karen had grown so thin it is far more likely that she was not eating properly. He suggested some injections—an idea that did not appeal to her after her blood poisoning episodes of 1914 and 1920.

Her great friend Gustav Mohr, who had followed the deteriorating state of her finances and her health over the previous year, was distressed. He visited her frequently while Denys was on safari, and grew more disturbed at her extreme thinness, her nervous preoccupations, and her obvious difficulty at thinking through her problems. On February 3, 1931, he came to the farm in the company of Dr. King, and together they persuaded her to enter the hospital for a few days.

Karen's severe anemia was perhaps attributable to a constellation of causes, in addition to vitamin deficiency. She appeared to be suffering from amebic dysentery, which results in a certain loss of blood. Further, she was extremely run-down. But the decrease in the reflexes in her extremities, the occasional numbness and tingling in her hands and feet, and a portion of her anemia were perhaps due to the steady, small doses of arsenic she was taking as a tonic.

* 2 *

Drought in Africa favors years of locusts, since the eggs of the insects go undisturbed by rain. The plague takes its form in dry regions and works its way steadily toward more fertile climes, destroying lush growth in areas innocent of breeding sites. In February 1931, during the final weeks of Denys's absence, rumors reached Karen of clouds of insects devouring everything green on farms to the north. When the plague failed to appear at Ngong, Karen adopted the hope that her farm would be spared. But soon grasshoppers began to fall onto her veranda, and appear on the road, and thump into the glass of her windows. When the eye of the cloud reached the farm, the locusts were so thick she could not walk outside without crushing them under her feet. They flew into her hair, landed on the back of her hands, and spat brown stains onto her clothes. The gnawing sound of millions of insects, resembling the roar of a rainstorm, brought to the farm the taunting augury of doom. The leaves of the coffee bushes were spared, since they were too tough to appeal to the insects, but otherwise the farm was stripped of the last vestige of green.

When the locusts had gone and silence settled on the farm, Karen had little left to wish upon. She agreed with her solicitors upon a date for a sale. But strangely, she did not for one moment believe she would be required to go through with it. She says in *Out of Africa* that she developed a demented strategy for pretending to agree to sell, while never believing it would happen.

Yet a buyer interested in the property had approached her solicitors with an offer, and they were only too glad to forward the offer to the corporation in Denmark. Until the end the shareholders had held themselves open to any proposal that would salvage the farm for Karen. She had sought help in buying the farm from many sources. But Uncle Aage wrote her on March 4, 1931: "Yes, for KC the end appears inevitably to have arrived. There is a much too hopeless distance in the various parties' proposals and conditions. But the fault was not yours. We realize that you have fought the long battle with exceptional ability and endurance" (*PA*, 35).

The final sale, held during the second week of March 1931, was a quiet affair. Karen did not attend. The buyer, a young real estate investor called Remi Martin (incorrectly spelled "Remy" Martin in earlier accounts) brought his solicitor. Another man, named Cartwright, had been invited to offer an opposing bid, although it was agreed in advance that the land should go to Martin. On April 1 the final papers were signed in Copenhagen. When the corporation was liquidated, it was revealed that the sale had not yielded even enough to cover the legal costs of selling (*LFA*, 415).

Young entrepreneurs in Nairobi, who had heard gossip about Karen, knew she had tried to make a success of the coffee farm after her husband left her. They knew that she had had a long-term liaison with Denys Finch Hatton and that she was mentally off-balance as a result of the financial collapse of her farm. They had seen her in Nairobi wearing torn sweaters and decrepit shoes but still carrying herself like an aristocrat. Many were scornful of how she had managed her farm. At the time of the sale there were 153 African families living there. Some dared to say that one should not have expected to make a profit from land with all those Africans hanging about.

* 3 *

Karen had had a new love in her bed over the past few months, and this was Saufe, the three-year-old son of Farah Aden. Since she had agreed to sell the farm, it was difficult for her to sleep, and Saufe's quiet breathing kept away the nightmares. In the daylight hours, he was one of the few who, in these difficult times, could make her laugh. He was a healthy, round-faced boy, and delighted Karen with his mischief. One day he shaved his head and came in pretending to be Denys, saying, "Good morning, good morning!," and chuckling merrily at his own cleverness.

Karen's immediate concern after the farm sale was not for her own plans but for the fate of the Africans on the farm. Their work contracts did not expire until May 1931. By law they would then have six months before they had to leave. In the intervening time Karen hoped to receive word from the government about land where they could resettle together. She had been spending her time going around the government offices of Nairobi in a fever to find a new home for them.

The offices—located for the most part in corrugated tin bungalows—were stuffy cubicles with slatted shutters, cement floors, and walls soiled with the region's characteristic red dust. Wooden tables that served as desks were piled with chits and ledgers, and stained from years of oily palms carrying on the affairs of the colony. Karen was shuttled from one functionary to another, each dressed in khaki shorts and puttees, each wrinkling his mustache uncomfortably and shifting on his wooden chair. Each would clear his throat sympathetically and state that, unfortunately, regulations tied his hands.

The Africans had weathered the jostlings of power and accepted bewildering British regulations; they had worked for the white man to pay the white man's taxes; they had had their customs systematically extinguished by British law; they had patiently allowed their dances, their attire, their burial rites, and their religious practices—the customs of centuries—to be curtailed by the whims of a bumptious white race who had lived in East Africa barely thirty years. But, with all this, they had thought to go on living in surroundings

312

familiar to them. Now the Msabu's selling the farm—a catastrophe they could not fathom—had made them homeless.

While Karen continued to make the rounds of the government clerks of Nairobi on behalf of her African staff, she accepted Remi Martin's offer to allow her to remain in her house for the time it would take to settle her affairs. She paid him a shilling a day in rent for legal reasons, to avoid being completely at the whim of charity (*OA*, 374). It was difficult for her to imagine any life for herself beyond Africa. One can go on living after one has had one's arms or legs cut off, she thought, but what kind of life will it be?

Her illness—amebic dysentery, anemia, and depression—prevented her from thinking clearly. She would forget what she was saying in mid sentence, and could not seem to move with any energy. She agreed with herself not to think beyond the task of the moment, since she was incapable of thinking further (*LFA*, 424–5). She had done nothing about packing her things, and had given little thought toward what to do with her furniture. In the end Denys had not requested, nor found the means, to buy the house and grounds.

He came home from safari toward the middle of March and found her fussing over the future of her house staff and squatters. Without having made any plans for herself, she was spending her days helping various of her servants to get legal questions and court cases settled; teaching one of them, Ali, how to drive so he could get a chauffeur's license; worrying about Halima, the wild Somali girl, and her marriage prospects—"Her beastly father has promised her in marriage to a man here in Kenya who is said to be unpleasant;"—and fretting over the future of Kamante—"I am doubtful whether he will get another post; he is really rather lacking." As for Sirunga, the little epileptic boy, she said, "One feels so strongly that this kind of *toto* ought to be shot, just like a little dog with a broken leg that one has to go away from" (*LFA*, 424–5).

Denys must have listened sadly to her say these things. She was simply not well. He evidently tried to joke with her. Did she not remember how they had laughed together at the idea that the Kikuyu might believe white people were completely dependent on them and could not live without them (*OA*, 275)? Did she truly think the Africans depended on her more than she on them? (She implied in several fictional tales that he spoke to her gently, as one might speak to a child.) Was she not exaggerating in her mind how important she was to the Africans?

But Karen insisted, "They stay here the whole time and come running after me when I am walking or riding on the farm; they say: 'Why do you want to go away? You mustn't go, what will become of us?'" (*LFA*, 416).

They will ask questions as long as you answer them, Denys might have replied. But in their hearts they already have the answers—and, anyway, they will not be satisfied with the ones you give them.

Karen had never felt so happy as when Denys took her flying, but it was a final ecstasy. She was reminded of her parting from Bror. She said, "I have before seen other countries, in the same manner, give themselves to you when you are about to leave them, but I had forgotten what it meant" (*OA*, 343). At the same time, she felt at odds with Denys because he could not understand her point of view. She spoke of her "friends," but she really meant Denys when she said, "my isolation from them felt very strange, and sometimes like a physical thing,—a kind of suffocation. I looked upon myself as the one reasonable person amongst them all; but once or twice it happened to me to reflect that if I had been mad, amongst sane people, I should have felt just the same" (*OA*, 343).

She worried her friends with her talk of preferring to die rather than go home. When they protested, she went on proclaiming lyrically, "I have had so infinitely much that was wonderful . . . I have looked into the eyes of lions and slept under the Southern Cross, I have seen the grass of the great plains ablaze and covered delicate green after the rains, I have been the friend of Somali, Kikuyu, and Masai, I have flown over the Ngong Hills . . . " (*LFA*, 416).

Denys had a serious conference with Gustav Mohr over their concern that Karen would not, or could not seem to, place any hope in the future. Finally, together, they sat down with her and urged her to work out a plan for herself. They told her that they thought she was very ill, that she should try to see things in a more optimistic way, that she must try to look ahead to what she might do. She insisted it was a certain love of greatness that had kept her working at making a success of the farm all these years, and now she had no idea what she might do to achieve something (*LFA*, 416). Could not her brother help her to find a role for herself in Europe? they suggested. She answered that she had thought of opening a restaurant, or getting a post as a cook—but not at home: she could not bear the thought of living at home. Perhaps somewhere in Italy, or France. But times were hard; such a position would be difficult to find (*LFA*, 419).

Mohr wondered why she did not dedicate herself to writing. He had given her the name of a publisher he knew, named Morley. She had told him she was writing down some stories. Writing was always what the Dinesens did when they had nothing else to fall back on. She had sent some stories to Morley, who replied to her from England, "The leisurely style and language are exceedingly attractive" (*LFA*, 419). She was writing in English, in order to have a wider audience. Perhaps she might find an opening somewhere in journalism. But until she had seen to the problems of the Africans on the farm, and settled the matter of where they would all go, she said, "I have neither the strength nor the time to manage to do anything for myself" (*LFA*, 416).

* 4 *

Once or twice, Karen had asked Denys where he planned to live when she was gone, and he could not say. One day he had been to Nairobi to look at the bungalows for hire, but they had so disgusted him that he would not even talk about them. Their mutual friends had persistently advised him to find some other place to live (*OA*, 356). This was not for his own sake, for he could take care of himself, but for Karen's. But when she broached the subject of what he would do, he interrupted her to say, "Oh, as to me, I shall be perfectly happy in a tent in the Masai Reserve, or I shall take a house in the Somali village" (*OA*, 357).

One evening she told Denys that she needed to give her employees gifts before leaving. She began to give Denys an example of her despair: she could not afford a gift for Pooran Singh, her mill hand. As she said this, she fondled the gold ring Denys had given her, and went on to say that she had asked Pooran Singh what he desired. He had replied, "A ring." It was fortunate that Denys had chosen a ring adjustable to the size of her finger. She had been quite plump at times, but now she was so thin the ring might have, with a gesture, flown off her hand. Denys, accustomed for many months to her unreasonable behavior, now concluded she meant to give his ring to Pooran Singh. Karen may have felt a flutter of daring at creating this misunderstanding, since she had before from time to time tested the men she loved. But she had not counted on the violence of his reaction. He demanded she take the ring off and give it back to him. Then he put it on his own hand (*OA*, 379).

Denys would have been particularly angry at this moment for several reasons. The thought of her giving away his ring exasperated him, so wildly ridiculous did it seem. For some years he had complained that she was always giving away his gifts (*OA*, 379). He attributed this to her love for the great gesture; she always preferred the giving of a valuable thing to the owning of it.

She had blithely presented a box of his cigars to Old Aarup, the blind drunkard, who was only on the farm a few months. As for the skins from the lions Denys had killed for her: Karen had bestowed one of them on the Indian high priest and sent the other to the King of Denmark.

From Karen's point of view, Denys could not go on being one more person on the list of people for whom she must find new homes. How could he expect her to think about leaving, when he had done nothing to find a place for himself? It was time he went; she had had it in mind to ask him to go for over a year, ever since he had betrayed her by taking Bror and Cockie on a second safari with the Prince of Wales.

Denys was slow to anger, and once angered he was not impetuous. For weeks her disturbing conversation had made it difficult to live with her, but leaving would mean abandoning her when she was ill. However, he should have understood earlier that she would not make plans for her future as long as he was in her house.

He eventually agreed to move in with Hugh Martin. Karen had visited Martin's house in the first part of April 1931 (*LFA*, 423), and perhaps returned with the opinion that it was not so disagreeable as some of the regulation Nairobi bungalows. Denys could have taken a cottage at Muthaiga (where Beryl Markham and others were living semi-permanently), but he had been at Oxford with Hugh, and along with Karen, enjoyed his conversation. Hugh was drinking more since his wife had left him (*OMS*, 46), and might appreciate someone to share his lonely house. Denys also knew that several of Karen's obligations were dependent on Hugh's decision. She had regularly sought his help at the land office, and too often failed to find him there. In fact, she had dared to be rude the previous week, by showing up at his house at eight o'clock in the morning, before he could escape (*LFA*, 423). Perhaps Denys could keep him sober long enough to act on the needs of Karen's Africans.

Denys gathered his things together, taking some of his books: the works in French of Proust and Anatole France, his collection of Shakespeare, the book *China Under the Empress Dowager*, and fifteen volumes of an illustrated Italian dictionary of sculpture (*SWS*, 315). He said he would come back for the rest of the books, but, for the moment, he told her, "You keep them; now I have no place to put them" (*OA*, 356).

The exact date that Denys left the farm is not certain, but in the second week of April 1931 Karen wrote to her mother that Rose Cartwright was staying there with her. Because Karen's attacks of anxiety and her comments about suicide had become frequent, Denys habitually called upon Rose or Ingrid Lindstrom, or whomever else he could recruit, to stay with Karen when he was not there (*SWS*, 212). Only recently a disturbing incident had caused Karen to dissolve into weeping in the Kikuyu village on her farm. For some weeks she had been giving medical treatment to a small African boy with burns on his legs, but on this day he ran away from her. Unable to accept the idea that he no longer needed her, she chased him. She finally caught up with him inside his hut, where she attempted to force medicine upon him, and when he rejected it, she says in *Shadows on the Grass*, "the world round me grew infinitely cheerless, a place of no hope. I had ventured to believe that efforts of mine might defeat destiny. It was brought home to me how deeply I had been mistaken; the balance-sheet was laid before me, and proved that whatever I took on was destined to end up in failure" (*SOTG*, 468–9).

Gustav Mohr had written Karen's brother Thomas an anxious letter asking if he could not come to Kenya to help his sister get back to Denmark. Together Denys and Mohr had tried to reason with her, but she seemed too ill to understand them. She had gone on raving about her Africans, foregoing food and sleep, and saying she would like "now quite calmly to retire from life together with everything that I have loved here" (LFA, 418).

* 5 *

For months Karen had been drawing up the inventory required by the government before it would consider resettling the Africans from her farm. She was to provide a list with the name of each worker, how many wives he had, how many children and sheep and cattle, and how long he had lived on the farm (LFA, 422). As for Africans who had come to the farm to work to pay their taxes, copies of the inventory would be sent to the district commissioners of their home regions , to determine if they would be allowed to go home. But those who were born on the farm, whose ancestors had owned the land, must leave and find some other home.

Every day the Kikuyu and the Masai, the Luo and the Kipsigis, classified as "squatters" on the farm by the colonial government, would come to sit on the lawn expectantly, wondering what was to be done. Rarely did the women come with babies on their backs and small children. Not comprehending they would have to leave, they stayed at the shambas, bent at the waist weeding the maize, or sweeping with shocks of grass the bare earth in front of their huts.

From where they gathered in the shade of trees in Karen's park, the men filed into Karen's office, one by one, to recite the particulars of their families. They leaned on their sheep staves and frowned, trying to make some sense of the questions the Msabu was asking. Reddish cloaks did not fully cover their dusty bodies. They held a musty smell, of the livestock they tended. There were fragments of dried grass in their woolly hair. The old men had fine wrinkles in their legs, and their toes and bare feet were coarse. As Karen questioned them, they answered quietly, in Swahili syllables. Their eyes widened gravely, and the bobbing of their heads as they spoke made their long earrings sway.

1931

Afterwards, they sat on the ground outside, their arms resting on their knees. They chewed sugar cane and spat out the fiber, and flicked flies as they waited. There were silences broken by an occasional tonal comment. Hours later they might come to Karen's door, saying softly, "Please, Msabu . . . ," anxious to correct what might have been a wrong calculation. Often the first figure was correct, but they had begun to imagine they had said the wrong thing. The white man's system had no meaning for them; they did not understand what was expected.

Karen explained that they would be allowed to stay on the farm until the end of the month of May. The land no longer belonged to her, but to men in Nairobi. She had a right only to the coffee now ripening on the bushes. When it was harvested and sent away to London, the coffee trees must be uprooted. The land would be used for country houses, and the Africans must leave. By the Englishman's law, they would have six months to find a new place for themselves. They could not all go to one farm. There was not room at any one place for all of them.

Karen could see no end to the negotiations for resettling the Africans, and reluctantly assumed she would have to leave before the matter was decided. She had spoken about this to Andersen, the Danish consul in Nairobi. He was not merely unsympathetic, but told her in no uncertain terms that the squatters must be off the farm by the time she left, and that he would not tolerate further procrastination. Karen left his office calling him a "cad and bounder" (*LFA*, 421), so he arranged for the police to send her a warning, accusing her of encouraging Africans to break the law by allowing them to make *tembo* on the premises. Karen then stomped to the office of the D.C. and, demanding to know what penalty could be had for brewing *tembo*, discovered that no one could be sent away from the farm for such a minor infraction of the law, merely fined.

In these last days she had a particular fear of the authorities. It was as though she thought a misstep could ruin her efforts on behalf of the Africans. In the eyes of the British authorities, she was a foreigner, like the Africans. She regarded the power of the police as ominous and unpredictable. She remembered the Englishwoman who threatened to have her cook detained during the war, for no other reason than that he chose to work for Karen. Fear of the police now contributed to her general difficulty in thinking clearly. When she was called to the bedside of a dying friend, Chief Kinanjui, she sacrificed friendship out of fear. Kinanjui pleaded with her not to make him die in the hospital. A hospital bed, so alien to the way he had lived, would rob his death of dignity. But fearing that the authorities would blame her for his death, Karen refused his last request. Reluctantly she sent him to the Scottish mission, where he died soon afterwards (*OA*, 346-54).

She finally finished her inventory in mid April, after Africans had come in to her to make corrections a hundred times. In all, the document took up twelve pages, and she typed and sent copies to the D.C.s in Nairobi, Kabete, Kiambu, Dagoretti, Fort Hall, Nyeri, and Machakos, and to the Native Affairs Department (*LFA*, 422). When this had been done, and her outstanding bills paid and obligations fulfilled, she knew nothing was going to happen to change everything back. She continued to say to her family and friends, "To me it would seem the most *natural* thing to disappear with my world here, for it seems to me to be, to quite the same extent as my eyes, or as some talent or other I might have, vital parts of myself, and I do not know how much of me will survive losing it" (*LFA*, 418).

Meanwhile, Denys settled in with Hugh Martin and began taking care of business neglected during his safari. He paid his bills, had his teeth repaired, and discovered the dentist, Jack Melhuish, had a darkroom in his house. It so happened that Denys had two years' worth of undeveloped film. He struck up an acquaintance with Melhuish and his live-in companion, Joan Waddington, and they were only too glad to offer him the use of their darkroom (*SWS*, 305).

A day or two after Denys left Karen's house, he sent his servant Kamau to her with a brief note and a bottle of claret. Perhaps he also sent Karen a more private message in the voice of Kamau, since it was their custom to send messages of a secret nature, not in writing, where they could fall into the wrong hands, but by word of mouth, with an accompanying note so that the receiver might be sure of the authenticity of the message.

1931

Karen accepted this peace offering and may have invited him to visit, because a day or two later she received another note from Denys, signed in a most uncharacteristic way. It said:

> I meant to come out with Hugh to visit you this afternoon, but I have been engaged in bailing out Matiano from prison and preparing his defense for tomorrow, a case of assault. I am glad to say a Somali got his head cracked in the encounter. I will be here for a day or two still I think, papers, teeth, and some business.
>
> I find it very convenient to be on a telephone. I have found 1800 feet of film dating back 2 years which I am trying to save in developing.
>
> May I come out to you later on in the week? and let me know anytime you would like me to run out if you have anything to arrange in your own plans in which I could help. I have a book here I want you to read. I will bring it out. Best love—Denys. (DFH to KB 4-?-31 #2:KO, 15)

Even at the height of his infatuation with Karen in 1926 and 1927, when he had written to her erotically from England, he had not signed a letter to her with the word love. Throughout the previous months she had grown accustomed to his speaking to her gently, as one would speak to a child. Customarily, during their friendship, he had often had a book for her to read. Sharing books had been one of their chief means of understanding one another. In his delicate inquiry about coming to see her, he was not assuming she had forgiven him. But he was firm that she not worry about where he was living. He wished her to concentrate on her own plans. Saying that it was convenient to be on the telephone was his way of letting her know he was making the best of living elsewhere.

* 6 *

In early May, 1931, like a sudden bright portent, Karen received word from the government that Africans from the farm could resettle together. They had been allotted a small section of land in the Dagoretti Forest Reserve, only a few miles from Ngong. Karen had never expected such munificence; Ingrid Lindstrom said she would not have been more amazed if Queen Victoria had offered Mount Kilimanjaro as a gift to the German Kaiser. Karen joyfully interpreted the news as a sign that fate could be kind, after all.

At last she began to feel her old self. She was still weak from bouts of diarrhea, but she had received a most encouraging letter from Joanie Grigg, the wife of the former governor, recommending a clinic in Switzerland where she herself had gone to recover from amebic dysentery; Karen would find it perfect for her recuperation. This suggestion—a first concrete step to which Karen could reach—became the starting point for her future plans. Spending a few weeks in Switzerland seemed a heavenly idea. Now Karen actually began thinking about arrangements for sailing home. She decided to book passage on an Italian ship leaving on June 9; this boat would take her to Venice, where Thomas could meet her. On May 13, 1931, she wrote her mother that it appealed to her to "land at a different place from the other times," and "to spend a week in Venice and then travel quite slowly" through northern Italy (*LFA*, 429).

And so it was decided, and Karen at last began to advertise her furniture for sale and to have the things she wished to keep put in crates. Her friends were relieved at her change of attitude. Denys came out to the farm most evenings for dinner and kept himself apprised of her plans.

In March 1931, the East African *Standard* reprinted the notice of Denys's first arrival in Kenya in their "Twenty Years Ago . . . " column, and on April 24, he turned forty-four years old. Aside from occasional funks, recognized only by those close to him, he had accepted middle age gracefully, although in his latest trip to England his nieces had noted he was a little vain about his age. He had challenged Toby's daughter Diana to guess how old he was, and when she replied, "Oh, I should think about thirty," he was almost childishly delighted (*SWS*, 298).

In early May 1931, he was reorganizing his safari equipment and spending as much time as he could on short flights out of Nairobi. Safari life had accustomed him to getting up before dawn, when he sometimes went out to the airfield to tinker with his plane or go up for a spin before breakfast. Afterwards he went about the dusty streets of Nairobi, checking in at his solicitors', seeing about new safari equipment, stopping in at Indian shops to be measured for new hunting khakis, and occasionally threading his way through the crowded Somali bazaar with his servant Hamisi, looking for new gun bearers. Sometimes he had lunch at Hugh Martin's, or at Muthaiga. Often he would go to the Norfolk Hotel, where he might run into Lord Delamere, or some other old friend from the early years. The shops and businesses in town closed from twelve o'clock to two, and this time was used for leisurely conversations about the state of the colony, during which Denys usually had some wry remarks and jokes.

Before dusk Denys often took Karen up in his plane. After they had been in the sky one day, a Kikuyu asked them if they had seen God. They had not. But in *Out of Africa* Karen said that the view from an airplane gave her a sudden perspective on her problems. In this third dimension, the air, her own difficulties became small, like features of the landscape. She was delirious, like a person drugged, and could not believe everything must change.

* 7 *

In the second week of May 1931, Denys announced he was going to take a brief holiday at his house on the coast, at Takaunga. (In *Out of Africa* she says they discussed the plan over dinner, which would have been well after dark, yet the other events she relates took place in daylight.) He said he would be gone only a week, so as to return well before she left for Denmark. He was going to work on his house and to plant mango trees. He was fond of the succulent red-orange fruit, a little piney to the taste. (In fact, Denys loved any kind of fruit, especially oranges, which he once declared to Kermit Roosevelt he could live upon exclusively in preference to the cuisine aboard ship.)

His cottage near the ocean had a small veranda made from gray coral; Denys sometimes slept there, listening to the sound of the waves. He had been silent and self-absorbed for several days (*OA*, 359); perhaps he needed the change of air to sort out his thoughts. Karen had asked him what was the cause of his melancholy, but he had only laughed. It was not the way of the English to lay bare their uncertainties; Karen had often noted Denys's lack of self-consciousness. When she was annoyed with him, she called this trait "heartlessness," for he seldom revealed his feelings. In "The Dreamers" she describes a character like him who seems incapable of feeling much difference between pleasure and pain; they were the same to him (*SGT*, 285). But even if Denys had been one to discuss his misgivings, he had not found it possible to converse rationally with Karen for months. She insisted on assuming the burden for the fate of everyone around her. Any expression by Denys of sadness that she was leaving would have fueled her uncertainties and indecision.

Although, to help her escape from her *shauries*, Denys had sometimes urged Karen to go to the coast, he would not have recommended that she go now, in her delicate state of health. The blue seas and white beaches, the green palms and yellow weaver birds were not beautiful enough to make up for the sultry heat. So it surprised him when this time she asked to accompany him.

First he said yes, and then he said no. This was the reason he gave her: he had decided to land at Voi, and camp there on his way back, so that he could look for elephant from the air. He told her he was unsure of the territory, and thought camping would be difficult—he could take very little with him, and would have to sleep on the open ground. She should wait until he had scouted the area; then he would take her to view the elephant. She said she dreamed of going on one last safari before she left Africa forever.

On this particular afternoon, as he climbed into his Hudson, he told Karen he would be back—in time for lunch the following Thursday. She seems to have admonished him, in the name of God, to be careful. In a vivid moment in the tale, "The Old Chevalier," a character acting very much like Denys quotes flippantly from

Sophocles's Ajax, "You worry me too much, woman. Do you not know that I am no longer a debtor of the Gods?" (*SGT*, 86).

He started to drive away, then came back, and leaving the car running, came inside to look for a volume of poetry he wanted to take with him: a collection of poems written by his friend Iris Tree. "Listen to this," he said as, with one foot on the running board of his car, he opened the book:

> I saw grey geese flying over the flatlands
> Wild geese vibrant in the high air—
> Unswerving from horizon to horizon
> With their soul stiffened out in their throats—
> And the grey whiteness of them ribboning the enor-
> mous skies
> And the spikes of the sun over the crumpled hills.
> (*OA*, 360)

Karen describes partings in several tales. In "The Old Chevalier" there is no kiss, but, in a gesture never forgotten, the lover offers an encouraging, consoling glance (*SGT*, 103). In "The Dreamers," the lover says, "Do not ever bear me any grudge. I have tried to do you good" (*SGT*, 301). Perhaps Karen imagined that is what Denys would have said had he known he was going away forever. He eased his long legs into the Hudson, gripped the door by the open window, and slammed it with his large hand. Then he pushed his wide-brimmed hat back from his forehead. He wore a khaki shirt, open at the throat, with a ringed scarf around his neck, like a tie. As usual, his sleeves were folded to his elbows. He waved a long, tanned arm to Karen as he drove off.

* 8 *

Denys planned to leave for Mombasa at dawn the next day, the eighth of May 1931. If the weather were good—and with all likelihood it would be, the rainy season having ended—he should be at the coast by mid afternoon. Fog could delay his departure, but it would burn off early. He related his plans over dinner at Jack Melhuish's house, and he jokingly asked Joan Waddington if she would like to go along. She giggled, "Good God, Denys! Do you want me to commit suicide?" (*SWS*, 306)

His servant Hamisi was to accompany him to the coast—in spite of Hamisi's protestations, since he was terrified of flying. (In *Out of Africa*, Karen says the Kikuyu Kamau accompanied Denys on the flight, but Denys always traveled with a Somali, and in *Longing for Darkness* Kamante confirms that the Somali, Hamisi, went with Denys [*LFD*, Ch. 16].) Denys did not entertain the idea of going away for the entire week without a servant. His invitation to Joan Waddington had been strictly tongue-in-cheek, for there was no room for her in the airplane.

The flight to the coast was uneventful, but coming down onto the coral airstrip at Vipingo, near Mombasa, Denys made a rough landing and broke his plane's propeller. He wired Tom Black for a replacement, which was installed, and a test flight made without incident. After spending a few days at his house by the ocean, Denys returned via Voi, where he scouted elephants from the air. Later he accepted an invitation to spend the night at the home of the District Commissioner. When he taxied off the next day, he had in his plane a bundle of oranges, picked by the D.C.'s wife in her orchard. She later reported that his airplane rose into the air without difficulty, circled the field twice, and banked in the direction of Nairobi. Then suddenly, without explanation, the engine died, and the aircraft plummeted groundward.

Denys's friend, J. A. Hunter, who was just getting into his truck a quarter of a mile away, saw the flames of the exploding gas tank. He drove as fast as he could to the burning wreck, but when he arrived, nothing survived but a few charred oranges that had rolled free of the plane.

* 9 *

On the morning of May 14, 1931, Karen waited for Denys to appear for lunch as he had promised. He had said he would be there early. As the minutes drew closer to noon Karen was seized by the conviction that he was not coming. Steadier individuals might have placed less significance on his failure to appear, but she viewed it ominously. To her it was another betrayal, a punishment for her own shortcomings, a harbinger of doom. She dissolved into panic. In *Out of Africa* she says, "During my last months in Africa, when everything was going wrong with me, it sometimes suddenly fell upon me like a darkness, and in a way I was frightened of it, as of a sort of derangement. On this Thursday . . . the nightmare unexpectedly stole upon me, and grew so strong that I wondered if I were beginning to go mad" (*OA*, 362). She could not escape the idea that Denys was letting her down in a final and disastrous way. Unable to bring herself around to sensible thinking, nor to convince herself her terror was foolish, she sent for the car and headed to Nairobi.

When she was overtaken by panic, she often fled from her house. She seems to have been afraid to be in the large rooms. On the open plains she felt menaced, but she was not afraid in the woods. Indeed, in her writings she describes the woods as a place of comfort and consolation. At night she would sometimes run outside without a coat, while Farah pursued, afraid she might be seized by a leopard (*OA*, 335). Over the years she had developed a method for dealing with her attacks of panic, and this was to find some reasonable, clear-thinking person to talk with, on whatever trivial subject, long enough to cheat anxiety of its hold on her mind. "We will talk and behave sensibly," she would think (*OA*, 363). Her African servants would not do because, she said, "their ideas of reality, and their reality itself," were different (*OA*, 362). At night she would run as far as the smithy and speak to Pooran Singh, or visit the school teacher to converse about his pupils, or call out Dickens to discuss some minor matters concerning the farm. But when she was seized by anxiety in broad daylight, especially in the difficult early years, when Northrup McMillan was alive, she had often fled to Chiromo. So, out of ancient habit, while struggling to render balance to her mind, she made an unannounced appearance at the home of Lady McMillan.

Lady McMillan was entertaining guests for luncheon. She was not expecting Karen, since Karen was supposed to have lunch with Denys at Ngong. Karen was most welcome to join them at table, but she had the feeling from their silence that they had been talking about her. How was it that her friends had turned against her? She had fallen into some unfathomable disgrace. Perhaps they perceived her imbalance of mind. Ever since the years when she was suspected of being a German sympathizer during the Great War, Karen had experienced a recurring nightmare. In this dream she would arrive in Nairobi for shopping, but wherever she went—along the street, in shops, at Muthaiga—everyone, even those who had been her friends, shunned her. There was a strange aura of silence surrounding the people and town, the kind of silence that occurs in a dream. In *Out of Africa*, she describes the nightmare as though it really occurred on this day.

When her friends regarded her with fright and behaved as though they were unwilling to talk to her, the nightmare was real. As soon as they finished eating and—as though fleeing—excused themselves to the drawing room, Lady McMillan invited her into the library. She began by saying, "My dear, it's Denys . . . ." Karen later said, "It was then as I had thought: at the sound of Denys's name even, truth was revealed, and I knew and understood everything" (*OA*, 363). She accepted the news as fulfillment of a premonition, as vindication of the seemingly unreasonable state of panic she had experienced, and, ultimately, as justification of years of anxiety over how it all might end. She had dreaded such an ending not merely for hours, but for an epoch.

Lady McMillan explained the terrible details. They had only just received word from Voi before Karen arrived at Chiromo, and had not had time to send someone to her. In truth, they were at a loss how to tell her of Denys's death, half-crazed as she already was over losing the farm. In "The Old Chevalier," as if describing her feelings under such circumstances, Karen suggests that at that moment she had no thought but to go and get him back. "I think," she says, "that I went, in those minutes, through the exact experience, even to the sensation of suffocation, of a person who has been buried alive" (*SGT*, 105).

Word was that Tom Black was going to Voi to investigate the crash. Desperate, and unwilling to believe Denys was really dead, Karen insisted that she must see the evidence, and directed Farah to drive her immediately to the airfield to accompany Black. But when they arrived, his airplane had already lifted into the air. Later Black reported that the skulls of both Denys and Hamisi had broken with the impact of the crash, so they did not feel the flames (*SWS*, 313).

One person went straight to the farm as soon as he heard the news, and this was Gustav Mohr. He was with Karen when Denys's remains were brought to her from Voi. There was no question about who was to plan Denys's funeral, since Karen and Denys had lived virtually as man and wife for the previous five years. They had fantasized about making their graves on top of the Ngong Hills, with views of the farm and the game reserve in the distance. On the morning of the funeral, Karen, Mohr, and Farah drove the car up the steep hill in a dense fog. They did not attempt to reach the summit, since the road was risky for cars beyond a certain point, and mourners could not be expected to proceed to the top on foot. Although the fog was bound to lift in time for the burial, a site must be chosen beforehand, and a hole dug. Just as Karen despaired of getting the right bearings, the clouds parted long enough for her to be sure of the site. Actually, any site high on the east face of the hills was likely to give the view she sought, but here the slope widened as though forming a terrace or receiving area. Here was room for admirers and pilgrims. She instructed her boys to dig.

The group of mourners was not a legion, for Denys had been a private person, but those who came to the funeral believed him to have been the most witty and blessed of men. Although Denys had never put down roots, nor held what the world might regard as a profession, he had been an admirable friend, a warm student of nature, a great sportsman, and an incomparable human being. He had led his life gracefully in a way that inspired those who knew him. His tall, lithe presence in hunting khakis and double *terai* would be missed in Kenya, as would his crooked smile and his gentle teasing. Denys had led a steady life. Karen had called him a wanderer, but she knew he was not that: he had preferred to have a home, and had never left his moorings for more than a few months at a time. For twenty years, except for the upset of the Great War, he had kept the same schedule: spring and summer in England, fall and winter in Africa. He had never ventured to India or America, despite the urgings of friends, and had been content to travel back and forth over the route between England and Africa, stopping at countries along the way as a diversion from life aboard ship. The schedule he maintained, sharing himself alternately with friends and family in two countries, had given his life shape. He had felt the burden of expectations all his life, yet he had never done, as Karen said, "but what he wanted to do" (*OA*, 234).

* 10 *

For some days after Denys's funeral, Karen stayed at Chiromo with Lady McMillan. She was afraid to be in her house alone— overcome by an anxiety she had experienced through the years, but this time more grave and more prolonged. In her silent house she felt accused of eighteen years of *shauries* and failure.

In the first days following Denys's death she went about in a stupor, sometimes going to Muthaiga to sit in his favorite chair (*SWS*, 315). She clung to the belief that if she frequented his old haunts, surely he must reappear. His death must be something she had dreamed, an exaggeration of the nightmares she had experienced ever since the farm was sold. She seemed to feel as she describes in "The Old Chevalier," that if she went down to the same place at the same hour where she had met him, she was bound to see him again. She says, "This state of mine lasted for some time . . . I attached much hope to this idea, which only slowly died away" (*SGT*, 105). In the same story she appears to brood upon Denys's plane crash, and to wonder if he committed suicide—since he had so recently made out his will—but she certainly dismissed the idea of suicide as melodramatic, for Denys would not have taken Hamisi down with him. However privately disappointed Denys was at the sale of her home, or however preoccupied in his last days, or dispirited by the futility of his middle years, Denys had given no one reason to believe that he would take his life. His overriding characteristic had been lack of concern about the future. Karen may have been convinced, as she hints in an elaborately symbolic passage in "The Old Chevalier," that Denys was caught up with, and dragged down by, somebody else, for if he had been alone in the airplane the accident might not have happened. That other person was perhaps somebody who held him, and yet was unable to help him, someone helpless, like a child—like Hamisi. Left to himself, Denys might have somehow floated down safely, but an hysterical Hamisi could have distracted him from preventing the crash (*SGT*, 104).

330

1931

When Karen finally accepted that Denys was gone forever, she left a suicide note and slit her wrists. The note, which survived for many years, has since been lost, but evidently it was Lady McMillan, alert for such a development, who rescued her and brought a doctor. There had been ample reason to fear such a possibility. In addition to her depression and veiled references to suicide over the past months, she had wired Thomas, who had sent word that he was coming to accompany her to Europe, not to come (*LFA*, 430). Indeed, he had made his offer before Denys's death, but Karen had refused. It is likely she was retaining her option to commit suicide, and wished to spare Thomas from having to bury her.

Now her friends banded together to help her complete the sale of her furniture and to pack. She had only begun to advertise her household things a few days before Denys's death (*LFA*, 430). He never ate with her on packing crates, in spite of what she says in *Out of Africa*, although other people did. Because there was so much furniture, selling everything took several weeks, and Mohr and some others dined with her until she was ready to leave. Some of her dining room pieces she gave to Lady McMillan for the neoclassical pillared library she was having built in honor of Sir Northrup in the center of Nairobi. Some things, like Karen's crystal wine glasses—the ones Berkeley and Denys had piled into pyramids to tease her—she sold, and then, panicking at the thought of selling something of such great nostalgic value, asked for them back. Eventually, after the larger pieces of furniture had gone, and miscellany still cluttered her house, she ordered the boys to put all the remainder in crates, since she was incapable of making further decisions. Thus a great many relatively worthless items made their way by ship to Rungstedlund, at the expense of Thomas Dinesen. In all there were twenty-five crates; Karen begged Thomas not to be angry when he viewed their contents (*LFA*, 432).

From time to time while she was packing, Karen would go outside and peer in the direction of Denys's grave in the Ngong Hills. She and Farah had erected there a canopy made from a white sheet mounted on poles—from a distance, like a flag—so that she would know in which direction to look. As years ago she had depended upon the spirit of her dead father for strength, now she developed the idea

331

that Denys was watching over her packing, and urging on her plans. Once when she drove up with Farah to the grave she found Hugh Martin there. He had grown close to Denys in the weeks they lived together. Hugh had brought a young girl to lay flowers on the grave because, he said, he himself was not worthy enough (*SWS*, 316).

* *

Whatever Denys's sexual preference, Karen seems to have retained faith that his affection for her was genuine. In the tale "The Poet," she says of a stormy relationship resembling theirs: "Indeed it was doubtful whether, amongst all the women he had met, he did not like [her] best" (*SGT*, 381). She received a consolatory letter from Lady Northey, now living in England, which expressed the emotions of many: "With Denys's tragic death the great love of your life has gone and with it all your happiness . . . But my dear, do you realize your own great charm and the affection of your friends?" (*ID*, 248).

In the months following Denys's death, while trying to find meaning in what had happened, she wrote "The Dreamers" (*TP*, 35). The tale is so like a troubled dream or nightmare that one pictures its images coming to her as she tossed in bed at night. Bror plays a prominent role in the story, as Baron Guildenstern of Sweden, racing in the dark against the narrator, along a mountain road in a windstorm, in competition for the favors of a lover. (The outcome of this chase scene strongly resembles Karen's kindly attempt to force medicine on the African child; the intended beneficiary is horror-struck.) Denys became the model for the "woman" who frequently leaves: "'She' could fly" (*SGT*, 286), and when they were together "it seemed to me that I had, somehow, got up very high outside the world in which I used to live, and that I was now quite alone there, with her." "She" stayed with the author "when 'she' was not travelling," in her villa outside a certain city, where they entertained friends and walked together in the garden.

Karen actually seems to have begun the introduction to "The Dreamers" and the early description of its principal character, Pellegrina Leoni, in the first months of 1926. The narrator, Lincoln Forsner, as physically described, is Berkeley Cole; the setting, a dhow sailing on the monsoon—Karen's tribute to their friendship. The language parallels statements in her letters in 1926, the emotional period after Berkeley's death, when she was afraid of "being put on the shelf" by Denys in favor of younger friends (*SGT*, 304). In the story Karen establishes Pellegrina Leoni as the personage she would like to imitate in life—a heroine who as described throughout bears the traits of character of Denys Finch Hatton. Like Denys, Pellagrina travels and takes risks—as Karen was never able to do.

The story appears to give several views of her parting from Denys, all written allegorically, as if she is pondering the event over and over, seeking truth. The story is suffused with guilt, an emotion commonly felt in the early stages of grief. In parting, the Denys-like character is always devoid of feeling, as though "she" does not experience pleasure or pain—as though she does not care as much as the author how it ends. Karen appears to accuse herself of grasping at the relationship like "a python" and killing it through force of embrace.

It seems clear that her notion that she had suffocated the relationship was a delusion of her grief. By the time she writes another allegory about their parting, "The Old Chevalier," guilt plays no role. In this tale Karen reviews the relationship symbolically, from meeting to parting. While again the character representing Denys, a young prostitute just learning her trade, leaves for good without showing any emotion, the narrator does not take it personally, but rather attempts to understand the loss as destined.

In "The Dreamers" Karen consolidates the philosophy announced in "The Roads Round Pisa." Pellegrina Leoni—a "lioness" of the operatic stage—finds her voice ruined by the effects of a great fire. The loss of her great loves, career and audience (the farm and Denys), is such a tragedy that she resolves never again to become emotionally attached to a person or situation. Henceforth she will seek many roles in life, behaving like a character in a play, forgetting the role when she walks off stage. So the agonies of life will have no more power over her. "The time has come," she says, "for me to be that: a woman called one name or another. And if she is unhappy we shall not think a great deal about it" (*SGT*, 345).

In the last week of July 1931, her friends accompanied her to the Mombasa train. Hugh Martin was there, and Lord Delamere, Lady McMillan and Gustav Mohr, and a large group of Somalis. Dressed in an old cardigan and torn stockings, she boarded the train. Her friends had a last look at her as she wryly waved good-bye. She was suffering from jaundice, anemia, and the effects of chronic doses of arsenic. To cover her hair, which had begun to fall out in clumps, she wore a close-fitting hat that looked like a turban, and thick make-up to mask the discoloration in her skin caused by years of using arsenic. She was so thin and her eyes were so sunken that her face resembled a bare skull, and her nose protruded like that of a witch.

As the train made its way southeast over the Athi Plains, smoke from the wood-burning firebox met her eyes. To the northwest she could see the Ngong Hills watching over what had once been her land. Then the hills disappeared behind the horizon as though, like her farm, they had ceased to exist. It was as if she were going away from the one real place and hour of her life (*SGT*, 3).

Epilogue

From early youth Karen had envisioned her life as a drama on a stage. She imagined herself swept along through happiness and adversity in the manner of an actor who must play out her role. She could not control events—the script had been set by fate, an infinite power with a strange sense of humor. But some actors are greater than others and some roles more meaningful; and she had determined that her performance would be memorable and her character never forgotten.

She arrived at Marseilles on August 19, 1931. Later she said that when her brother Thomas bought her some silk stockings to replace the torn ones she had worn on the return from Africa, she suddenly saw hope for the future. She was as exhausted—and as relieved—as an actor who has just completed a difficult part in a tragedy.

She did not yet understand the meaning of what she had gone through and what might be her next role in life. From time to time, in periods of depression, she had said that she could not face the idea of living at home and had alarmed her mother, especially, with this talk in the months before her final departure from Africa. She had railed against her family, claiming that they did not understand her and that she could never be happy living with them. But these ideas were inspired by depression. If she had thought carefully, she would have remembered that she had nearly refused to leave Denmark at the end of her home leave in 1925, and again in 1929. She had looked forward to Africa only when going there to join Bror; and even in the early years she had taken longer home leave than Bror or Denys. Her avowal that she could not live "at home," made while she was in Africa, was little more than stubbornness. If she had really been unwilling to return to Denmark, she could have found work in the colony, as others did. Cockie Birkbeck, after Bror left her a few years later, ran a dress shop. Karen had spoken of opening a restaurant or running a hotel, but these were fantasies for which she did not have courage or funds. She had been homesick for Denmark throughout much of her stay in Africa. In May 1930 she wrote her mother, "I find myself longing for Denmark . . . with dew on the grass, cowslips, and the sound of waves from the Sound, in a way that sends me completely wild" (*LFA*, 407). That she must live at home was by no means the tragedy she had implied in her letters.

Through tales, essays, and long letters from Africa, she had maintained a habit of writing, more intensely in direct proportion to her emotional distress. Her fantasy life, like an hypnotic spell, had sustained and protected her. The reliance on writing to maintain her mental balance continued upon her return to Denmark. In two years she readied a dense book of stories, *Seven Gothic Tales*, and only a year later, in 1934, it was published, although she was an unknown author. It seems unlikely that this complex work could have been completed in such a short time unless much of it was written in Africa. A comparison of the language in the tales to that in her letters (as indicated previously) allows a reconstruction of the dates when the tales were begun: "The Roads Round Pisa," 1923; "The Monkey," 1926; "The Deluge at Norderney," 1928; "The Poet," begun in 1928, completed in early 1931; "The Dreamers," begun in 1926, resumed in mid 1931; "The Old Chevalier," probably begun in 1930 (during the period of emotional separation from Denys) and completed after Denys's death; "The Supper at Elsinore," probably begun in 1929 (it seems clearly to have been written in Denmark) and completed after Denys's death. "The Caryatids," which can be dated to 1921 since it refers to a marriage troubled after seven years—but not ended—and "Carnival," begun in mid 1926, did not appear in *Seven Gothic Tales*. Four tales were deleted from the 1932 manuscript, while two new ones, evidently completed in the interval, were inserted. One may suspect that those not published appeared later in another form and may have been early allegories about her relationship to Bror—"Peter and Rosa" and "The Pearls," among them. The facts remain that *Seven Gothic Tales* was a sophisticated first publication by an unknown author, and Karen did not write it in the interval after her return from Africa, but over many years. The sheer volume of her writing in all forms—tales, letters, and essays—whether her life was going poorly (1923), or well (1928), indicates that writing had become a habit long before her return from Africa.

She relied upon her memories of Denys to inspire her life and writing, in the same way that she had imagined her father's spirit lending strength to her in earlier years. Many conversations between herself and Denys seem to appear in the tales; and *Out of Africa*, published in 1938, resembles the voice of Denys himself. In this book appear anecdotes probably related over dinner at Ngong; and the voice, so different from Karen's fictional collections, is almost identical to the Oxford lilt of Llewelyn Powys, Denys's friend who wrote about Kenya in *Black Laughter*, published in 1925. *Out of Africa* celebrates Denys's forte, the anecdote—stories taken from life—whereas the usual focus of Karen's writing was on fictional tales. She would have done well to continue writing in the form of memoir, for *Out of Africa* is superior to her other writing, both in its lyricism and in its clear portraits of human beings. Her collection *Winter's Tales*, however, is a splendid elegy of her life with Bror Blixen, and may have struck him as a love letter. One story in it, "The Pearls," offers a superb testament to her tenderness for Bror, which lasted to the end of her life.

* *

Karen Blixen's career as a writer was plagued with interruptions from crises of abdominal pain similar to that she had experienced in Africa. The pain, which had first bothered her in late 1921 when her sister Ea was dying, recurred after the death of her mother in 1939, and troubled her intermittently for the rest of her life. She insisted the pain must be due to syphilis, although tests of her blood and spinal fluid showed no evidence of the disease. Her doctor, Mogens Fog, found some slight neurological damage in her legs, which never worsened, and she was treated with various remedies for syphilis, including fever treatments—being placed in a steam bath for several hours to raise her body temperature—and surgery to cut pain fibers in her spine. All these efforts failed to relieve her symptoms.

By 1956 her physicians were certain her continuing pain was not due to syphilis (KBS) and decided a stomach ulcer might be the source of her difficulties. The operation to remove the ulcer eliminated a third of her stomach, and she was never able to eat normal amounts of food again. Afterwards she lost weight dramatically, and malnutrition rendered her an invalid.

Her abdominal pain was certainly real but may have arisen from psychological factors. While she was usually able to function in a normal way, her behavior often puzzled and fascinated her associates. After she had become a successful author, she sometimes pretended to be a sorceress. Two young writers who claimed to have fallen under her spell describe bizarre incidents. Thorkild Bjornvig, with whom she established a pact in which she was to play inspirational god to his writing genius, says that one evening after dinner she pointed a revolver at him theatrically as part of a game, the theme of which he was too drunk to understand. Aage Henriksen says that she would call him at odd hours of the night, talk rapidly for two to three minutes, then abruptly hang up without allowing him to respond. Her mood swings—agitated nervousness changing in the space of a few minutes to exaggerated graciousness—strongly suggest drug dependency. At least as early as the 1940s she was taking amphetamines (*ID*, 316). There can be no doubt that they exaggerated her natural tendency to be dramatic.

There is little evidence, however, to support the idea that she was peculiar, naturally histrionic, or false in Africa. Denys Finch Hatton held hypocrisy in contempt and would not have devoted thirteen years of friendship to Karen Blixen if she had been insincere or self-aggrandizing. The aesthetic of Karen Blixen's era required that artists establish a persona. Ernest Hemingway, Marianne Moore, and Gertrude Stein were among the many who exaggerated their personal quirks to solidify their reputations. This was a tactic Karen Blixen recognized from childhood, for she had followed the career of the flamboyant Georg Brandes and certainly had noted how Oscar Wilde's habits had attracted attention to his work. As a writer she strove to establish a mysterious, dramatic persona, characterized by her aura as aristocrat and by certain excessive—therefore calculatedly memorable—gestures, such as flaunting a bearskin coat and insisting upon being addressed as Baroness. She accomplished the goal of artists of the time: becoming controversial, thus providing a stimulus for conversation. She had always taken an individualistic approach to life and been eccentric by some standards. Her attitude arose naturally from contempt for the bourgeois—by definition, whatever is achieved by imitation. In her time she was criticized and regarded with suspicion by Danes, but not deprecated. The task of deprecation has been left to those who do not understand her character or her era.

As she grew older certain characteristics of her nature resulted in conflicts that resembled her struggle with Bror. She tended to consider herself the central figure in any drama and wished to direct as well as to star. Unfortunately the supporting actors were not always malleable. There were tensions between her and her brother Thomas, as well as with newspaper critics and her brother-in-law Knud Dahl, a publisher.

Her later years were marked by acclaim in the English-speaking world, and indifference on the part of the Danish literary intelligentsia (because she had not written in Danish). The young male literary aspirants whom she courted and counseled were alternately fascinated and repelled by her illusion of grandeur. She had created herself in the image of an aristocrat and strove to proffer hospitality equivalent to that of the great nineteenth century French literary salons. At base, however, she had never severed her bourgeois roots and until she died was plagued with insecurities.

In the end she was adored because of her characteristic playfulness. The roles assumed, the striking clothes, the elaborate dinners, most of all the fantastical conversations and word-games, arose from a love of theater. She transformed love and tragedy through imagination. When her relationships succeeded—with Bror, Berkeley, Denys, her family, and other friends and writers—it was, as her mother said, because of her talent for making life festive (*LFA*, 427).

Toward the end of her life Karen Blixen's face revealed the severe pattern of lines characteristic of heavy smokers, accentuated by her great loss of weight. Her eyes glowed with the defiant expression of a witch. Chronic smoking had deepened her voice, which enhanced the mood of stories she recited over the radio. Despite the difficult years of illness in Africa, the cigarette addiction, years of amphetamine use and several surgical operations, Karen Blixen lived to be seventy-seven years old.

She was preceded in death by Bror, who was killed in an automobile accident in 1946. Legend has it that as he died, he embraced his fiancee to protect her from the crash. He was sixty years old and had never, so far as anyone recognized, developed late symptoms of syphilis. (Up to two-thirds of untreated victims of syphilis show no further symptoms.) His second wife did not learn that he had had syphilis until after his death. In later years Bror's face was nearly as smooth and serene as the face of a child. He had married three women, and was engaged to a fourth at the time of his death. Karen grieved when Bror died as she had years before when he divorced her.

In the thirty-one years that remained of her life after she returned from Africa, Karen devoted herself to writing, eventually becoming a literary lioness in Denmark. She chose the pen name Isak partly to hide the fact that she was a woman, for critics were less likely to treat seriously the work of female writers. She was nominated for the Nobel Prize for Literature on two occasions, but it was won first by Ernest Hemingway and then by Albert Camus.

From the viewpoint of a storyteller, Karen Blixen says of Mira Jama in "The Dreamers," "dreaming is the well-mannered people's way of committing suicide" (*SGT*, 277). Dreaming or creating a story was her means of looking back, living in the past. Some believed that she had died spiritually when Denys died and spent the rest of her years reliving her life on the farm. It is said that every evening before going to bed she opened the south door of her house and looked toward Africa.

EPILOGUE

Her various plans to visit Africa again never materialized. Once she received a private travel grant, the Tagea Brandt Fellowship, which would have—modestly—covered her expenses for the trip, but she never used it. In 1939 she made arrangements to travel to Mecca with Farah, but World War II broke out, and Farah died. Karen's desire to revisit was likely a fantasy. Once having returned to Nairobi she might well have perished from the force of terrible memories. In the end she chose the woods at Rungstedlund for her grave—a site well away from the resting place of lions atop the Ngong Hills.

When Karen Blixen's family insisted that she publish her letters from Africa, she could not take them seriously. She had always said that her conversation was far better than her letters. In many ways, her tales represent the conversations for which she thought herself famous, while *Out of Africa* was, like the letters, not written in the style she preferred. She liked to dissociate herself from contemporary writing, saying she had no interest in tales of poverty and ill luck. "That is not the sort of story Mira Jama [herself] tells," she says in "The Dreamers" (*SGT*, 275). Rather, she thought of herself as a fiction writer, and believed her talents lay more in the art of fascination than in description of reality. *Out of Africa* might never have been written had it not fulfilled the motto she carried with her in the years in Africa: "I will not let thee go unless thou bless me." By writing about those years, she reshaped the struggle in order to exorcise her bitterness and to forgive. Toward the end Denys had suggested some advice it behooves a storyteller to take—a twist on an old verse: "You must turn your mournful ditty to a merry measure, I will never come for pity but for pleasure" (*OA*, 356). When Karen was in despair at leaving the farm, his words annoyed her, for they seemed heartless. She was dismayed to be forced into cheerfulness. In "The Poet" she accuses his kind of attitude of reflecting an "extreme disregard of truth" (*SGT*, 398). He was asking her to take "a short cut to happiness by declaring things to be" what they were not. But later she realized that, through acceptance of fate, such a philosophy is sublime and necessary to the art of a great writer. Transformed by means of the imagination, the most desperate and tragic events may seem to follow the romantic ideal.

In "The Roads Round Pisa" she says, "Why does my life seem to me so terribly important . . . " (*SGT*, 168)? But when she

341

wrote *Out of Africa*, she meant nothing more than to bless those years, and to gain perspective upon the stork—the pattern of beauty underlying the struggle and failure of her life in Africa. She had written to Thomas in 1926, "If only someone would tell me how it all ended!" (*LFA*, 289). The story still fascinates us, more than a half century later.

Karen Blixen died of malnutrition on September 7, 1962, at Rungstedlund in Denmark, where she was born.

Author's Note

All interpretations in this work of Karen Blixen's tales are based on the new analysis of her life presented here.

Appendix

On Isak Dinesen's Medical History

Isak Dinesen, who prided herself upon being the mistress of illusion, convinced her friends and even some of her doctors that she suffered from syphilis in her later years. She certainly suffered from *something*: she was plagued by paroxysmal attacks of abdominal pain, which never prevented her from doing the things in life that mattered but were a constant trial. Audiences who saw her during her tour of America in 1959 were shocked at her emaciation. She was carried on stage and settled in her chair like a paralytic—although she was in no way paralyzed and could walk perfectly well on other occasions.

What was the cause of her symptoms, and what transpired during these periods when she seemed so dramatically debilitated? Many readers will tell you earnestly and confidentially that she suffered from syphilis and this was the reason for all of her troubles. It is true that her husband gave her syphilis in the first year of their marriage, but her own physicians state Karen Blixen did not suffer late in life from syphilis. Still, her every episode of illness over nearly fifty years has been ascribed to syphilis by one account or another.

While syphilis is known as "the great imitator" of other diseases, leading physicians astray in its diagnosis, it is also true that symptoms shared by syphilis with other diseases are more often found in those other diseases. There is a saying in medicine, "When you hear hoof beats, do not expect zebras." Although Karen Blixen suffered from, and was treated for, syphilis in her early adulthood, all of the symptoms she later presented could be accounted for by much more common medical problems. How did the process begin of labeling all Karen Blixen's symptoms as syphilis?

In 1915, when Karen Blixen was thirty years old, she left her coffee farm in Africa and went to Paris, ill with what was described as a case of syphilis so severe as to rival that of any soldier in the ranks. An army doctor in France told her he doubted very much if she would ever recover, and she believed him.

Syphilis is a disease that progresses through three stages: a prodromal period of two or three weeks followed by a skin sore called a chancre, which is painless but infectious to sexual contacts; a second stage of illness arising within several weeks in which the patient has rash, skin sores, fever and enlarged lymph nodes, and is extremely infectious to sexual contacts and to a baby in the womb; and, in a limited number of cases, a third stage of disease that appears twenty to thirty years after the initial infection, in which there is deterioration of the blood vessels (cardiovascular syphilis) or the nervous system (late neurosyphilis), or both. Neurosyphilis may include general paresis, ie. widespread damage to the brain and cranial nerves; and/or *tabes dorsalis*, ie. syphilis of the spine.

The second stage of syphilis may last months or up to a few years. Karen Blixen had been suffering from the second stage of the disease for at least three months when she arrived in Europe in 1915. She eventually was treated in Copenhagen by a specialist in venereal diseases, Dr. Carl Rasch. He gave her two series of injections with Salvarsan, an arsenic preparation developed by the German Paul Ehrlich in 1910—a treatment, later dubbed "the magic bullet," that proved in the majority of cases to be dramatically effective in curing syphilis. A Wasserman test of Karen Blixen's blood was initially positive, indicating that she did indeed have syphilis when treatment was started, but a series of later tests were all negative, suggesting that the disease was halted in the infective stage. Before treatment many white cells were found in her spinal fluid, confirming that syphilis had entered her central nervous system, but subsequent spinal taps were all normal, which seemed to underline the fact that the Salvarsan treatment had effectively eliminated her syphilis.

In 1919 and 1925 she was reexamined by Dr. Rasch and no further evidence of syphilis was found. (Even without treatment, in possibly two-thirds of such cases there is no progression of disease to late-stage syphilis.) However, in the intervening period Karen Blixen's letters to her family from Africa make it clear that she continued to dose herself with an elixir of arsenic whenever she experienced symptoms she felt merited it. Despite Dr. Rasch's assurances, she remembered the words of the physician in Paris and believed she would never recover.

A few years after her treatment for syphilis, in late 1921 and again in early 1922, when she was thirty-six years old, she was hospitalized by paroxysmal abdominal pain. Although she was convinced she was dying, three physicians were unable to determine the cause of her pain. Her sister Inger (Ea) was at the same time hospitalized in Denmark with a difficult pregnancy from which she died a few months later. Karen Blixen herself later attributed her own symptoms to emotional strain because of the failed coffee crop that season, but a more salient fact was that her estranged husband, Bror, was preparing to ask for a divorce, which he did only a few weeks after Karen Blixen's hospitalization.

While living alone afterwards on the African coffee farm, Karen Blixen suffered from panic attacks. She herself never labeled them as such; they would have been called "neurasthenia" or "anxiety neurosis" in her time (Freud). She suggested to her mother that something was the matter with her nerves, and said she felt at times that she was going mad. Her mother was alarmed and insisted she needed the "peace and quiet" of Denmark, and her physician, R. W. Burkitt, told her that she "must and should" go home.

In *Out of Africa* the panic attacks are described in a manner unmistakable to physicians: "Whenever I was ill in Africa, or much worried, I suffered from a special kind of compulsive idea. It seemed to me then that all my surroundings were in danger or distress, and that in the midst of this disaster I myself was somehow on the wrong side . . . when everything was going wrong with me, it sometimes suddenly fell upon me like a darkness, and in a way I was frightened of it, as of a sort of derangement . . . " (*OA*, 361–2). She speaks of being awakened by "a great feeling of terror . . . as if someone had been trying to choke me . . . I got up in a real panic . . . " (*OA*, 70). In letters to her mother she describes fears of going hunting on the open plains, and of surreal feelings of being buried alive in her own grave. In the memoir *Shadows on the Grass* she explains that these fears, accompanied by paroxysmal weeping, arose from the sudden conviction that "everything I took on was destined to end up in failure" (*SOTG*, 469).

Panic attacks are the manifestation of sudden irrational terror in which dread, fear of incipient madness, feelings of unreality and impending doom, physical symptoms such as choking and hyperventilation, and consequent agoraphobia, or fear of certain situations, are hallmarks. (The Danish critic Aage Henriksen points out that panic is a central element in Isak Dinesen's fiction, a means to self-realization.) In many individuals panic attacks arise from a severe childhood loss, and Karen Blixen's father had committed suicide when she was ten years old. She herself attempted suicide at least once (1931), probably twice (1915), in Africa; she threatened suicide many times. She seems first to have suffered severe anxiety or depression at the age of twenty-four after being disappointed in love (she speaks of being thrown "completely off balance"), and throughout her life she was unable to be alone for any stressful period. Her brother Thomas lived with her for two years in Africa after her husband left the farm and his visit was followed by that of a series of extended house-guests, including Denys Finch Hatton.

Just how panic attacks may have related to Karen Blixen's abdominal pain suggests an interesting theory. Panic attacks sometimes disguise themselves as abdominal pain; when this occurs they are often associated with a process known as somatization—adopting the symptoms of a loved one as a means of dealing with threatening circumstances. Her sister was dying of a probable kidney ailment in 1921 when Karen Blixen's pain began.

Whatever her physical symptoms in 1921 and 1922, they seemed unrelated to any known syndrome recognized by her doctors. She did not have appendicitis, bowel obstruction, gall bladder disease, torsion of an ovary, or stomach ulcer—illnesses that might be expected to cause such pain in a thirty-six-year-old woman. She was not suffering from any progressive disease, such as carcinoma or inflammatory bowel disorder, nor did there seem to be any infectious cause of her ailment. Syphilis was certainly not at fault; any symptoms of late syphilis would not occur for fifteen or twenty years. She might have taken an overdose of arsenic; that seems to be the most likely possibility, but surely her physicians would have noticed the telltale signs: nausea and vomiting, diarrhea, burning of the mouth and throat, later pigmentation and scaling of the skin, hair loss, and white striation of the nails.

Physicians are wary of assigning a psychological cause to pain until all other possible diagnoses have been ruled out and until a pattern is established over time to demonstrate that no life-threatening illness is at stake. There was no recurrence of Karen Blixen's abdominal pain for some years, so the early diagnosis remained unknown. Her next episode, if indeed the symptoms were the same, seems not to have occurred until eighteen years later, when she was fifty-four years old. When her coffee farm had failed and she returned to Denmark in 1931, she was suffering from several medical problems, diagnosed variously by doctors in Africa as amebic dysentery, severe anemia, and even pernicious anemia; but by 1939 these complaints had resolved. She had become a successful author, and she had been living in Denmark with her mother for eight years. Her mother died in January 1939 (aged eighty-two) and shortly afterwards Karen Blixen's severe episodes of abdominal pain began to recur.

She was eventually referred to a neurologist named Mogens Fog. She gave him a history of repeated episodes of pain, appearing paroxysmally, often at night. The pain actually caused her to double over in Dr. Fog's office and required her to lie down. This pain could last four to five hours and might be intermittent over several weeks, followed by months without symptoms. It was accompanied by diarrhea and often by vomiting. The discomfort would begin near the central abdomen and spread circumferentially, sometimes extending to the lower limbs.

Dr. Fog examined her and made the following significant physical findings: the deep tendon reflexes in her lower extremities were diminished, and the pain and temperature sensation was impaired. Her weight was considered normal for a slender, chain-smoking female aged fifty-four.

Judging by the objective evidence, Dr. Fog's initial impression was that Karen Blixen might be suffering from the lightning pains sometimes seen in tabes dorsalis, late syphilis of the spine. This stage of syphilis, associated with demyelinization of nerves, develops twenty-five to thirty years after the initial infection. Tabes dorsalis is characterized by peripheral nerve damage and by abdominal crises with lightning pains named for their paroxysmal occurrence. To arrest what might be ongoing syphilis, Dr. Fog tried various regimens. Karen Blixen was immersed in a steam bath to undergo the so-called "fever treatment"—thought to kill spirochetes, which cause the infection, by raising the body temperature for extended intervals; but after four to five hours she became claustrophobic and refused to continue. We may assume that she was also treated with penicillin, developed in the 1940s, with no relief of symptoms. By 1946, her pain had become intolerable, and she underwent a cordotomy—section of the antero-lateral portion of the spinal cord—to sever the pain pathways to her abdomen. This operation relieved her symptoms only briefly.

For another ten years Dr. Fog continued without success to search for the cause of her pain. At surgery some scarring had been found near the spinal cord around the blood supply to her digestive tract. The vagueness of Dr. Fog's description suggests that the pathological findings were limited and non-specific. He now began to theorize that Karen Blixen suffered from gummatous scars localized to the abdomen—in his words, like tuberculosis of the spine. (Whether caused by syphilis, tuberculosis, or some other disease such as leishmaniasis, a parasitic disease found in Kenya, such scars are often indistinguishable from each other.) Gummas—granulomas due to syphilis—are thought to arise as a hypersensitivity phenomenon to spirochetes. (Today there is some evidence that gummatous disease is the result of *reexposure* to syphilis—an unlikely cause of Karen Blixen's symptoms). Tabes dorsalis, a degenerative disease of nerves that may be associated with an inflammatory response, or endarteritis, of small vessels, involves a different process that than of gummatous disease.

One would expect tabes dorsalis to be progressive, but Karen Blixen's neurological signs remained unchanged throughout her time in Dr. Fog's care. After she underwent a revision of the cordotomy in 1955, he was convinced that her remaining symptoms could not be ascribed to syphilis and turned the case over to another physician.

Late in 1955 Karen Blixen developed a new pain, a discomfort under the rib cage in the area of the stomach. To treat what was diagnosed as a duodenal ulcer—a finding not related to syphilis but highly correlated with heavy smoking—Dr. Torben Knudtzon suggested another surgical procedure. He resected the ulcer, and with it, a third of her stomach. The operation was designed to eliminate her pain and to reduce the amount of stomach acid causing the ulcer. However, the result presented a complicated prognosis, for Karen Blixen could no longer eat normal quantities of food; this caused her health to undergo a dramatic change. She proceeded to suffer from malnutrition, malabsorption, and weakness that repeatedly hospitalized her until her death in 1962, at the age of seventy-seven. The night before she died she had played cards, written a birthday note, and walked, with aid, upstairs to her bed. Thus, contrary to signs normally seen in late syphilis, her mental and neurological status, except for the few findings mentioned, remained intact to the end.

Chronic abdominal pain of uncertain etiology presents a diagnostic challenge for the physician. It is not uncommon for patients with unexplained symptoms to undergo numerous operative procedures over time, only to have their pain inexplicably return. The story of Karen Blixen's recurring pain is of particular interest because her severe episodes of pain in later life began in 1939 shortly after the death of her mother, the person closest to her in life; and the pain was exacerbated after she failed to receive the Nobel Prize for Literature in 1954. Although her pain was certainly real, a strong association remains between her symptoms and stressful events in her life.

If panic attacks and not syphilis were the source of her abdominal distress, then what caused the neurological damage in her legs? If Dr. Fog knew about her arsenic tonics in Africa, he did not mention them in his published report of her medical history in 1978. Karen Blixen was known for wearing heavy make-up and a variety of hoods, hats, and turbans; one observer remarked that he never saw her without a hat. Chronic arsenic use would have left blotchy areas of increased pigmentation in her skin and thinned her hair, and could even have caused intestinal ulcers, although it is not clear if she used arsenic after she returned to Denmark in 1931. Arsenic exposure in Africa could have permanently impaired the deep tendon reflexes and sensation in Karen Blixen's distal extremities, causing the syndrome known as *pseudotabes*; like syphilis, arsenic toxicity produces demylenization of nerves, first affecting the feet and lower limbs, where Dr. Fog made his findings. A similar pattern of damage—loss of deep tendon reflexes and pain and temperature sensation—may be seen in pernicious anemia—absence of intrinsic factor, the enzyme needed to absorb Vitamin B_{12}—the incorrect diagnosis suggested by Karen Blixen's Nairobi doctor in 1931.

Karen Blixen's panic attacks would have been aggravated by amphetamines, which she took liberally in her later years. Drug use was common among members of her social set in Africa; in a story called "The Dreamers" written in 1931 Karen Blixen makes an allusion to the amphetamine-like *miraa*, a chewable plant easily available in Kenya.

Dr. Fog's report makes no mention of Karen Blixen's psychological behavior, and it seems apparent that doctors in Denmark categorized her abdominal pain strictly on the basis of physical symptoms. However, the fact that her pain was intermittent over years and there was no progression of her neurological signs perhaps should have alerted physicians that she was not suffering from operable disease. The diagnosis of tabes dorsalis, characterized by progressive impairment of neurologic function, does not explain her symptoms. Karen Blixen never had incontinence of urine, often seen early in tabes, nor any of the diverse manifestations of late syphilis: ataxia, Argyll-Robertson pupil, traumatic ulcers of desensitized skin, Charcot's joints, optic atrophy, or general paresis.

She convinced many associates that she suffered from late syphilis, despite the fact that her symptoms did not fit a recognizable pattern for the disease. The Danish writers Aage Henriksen and Thorkild Bjornvig both discuss her illness in their memoirs. She herself believed, perhaps romantically—her father and the great philosopher Nietzsche had both suffered from syphilis—that she had not been cured. Dr. Fog's final assessment was simply that "hers was a *painful* disease"; he states explicitly that she was *not* suffering from syphilis at the time of her death. The weakness and emaciation audiences saw when she visited New York City were due to her inability to eat normal amounts of food after her operation for the stomach ulcer. When she was hospitalized and rehydrated and fed intraveously, she regained her ability to walk and could function normally.

Karen Blixen's medical tests after the age of thirty-one were never again positive for syphilis. She certainly suffered from a panic disorder that would have explained her unusual abdominal pain conforming to no known medical syndrome. Her history of taking an arsenic tonic for years in Africa—at least once described as an overdose in *Shadows on the Grass* (*SOTG*, 486)—suggests that her few neurological signs related to arsenic intoxication and had nothing to do with tabes dorsalis.

Perhaps to Isak Dinesen the author, panic attacks were too bourgeois an explanation for her symptoms. She strove to maintain the image of herself as an aristocrat. Judging from the quantity of widely propagated misinformation about her medical illnesses, she succeeded in fooling herself and her public.

References

Alpers, Bernard J., and Elliott L. Mancall. *Clinical Neurology*. Philadelphia: F. A. Davis, 1971.

Bjornvig, Thorkild. *The Pact: My Friendship with Isak Dinesen*. Trans. Ingvar Schousboe and William Jay Smith. Baton Rouge: Louisiana State University Press, 1983.

Comprehensive Textbook of Psychiatry / V. Ed. Harold I. Kaplan and Benjamin J. Sadock. Baltimore: Williams & Wilkins, 1989.

Dinesen, Isak. *Letters from Africa, 1914–1931*. Trans. Anne Born. Ed. Frans Lasson. Chicago: The University of Chicago Press, 1981.

Dinesen, Isak. *Out of Africa* and *Shadows on the Grass*. New York: Random House, 1938 and 1961. Vintage Books, 1985.

Dinesen, Isak. *Seven Gothic Tales*. New York: Harrison Smith and Robert Haas, 1934.

DeVaul R. A. et al: Persistent pain and illness insistence. *Am J Surg* 135:828, 1978.

Drossman D. A. Patients Psychogenic Abdominal Pain: 6 years observation in the medical setting. *Am J Psychiatry* 139:1549, 1982.

Eisendrath, S. J., L. W. Way, J. W. Ostroff, et al. Identification of psychogenic abdominal pain. *Psychosomatics* 27:705, 1986.

Fog, Mogens. "Karen Blixens Sygdomshistorie." *Blixeniana, 1978*. Copenhagen: Karen Blixen Selskabet, 1978.

Gomez, J., P. Dally. Psychologically mediated abdominal pain in surgical and medical outpatient clinics. *Br Med J* 1:1451, 1977.

Gosselin, Smith, Hodge. *Clinical Toxicology of Commercial Products*. Baltimore: Williams & Wilkins, 1984

Harrison's Principles of Internal Medicine. Seventh Edition. New York: McGraw-Hill, 1974.

Henriksen, Aage. *Isak Dinesen/Karen Blixen: The Work and the Life*. Trans. William Mishler. New York: St. Martin's Press, 1988.

MacDonald, A. J. et al. Non-organic gastrointestinal illness: A medical and psychiatric study. *Br J Psychol* 136:276, 1980.

Principles of Surgery, Fifth Edition. Ed. Seymour I. Schwartz. New York: McGraw-Hill, 1989.

Sarfeh, I. J. Abdominal pain of unknown etiology. *Am J Surg* 132:22, 1976.

Sheehan, D. V. Current concepts in psychiatry: panic attacks and phobias. *N Engl J Med* 307 (3):156–8, 1982.

U.S. Dept. of HEW. "Syphilis." Public Health Publication No. 743. Washington, D.C.: U.S. Government Printing Office, 1960.

Vick, Nicholas A. *Grinker's Neurology*. Springfield, Ill.: Charles C. Thomas, 1976.

Woodhouse, C. R. J., S. Bickner. Chronic abdominal pain: A surgical or psychiatric symptom? *Br J Surg* 66:348, 1979.

Glossary

Bedar: "The Bald One," one of Denys Finch Hatton's African nicknames, according to Karen Blixen, although this is not the standard term for bald in Swahili.

Bwana: "Sir," "Master."

boma: A barricade or fence, usually made of thorn branches.

duka: Native shop, often a shanty.

kanzu: Floor-length, light-weight tunic worn by a man; Muslim garb.

kiboko: Whip, often of hippopotamus hide.

Kikuyu: Agricultural tribe of the hills of central Kenya.

Kipsigis: Agricultural tribe of western Kenya.

Luo: Tribe inhabiting the region near Lake Victoria.

Makanyaga: "Master-of-the-Putdown," another of Denys Finch Hatton's African nicknames.

manyatta: Rectangular Masai dwelling with a rounded roof made from mud and cattle dung.

Masai: Pastoral tribe inhabiting the plains of central Kenya.

Mbagathi: Karen Blixen's first home in Kenya.

Mbogani: Karen Blixen's estate house in Kenya.

Memsahib: "Mistress," Swahili term used by servants to address the lady of the house.

moran: Tribal warriors, usually spear-carrying Masai warriors.

Msabu: "Madame."

Nandi: Tribe of western Kenya.

ndito: Young woman.

ngoma: Tribal dance, usually lasting several hours.

Nzige: "The Grasshopper," Denys Finch Hatton's airplane.

posho: Maizemeal porridge.

shamba: Farm, garden, field.

shaurie: (Standard spelling is *shari*) Trouble, conflict, falling out.

shenzie: (Usually, *shenzi*) Fierce, wild, mongrel.

syce: Servant who grooms the horses.

tembo: Native beer made from millet and sugar cane.

terai: (Usually, "double terai.") Soft, wide-brimmed felt hat.

toto: Child.

Wahoga: "The Wild Goose," Bror Blixen's African nickname.

Select Bibliography

Note: The letters of Denys Finch Hatton to Karen Blixen are found in Brundbjerg's "Kaerlighed og okonomi." The letters and diary entries of Aage Westenholz are found in Anders Westenholz's *The Power of Aries.* The letters of Karen Blixen concerning Beryl Markham are found in Lovell's *Straight on Till Morning.* The letters of Denys Finch Hatton to Kermit Roosevelt are found in the Roosevelt family papers, the Library of Congress, Washington, D.C.

Alpers, Bernard J., and Elliott L. Mancall. *Clinical Neurology.* Philadelphia: F.A. Davis, 1971.

Anderson, Isabel. *Circling Africa.* Boston: Marshall Jones Co., 1929.

Aschan, Ulf. *The Man Whom Women Loved: The Life of Bror Blixen.* New York: St. Martin's Press, 1987.

Bell, Quentin. *Virginia Woolf: A Biography.* New York: Harcourt Brace Jovanovich, 1972.

Bjornvig, Thorkild. *The Pact: My friendship with Isak Dinesen.* Trans. Ingvar Schousboe and William Jay Smith. Baton Rouge: Louisiana State University Press, 1983.

Blixen-Finecke, Bror. *African Hunter.* New York: St. Martin's Press, 1986.

Blixen-Finecke, Bror. *The Africa Letters.* New York: St. Martin's Press, 1988.

Bohannan, Paul, and Philip Curtin. *Africa and Africans.* Garden City, N.J.: The Natural History Press, 1971.

Brundbjerg, Else. "Kaerlighed og okonomi," *Kritique* 66 (1984).

Dinesen, Isak. *Anecdotes of Destiny.* New York: Random House, 1958.

———. *Carnival: Entertainments and Posthumous Tales.* Chicago: The University of Chicago Press, 1977.

———. *Daguerreotypes and Other Essays.* Trans. P. M. Mitchell and W. D. Paden. Chicago: The University of Chicago Press, 1979.

———. *Last Tales.* New York: Random House, 1957.

———. *Letters from Africa, 1914–1931.* Trans. Anne Born. Ed. Frans Lasson. Chicago: The University of Chicago Press, 1981.

———. *On Modern Marriage and Other Observations.* Trans. Anne Born. New York: St. Martin's Press, 1986.

———. *On Mottoes of My Life.* Christiansborg: Royal Danish Ministry of Foreign Affairs, Press and Information Department, 1962.

———. *Out of Africa* and *Shadows on the Grass.* New York: Random House, 1938 and 1961. Reprint. Vintage Books, 1985.

———. *Seven Gothic Tales.* New York: Harrison Smith and Robert Haas, 1934.

———. *Shadows on the Grass* (see above).

———. *Winter's Tales.* New York: Random House, 1942.

Dinesen, Thomas. *My Sister, Isak Dinesen*. London: Michael Joseph Ltd., 1975.

Dinesen, Thomas. *Boganis: Min Fader, Hans Slaegt, Hans Liv og Hans Tid*. Copenhagen: Gyldendal, 1972.

Dinesen, Wilhelm. *Letters from the Hunt*. Boston: Rowan Tree Press, 1987.

Donaldson, Frances. *Edward VIII*. Philadelphia: J.B. Lippincott Company, 1975.

Finch Hatton, Denys. Letters to Kermit Roosevelt. Roosevelt family papers. Library of Congress, Washington D.C.

Fog, Mogens. "Karen Blixens Sygdomshistorie." *Blixeniana, 1978*. Copenhagen: Karen Blixen Selskabet, 1978.

Fox, James. *White Mischief*. New York: Vintage Books, 1984.

Fox, James. "Who is Beryl Markham?", *Observer Magazine*, 9–30–84.

Gatura, Kamante. *Longing for Darkness: Kamante's Tales from Out of Africa*. Collected by Peter Beard. New York: Harcourt Brace Jovanovich, 1975.

Goodrich, Joseph King. *Africa of To-Day*. Chicago: A.C. McClurg & Co., 1912.

Gosselin, Smith, Hodge. *Clinical Toxicology of Commercial Products*. Baltimore: Williams & Wilkins, 1984.

Haarer, A.E. *Modern Coffee Production*. London, Leonard Hill Ltd., 1956.

Handbook of British East Africa. Nairobi: Ward & Milligan, 1912.

Hannah, Donald. *'Isak Dinesen' & Karen Blixen: The Mask and the Reality*. London: Putnam, 1971.

Harrison's Principles of Internal Medicine. Seventh Edition. New York: McGraw-Hill, 1974.

Henriksen, Aage. *Isak Dinesen/Karen Blixen: The Work and the Life*. Trans. William Mishler. New York: St. Martin's Press, 1988.

Hobsbawm, Eric. *The Age of Empire.* New York: Vintage Books, 1987.

Hunter, J.A., and Daniel P. Mannix. *Tales of the African Frontier.* New York: Harper & Brothers, 1954.

Huxley, Elspeth. *Out in the Midday Sun.* New York: Viking, 1985.

———. *White Man's Country.* 2 vols. New York: Frederick A. Praeger, Inc., 1968.

Huxley, Julian. *Africa View.* New York: Harper and Bros., 1931.

Johannesson, Eric O. *The World of Isak Dinesen.* Seattle: University of Washington Press, 1961.

Johnson, Osa. *Four Years in Paradise.* New York: J.B. Lippincott Co., 1941.

Kenya, Colony and Protectorate of. Dept. of Agriculture. *Annual Report.* Nairobi, 1926.

Kenya. Insight Guides ed. by Mohamed Amin and John Eames. Singapore: APA Productions, 1987.

Kenyatta, Jomo. *Facing Mt. Kenya.* New York: Vintage Books, 1965.

Langbaum, Robert. *Isak Dinesen's Art: The Gayety of Vision.* Chicago: The University of Chicago Press, 1975.

Lasson, Frans, ed. *The Life and Destiny of Isak Dinesen.* Text by Clara Svendsen. London: Michael Joseph, 1970.

Lerner, Robert E., Standish Meacham, and Edward McNall Burns. *Western Civilizations: Their History and Their Culture,* Volume II. New York: W.W. Norton & Co., Inc., 1988.

The Living Bible Paraphrased. Wheaton, Ill., Tyndale House Publishers, 1971.

Lovell, Mary. *Straight on Till Morning.* New York: St. Martin's Press, 1987.

Ludwig, Emil. *The Nile.* New York: The Viking Press, 1937.

MacColl, Gail, and Carol McD. Wallace. *To Marry an English Lord.* New York: Workman Publishing, 1989.

McDonald, J. *Coffee in Kenya.* Nairobi: Government Printing Office, 1937.

McGraw-Hill History of Science and Technology. New York: 1982.

Markham, Beryl. *West with the Night.* San Francisco: North Point Press, 1983.

Middleton, Dorothy. *Victorian Lady Travellers.* New York: E.P. Dutton & Co., 1965.

Migel, Parmenia. *Titania.* New York: Random House, 1967.

Miller, Charles. *The Lunatic Express.* New York: Ballantine Books, 1973.

Moorehead, Alan. *No Room in the Ark.* New York: Harper and Bros., 1957.

———. *The White Nile.* London: Penguin, 1973.

Mosley, Paul. *The Settler Economies.* Cambridge: Cambridge University Press, 1983.

New Webster's Universal Encyclopedia. New York: Bonanza Books, 1985.

Pelensky, Olga Anastasia. *Isak Dinesen: A Biographical Study of Her Artistic Imagination.* Ann Arbor: UMI, 1983.

Powys, Llewelyn Powys. *Black Laughter.* London: Grant Richards Ltd., 1925.

Principles of Medicine in Africa. E.H.O. Parry, ed. Oxford: Oxford University Press, 1976.

Sikes, Christopher. *Nancy: The Life of Lady Astor.* Chicago: Academy Publishers, 1984.

Skidelsky, Robert. *John Maynard Keynes: Hopes Betrayed, 1883–1920.* New York: Viking Penguin, Inc., 1986.

Sprott, F.H. *Coffee Planting in Kenya Colony.* Kenya: 1927.

Tannahill, Reay. *Sex in History*. New York: Scarborough Books, 1982.

Thurman, Judith. *Isak Dinesen: The Life of a Storyteller*. New York: St. Martin's Press, 1982.

Trzebinski, Errol. *The Kenya Pioneers*. New York: Norton, 1986.

———. *Silence Will Speak*. London: Heinemann, 1977.

U.S. Dept of HEW. *Syphilis*. Public Health Publication No. 743. Washington, D.C.: U.S. Government Printing Office, 1960.

Vick, Nicholas A. *Grinker's Neurology*. Springfield, Ill.: Charles C. Thomas, 1976.

Westenholz, Anders. *The Power of Aries: Myth and Reality in Karen Blixen's Life*. Trans. Lise Kure-Jensen. Baton Rouge: Louisiana State University Press, 1987.

Windle, E.G. *Modern Coffee Planting*. London: John Bale, Sons & Danielsson, Ltd., 1933.

Wolf, Eric R. *Europe and the People Without History*. Berkeley: University of California Press, 1982.

Acknowledgments

Early in my research, I was told of a woman in Montana named Danette Wollersheim. Danette had a marvelous friend in Copenhagen, Eva Arnesen, and without Eva I could not have located the letters of Denys Finch Hatton to Karen Blixen. More importantly, without Danette's help, this book might not have been written.

Danette had traveled to Kenya on a wild whim and succeeded in meeting and spending a few days with Beryl Markham. In a long telephone conversation between Montana and Iowa, Danette gave me information I could not have learned elsewhere.

A few years later, just as I was thinking about putting together the acknowledgments for this book, I went with my family on our first skiing vacation to Colorado. At a tiny resort named Cooper Mountain (over the Continental Divide from Copper Mountain), late on a Sunday afternoon, I was invited forward in the line for the ski lift to ride with a woman I did not know. Our conversation was animated; it seemed we were interested in all the same subjects. When she said she was from Montana, I could not resist the silly question, "Did you ever meet Danette Wollersheim?" At this, the woman nearly fell off the chair lift, screaming "I am Danette Wollersheim!" She, too, had never been to Colorado before.

I thank Danette, and the friend who gave me her name, Dorothy Fawcett. Pat Cain's curiosity sparked the writing of this book. Eva Arnesen drove me all over Copenhagen and was a force in my starting this writing project. I thank Ingeborg Dinesen (Thomas Dinesen's daughter) for giving me an impromptu tour of Rungstedlund, years before it was open to the public.

In Kenya, thanks to Genepher Owino, Bruno and Katelijn Goddeeris, and their friends Mark and Marcine at the Belgian Embassy, Douglas and Elspeth Whitelaw, Paddy Migdoll, Michael Blundell, Remi Martin, Ruth Hogar, Ruth Holt, and Blixen scholar Armelle Webster.

For responding to inquiries, thanks to Clara Selborn, Frans Lasson, Anne Born, Mary Lovell, Erroll Trzebinski, Else Brundbjerg, Susan Hardy Aiken, and Robert Langbaum. Thanks also to Susan Rabiner, Vaughn Kirchhoff, Barrie Van Dyck, Claire Wachtel, Brian Pingel, Mary Nilsen, Norman Sage, Trackless Sands Press, and the University of Iowa Press. Thanks to readers Marianne Gould, Kay Colangelo, Diane Krell, Dawn Dillman, Anne Marie Mast, and Trish Koza. Special thanks to Christina Donelson.

Thanks to Paul Englund, Chris Squier, Lesley Menninger, Donna Rodnitsky, George Cain, George and Kathy Cook, Von Pittman, Hilke Breder, Stephanie Solomon, Richard and Marit Hamilton, Raji Padmanabhan, Mike Lenardo, Phyllis Nelson, Ruth Pettengill, Mimi Gormezano, Sally Staley, Wanda Boeke, Clark Kenyon, Amy Klion, Suzanne Gleeson, and Susan Okie.

A grateful thank you to Judith Pendleton who gave me the road signs for editing this book.

A special note of thanks to Maud Hart Lovelace.

Index

Telephone orders: 1-800-625-7452

Send mail orders to: Coulsong List
                          P. O. Box 1938-B
                          Iowa City IA 52244

Name

Address:

Telephone #:

Visa or Mastercard #:

About the Author

Linda Donelson is a medical doctor who has lived on a farm overlooking the Ngong Hills of Kenya.

Printed on recycled paper by Thomson-Shore, Inc.,
Dexter, Michigan U. S. A.
426 Pages